Exits and Entrances

a memoir by

Robert Fisher

one of Mr Wesley's preachers

Design, typesetting and publishing by UK Book Publishing

www.ukbookpublishing.com

ISBN: 978-1-915338-33-4

For

Kath

Bobbi and Liz

and those who come after...

FOREWORD

This memoir began as a talk to introduce myself when I first joined a Rotary Club in Blackburn and later when I joined the Rotary Club in Newcastle-under-Lyme. It was subsequently adapted to fulfil the same purpose when I was first invited to address a succession of women's groups when I retired to Crook.

Writing this has been a fascinating exercise, undertaken partly because of the 'lockdown' that began in March 2020, the consequence of the Covid 19 pandemic first identified at the end of 2019. This gave me time to fill. To help me I had to hand, a collection of Christmas 'round robins', some audio and video diaries, and, of course, my memories.

That may explain where the material came from but doesn't adequately answer the question 'Why'! It certainly wasn't intended to be an autobiography, nor a 'journal', spiritual or otherwise. It is what it is, a collection of my memories. I suppose, for me the process of putting it together was a way of evaluating the life I have lived. To quote Sinatra – 'regrets I've had a few', but by and large I feel my life has been worthwhile and this was my way of reviewing it.

I suppose, also, at the back of my mind, given the prevalence of dementia today, I was mindful of the fact that should I fall foul of that dreadful disease this record might serve to help me recall some of the events that have shaped my life. I guess I also hoped that perhaps, at some future date, a descendant might find it of interest to read about a fairly ordinary life that spanned the twentieth / twenty-first centuries.

I have always found that some of the most inspirational quotes that have lodged in my mind have been from Shakespeare and not, as might be assumed, the Bible. It was Shakespeare that provided me with the structure for this memoir. Specifically, Jaques' famous speech from As You Like It. I quote it in full below.

I suppose that the opening words of Jaques' speech "All the world's a stage" reminded me of John Wesley's assertion that "The world is my parish". Both, in their own way challenge us to avoid falling into the trap of seeing ourselves as the centre of our own particular universe. We are part of something bigger than our immediate environment, and we are human and thus mortal. How do we accept our humanity and still impact on the world at large?

'Stage' is clearly the operative word. As I was writing this memoir, I was conscious, again, of the perceptiveness of Shakespeare. He had Jaques observe "... all the men and women merely players; They have their exits and their entrances." As we go through life our lives interact, albeit sometimes only briefly, with those whom we encounter along the way. This memoir is an account of my life with reference to those I have encountered over the years.

And then someone suggested I should publish it . . .

"All the world's a stage"

by WILLIAM SHAKESPEARE
from As You Like It [Act II Scene VII]
(spoken by Jaques)

All the world's a stage,
And all the men and women merely players;
They have their exits and their entrances;
And one man in his time plays many parts,
His acts being seven ages. At first the infant,
Mewling and puking in the nurse's arms;
And then the whining school-boy, with his satchel
And shining morning face, creeping like snail
Unwillingly to school. And then the lover,
Sighing like furnace, with a woeful ballad
Made to his mistress' eyebrow. Then a soldier,
Full of strange oaths, and bearded like the pard,
Jealous in honour, sudden and quick in quarrel,
Seeking the bubble reputation
Even in the cannon's mouth. And then the justice,

In fair round belly with good capon lin'd,
With eyes severe and beard of formal cut,
Full of wise saws and modern instances;
And so he plays his part. The sixth age shifts
Into the lean and slipper'd pantaloon,
With spectacles on nose and pouch on side;
His youthful hose, well sav'd, a world too wide
For his shrunk shank; and his big manly voice,
Turning again toward childish treble, pipes
And whistles in his sound. Last scene of all,
That ends this strange eventful history,
Is second childishness and mere oblivion;
Sans teeth, sans eyes, sans taste, sans everything.

By way of Introduction...

When I finished my 'memoir' it dawned on me that to make sense of what follows probably means that you, the reader, will need to have a basic knowledge of Methodism and its structure. So here goes, and I will try to be brief.

'**Methodist**' was originally a nickname applied to a revival movement in 18th century Britain, based within the Church of England and led by, among others, the brothers John and Charles Wesley. Born into the large family of Samuel Wesley, Rector of Epworth in Lincolnshire, **John [1703-1791] and Charles [1707-1788]** owed a great deal to their remarkable mother Susanna, as well as to the Puritan background of both parents.

Both brothers studied at the University of Oxford (at Christ Church) and both went on to be ordained as priests in the Church of England. In the early 1730's, lead first by Charles, then later by John, a small group of students met regularly for Bible study and prayer, received Communion frequently and undertook works of charity; such devout behaviour was unusual in those times and they were soon ridiculed. They were known by their fellow students by various nicknames – 'Bible Moths', 'Sacramentarians', 'Enthusiasts', 'Supererogation Men', 'The Holy Club', and, the one that stuck – 'Methodists'. Among others in the group was George Whitefield who would become the greatest preacher of the time. The Wesleys, Whitefield and other leaders were mostly ordained clergy of the Church of England.

In 1735 the Wesleys responded to an invitation to serve as chaplains to American colonies; this was unsuccessful, and both returned to Britain by 1738. Although neither returned to America, some 50 years later their followers (such as Francis Asbury and Thomas Coke) did, and so Methodism spread to the 'New World'.

Influenced by the Moravians the Wesleys joined in a 'Religious Society' in London, and in May 1738 both underwent a profound spiritual experience. John famously described this in his Journal for 24th May 1738:

"In the evening I went unwillingly to a society in Aldersgate Street, where one was reading Luther and preface to the Epistle to the Romans. About a quarter to nine, while he was describing the change which God works in the heart through faith in Christ, I felt my heart strangely warmed. I felt I did trust in Christ, Christ alone for salvation, and an assurance was given me that he had taken away my sins, even mine and saved me from the law of sin and death."

The next year Whitefield invited John Wesley to preach to crowds of working classes in Bristol in the open air. Since such people were often excluded from the churches. John finally agreed and recorded in his Journal for 2nd April 1739:

"At four in the afternoon I submitted to be more vile and proclaimed in the highways the glad tidings of salvation, speaking from a little eminence in a ground adjoining the city, to about three thousand people."

'Field preaching' became a key feature of the revival, and Wesley recorded addressing gatherings of many thousands. His published Sermons became and remain the doctrinal standard of the Methodist Church.

John Wesley was a genius when it came to organising his converts into local societies, originally modelled upon the 'Religious Societies' and his Oxford group; they were also subdivided into 'classes' which met weekly. Every year, by horse or carriage, John Wesley travelled the country to visit, encourage and admonish the societies, as well as preaching. John had no intention of setting up a church to rival the Church of England and he insisted that Methodists regularly attend their local parish church as well as Methodist meetings.

For the Wesleys, 'works' as well as faith were essential to the whole of Christian living, and caring for the poor, for prisoners, for widows and orphans mattered a great deal. Methodists were not only interested in welfare, they were concerned to remedy social injustice, and John Wesley's last known letter urged the abolition of 'that execrable villainy'; black slavery. The Wesleys were an influence in prison reform and, inspired by Susanna Wesley, they earned a reputation as pioneers in education. John Wesley wrote, edited or abridged some 400 publications.

Charles' contribution to the Methodist movement was as a hymnwriter. In his time, he penned in excess of six thousand hymns, some of which are still to be found in hymnbooks today. This was at a time when hymn singing was virtually unknown in the established church. After his marriage in 1749, Charles remained mostly in London and Bristol.

Although Wesley declared, "I live and die a member of the Church of England", the strength and impact of the movement made a separate Methodist body virtually inevitable. After John's death there began a series of breakaway movements including Primitive Methodism which began with 'camp meetings' in 1807 and was organised into a separate body in 1811. The Methodists grew to be a large, respectable and influential section of society; characterised by the 'nonconformist conscience' and also the 'temperance movement' and many members with poor origins became prosperous. The missionary movement also spread the Methodist message around the world. In 1932 the three main Methodist groups in Britain came together to form the present Methodist Church.

The Structure of Methodism

As the number of Methodist societies increased, some way of keeping in touch and organising them was needed. John Wesley held what became an annual conference of Methodist preachers. In 1784 he made provision for its continuance after his death when the leadership of the movement passed to the Methodist Conference. Conference appointed a minister as a President who would serve in that post for one year.

The Methodist Church has a Connexional structure rather than a congregational one. This is where the whole church acts and decides together, a local church is never independent of the rest of the Connexion. Everyone who becomes a member through confirmation is a member of the Methodist Church as a whole, not just their local church.

The Methodist Church in Britain is divided into circuits, each of which is made up of a number of local churches, each with their own Church Council. Each minister in a circuit is likely to have responsibility for several local churches. A Superintendent Minister is appointed to provide pastoral leadership to a circuit and chair the Circuit Meeting which usually meets twice each year. A number of circuits make up a district. There are 33 districts in the British Methodist Church. Each District has a Chair (in some regards like a Bishop in the Anglican Church) whose job is to provide leadership within the district and chair the District Synod which usually meets twice each year. The Synod decides policy for that district, within the parameters laid down by the annual Conference

It is difficult to be precise when it comes to establishing the number of members of the Methodist Church worldwide today. It appears to be somewhere in the region of sixty to eighty million, a figure which is similar to the number of Anglicans worldwide.

I did try to be brief! Honest! I hope that this 'brief' introduction to Methodism will prove to be sufficient to enable you to make sense of much of what follows in this memoir.

Background

[1947-1954]

My dad was manager of the Co-op store in Winlaton when I was born. He had been there during the war years (1939-1945). He had volunteered for service but failed his medical because of high blood pressure. Mam and Dad lived in the flat above the shop.

I should have been the youngest of four boys, but Mam lost the first three late in each pregnancy. They were stillborn and were delivered at home in each case. It fell to my dad to destroy the dead foetus by throwing it onto the fire in the living room. I only discovered this not long before Dad died. To ensure that I survived her fourth pregnancy Mam was confined to bed for several weeks before the due date. It worked. I should have been born on 4th July. The date came and went but there was to be no delay, so I was delivered by caesarean section at Newcastle Royal Victoria Infirmary just a couple of days later.

My dad's father owned a hunter pocket watch which was engraved RF on the case and Robert Fisher inside. At the time when my grandfather died it was traditional for such a pocket watch to be passed on to the eldest son. But, given that it was engraved 'Robert Fisher' my uncle Jim, who was the eldest, insisted that it should go to my dad. So, my name was decided even before I was conceived! I was born on 6th July 1947 and I was baptised 'Robert' by the Revd Jack Cullom at the Methodist Church in Blaydon on 24th August – all because of the pocket watch!

My paternal grandfather was a colliery blacksmith, responsible for shoeing the pit ponies. He died at the age of 67, a couple of years before I was born. Apparently, he went to bed one Sunday afternoon for his usual 'nap' and simply didn't wake up! My father was born South of the Tyne and recalled, as a youngster, seeing the last race ever run on Blaydon Racetrack, watching, with his father, from a hill outside the ground. "Blaydon Races" was, and still is, a popular Geordie folk song. Dad also recalled his dad taking him to a football match to see Sunderland play. He was lifted over the turnstile, as often happened in those days where youngsters were concerned.

Dad's mother, my 'Big' Grandma, was a Clapperton by birth. She originated from St Bees on the west coast of what is now Cumbria. Her sister emigrated to Canada. I have a photo of the two of them under the whale jawbone at Whitby before Grandma's sister emigrated.

My father wasn't the eldest, the 'first born' was my uncle Jim

(James), married to Aggie. They had one son, Roddy. Then there was a sister, Margaret. She married Jack Toothill and they had two children. I don't recall much about that family except that the children emigrated to Canada when I was quite young. Then came my father, then three more brothers Stevie (Stephen), Charlie (Charles), and Tot (Thomas) – always regarded as 'the black sheep of the family, although I never discovered why. Stevie and Charlie married two sisters Edie and Elsie and each couple had one daughter; one from a previous marriage, her first husband having died. They lived next door to each other and regularly changed their cars together, buying identical new models separated only by one digit on the licence plate! The cars I recall were the revolutionarily designed Ford Anglia, in yellow, and the Lada, when they first appeared on the British market.

At a school careers evening Stevie's stepdaughter said she wanted to 'marry a rich man' – she subsequently married a very wealthy owner of a DIY store in Ware. At the same evening Charlie's daughter told the careers teacher she wanted to be a brain surgeon. She did so well, academically, that she was fast-tracked at University where she studied medicine. She worked as a brain surgeon in both the United States and latterly in Edinburgh.

My father's family was 'nominally' Anglican. In their late teens my grandfather gave the family a choice, either a motorbike each or a bus between them! I still have the drawing my dad did of what was then the latest model of a charabanc bearing the logo 'R. Fisher & Sons' and the destination board reading 'Newcastle – London'. It would have been the first Newcastle

– London Service! All, apart from my dad, wanted a bike, so a bike each is what they had. Still, I was told, it came in handy for courting!

Whilst all his brothers followed their father down the pit Dad chose to work at the local Co-op beginning on what today we would call the 'deli' counter at the age of 13. He used to tell the tale of one customer who would always come into the shop on a Friday night at five minutes to eight, just before the shop closed. This particular Friday night she came in with a pack of bacon she'd bought a couple of days earlier complaining that it was covered with maggots and insisting that it be replaced. All the machines had been cleaned down, so my father took the pack of bacon through to the back shop and carefully washed each rasher, ensuring that all the maggots were removed. The bacon was rewrapped and given back to the customer. On the Monday she returned demanding some more of the bacon she'd been given on the Friday night as it was the tastiest bacon she ever eaten! Dad went on to become a manager in several different Co-op stores and opened the new Co-op at Westerhope as manager.

Dad met my mother at the local Primitive Methodist Church tennis club when he accidently knocked her out with a tennis racquet! My mother's father apparently had had a very dramatic conversion experience and the family began attending the local Primitive Methodist Church. Mam was the second oldest of seven children. Eva was the eldest, then after Mam, came Lila, Ruth, Albert, James (Jim) and Norman. Mam worked as a secretary at Lemington Glass Works after leaving school until, like most women at that time, she was married and gave up work to be a housewife. As a wedding present she was presented with a set of six handblown water tumblers. They were kept in the original box for years and they are still around somewhere although one was broken when I was a youngster. Mam was an excellent cook, I can still taste her Rabbit and Black Pudding pie, and her cheese scones were to die for. We were frequently in touch with her siblings and their families as I was growing up, more so than with my father's.

Along with a group of other lads my dad would hang about outside the Church waiting for the girls to come out after the evening service. Eventually they decided to go inside where it was warmer – I'm not sure that that was what John Wesley had in mind when he talked about his heart being 'strangely warmed' after his Aldersgate Street experience, recorded in his Journal on 24th May 1738, but it was the beginning of a lifetime of Christian commitment as far as my dad was concerned. So, Robert (Bob) Fisher and Elizabeth (Betty) Turnbull married at Algernon Road Methodist Church in Lemington on 1st January 1935 – it rained! They had a week's honeymoon in a cottage in Bamburgh. It belonged to the Carses, who were family friends. It is still there, as you drive south out of the village, one of several wooden bungalows, painted green!

They were on holiday in Scarborough in 1939 and on the Sunday, they went to the Methodist Church for the morning service. At the end of the service the minister announced that Britain was now at war with Germany. When they got back to the boarding house where they were staying, they found all the other guests packing up to go home. They couldn't understand why Mam and Dad had decided to stay for the rest of their holiday. Typical Dad!

When they were first married, they bought a house in Lorraine Terrace in Lemington. It was a three-storey mid-terrace house. They had little furniture. My mother had always wanted a piano. She got her wish, and the front room of their newly purchased house contained the piano, plus, I was told, a step ladder, and nothing else! Dad recalled how, not long after they moved in, they smelled a gas leak and called the Gas Board. When the gasman arrived, he asked Dad for a candle so he could better see the gas meter in the cupboard under the stairs!

They used to regularly meet up with friends at the end of each week to play Mah Jong, so Dad purchased a genuine antique set. Unfortunately, there were no roman numerals on the tiles so Dad laboriously, using a pin, scratched the correct number of each tile using Indian Ink to make it legible. He also made a box to house them in. I still have the Mah Jong set. He was, apparently quite adept with his hands and during the General Strike made a pair of turned candlesticks and a cabinet comprising a lot of small drawers made from the wood of butter boxes. When, in later life he became an Insurance Agent it proved invaluable as a 'filing cabinet' to store various forms for his job. His eyesight wasn't bad either. He could draw around a silver threepenny bit, (about the same size as a 'modern' 5p) and write The Lord's Prayer within the circle. It required a very sharp pencil, a steady hand and a sharp eye! With a succession of promotions, each coming with a 'tied house' the house on

Lorraine Terrace was rented out until they eventually moved to Durham when it had to be sold, complete with the full-sized billiard table in the attic. No-one knew how it got up there, it was there when they first moved in, and no-one could work out a way to get it out!

The minister had tried to persuade my Dad to go into the ministry, but my mother insisted she could never be a minister's wife. However, he was given 'a note to preach'. The exams were far more demanding than in later years, and, as well as Old and New Testament studies, Church History and Theology they included Primitive Methodist Law and Polity, and English Grammar! When Dad was taking his final exam in English Grammar, in the minister's study, the minister saw him struggling and took a book from his shelves with the comment that "such matters should never prevent someone from preaching the Gospel!"

Dad came 'On Full Plan' (became a 'Fully Accredited Local Preacher') in 1932, in the Primitive Methodist Church, in the last Quarter before Methodist Union when the Wesleyan, Primitive and United Methodist Churches came together to form the Methodist Church of Great Britain. He was not in favour of Methodist Union which he felt was too heavily weighted in favour of the Wesleyans who were less inclined to favour the laity. He was however always a democrat, so when invited to preach at a society that had refused to enter the Union he declined, much to their surprise. He was an excellent preacher! He also served in a number of Offices in the Church including Circuit Steward, before I was born, and Youth Club and Youth Fellowship leader when I was a youngster.

During the war years Dad continued as a Local Preacher. He recalled how, after one service he took there was a short Prayer Meeting. One elderly gentleman got to his feet and began to pray. "Lord, you told us that we had to pray for our enemies so tonight I am praying for Hitler. Last year I prayed that you would freeze him to death in the arctic. This year I am praying that you will burn him to death in the Sahara." I don't think he'd quite understood what Jesus had meant!

I recall a number of tales Dad told about the war years when everything was rationed. On one occasion when he had a number of odd items of crockery that he simply couldn't get shift he put a notice in front of them that read 'Only one item per customer'. They all sold within an hour. Next day one purchaser returned wanting to know what she could use her purchase for as she had no idea!

Dad was usually on 'Firewatch', especially at night when the bombers came over to bomb the nearby Blaydon tar pits. On one occasion a nearby barn was bombed and a group was despatched to rescue what animals they could. One young lad came out of the blazing barn with a hen under each arm. "What should I do with them now?" he asked. The reply startled him, "Let the buggers go, they'll either fly or run!" On another occasion my parents went to bed but didn't hear either the air raid siren or the bomb that was dropped nearby. When they went to bed the blind was on the inside of the huge plate glass window at the front of the store. When they came down in the morning to open up the blind was on the outside of the window! The blast from the bomb had lifted the plate glass window out of its frame, flipped the blind to the outside and then replaced the glass!

Despite rationing many people, apparently, were still fussy about branded goods that were available. On one occasion Dad called in at Blaydon Flour Mill. The milled flour travelled on a conveyor belt which split at the end and the flour was fed into a variety of branded bags, Bero, Hovis, Co-op, etc. Try telling his customers that despite the label on the bag the flour was exactly the same! I used to think this was a bit of a tall tale until I experienced something similar when I was delivering orders for the Co-op in Durham during one of my University vacations. But more of that later.

The first and second ages...

At first the infant,
Mewling and puking in the nurse's arms;
And then the whining school-boy, with his satchel
And shining morning face, creeping like snail
Unwillingly to school.

My Earliest Recollections – Prudhoe

I don't recall anything of living in Winlaton, I guess we must have moved from there when I was only two or three years old.

My earliest recollections are from the time we lived in Prudhoe. During the 1930s, with a view to self-improvement Dad attended evening classes to gain qualifications in book-keeping and accountancy. By the time he was 40 my Dad had worked his way up to be Manager of quite a big Co-op branch in Prudhoe, with grocery, butchery, drapery, and hardware departments. We lived in the Manager's house which was attached to the Co-op where my father was both Branch Manager and manager of the Grocery Department. Facing the Co-op was St John's Methodist Church, a typical ex-Wesleyan building. The manse was on the same site. Dad became good friends with the minister, the Rev'd Walter Best, and his son Geoffrey became my best friend.

I remember the day after bonfire night, I guess I was about five, Geoffrey and I combed the Manse garden to find as many of the empty firework tubes from the celebrations of the night before. They each contained a little gunpowder. We tipped them all into one tube and put a twist of paper in the top. We then went to find Geoffrey's mam to get some matches. Needless to say, we didn't get any! On another occasion we were given some chewing gum that we chewed and promptly swallowed. When we asked for more none was forthcoming. I lost track of Geoffrey when we moved to Durham when I was six. I didn't come across him again until, in my seventies I kept regularly seeing a post on FaceBook from a Geoffrey Best. He eventually 'messaged' me to ask if I was the same Robert Fisher who had played with him the manse garden in Prudhoe! Remarkably he seems to share the same political and theological views as myself. Perhaps an inheritance from our fathers who, when we were children, were such good friends.

My earliest recollection is, at about the age of 4, reciting my 'piece' at the Sunday School Anniversary at St. John's Methodist Church in Prudhoe:

'Buttercups and Daisies
All the pretty flowers
Coming in the Springtime,
They tell of happy hours.'

My earliest recollection of school was at Prudhoe. I guess I was about five years old. We'd all taken fruit and veg for the Harvest Festival and this was then auctioned off to the children. I don't know how much money my mother had given me, but I bought so much produce home I couldn't carry it, dropping a cabbage in the middle of the road I had to cross when walking home.

I remember I had a blue pedal car, before I was bought a tricycle. I had a habit of leaving it in the unmade drive that ran alongside the Manager's house. I was warned, umpteen times, that it was liable to be stolen, even though there was a substantial gate at the end of the drive. One day it disappeared, and only re-appeared when I finally confirmed that I had learned my lesson! Dad had hidden it in the Store yard. Dad would tell the story of when he found me painting the step at the side entrance to our house. Apparently, I had found a tin of silver paint and a small twig with leaves on it that served as a paintbrush and I had set about transforming the step. I honestly don't recall that particular incident.

At some point my parents must have opened a savings account

with National Savings as I recall, on occasion, buying the saving stamps which featured a picture of a very young Prince Charles on them and sticking them in the savings book. I recall that the stamps were predominantly blue in colour. I have no idea whatever happened to the account.

It was while we were living in Prudhoe that my parents realised that my eyesight was not as it should be. It turned out that I had virtually no sight in my left eye, I could only distinguish dark and light, and I was short sighted in my right eye. So National Health horn-rimmed glasses became the fashion icon of choice for many years. And for many years, in fact into my teens, regular visits to the eye hospital in Newcastle became common place. No-one could explain the cause of the blindness in my left eye.

While we were living in Prudhoe Dad decided to buy the 'Mickey Mouse' comic each week for me. I kept every issue over the years, much to my mam's annoyance. I only stopped collecting them when 'Mickey Mouse' merged with 'Dan Dare'. I took 'Dan Dare' for a while although I didn't save any issues. The box with the 'Mickey Mouse' comics lodged in the top landing cupboard in Durham until I was in University and Mam asked whether she could now get rid of it. I agreed, but several weeks later regretted my decision when it was reported in a newspaper that a complete set of 'Mickey Mouse' comics had sold for several thousand pounds! Maybe my obsession with collecting things began with 'Mickey Mouse'!

One of the ladies at church was a Mrs Yielder. She lived not far from our house. She was crippled with arthritis but still persisted in crocheting. I recall taking my cousin Ruth to visit her when my Auntie Lila, Uncle Graeme, and Ruth and Gwenneth were visiting from Flixton. Ruth sat in a pram, fastened somehow to the back of my tricycle and I towed her down the street but couldn't manage the hill up to where Mrs Yielder lived!

Dad bought our first car when we lived in Prudhoe. It was a 1938 Ford 8 that had served as a Police car during the Second World War. It belonged to Billy Bewick, who was the Butchery Manager in the Store where my father was Branch Manager. Billy had kept the car immaculate. It lived, under cover, in the yard behind the Store. I recall on one occasion Dad went out into the Store yard one Saturday and found Billy washing and polishing the car even though he had sold it to my Dad months earlier. He just couldn't bear to see his pride and joy being neglected.

Where the counter met the manager's office there was a section that lifted up allowing access via a 'half door' to the area behind the counter. I am told, though I don't recall the incident, that on one occasion Dad caught me swinging on the half-door telling all the customers that the next day we were off on holiday. Apparently, many of them gave me some spending money. Dad was not amused!

We were still living in Prudhoe when the Coronation of Elizabeth II took place. Mam and Dad bought a TV for the occasion – a Murphy with a 12" screen. On the day there was no public transport and Dad and I drove through from Prudhoe to Lemington to bring his Mam, my 'Big' Grandma, back to watch the Coronation on our new TV. We passed two young women hitching a lift and Dad stopped to pick them up. When we dropped them off, they gave me a sixpence! The roads that day were deserted. By contrast our front room was packed with family, friends and neighbours to watch the ceremony on our new TV!

When I was growing up, I saw quite a bit of my cousins, especially those on my mother's side of the family. On Sundays when we were living at Prudhoe, we would often visit my Auntie Eva and Uncle Bill, who lived not far along the road in Halfway, for Sunday tea. So Melville, who was the oldest of my cousins, and I would play together, or go into the cellar to watch my Uncle Bill's budgerigars which he used to breed. Auntie Ruth and Uncle Ridley had two children, Norman and Paul. There were quite a few years between them, so when I was in my teens and living in Durham, first Norman (until he discovered girls) and then Paul would come through from Newcastle to spend a Saturday with me. A little later John, Auntie Elsie and Uncle Jim's son, did the same, coming through from Windy Nook. Later on, when I had left home, John lived at Mam and Dad's, with his friend George Curry, while they studied for their degrees at Durham University.

Uncle Albert and Auntie Ella lived on a farm in Northumberland. They had four children, James (Jim), Elsie, Trevor and Hazel. We didn't see so much of them as it was a bit of a trek to Heddon-on-the Wall and later to Ogle, near Ponteland. Uncle Norman and Auntie Rita and cousin Marion lived in Seaham

Harbour. Again, we didn't see so much of them but always looked forward to visits with them as Auntie Rita was a Home Economics teacher, so her baking was first rate! That only leaves Auntie Lila and Uncle Graeme (who was profoundly deaf), Ruth and Gwenneth, who lived in Flixton near Manchester. Once we had a car, we would go to visit them for a week's holiday most years.

When I was six, we moved to Durham. My father, rebel, visionary, and man of principle resigned as branch manager of the Co-op in Prudhoe after a theft of cigarettes. They'd been checked off the wagon but when Dad went back into the shop the driver loaded them all back on the wagon and 'did a runner'. He was caught, but the management committee were constantly 'checking up' on my dad after that to the point where he decided he had had enough. If they couldn't trust him, he would go elsewhere. He was 'on the dole' for six months before getting a job as an Insurance agent – for the Co-operative Insurance Society, in Durham, so we moved!

Durham

[1954 – 1965]

The house my parents bought had a magnificent view of the Cathedral. It was a three storey mid-terrace – 5 Palatine View. It needed a lot of work doing to it and over the years I helped my Dad and honed my own DIY skills in the process.

Not long after we moved in Dad began the work of improvement. In the back yard there was a coalhouse, a storage outhouse, and an outside toilet. After getting planning permission he turned the toilet round and brought it 'inside' by adding it on to the end of the kitchen. The other buildings were demolished, and a garage was built. The garage was quite unique in that it was built parallel to the back lane which meant doing a parallel park to get the car into the garage. Since the back lane was higher than the backyard Dad created a 'pit' beneath the car and a coal hole, accessed from both the garage and the back yard. Coal fires were still the principal form of heating and we regularly had the chimney sweep come around. I remember playing in the back lane which was surfaced with a concrete and pebble mix. On one occasion when I fell, I took a lump out of my knee. I still have the scar!

Those were the days of the travelling shop. The local Co-op had several. We were regularly visited by the Grocer, Greengrocer and Butcher. And, of course, if you sent your order in it would be delivered to your door. I don't recall whether or not Mam phoned it in, but I still recall our Durham phone number – Durham 2335 – one digit more than our Prudhoe number – Prudhoe 223. I find it amusing that the 'modern' Superstores have now begun delivering orders as if it was something new that they had invented! Truly there is nothing new under the sun! The same is true where loyalty cards are concerned. The Store (the Co-op) always paid dividends to its members each year. Whenever you shopped there you gave them your divi number – Mam's was 12372 – and you were given a slip of paper, a bit like a cloakroom ticket. Over the year they added up to a nice little bonus.

By my teens Dad had had two Dormer windows fitted in the attic and those two rooms became my – almost – self-contained flat. By then Dad had also altered the back bedroom on the first floor to create a bathroom and a smaller bedroom. The front little bedroom, which was mine before I moved into the attic, had the most magnificent view of the Cathedral. In the fashion of the day Dad 'modernised' the doors by covering them with a sheet of hardboard edged with simple beading. He also boxed in the staircase. Cutting and bending the hardboard to go around the bends, on the rise, proved quite a task! Downstairs the wall between the front and back rooms was removed and glass sliding doors were put in making the back room much lighter. Because it was too easy to walk into the glass door, plastic doilies were glued on at head height as a reminder when the doors were closed. Although Mam and Dad usually did their own decorating when it came to the front room, they had Billy Fenwick do it. He was a Painter and Decorator who lived on Crossgate with whom my Dad had insurance business. He did a remarkable job. The paper they chose was basically pale grey with white and lemon sprays of flowers on it. Billy picked out some of the cornice and ceiling rose in pastel lemon. The effect was impressive.

On more than one occasion we went on holiday – to Tynemouth! We rented a top floor flat in a mid-terrace overlooking the green. There was a fabulous Crazy Golf course near the hotel at the seafront. I've never seen one as good since. Every hole was amazing – a windmill, a helter-skelter, a French horn – every one brightly painted. I recall on one occasion, when it was raining, being taken to the cinema in Tynemouth to see the recently released 'Wizard of Oz'. It was impressive. I also recall spending time on the beach and in the outdoor swimming pool nearby.

Palatine View was a fairly friendly neighbourhood. The Bests lived at number 1. They were also a Methodist family who attended Jubilee Methodist Church. Bob was a local preacher, with Annie his wife they had two children, John and Margaret. They were a year or two older than me, so I didn't mix with them much apart from at church.

Bob was also the scout leader of a local troop and he pestered me endlessly to join the Scouts. They met above the Market Hall and I went once and decided never again since the most exciting thing we did that night was to go out into the town and collect things beginning with the letter 'C'! Sadly, Bob died, relatively young I guess, and Annie decided that the body should be taken straight to the undertakers, rather than being available to view in the house. Her decision caused quite a bit of comment in the neighbourhood, as such a decision was unusual at that time.

Ian Atkinson lived at number 2 along with his mam and gran. We grew up believing that his dad had died but learned many years later, after I had left Durham, that in fact he was illegitimate, his father was a Police Inspector who was married when Ian was born. Keeping such a secret was just what you did in those days. Ian was a bit younger than me, but we often played together, especially during Junior School years.

'Nellie' lived in number 4. She was single, elderly, and a recluse. The House was dirty and smelly. We saw virtually nothing of her. The guy who lived at number 6 bred guinea pigs. He had a couple of huts on his allotment in which he housed them. The allotments occupied the land facing Palatine View next to St Margaret's Primary School, separated from St Margaret's graveyard by a narrow pathway that led to South Street which was immediately across the river from the Cathedral.

The Svensons lived at number 7. They had two children, a boy and a girl, about my age, with whom I used to play. I don't recall their names, but the parents were called David and Sylvia – I remember that clearly since that was how their children addressed them! At that time such familiarity was almost unheard of! They came to Durham from Tripoli. What the parents did, I never did find out. I suspect they were involved at the university.

Summerville separated numbers 3 and 4 Palatine view. Two girls, we often played with, lived in Summerville, Sonia Spedding and Lilian Johnson. We kind of lost track when we began our Secondary Education since the Grammar Schools were single sex although the Secondary Modern was mixed. David and Ethel Edwards also lived in Summerville. My parents befriended them, though I don't know why. David, who was Welsh, was a retired sea captain. He captained the last of the clipper ships that were in commercial service. Ethel was virtually blind. In my teens I used to go, each week, to the library to choose books for David, thrillers mainly. After he died, I used to put into practise the DIY skills, learned from my father, by 'modernising' the house to make it better for Ethel. I recall cutting out the top of the kitchen door that led into the back yard and putting a window in it to lighten the kitchen for her. She had a beautiful long-case Grandfather Clock that she promised to leave me in her will! I never did discover what happened to it. To the best of my knowledge they had no family.

On the other side of 1 Palatine View was a huge orchard. We never did discover who owned it. It was enclosed by a high wall with a gated entrance that led to some derelict outbuildings then opened into the orchard. It was permanently locked, and the gate was too high to climb over. Nevertheless, we managed to find a way in, and it became our playground on sunny days in the school holidays. In the winter we would make our way to Observatory Hill, beyond Durham School to go sledging. Dad had used the steel runners he had found on an old sledge to make me a new one from a design by Barry Bucknell that appeared in the Radio Times. It worked remarkably well.

Primary School

The primary school I attended was, literally, just across the road. St Margaret's C of E Primary school. I began in the Infant Department which was housed in 'temporary' classrooms on one side of the School yard. All I remember from my time in the Infants was doing a drawing of the three crosses of the crucifixion in crayon on sugar paper. It measured c. 3" x 3" and I covered it in transparent adhesive tape. It's still around somewhere.

The Headteacher was a Mr Robson. I think I twice had the cane, though I cannot now remember why. Miss Boxall was the first teacher I encountered in the Junior School. I remember her being very strict, and I remember there being a roaring fire in the corner of the classroom. I have clearer memories of the top two classes. In Mr Pallister's class I remember losing a penny behind the door at break time as an excuse to kiss Jennifer Wilson – we were caught, and the kiss never happened! Charlie Pickering, who taught the top class, wrote in royal blue ink in the most beautiful copperplate writing – something I always tried to emulate, though not terribly successfully. In his class I sat next to Geoffrey Walker, who was always in trouble. As a consequence, I had the record for getting the strap during my year in Mr Pickering's class, largely because of Geoffrey!

At some point during my time in Junior School I started learning to play the piano. My teacher was a Mr Foster who was the organist at Croxdale Methodist Church. I presume Dad had preached there at some point and 'discovered' him. He was very pedestrian. I can't say I enjoyed learning the piano under his tutelage but to his credit he got me through a whole series of exams, up to the highest grade. Eventually, when I was in secondary education, I gave up the piano and instead started playing the violin at school and for a while was leading second violin in the school orchestra. Eventually I abandoned the violin and in the sixth form decided to take up the piano again. My teacher, whose name I cannot now remember, was again a church organist, but much younger and more enthusiastic than my previous teacher! No exams to practice for and I thoroughly enjoyed playing this time. Sadly, after leaving school my practicing lapsed. It is one of the things I most regret.

From a very early age I found that I thoroughly enjoyed reading. I suppose it began in Prudhoe when Dad started buying me the Mickey Mouse comic. It was after we moved to Durham that it merged with the Eagle, which, interestingly was founded by Marcus Morris, an Anglican vicar from Lancashire. He edited a Southport parish magazine called 'The Anvil' but felt that it was not communicating its message effectively. He was also disillusioned with contemporary children's literature, so he and 'Anvil' artist Frank Hampson created a comic based on Christian values. It was first published in 1950 and ran until 1969. Dan Dare was inspired by the biblical story of Daniel. By my teens I was bored with comics but there was no alternative available for boys. Consequently, each week, when I was in town, I would call in at the little newsagents in Milburngate to buy a copy of both Bunty and Judy, girls' publications, but with 'proper' stories!

Secondary School

I passed the Eleven Plus, largely, I think, because of the 'weighting' as I was one of the youngest in the class. So, in September 1958 I began my Secondary Education at the Johnston Grammar Technical School at Crossgate Moor. It was a very new building, having recently moved there from the bottom of South Street where a new County Library was built on the vacated site.

One of my earliest recollections from that first term at the Johnston School was the last execution at Durham Prison in December 1958 when 18-year-old Brian Chandler was hanged for battering 83-year-old Martha Dodd of Darlington to death. An eerie silence descended over the whole city when the time of the execution arrived. Although nothing was said we were aware of it in our classroom. Brian was registered as a 'Methodist' so our minister, the Rev'd Harold Stanaway had to witness the execution. I learned later that after the execution he wrote to the Home Secretary to protest against the continued use of capital punishment. It must have been a truly traumatic experience. It wasn't until 1965 that the death penalty for murder was banned in England, Scotland and Wales. Northern Ireland outlawed capital punishment in 1973. However, several crimes, including treason, remained punishable by death in Great Britain until 1998.

I tried school dinners for a term and decided that I wasn't keen. The lunch hour was long enough for me to walk home for lunch and catch the bus back in time for afternoon school. At some point during my secondary school years Grandma, my mother's mother came to live with us. She and Grandpa had lived in a bungalow in Throckley, then with my Auntie Ruth and Uncle Ridley in Ryton. After Grandpa died it was decided that each of the children would have Grandma live with them for a few weeks each in turn. It didn't quite work out as intended and she came to live with us on a semi-permanent basis! She drove Mam to despair as she never moved from her rocking chair beside the fire. This particular day Mam must have lost it and Grandma put her hat and coat on and went off in a huff without saying where she was going. When I got in for lunch I was despatched to see if I could find where she was but without making any contact! I found her sitting of a seat halfway in the Peth. I returned home for my lunch. Grandma finally came home after I had gone back to school. She never went walkabout again!

My academic career in secondary education was one of steady decline. From being third in the class in my first year to being bottom of the class by the end of my third year. We then had to choose which class we wanted to be in for GCEs. 4E (or was it 4L?) meant taking two languages – French and German. 4S meant taking three sciences – Physics, Chemistry and Biology. I can't remember the designation of the third class, but it meant taking Woodwork, Metalwork and Tech Drawing. 4C (which for some reason meant 'Commerce') meant taking one language, one science, and one technical subject. I chose 4C.

I guess like most people my age looking back, I only remember some of my teachers at the Johnston School, for a variety of reasons. 'Massa' Reece – not sure about the spelling – was a Welshman who taught us Latin in our second year. We didn't make life easy for him. I remember pinning an 'L' plate of the back of his gown (all the staff wore gowns) where it remained in place through several lessons that morning! Then there was 'Tut' (as in Tutankhamun) Harbottle who taught history. I'm ashamed to say we made his life hell, even to the point of discovering his home address and ordering a greenhouse and several tons of manure to be delivered there. His colleague, Mr Harrison, who also taught history was made of much sterner stuff.

'Arty' Brown, unsurprisingly, taught art. He was ex-military, and it showed! We were never allowed to leave the art room unless it was immaculate. Not a spot of paint anywhere and every paintbrush clean and in its place. He was a great teacher. Sadly, he died suddenly of a heart attack, during either my second or third year. I don't remember the name of the teacher who replaced him, but I do remember that the art room was never clean or tidy again!

Dave Lishman taught me Maths for the two years I was studying for my GCE. I remember a lesson in the Tech Drawing Office when I had to go to his desk to explain why I had the correct answers to the eight algebra problems he had set for homework but hadn't shown any working. I had worked them out by mental arithmetic – I never could make sense of algebra. Needless to say, I failed my GCE Maths gaining a grade 9 – 'if a thing is worth failing, it's worth failing well!'

I was equally unsuccessful with French. When it came to the oral, the examiner became so frustrated with my inability to respond, in French, to any of her questions that she finally pointed out of the window to a bird on the grass outside and said, somewhat aggressively, "Qu'est-ce que c'est?" to which I finally managed to respond, "un oiseau"! Like Maths I gained a grade 9!

Anyway, I did pass six 'O' levels. I was awarded a Grade 1 for Divinity and English Literature ... six passes were enough to gain an award at 'Speech Day'. Those who did were entitled to receive a book of their choice. I chose "The Methodist Story" by Cyril J Davey. Needless to say, it had to be ordered specially. So, while everyone else was given the book of their choice on the day I received a 'dummy' book and had to wait to receive mine later.

Six passes were also sufficient to enter the Sixth Form. However, when it came to taking 'A' levels, because I wanted to take English and RE, I had to take French. Mr Turnbull persevered with me for about a term and then agreed that I could drop the subject. So, I ended up filling in my time in the woodwork and metalwork workshops. Among other things I made a projector stand and a turned bowl for my mam!

I also managed to make a copy of the school master key in the metal workshop. It worked, and that led to a number of pranks being played on our Sixth Form tutor, Tom Greener. Our form room was a small classroom at the beginning of the bottom corridor to the right of the main entrance. It was locked during the lunch hour. No problem. On one occasion we got in and moved all the desks and chairs into the, locked, stockroom. We repeated this on another occasion, this time placing the bust of the school's founder, with a cycle tyre round its neck, in the centre of the empty room. The bust normal resided outside the library on the first floor at the other end of the building. On another occasion we stacked the desks between the window wall and the door so that the door couldn't be opened, intending that one of us would exit via one of the small opening windows that were at ceiling height on the corridor side of the room. It didn't quite work as none of us was small enough to squeeze through the window so the desk nearest the door had to allow for someone to squeeze through the door. Tom Greener was not amused by any of our pranks!

Through my Secondary School years, with just a couple of exceptions, Scripture was taught by Tom Greener. He also ran a lunchtime SCM Club. Much later I discovered that most schools ran Christian Unions, supported by IVF and latterly by Scripture Union. Christian Unions were largely conservative evangelical groups. SCM was theologically progressive. Looking back being a member of an SCM group undoubtedly played its part in my own Christian formation. Tom was a member of our Church, and a Local Preacher. When it came to GCE 'O' and 'A' levels Tom was our teacher. The two exceptions were when we were taught for a brief spell by a Church of Scotland minister (I don't recall why) and a young Maths teacher who also happened to be a Methodist, attending one of the other churches on the outskirts of the city.

Every year the school put on two productions, a Shakespeare play and a Gilbert and Sullivan operetta. The two I remember were Henry V and The Pirates of Penzance. Remember, at the time it was an all-boys school so, in keeping with tradition, all the female parts were played by boys. I had no ambition to perform but enjoyed being part of the stage crew.

I only ever skived off school once, and then it was only for an afternoon. Dad was a fairly keen supporter of Sunderland AFC. He rarely went to a match but every Saturday evening I would go with him to Durham Bus Station to buy a copy of the Sunderland Echo for the report on the latest match. If Sunderland remained in the First Division, the paper was pink. On the occasion when they were demoted to the Second Division, the paper was green!

The year I was in the Lower Sixth Sunderland were playing Manchester United in the F.A. Cup 6th Round at Roker Park. They had met at Old Trafford and the game was a draw, so this match was a replay. Although the official attendance was given at just under 47,000, eyewitness spectator accounts estimated that there could have been as many as 80,000 inside Roker Park at kick off time. It was also estimated that as many as 40,000 were 'locked out' of the game. Dad was one of those who was 'locked out'! The game finished 2-2. So, United had to face Sunderland for a 3rd time but this time on the neutral ground of Huddersfield Town 5 days later.

Clifford Turnbull, Joe Kidd and my Dad decided to go to the 2nd replay and Joe's second son, David, who was also in the Sixth Form, and I, decided to go with them. It meant missing afternoon school. Clifford took his car. We got to the ground with enough time to spare to gain entry. The crowd was officially recorded as 54,952. Everyone was wearing red and white scarves, the colours of both teams. We managed to get a position quite high up in the stands. It quickly became apparent that we were in the middle of a huge contingent of Manchester United supporters. It was a good game which Manchester United won 5-1. The crowd was remarkably good natured. As we left the ground those who were near us commiserated, some even saying, quite sincerely, that Sunderland should never have lost by that scoreline as they had played well. Some even said that Sunderland were the better team on the pitch! Such good-natured rivalry would be hard to imagine today!

In the school holidays I would often go with Dad when he went out collecting insurance on Mondays, Fridays and Saturday mornings. Mondays were fine. The houses we went to were on the Sunderland Road Estate and its environs. Saturday mornings were fine, Carville and Belmont and then nearer into the city. The car was essential on a Saturday. Fridays however were a different matter. Most of his round on a Friday was around the Sherburn Road Estate. The estate had been built to move families from the slums in the Framwellgate and Milburngate areas in the town centre which were scheduled for redevelopment. The new estate quickly deteriorated as families seemed unable to change their lifestyles. One house we went to used the bath in the downstairs bathroom to store their coal. Access to the first floor was via a ladder, the stairs having been removed and chopped up for firewood. Another house, one I refused to go into after my first visit, stank, and your shoes stuck to the lino in the kitchen because of the urine that had impregnated it. I got to know his round so well that in the year before he retired, when he contracted a severe case of 'flu, and I happened to be home because it was during one of my University vacations, I did his round for two weeks since otherwise, because he was paid solely on commission, he would have had no income that fortnight.

I went on my first trip abroad when I was at the Johnston School. It was to Annecy in France. It was a wonderful experience. One thing I particularly remember was a visit to a glacier. We were able to go through a tunnel that took us right to the centre. It was surreal with ice all around. The tunnel had to be dug out afresh every year to allow for the glaciers slow but inexorable movement. We also crossed the border into Switzerland to visit Geneva. In Annecy I remember being fascinated by the shops. Everything was so different, from food to stationary.

In the summer holidays after fifth form (Year11) I was one of several students from across Northumberland and Durham to meet up with a group of students from Czechoslovakia. We joined them at a Secondary School in Newbiggin-by-the-Sea where we spent two weeks with them, sleeping on the floor in various classrooms and making various trips out around the region. At the end of the fortnight, we exchanged gifts, and hoped to meet on the next occasion, in two years' time, in Czechoslovakia. Whether it happened I don't know, as two years on I was off elsewhere!

The Sixth Form Dance was the highlight of seven years in Secondary School. For many, it was a problem to know who to invite. Being in an all-boys school meant most of us had little contact with suitable girls! Being involved in Church helped as I knew a number of girls of my age in various Churches in the town an in the end, I invited a girl who attended St Nicholas' C of E Church. Dad had insurance business with her parents. To my shame I can no longer recall her name as that was our one and only date. A year or two later Dad told me her parents had divorced. They'd not spoken to each other for years but had stayed together for the sake of their daughter! However, once she went off to University they decided to split up. So sad.

Church

When we first moved to Durham, we attended Jubilee Methodist Church. It was the ex-Primitive Methodist Church, situated at the bottom of North Road near Framwellgate bridge. Elvet Methodist Church was ex-Wesleyan and Bethel, at the top of North Road next to the Bus Station was ex-United

Methodist. Mam and Dad had been Primitive Methodists so not surprisingly they opted to attend Jubilee. Methodist Union had only happened in 1932, only 20 years before we moved to Durham.

The Trotter family were the leading lights at Jubilee. Four sisters, as I recall, and one brother. They lived on The Peth. Only one of the sisters, Winnie, was married, to Clifford Turnbull. They had a son, Michael, a couple of years younger than me, and a good friend when we were growing up. Clifford was a Local Preacher. I was given a 'Note' to preach, when I was sixteen, and was placed 'on Note' with Clifford. He was an excellent preacher, one of three of the best in the Circuit when I was growing up. Joe Kidd, from Sherburn, and my Dad were the other two.

The Trotters ran the Sunday School between them. Despite what may seem to be implied, they were all very good. One of the Trotters was also in charge of the Junior Christian Endeavour, which met on a Tuesday evening. Clifford was one of the Youth Fellowship leaders, along with my Dad. Sunday School was at 2.00 pm on a Sunday afternoon. When you became too old for Sunday School it was time to move into the Bible Class. This met in the Church at the same time as Sunday School and was led by Tom Greener. Tom was also an excellent Local Preacher, a bit more 'academic' than the other three, perhaps because he was the RE teacher at the Johnston School.

Tom and his wife, Flora, had two children, John, quite a few years older than me, and Anne, just a couple of years older than me. I remember having to sing a duet with Anne at a Church concert – 'Are you going to Scarborough Fair?' Every Christmas we had a Nativity Play and, because I had a good singing voice, I was usually cast in the role of one of the kings, as we always sang 'We three kings of Orient are'. One year I objected, insisting that I should be cast as a shepherd. That was fine, but the next year I was back to being a king once again!

Sundays meant Morning Service at 10.30 am; Sunday School / Bible Class at 2.00 pm; Evening Service at 6.00 pm; then, in your teens, Youth Fellowship at 7.30 pm. As a fan of 'The Goons Show' and 'Hancock's Half-hour' which were broadcast on Sundays between 1.00 pm and 2.00 pm on the 'Home Service', later 'Radio 4' I had to run from home down Crossgate to Jubilee usually arriving – out of breath – just in time for the beginning of Sunday School. I remember over a number of years being entered for the Scripture Exam. That undoubtedly gave me a real grounding in Scripture that would prove to be invaluable in the years that followed. For some reason, I know not why, the time of the morning Service was changed from 10.30 am to 10.45 am. Joe Bradley, the Youth Club leader always arrived at 10.35 am. Everyone expected that with the change in Service time Joe's tardiness would be a thing of the past. Not a chance! He subsequently arrived each week at 10.50 am!

From starting Sunday School, I began collecting for JMA (it came to be known as 'Junior Mission for All' although when I was a youngster, I think the initials stood for 'Juvenile Missionary Association). You were given a little book in which to record the names of family, church members, and friends who committed to give you a small sum of money each week for missionary work. Most of my friends had only a handful of family member contributors. Typically, I had lots of names of church folk as well, so I usually collected the most money over the year. At the end of the year you received a Certificate and, the first year a medal, and subsequent years a bar to add to the medal's ribbon. The other thing I remember from Sunday School days was selling Sunny Smiles on behalf of NCH (National Children's Homes, now 'Action for Children'). You were given a small booklet full of pictures of individual smiling children's faces and you were expected to sell as many as possible to family and friends. They chose a picture, tore it out to keep, and gave you a donation for NCH. It was a good way of encouraging a child to think of others apart from themselves.

I have a newspaper cutting from the Durham County Advertiser from the 1950s, taken on the occasion of Overseas Missions Sunday. It shows members of the congregation on the steps outside Jubilee Methodist Church. Dad took the morning service for the Revd Harold Stanaway, who was ill. Miss Edna Konote Ahulu from Ghana gave a talk on missionary work and presented JMA awards. Dad is pictured on the left towards the back and I am on the front row second from the left. I became a member of the Methodist Church at Jubilee in the late 1950s when the Rev'd Harold Stanaway was the minister.

Youth Club met on a Thursday night. We did all sorts of activities. I was one of several who were entered in a Public Speaking Contest over a number years. Again, one of those things that undoubtedly played a part in preparing me for my later life. Joe also arranged a number of visits 'out'. One that particularly sticks in my mind was a visit to the offices of the Durham County Advertiser, where we saw the way the paper went to press.

I mentioned the Junior Christian Endeavour a while back. I took over the running of it in my early teens. I organised it into four 'houses', awarded points for attendance among other things and presented the 'winning' house with a cup each month. I quadrupled the attendance in a very short time. It was fascinating, when we retired to Crook in 2012 to come across several people who still recalled fondly my time in charge of the Junior Christian Endeavour. At about the same time I set up a 'Town Youth Fellowship' so we got to know other young Christians who attended churches of other denominations in the city. The guy who owned and ran 'The House of Andrews' bookshop on Saddler Street let us use the Coffee Shop (to which there was separate access) on one evening a week as a 'drop-in' coffee shop, without adult supervision! At that time, I also began producing a 'magazine' called 'Logos', using covers produced by the Bible Lands Society.

Ministers I remember while I was growing up included the Revd Wilfrid Billington, who was a good preacher and a very conscientious visitor, though, unless you could talk cricket, conversation was a bit limited. He was followed by the Revd Harold Stanaway, who was an excellent visitor, and a well-prepared, though not a terribly inspiring, preacher. When Jubilee amalgamated with Bethel, more of that in a moment, the Revd Geoffrey Kemp became our minister. He was excellent at conducting worship, and also excellent when it came to administration. Pastoral visiting was not his forte. I realised that ministers could not be all things to all people, that one of the strengths of Methodism was that successive ministers brought different gifts and that by playing to their strengths churches could gain much.

One thing that made a lasting impression on me was the fact that Geoffrey always wore a cassock and preaching bands. It confirmed the feeling that I had that preachers should wear preaching gowns. One hung behind the vestry door in Elvet Methodist Church for the use of Local Preachers. I felt then, and still feel now, that worship should not be about the fashion sense of the person conducting worship, but about the office. I recall one Local Preachers Meeting when I was 'On Trial'. The issue of preaching gowns came up. I said I was in favour of wearing them. One of the preachers immediately responded, "If you turn up at my church wearing a gown I'll walk out." With all the arrogance of youth I responded, "And if my dad turned up wearing one?" To which there was no reply!

The same is true of choirs. Mam and Dad took me on holiday to Margate one year. As was our custom on holiday we went to other than a Methodist Church. On this occasion a Baptist Church and a Congregational Church. We were surprised to find at the morning service that the choir was robed. The same was true at the evening service. Same style robe, different colour. When Dad commented we were told that all the Churches in the town had robed choirs. Each church choir had a different colour. After the evening service the choirs came together, robed, to lead an open-air service on the seafront. We went along. Not only was it a good service, but the colours of the robed choirs made an amazing visual impact. I was even more convinced then of the importance of robes in worship. At North Road the few minutes before the service were often marked by comments about the choir – "I see Mrs So-and-so has a new hat", "I don't like Mrs So-and-so's new twin set" and the like!

Geoffrey Kemp's oldest son, Peter, was the same age as me and also attended the Johnston School. We were good friends – most of the time – but when we fell out it could be weeks before he spoke to me again! We both had model railways and we combined them in my attic room to make a much bigger layout. We had a lot of fun. My other two 'best' friends during my teenage years were Kenneth Everard and Kenneth Maggs. The former lived at Neville's Cross. He had a very young brother who followed him everywhere. One evening when he was delivering papers on his paper round, unbeknown to him, his young brother had followed him on his tricycle. When Ken crossed the main road, his brother, unnoticed by Ken, did the same and was, tragically, killed by a car. It was a traumatic experience.

Ken Maggs lived near Waddington Street Presbyterian Church. Like me he was a keen photographer. We often developed and printed the photographs we had taken. Those were the days when all photography was black and white. The advent of colour posed problems and once we switched to taking photographs in colour, we had to have them developed and printed professionally. Not long after that I switched to taking slides and to that end bought a much more sophisticated camera.

One year, in my early teens, on the occasion of the Sunday School Anniversary, I refused to dress up as the Apostle Paul. I wore my suit, but my hands were bound in chains, a not unreasonable concession given that I 'won' my point! I remember the occasion well. Those were the days when you had new clothes for the Sunday School Anniversary. Because he was a Co-op employee Dad had a concession card that allowed him to purchase things at cost price from the C.W.S. (Co-operative Wholesale Society) at Blandford Street in Newcastle. The top floor housed the drapery department and several times during my teens I had a made-to-measure suit from Blandford Street. One particular year I chose a green plaid – it was much nicer than it sounds. I wanted narrow trousers, but Mam refused. One Sunday afternoon, just before the Sunday School Anniversary, I went up into the attic where an old treadle Singer Sewing Machine resided and set about narrowing the suit trousers. Even Mam had to admit I had done a good job! That was the suit I wore when I played Paul in the drama.

Youth Fellowship was always stimulating. The first Sunday evening of the month we always met at the manse and the minister usually arranged for someone to come and talk about what it meant to be Christian in their particular employment. It was at one such session that I first heard about Voluntary Service Overseas. Another Sunday on the month was 'Circuit Youth Fellowship' when we met up with young folk from other Churches in the Circuit. If there was a fifth Sunday in the month we met in Church and one of us would do a kind of 'Desert Island Discs'. The Youth Fellowship also went on an annual trip. One year to the York Railway Museum, the next year to the Edinburgh Military Tattoo and the next to Windermere including a trip on the Lake, the cycle was then repeated. I can still taste the fish and chip we stopped for in Barnard Castle on our way back from the Lakes!

I remember one Youth Fellowship Weekend when we went to Ireshopeburn. We stayed in a very large guest house. Being typical teenagers, we waited until the leaders were in bed and asleep and then we sneaked out of our rooms to meet up on the landing. In those days of innocence, we did nothing more than talk. The guest house was just around the corner from High House Chapel where we met for our study sessions. High House was the oldest Methodist building in continuous use. It was opened in 1760. John Wesley visited 13 times. As a seventeen-year-old Local Preacher on Trial I preached at High House, from the pulpit from which John Wesley had preached; I considered it to be a tremendous privilege. The Gospel passage I used was John 3:1-21. I preached there again when I retired to Crook, fourteen times, the first time on 9th August 2013 and the last time on 7th April 2019. The pulpit was no longer used, instead worship was conducted from a rather unsteady lectern located on the ground floor between the communion rail and the pews. Sadly, worship ceased in 2019. The Weardale Museum, located in the old manse, attached to the Chapel, bought the building and is currently in the process of renovating it.

On Christmas Eve the members of the Youth Fellowship would go round t the houses of church members where they would sing Christmas Carols. Some folk would invite us in for a mince pie and a glass of ginger wine, non-alcoholic of course, or a cup of coffee. On one occasion, I recall, it snowed, and the temperature dropped dramatically making the road surfaces icy. We were walking up Sutton Street, it was nearing midnight, and we heard a car struggling to get traction as we crossed Allergate. We offered to help. We pushed gently on the rear end and the car turned through 180 degrees with no effort, and then drove off back down into the city! When one or two of us had passed our driving tests we were able to venture further out of the city to sing carols to members who lived beyond our normal walking route. On the Sunday nearest Christmas, we would go carol singing to the Blind Hostel, near St Oswald's Church. It was there that I was introduced to the tune 'Sweet Chiming Christmas Bells' to 'While shepherds watched their flocks by night' as it was requested every year!

The two big events in the year were the Miners Gala and the Methodist Big Meeting. For the Miners Gala the churches in the town served food and cups of tea or coffee, from early in the morning until early in the evening. The town was closed to traffic. We used to stand at the front of Jubilee to watch the collieries march past with their banners, sometimes draped in black if there had been a fatality in the pit that year. Each colliery was usually preceded by either a brass band or a pipe band. I remember one year, before the procession started standing at the back door of Jubilee, on Crossgate, seeing a man come out of the Working Men's Club, a few doors up from the Church. (Anywhere serving alcohol had an all-day licence for the day.) It was about 10.00 am. He was absolutely 'plastered'. He tripped and rolled all the way down Crossgate, past where I was standing, finally coming to rest at the bottom of the street where North Road crossed Framwellgate Bridge. He got up, dusted himself off and set off across the bridge as if nothing had happened! There was a Cathedral Service in the morning, followed in the afternoon by political speeches on the Racecourse, given by leaders of the Labour Party and the Trades Union movement.

The Methodist 'Big Meeting' took place a few weeks after (or was it before?) the Miners' Gala. It began, so I was told, when the Rev'd Dr Donald Soper, an active member of the labour party, leapt onto the back of the wagon that had been the used as a platform for the political speakers at the Miners' Gala, and before the crowd had dispersed he commandeered the microphone, clapped his hands to attract the crowd's attention and told them, "Don't go – the best is still to come" and promptly preached a sermon!

Thereafter, every year, Methodists from across the County gathered in Durham for the 'Big Meeting'. There was a procession through the town in the morning – the roads were closed to traffic – up to the Cathedral. The Dean and Chapter gave the Methodist's the use of the Cathedral free of charge with the only proviso that they used the Cathedral organist! The Cathedral was always packed, apparently the only time each year that it was filled to capacity. The singing was incredible. Every year the congregation finished hymns like 'And can it be' or 'Love divine' a verse or half a verse ahead of Conrad Eden, the cathedral organist, who, whilst an accomplished organist could best be described as pedestrian, or typically Anglican!

There was an open-air meeting on the Racecourse in the afternoon, in the fashion of the Miners' Gala. All day the churches were open for refreshments. In the evening there were services at the three Methodist Churches, Bethel, Jubilee and Elvet, plus the Congregational Church on Claypath and the Presbyterian Church in Waddington Street. The Miners' Hall on Redhill was used for a Youth activity. At each of the Churches there were two preachers, so the first in 'Church 1' was rushed to be the second at 'Church 2' and so on. Those were the days of well-known and recognised preachers. I remember hearing the Revd Brian O'Gorman on one occasion, and I can still remember his sermon – all about how the appearance of a Church on the outside said much about what went on the inside! He made reference to the number of churches that had untidy gardens, dilapidated notice boards and displayed out of date notices! I also remember hearing Howard Belben, then principal of Cliff College and I recall having a conversation with him about possibly gong to Cliff when I finished school – but more of that later!

My teenage years were, clearly, formative. As I have already noted I became a member of the Methodist Church at Jubilee Methodist Church when Harold Stanaway was our minister. We always had a Children's Address in the morning Service, and I remember one Sunday, after we had finished the second hymn, Harold Stanaway turned round to the organist, Joe

Parker, and asked him to play the hymn again, but to play it badly! Joe struggled to do as he had been asked, and Harold went on to make the point that learning to do the right thing in early life would ensure that good habits would carry on into later life. I confess I have used the same gambit on occasion, especially if caught out without a prepared children's address.

I think it must have been as part of the Centenary Celebrations that we had a Love Feast at Jubilee. I vividly remember Clifford's dad, Tommy Turnbull, who must have been in his 80s, recalling Love Feasts at Jubilee when he was a youth. He told us of the testimony of one of the first Labour MPs who declared that he was "a PM first and an MP second", in other words it was his faith that had led him into the realm of politics!

After we celebrated its centenary in 1961 Jubilee amalgamated with Bethel. It had been agreed that both churches would come together and build a new church at the bottom of the Peth on a piece of land that had been vacant for years. Both churches were put 'on the market'. The plan was that proceeds from the sale of whichever sold first would be used to begin the new build, meanwhile the two congregations would worship together in the remaining building. Unsurprisingly Jubilee sold first. It was a much more desirable site, at the bottom of North Road, much nearer to the town centre. Iceland bought the site and is still there as I write this. Before the new building even reached the planning stage a preservation order was placed on Bethel, at the top of North Road, making it virtually unsellable, and so the temporary became permanent and remains North Road Methodist Church to this day.

I was about thirteen, I think, when the Revd Dr Billy Graham came on one of his visits to England to conduct one of his campaigns. One of his crusade rallies was relayed to St Nicholas' Church in the Market Place. I was determined not to go forward when the 'appeal' was made after the sermon and I have no recollection of going to the front, but sure enough I found myself there committing myself to becoming a follower of Jesus. A decision I have never had occasion to regret although my understanding of what that means may have changed significantly over the years.

Shortly afterwards, I became friendly with Geoffrey Mundell who attended the local Baptist Church and who was in my year at school and had also 'gone forward' during the relay of Billy Graham's Crusade. Through him I got to know the Baptist Youth groups in Durham, Hartlepool and Esh Winning. The Hartlepool group went each year for two weeks to Keswick for the Convention. They camped in a field just outside the town. The first week was the week of Keswick Convention (it was only one week in those days) and the second was a 'holiday' week. I remember, on one of those holidays, hosted by a visiting Baptist minister who was on furlough from mission work in South America, being challenged to consider "full time service for the Lord". I recall thinking about that challenge as I fell asleep that night in my tent and waking next morning convinced that God was 'calling' me to the Methodist ministry. That week at the Convention Mission meeting I stood with others who had felt a similar call. I resolved, however, to say nothing but wait until I was invited to take a 'Note' to preach. I would consider that to be confirmation of my call, since to candidate for the

Methodist ministry required that one was a Fully Accredited Local Preacher.

I became a Sunday School teacher. I wasn't enamoured of the material that was being used although it was material supported by the Methodist Church and used in Methodist Sunday Schools the length and breadth of the country. After my experience at St Nicholas' Church, I made a point of buying various publications from the Billy Graham Association. It was so much more attractive than many similar publications available in the UK. The Sunday School material also provided 'handouts' for youngsters to take home with them. It's only in recent years that UK providers have finally caught up. I asked Clifford Turnbull who was Sunday School Superintendent if I could use the Billy Graham material with my class. He agreed. The youngsters really enjoyed it.

At about that time I discovered that there was a Christian Youth Rally held each month on a Saturday evening in Newcastle City Hall. I took to walking from Durham to Newcastle, some fifteen miles. I would meet up with a friend in Low Fell. I'm not sure now how I came to know him and, I confess, I have long since forgotten his name. We would have tea at his house before going to the evening meeting in the City Hall. I may have forgotten his name, but I have never forgotten the pork sausages we had, with baked beans, for tea. Decades later I came across them again in Kendal – Brennan's Pork Sausages, but no sooner had I re-discovered them when the firm went out of business. I can still taste them now!

One of the young people I met at that time was a girl from Esh Winning Baptist Church, Gwyneth Rewbury, my first 'serious' girlfriend! I was seventeen. I bought her a rather nice soft blue leather-bound Bible as a gift from Keswick Convention that year as she had not been able to go. She finished with me, with no explanation! However, she didn't formally break up with me until after I had taken her to the 'Son et Lumiere' at Durham Cathedral for which I had already bought the tickets! The 'show' was outstanding, and I can never understand why it has never been repeated.

Dad had two fountain pens which he always had with him along with a copying ink pencil. One of the pens was a Waterman which, I think, had been presented to him when he left Prudhoe. Waterman pens were, and still are, very expensive. One day he came in from collecting and announced that he had lost both his pens. I insisted that he go to the Police Station to see if anyone had handed them in. He refused since he couldn't believe anyone would bother handing in a couple of pens. I persisted over several days and in the end, merely to shut me up, he finally went to the Police Station. To his amazement someone had handed them in, and they were duly returned to him. I was disappointed after my parents died to discover that my mother had, apparently thrown them out after Dad had died.

Talking of things getting lost, on another occasion Dad came in from work having lost the fob off his pocket watch, or should I say his dad's pocket watch. The fob was solid gold and engraved with the initials RF. He thought he might have caught it when he was getting off the bus. He searched around the bus stop and even went to the depot to see if it might have fallen into the used ticket bin which was by the door of the bus, or indeed anywhere on the bus. All to no avail. It was never found. He did have a 'spare' fob which happened to be made of his birthstone and he attached this to the chain. He always intended to replace the one he lost but never did. I have seen similar in Jewellers' windows that feature antique gold and they are several hundred pound each so I don't think that I will be replacing it either.

Dad taught me to drive. I applied for my licence and received it in time for my seventeenth birthday. He had never had to take a test; they hadn't been invented when he first got a licence! Nevertheless, he was a good driver and to the best of my knowledge he had never had an accident. His insurance 'round' was on the other side of the city. He went out collecting on a Monday, Friday and Saturday morning. On those days he took the car, parking up from time to time as he went around each area he covered. He also used the car on a Wednesday when he went to the office in Stanley, to 'pay in'! Sometimes he would drive via Lanchester to pick up Joe Peacock, another agent who also happened to be a Local Preacher. On one occasion, after a TV programme on Free Masonry, when they got to the office door, the office was on the first floor above a shop, Joe took his jacket off, rolled up a trouser leg and a shirt sleeve and then went upstairs. Dad reckoned you could have cut the atmosphere with a knife!

He was often preaching on a Sunday and again he would use the car. Once I had my licence, whenever I was available and he was going out in the car, he handed over the car keys and I had to drive. Once he was satisfied that I was competent he arranged for me to have six lessons with a driving instructor to make sure I was aware of the things I might need to do in a test and which he might be unaware of never having had to take a test. Not long before I took my test Dad took me with him one Sunday evening to his preaching appointment. On the way back home, when we were out in the country, he asked me about emergency stops. I explained that the examiner would, without warning, hit the dashboard with his hand and say 'Stop'. Minutes later Dad hit the dashboard and said, 'Stop!', so I did! He nearly fell out of the door as he had had his left hand on the door handle unintentionally opening it! I hadn't heard him saying 'Like this?' I couldn't remember where this happened until we retired to Crook, and we were driving on the B6301 out of Tow Law and I instantly recognised the road.

I took my test in the November and passed first time! I remember the occasion well. The test centre was in New Elvet and that day there was a thick fog that covered the 'peninsular', although the rest of the city, where most of the test took place, was clear. (The River Wear winds around the city so that the Market Place, Castle and Cathedral are situated on what, from the air, appears to be a peninsular.)

Shortly after I passed my test Dad let me take the car to drive through to Newcastle with Ken Maggs to go to a performance of 'Doctor in the House' at the theatre in Jesmond. We got there fine, but returning home was a different matter altogether. I could not get any power from the engine, forcing me to drive at just a few mph in first gear. We pulled off the road and

contacted the AA. When the engineer arrived, he could find
nothing wrong. We limped home. Dad was still up waiting for
me, he wasn't happy. I'd not phoned him – no mobile phones
in those days. He took the car out on the next day, a Friday,
and the car was fine. On the Saturday he went by bus to do
his round. I was to meet him in the car park behind the Co-op
at the bottom of Claypath. The car struggled to get there but
when Dad arrived it was fine driving home. He took the car
with him when he was preaching on the Sunday and it was fine,
but on the Monday, he experienced the same problem. It turned
out that the valves were 'dirty' and consequently, on occasion.
were sticking.

On a Monday I would often meet Dad as he finished his round
about five o'clock. His last call was at Black's Herbalists, halfway down Claypath. Dad would buy me a half a pound of peanuts which would last me all week. On one occasion, when we
were about to go on holiday to North Wales Mr Black proised
that he would give me my usual half pound of peanuts free
if, when I came back, I could tell him the name of the town
which had the longest name of any town in the UK. Its full
name is Llanfairpwllgwyngyllgogerychwyrndrobwllllantysil-
iogogogoch, however it's usually abbreviated to Llanfair PG.
When we were in Wales, we visited Llanfair PG, I bought a
post card that showed the town's name in full, spent all week
learning how to pronounce it, recited it to him on the Monday
after we came home and collected my free peanuts.

My involvement with the Baptists gradually came to an end.
Geoffrey Mundell and several others had left the Church when

they had questioned the opening chapters of Genesis. They were told that if that was what the Bible said it was true and if you couldn't accept that then you had no business being in the Church! Thank God I belonged to a much more enlightened tradition. Many Methodists today, seem to equate Primitive Methodism with such a narrow view of Scripture however, thankfully, that was never my experience.

My teenage years were memorable for the Methodist / Anglican Conversations. In 1946 Archbishop Fisher invited the Free Churches to consider 'taking episcopacy' into their system. Only the Methodists responded positively to this and conversations began in 1955, with 12 Anglicans and 12 Methodists led by Bishop Bell and the Revd Dr Harold Roberts. By 1958 they were ready to propose that the two Churches should unite their ministries on an episcopal basis. Their 1963 Report included a strong Methodist 'Dissentient' section, resulting in the formation of groups such as the 'Voice of Methodism' who opposed the proposals, which they saw as a take-over of Methodism, and especially the 'Service of Reconciliation' which they saw as implying re-ordination. The eventual scheme of 1968 was accepted by the Methodist Conference but did not gain the required 75% majority in the House of clergy in the Anglican General Synod, largely because of the combined opposition of Evangelicals and Anglo-Catholics. In the Houses of Bishops and Laity the scheme did gain the necessary majority.

One of the signatories to the 'dissentient' report was the Rev'd Professor Dr Charles Kingsley Barratt who was a minister in the Durham Circuit and Professor of Divinity in the Department of Theology in the University of Durham. North Road was his home church. Bethel, as it was called before it joined with Jubilee, had originally been United Methodist before Methodist Union in 1932 and Kinsley had been ordained in the United Methodist Church. Not surprisingly the Durham Circuit voted against 'the Conversations'. Ironically the same year they opened a joint Methodist / Anglican Church in Newton Hall. The builders of Newton Hall Estate gave, free of charge, three sites to the churches. One went to the Roman Catholics, one to the Anglicans – they built a school on their site – and one to the Methodists. We did not have the funds to build a church on ours but with the help of the Anglicans we built a church which was shared. It still thrives.

I was in favour of 'the Conversations'. Had it been successful I would have been in the first cohort ordained in the United Church. Initially, Clifford Turnbull was against the scheme, arguing that we would quickly just become Anglicans – uniformity being the 'name of the game'. I pointed out that in the City of Durham there were several parishes in each which was a Methodist Church. Worship in each Parish Church covered a whole spectrum of styles. For example, St Nicholas' in the Market Place was very low church evangelical, St Margaret's was high church and very 'catholic'! In every Methodist Church in the city Sunday Worship was the same 'five-hymn sandwich'! Clifford revised his position!

I was sixteen when I was asked if I wanted a 'note' to preach. In my early teens I often accompanied my Dad to his preaching appointments. He would ask me to announce the hymns, or do a reading, or offer a prayer. I remember, on one occasion going with my dad, Clifford Turnbull and Joe Kidd into the Danby Circuit on LPMA Sunday. In those days LPMA (Local Preachers Mutual Aid) Sunday usually involved Local Preachers, en bloc, taking services in a neighbouring Circuit, the ministers were given a Sunday off! On this particular occasion Joe asked if I would like to go with him rather than go with my Dad. I agreed, and Dad said it was fine with him. Joe was the driver so dropped Dad and Clifford off before we reached the Church where he was the appointed preacher. Before we arrived, I asked what he wanted me to do in the Service. He replied that he would preach the sermon and I was to do the rest!

That Sunday was also memorable for the fact that when we went for lunch with a member of the congregation after the morning Service. The meal began with a plate sized Yorkshire Pudding the like of which I had never experienced before. My face must have been a picture because Joe had to explain that this was Yorkshire and the pudding was just the starter to which would be added the meat and vegetables!

It was shortly after this that I was given a 'note' to preach and Clifford Turnbull was appointed as my mentor. I was 'On Note' for two quarters before being recommended to go 'On Trial' and began studying for my Preachers' exams alongside my 'A' level studies. I recall that the Local Preachers Meeting, when I was given my 'note' was on a Saturday afternoon (they often were in those days) at Elvet Methodist Church. When Dad came home to tell me that I was now 'On Note' he also told me that there were six who had opposed the proposal. I promptly named all six! Chief among them was Tom Greener (by now I was in the Sixth Form studying RE and English at 'A' level and Tom was not only my RE teacher, he was also my Form Tutor). He had argued that I should be concentrating on my 'A' level studies – as things turned out maybe he had a point.

I recall, when I went 'On Trial', which meant that you were one your own, no longer just taking parts of the service of the preacher with whom you were 'On Note', being planned at North Road, my home church. Tom Greener was in the congregation. He had a habit of closing his eyes when it came to the sermon, not to doze off but the better to concentrate. It was rather disconcerting. Also in the congregation was the Revd Professor Dr Charles Kingsley Barratt. That too was rather disconcerting. He was an excellent preacher and always had a children's address that was always memorable. I recall one children's address he told, the story of the 'Biggest Pumpkin in the World'. I have used it many times since I first heard it, although I changed a pumpkin into a cabbage – in the 1960s pumpkins were not a familiar fruit in the UK.

The biggest Cabbage in the World

A long time ago, in a land far away, a poor old man grew an enormous cabbage. He didn't know what to do with it so decided to present it to the king who would surely be able to use it wisely. He loaded it into his wheelbarrow, just, and trundled off to the Royal Palace. The door was answered by the Vizier who was very intimidating. Having gained admittance to the King's presence the old man, stammeringly, explained his purpose. The King accepted his gift and the man turned to leave but the King stopped him and calling the Vizier over, whispered in his ear and then dismissed him.

The old man waited; the Vizier returned and handed a small bag to the King which the King in turn handed to the old man explaining that his generosity deserved to be acknowledged. It was a bag of gold coins. The old man went on his way.

The Vizier thought to himself, "If that old man could be given a bag of gold for a mouldy old cabbage, I wonder what I could get if I gave a gift to the King?" He went home to survey the many expensive objects that graced his house, paintings, ceramics, exotic silks and gold and silver ornaments. He was loathe to part with any of them. In the stables, out the back, there were many fine horses and one beautiful-looking, old white mare that was now only fit for the knacker's yard. He decided to give it to the King, after all the King would be deceived by its looks not realising that it was old and ill. When he gave it to the King, to his delight, the King explained that such generosity deserved to be rewarded with something unique. He called over one of his servants, whispered something in his ear, and dismissed him. The Vizier wondered what the King could possibly have in mind. A few minutes later the servant returned . . . . pushing a wheelbarrow containing the biggest cabbage in the world which the King then presented to the Vizier!

I recall one Local Preacher Meeting when my Dad raised the question of who was planned where and when, with particular reference to Elvet Methodist Church. During term time very few Local Preachers were ever planned at Elvet – the University Church! Those who were always had a degree. Dad was only rarely planned at Elvet and always when the University was on vacation. He did not have a degree. The next quarter Dad was planned at Elvet. It was term time. It never happened again!

The Methodist Church, in those days, used to organise a couple of days in one of their Theological Colleges for those considering ordained ministry. I applied for such a course and was directed to Headingly College in Leeds. It was a very worthwhile experience. Headingly was the most northerly of our five Colleges at that time. Sadly, by the time I was accepted for training for the ministry, Headingly had been closed.

I was now faced with a dilemma. I couldn't go from Sixth Form to University since I did not have a foreign language at 'O' level. I wanted to candidate for the Methodist ministry, but my Superintendent Minster refused to nominate me until I first did a 'job of work in the real world for at least a year'. I decided to apply to Cliff College (our Methodist Lay Training College). Howard Belben, the Principal, turned me down with the same advice. I had first met Howard Belben when he was one of the preachers at the Methodist Big Meeting, one of the two planned in the evening that year at the Congregational Church on Claypath. So, what to do? It was then that, at a Sunday evening Youth Fellowship meeting, I was introduced to VSO. I decided to apply. In those days they had a Cadet scheme for school leavers. Ken Maggs, one of my best friends at school, applied at the same time. He was turned down; we never did find out why. I was accepted – conditional on obtaining both of my 'A' levels.

I was appointed to teach at the Methodist Secondary School in Sibu, Sarawak. It was to be a one-year appointment. As soon as school finished, I had to attend a one-week course for all volunteers going to South East Asia. However, I had booked, and paid for a school trip to Paris as term ended. I consulted with the staff as I still wanted to go but would have to return early for the VSO course. It was agreed that I could return a day early under my own steam. I was really pleased not to have missed out as it was a great visit. On one of the days I, and another sixth-former, got up very early, around 5.00 am, to pay a visit to Les Halles, the Paris equivalent to Covent Garden. It was fascinating seeing all the vegetables and flowers arriving and being bid for by the various Parisian outlets. We finished off our visit in traditional fashion by having a bowl of French Onion soup in one of the cafés. The soup was very strong, with pieces of cheese on toast floating on top. As I recall I didn't finish it but it was definitely an interesting experience! I came home alone by train across northern France to the UK.

The course for VSO was held somewhere near London. I don't now recall exactly where. It was an intense course; we covered every eventuality including a half-hour lecture on how to deliver a baby in a situation where there was no other help available! Thankfully I never had to put theory into practice. Then it was home to pack.

I had applied to Cliff College and was accepted to begin my

studies when I returned from Sarawak, and my Superintendent Minister agreed to nominate me on my return, the one-year process of candidating would see me through Cliff. Then I found myself saying goodbye to my parents on Durham station platform as I headed to London to catch my flight from Heathrow. Dad's final words have always stayed with me "When I was your age, I thought I was going halfway round the world when I went to visit an aunt in Tarporley in Cheshire, and here are you literally setting off to go halfway round the world".

Sarawak

[1965-1966]

On the island of Borneo, Sarawak, along with Sabah, had joined with Malaya and the tiny, but prosperous, island of Singapore to form Malaysia. The federation was founded on 16th September 1963. However, Singapore left the federation on 9th August 1965. Since I was flying to Sarawak via Singapore at the beginning of August it was something of a tense time. The reason Singapore left was both simple and perfectly understandable. Malaya had entered the federation not as one, but as eleven States. Singapore was by far the wealthiest of the fourteen States, but that wealth was clearly in jeopardy as it had much to lose and nothing much to gain from being in such a federation. By contrast Sarawak and Sabah had much more to gain.

The flight chartered to take the volunteers to South East Asia was overbooked so four of us were booked onto a scheduled BOAC flight to Singapore with two of us booked on an onward flight to Kuching in Sarawak. I had never flown before and I thoroughly enjoyed the experience. Unlike today's budget flying, meals were set out on a menu and served with 'proper' plates and cutlery. We hit turbulence over Kuala Lumpur and landed in Singapore a little late – just in time to miss the onward connection to Sarawak. Because we had travelled with BOAC the company booked us into the Raffles Hotel, reputedly the finest hotel on the island. That, it transpired, was standard practice. Needless to say. I had no objections. However, one of my fellow volunteers had. He was a fellow Methodist Local Preacher, with a much stronger social conscience than me! So while he spent the first day contacting the British Council, I spent the first day sightseeing. He eventually prevailed so after two days in luxury, with air-conditioning, we were transferred to a dormitory room in a seaman's hostel – without air-conditioning!

Before I left the UK, I was aware that Singapore was the place to purchase electronic and photographic equipment tax free. During my four days stay in Singapore I therefore made two important purchases. I bought a cine camera and a portable tape recorder. At home the only portable tape recorder available to buy took three-inch tapes and recorded at one and seven-eighths inches per second. The first shop I went into I asked for a portable tape recorder that took five-inch spools and recoded at three and three-quarter inches per second! "Yes sir, we have three models you can choose from." Duty and tax free meant that, like the cine camera I purchased the next day, they were eminently affordable!

So, four days late, the two of us destined for Sarawak finally arrived in Kuching. However, it was a long holiday weekend and there was no connecting flight for me to get from Kuching to Sibu, so I was hosted by the British Council. It wasn't quite the Raffles, but it was a significant improvement on the Seaman's hostel. I remember that first evening buying a meal in the marketplace in Kuching, only to discover, a little later, that just a couple of yards away from where I had been seated, a terrorist bomb had gone off just two days earlier. Until then I don't think I had really appreciated that I had gone into an area that was so politically unstable.

Finally, I arrived in Sibu. I was met at the airport and driven the few miles to the Methodist Secondary School that was to be my home for the next twelve months. The school was English Medium. It had been Chinese Medium, although Chinese as the medium of teaching was being phased out in favour of English, however, not for long since, now that Sarawak was part of Malaysia, it was expected that Malay would become the medium of teaching, though that would take some time to introduce as there were very few Malay speaking teachers available at that time.

The School had a student population of around 850 students and 37 teaching staff. The Head Teacher was an English Methodist minister, the Rev'd Keith Wiltshire, and he and his family lived on site. The Head of English, the Rev'd David Johnson, was also an English Methodist minister. The rest of the staff were a mixture. One was a missionary from India, another a missionary from America. There was another from

America who was a volunteer with Peace Corps. There was several 'locals' – mainly English-speaking Chinese and one Malay, who taught Malay! Most of the staff lived in the locality.

I had a room in the boys' dormitory block! Most of the students in the school were Chinese. However, there were a number of Malays and a number Ibans. The Malays lived in the Malay Kampong on the edge of the town. The Ibans came from the villages in the surrounding jungle and they were boarders. As I settled in, I was quickly told I should have an Amah. This took me by surprise and at first, I was resistant. An Amah is a maid or servant, in this instance someone who would do my washing and ironing. It was explained to me that for the young woman such work was essential if she was to support her family, so I acquiesced. I cannot remember how much it cost me each week, but by UK standards it was negligible, even on my VSO allowance.

At first, I ate with the boarders, but the diet was incredibly monotonous. Rice, poor quality, that was supplemented with grain donated by American Charities, accompanied by locally caught fish that was almost tasteless, was served every day. I opted for an additional monthly grant that allowed me to either feed myself, I was given permission to use the facilities in the Home Economics Department, or cycle into town to eat at one of the many roadside stalls or 'cafes' where food was incredibly cheap.

The first evening I was in Sibu the head took me into town and bought me a Nasi Goreng at a local 'café'. I had no idea what it was, but it looked unlike anything I had eaten before. I decided that it was either 'eat or starve' and resolved there and then to eat whatever was put in front of me, no questions asked. If I asked before I ate, I knew there were some things I wouldn't even try and I would have missed out on so much!

If I went into town in an evening there was one food stall I frequented near the river side. He did a mean curry. When you arrived and placed your order, the proprietor selected a chicken from one of the cages behind his stall, slit its throat, plucked it, disembowelled it, and cooked it! The accompanying curry sauce was out of this world. Afterwards I would go around the corner and buy a small pineapple from one of the boats moored nearby. The guy who was selling them would expertly slice off the outer skin. They were, I was told, the finest pineapples in the world, and I could well believe it, but they were not produced in sufficient quantity to export.

If I was eating in town at lunch time, I would go down to a stall just outside the town's vegetable market. A clear soup followed by a chicken curry made a very satisfying lunch. It was delicious. I can still taste it as I write.

I also linked up with another, graduate, VSO who was living in the town and we would meet up occasionally at his place to eat. We invented 'Sarawak Special' which comprised of minced beef with chopped onions cooked with chopped chillies and baked beans then served over potatoes chopped up small. Delicious. I still make it quite often.

Because of my delayed flights in Singapore and Kuching I arrived a couple of days after the beginning of term. Consequently, I had no time to settle in. My first day, and I was in a classroom teaching. I was allocated a desk in the staffroom, which was situated near the School Shop, given a timetable and class lists, and I had to just 'get on with it'! One of the first things I did was obtain a bike, I can't remember now whether I bought it or borrowed it, but it proved invaluable since the school was a mile or so out of town.

Education in Sarawak was compulsory, and free, up to the end of Primary School. Thereafter every child paid a fee each month. It wasn't excessive, but some of the less well-off students used their 'free' time to tap rubber in the neighbouring jungle to earn their fees. Unlike the Malay mainland where there were rubber plantations with trees in serried rows, rubber trees in the nearby jungle were scattered randomly.

All textbooks, exercise books, pens and pencils and anything else needed in school had to be bought, hence the School Shop. Needless to say, books were rarely, if ever, lost or defaced by doodling on, or in, them. At the end of their third year in Secondary Education students sat the 'Sarawak Junior Examination'. Success meant they continued into the next two years to study for Overseas Cambridge 'O' level GCEs. Failure, and that was the end of their education. Succeed in 'O' levels and they could go on to study for 'A' level GCEs. Education was highly valued and the 'drop-out' rate was very small. Not long after I began my 'teaching career' I received the results of my 'A' levels – I had failed both RE and English. I began studying to re-take them the next year as an overseas candidate. I also set about studying to retake my Local Preachers Exam, which I had passed, but I was trying for better results.

One of the books I had to study for the 'A' level English Literature Exam was 'The Power and the Glory' by Graham Greene. The book's hero is an unnamed priest on the run from Mexican authorities after a state governor has ordered the military to dismantle all vestiges of the religion. Churches were burned. Relics, medals, and crosses were banned. The price for disobedience was death. While many clerics gave up their beliefs and accepted their government pensions, the unnamed priest travelled in secret, celebrating Mass and hearing confessions under the cover of night. However, he was also a gluttonous, stubborn, and angry man drowning in vices, and the religious ambition of his earlier years had been replaced with a constant desire to drink, hence Greene's term for him: the "whiskey priest." Tired of risking his life, the priest even prayed to be caught. Eventually he was caught so the last priest was finally removed from society. The novel ends, however, on an optimistic note, in the last scene of the novel, a new priest shows up. I found the novel, theologically both challenging and incredibly helpful.

I was a form tutor – Form 2B – and my form room was almost next door to the School Shop. I mainly taught English and RE, but also some local history and geography and some biology. Class sizes were around 40 plus! Discipline was never a problem as all pupils were keen to learn since education was valued as a means to ensure a decent livelihood. Many who gained 'A' level GCEs went on to study at Universities in Australia, the UK and the USA. I say 'all', but there was one exception, and he was in my Tutor Group, Neil Malia by name. He was English; his father worked in one of the multi-national companies based in Sibu. Remember most of the pupils in any class were Chinese, with a few Malays and a few Ibans. For all of them their learning was in a foreign language – English. At the end of my first term there were exams and the person who came out top in English was a Chinese girl, Teo Chean Chean with 98%! Bottom was Neil with 11%! In the end he was expelled, much to his father's annoyance. However, our school had a good reputation, and a waiting list, so there was no place for anyone not prepared to try their best.

On one occasion my students decided it would be a good idea to turn my name into a Chinese name. Robert Fisher became Lo Bau Fay Shr. It didn't work of course because Chinese names only have three syllables with the first being the surname and the second and third being the given name. One bright spark decided that if we made my name Bob Fisher and put the surname first it might work. It did. So, my Chinese name became Fay Shr Bau. Fay is a genuine Chinese surname and Shr Bau is a genuine Chinese given name. Interestingly Shr Bau means 'Famous in this world' which is almost the same as the meaning of Robert – 'Bright in fame'!

The nearest English-speaking Methodist Church was a mile or so up the road going out to the airport. It was a small congregation made up mainly of Europeans and Americans. Sarawak, before joining Malaysia, had been British, having initially been under the rule of a Briton called 'Rajah' James Brooke. He had divided the country into five divisions. To each division was allocated one Christian denomination. The nation's capital, Kuching, was in Division One which was Anglican, Division Two was Roman Catholic, and Division Three, with its capital Sibu, was Methodist. During the Boxer Uprising in China in 1905 many Chinese fled south through the Malay peninsula and settled in Sarawak around Sibu. They were Methodists as a result of mission activity among the Foochow people, and once settled, the community sent to America for missionaries to continue their missionary work in Sibu. After the death of Rajah Brooke, when Sarawak came under British rule, the denominational restrictions were abolished, so the boundaries became somewhat blurred. Although Division Three remained predominantly Methodist we had a Roman Catholic Secondary School in Sibu. Neil Malia transferred to that school when he left us.

The English-speaking Methodist Church was on the first floor of a building that was part of the Iban Methodist Theological College where Iban candidates were trained for ministry in their local communities. The College was small, and the buildings were basic. The area beneath the church was open-sided and it was there that a small Sunday School met. It wasn't long before I was persuaded to play the small organ for the hymns as they had no organist. Linked to the English Church was a fellowship / study group which I joined. It was an amazing experience.

That year John Robinson, the Bishop of Woolwich, had published his controversial book "Honest to God" and this formed the basis of one of our study series. It is a book which played a big part in my own spiritual development. In the book Robinson claimed that secular man required a secular theology, that God's continuing revelation to humanity is one brought about in culture at large, not merely within the confines of 'religion' or 'church.' The book also introduced the idea of situational ethics.

I remember on one occasion walking back from a fellowship meeting with one of the American missionaries, Doug Cool, I think, and we were discussing my future intention to candidate for the Methodist Ministry. "Can I give you some advice?" he began. "When you have an idea to introduce something new to your congregation, discuss it casually with one of the church leaders, and when they suggest it at the next Church Council commend them for coming up with the idea!" It was sound advice that I have had recourse to implement on more than one occasion.

In the town there was a thriving Chinese Methodist Church. It held several hundred people and was filled at each of its three services – two in Foochow and one in Mandarin. I was very friendly with one of the sixth form lads who was a member of the Chinese Church. Bear in mind that children couldn't start school until they were six years old, and sometimes they were older. Consequently, most of the sixth formers were my age, or older. I also only taught pupils in the first two years. Johnny Chien Pik-Un persuaded me to join the Mandarin Choir. I had no idea what was going on in the service, but Johnny transliterated everything we sang – hymns, anthems, the Lord's Prayer – so I was fully engaged. I had my white choir robes. I thoroughly enjoyed the experience. The Service was early, so I had time to cycle the two or three miles, past School to attend the English Service at the Theological College after singing in the choir at the Mandarin Service at the church in the town centre

One of my tutor group, an Iban boy called Dennis, invited me to visit his longhouse village during the first half-term. It was an amazing experience. A boat trip from Sibu down the River Rajang to Miri, an hour or so journey on a regular passenger boat, then a similar journey up one of the river's tributaries in an open 'canoe' propelled by an outboard motor, then an hour's walk on a narrow trail through the jungle! The longhouse was a series of 'rooms' with a wide, shared veranda – a bit like a terrace of bungalows! The toilet was communal – a hole in the ground dug some distance from the back of the longhouse. Dennis took me to see the travelling shop which turned out to be a well-stocked long boat. He also insisted on showing me the Methodist Church. It had recently been visited by the Bishop and was still decked out with flags and streamers. It was built of wood, on stilts. Inside was, sadly, so familiar – an altar table, lectern and pulpit, communion rail and pews!!! It seemed so incongruous. If it had been built of stone instead of wood, it would not have looked out of place in any English village! Meals in the longhouse were basic, but delicious. One, of plain boiled rice with roast wild boar, freshly caught, I can still taste as I write this. It was mouth-watering!

During my first term I developed toothache! We had been

advised by VSO to visit a dentist before we left the UK, so I duly went to our dentist in Old Elvet in Durham for a check-up and treatment a few weeks before I left for Sarawak. I had to have a filling so when I developed toothache I was puzzled. In Sarawak most dentists were unqualified Chinese practitioners. In fact, there were only three qualified dentists in the whole of the country, one of whom was a VSO graduate volunteer. These dentists were peripatetic so they would appear in a local hospital every few months for a week or two. It just so happened that when my toothache appeared the dentist was due at the hospital in Sibu. Coincidentally it was the VSO volunteer. I went to the hospital. The Waiting Room was full but having registered at Reception I was the next patient called through. I was not happy to receive preferential treatment but there was nothing I could do about it. The dentist was baffled as he could find nothing that might be causing my toothache. The only thing he could suggest was replacing the filling I had had done before leaving for Sarawak. When he did so he discovered that the dentist in Durham had failed to put a lining on the nerve before filling the tooth, so the filling was irritating the nerve. New filling – problem solved!

We had a strong Youth Fellowship at the School. It was made up primarily of Chinese students. It was not only a group that met for devotional and educational purposes, it was also committed to action in the community. It was arranged that, once term was ended, and before Christmas, the group were going upriver to Kapit to the Methodist Hospital there to dig out a fishpond. There were few roads in Sarawak at that time. The only way to reach Sibu was either by plane or boat on the Rajang River.

The same was true of Kapit, which was several hours by boat further inland towards the Indonesian border.

The Malaysian Government had ceased to subsidise missionary hospitals. In fact the only one was the one in Kapit. The fishpond we dug out was enormous, and messy – lots of yellow clay to remove. It wasn't ornamental. It was to be stocked with fish to supplement the available food in the hospital. It was the only hospital for, literally, miles around. Many who came for help would have had to hike for several days through the jungle to get there. We dug out the pond in the mornings then had a variety of activities in the afternoons.

One afternoon we hiked deep into the jungle. We spotted a young orangutan in the canopy before we stopped, for some strange reason, on a narrow rope bridge which crossed a gorge. The drop was c. 50 feet. Someone dropped a soda bottle which broke and cut my foot. I fainted. Fortunately, one of the missionaries who was accompanying us caught me just before I slid to my death below. We made our way back to the hospital and I was diagnosed with severe sunstroke and severe sunburn.! The sunburn was so bad that the cream they prescribed could only be used over a small percentage of skin or it became toxic. That evening, as part of an entertainment, I was involved in a sketch which involved my 'wife' shaking me by my arm at one point. I had to tell her not to touch me as my arms were so sore and tender. We spent several days digging out the pond before we returned, by boat, to Sibu. We never saw the pond filled with either water or fish, although we did hear later that the project was completed successfully.

It's only now, as I look back that I am aware of how my experiences in Sarawak were so formative. I recall on one occasion meeting up with a number of young folk from the MYF (Methodist Youth Fellowship)at a corner coffee shop in town; remember many of the students were as old, and in some cases, older than me. As the group broke up, I offered, in all innocence, to walk one of the girls home. She very politely declined and explained that the only Chinese girls seen alone with a white man were prostitutes! I had suddenly found myself on the receiving end of 'racism'! It was a salutary experience, and one I would never forget.

Quite early on I discovered that one of the shops in the town would, for a nominal charge, copy vinyl LPs onto reel to reel tapes. Illegal here in the UK but not, apparently, in Sarawak. So began my music collection that in time would include, vinyl, cassette tapes, CDs and memory sticks and cards!!! My other hobby that I indulged in whilst I was in Sarawak was stamp collecting. Because Malaysia was made up of a number of States even its definitives were interesting. Each value was identical in each State but as well as bearing the designation Malaysia, each bore the State name and either its crest or the head of Head of State. My interest in stamps must have got around as, on one occasion I was invited by the captain of a cargo vessel, temporarily moored up in Sibu to visit him in his cabin where he proceeded to show me his collection of stamps from all over Asia.

I also discovered the NAAFI. The UK still had an army base near the airport. I also met a nurse, Isobel, twice my age I should add, who had contacts with members of the forces stationed in Sibu, hence my introduction to the NAAFI. Because of those contacts I had an opportunity to visit the Indonesian border. There was still conflict between Indonesia and Malaysia, so initially I travelled by longboat, with outboard, upriver before setting off on foot through the jungle. En route we saw an orangutan – in the wild! I say we since I was only given permission to make the trip on condition that I was accompanied by an armed escort, in this instance a corporal and a sergeant. I discovered later that there had been some debate about whether or not I also should be armed!

On another occasion I had the opportunity to fly, in a two-seater, twin engine plane belonging to the Army Air Corps from Sibu to Kapit and back. The pilot was incredibly accommodating, flying quite low to allow me to capture the trip on film, one of the few times I used my cine camera. Film and developing was expensive, even in Sarawak, so I used it sparingly. I was none too pleased when I discovered that I had not captured any of the trip on film as the humidity had caused the film to jam. I never dared to tell the pilot.

For some reason one Sunday evening Isobel arranged a party in her apartment. One of the Army Captains and I went over early to help her prepare. She put on a veritable feast. I was whipping up the cream for the dessert course and in conversation suggested that we coloured the cream. We had been discussing how people were so easily conditioned to refuse food that didn't conform to their perceptions. So, I coloured the cream a delicate turquoise colour. I was right, virtually everyone avoided the cream because of its colour! All the more for me!

Because the school had a large school hall and was one of the
nearest buildings to the military base near the airport, we
were often used as a venue when arrangements were made to
entertain the troops. On one such occasion Acker Bilk and
his Paramount Jazz Band performed for the troops in our
school hall. The school staff were allowed to be present. It
was a fabulous evening. I got Acker Bilk's autograph, which,
sadly, I have since lost. One piece they played was particularly
memorable. One by one each instrumentalist dropped out of
the piece they were playing, leaving just the drummer who
performed on his own for several minutes before one by one
the other instrumentalists re-joined him. It was an outstanding
performance.

My parents wrote to me regularly and we exchanged the
occasional three-inch audio tape. During school holidays I used
to go with my dad when he went out collecting insurance, so
I got to know a lot of his clients. Apparently, some of them
regularly asked for an update on my time in Sarawak. As I
have already indicated British troops were still stationed in both
Singapore and Sarawak at that time. One of Dad's clients had
a married son stationed in Changi in Singapore and, although
I had never met them, they invited me to spend Christmas with
them in Singapore. Needless to say, I jumped at the chance. On
reflection I was probably a most ungrateful guest, as I spent
most of the week anywhere but with my hosts!

Almost immediately after returning from digging the fishpond at the hospital at Kapit I flew to Singapore. After settling in with my hosts I headed into the town to Wesley Methodist Church. There I linked up with the Youth Fellowship and, one way or another I spent the rest of my time in Singapore with one or other of the members of the MYF. On Christmas Eve I joined them as they toured the city. We had a lorry decked out as a stable, with a Chinese Mary and Joseph, a couple of Chinese shepherds, an Indian Sultan, a Chinese Mandarin and a European King. Guess who got to play the European King. Mind you, it was so hot that halfway round the 'actors' changed over, replaced by some of those who had been in the coach which followed the float. In the coach, with all the windows down, we sang Christmas Carols. It was a terrific experience. Christmas Day, I attended the service at Wesley in the morning and Christmas Day night four of the Youth Fellowship took me to one of the highest points on the island, Mount Faber, and then into Chinatown to eat. As I recall I did have Christmas lunch with my hosts.

With Christmas over it was back to Sibu and teaching my classes. I had decided to retake my 'A' levels, English Literature and Religious Education. In Sarawak it meant the Overseas Cambridge Board. That entailed a trip to Kuching in the summer of 1966 before I returned to the UK. To save money I travelled by boat overnight, sleeping on the deck – cheapest way to do it. Not surprisingly I failed them both. However, I will always be grateful for the opportunity since it introduced me to Graham Greene's 'The Power and the Glory'.

At Easter I visited a mission station an hour or so down river.

It comprised a house and modern church (though still very traditional in its layout – including pews!). As I have already said above Sarawak lacked a road system. Sibu had an extensive road system in the town itself with one road that went seven miles out to the airport and one that went thirty miles north into the jungle ending nowhere! On one occasion I borrowed the Mission's minibus and drove the road to nowhere. It simply stopped thirty miles from the town. So, another boat trip.

I stayed in the mission house with the English missionary. We had a sunrise service in the mission compound with a re-enactment of the first Easter followed by an Easter egg hunt for the children in the garden and then a service in the church. The church was pretty full, though where everyone came from, I have no idea as we appeared to be isolated on a rise overlooking the river and no township in sight.

Before the end of the year there was an Open Day at the school. I ended up buying several items produced by the woodwork classes. A beautifully turned plate made up of several different local woods. A lidded chalice and a gavel, which I confess I have never used. These were added to some Iban carvings I had already bought as souvenirs: a pair of busts, a 'trial' bust, a longboat with passengers, rowers and a pig, and a small household god. Given that I was flying home I was stretching my permitted weight limit to the extreme.

The year eventually came to an end. It had been a most enjoyable one, and undoubtedly played a very significant part in my subsequent development. I left England with no knowledge of any other world Faith, and within hours of landing in Singapore was visiting Hindu and Buddhist Temples and Shinto Shrines. In Sibu I was wakened every morning by the call to prayer broadcast from the Mosque down the road from the School. We had a significant number of Muslim students and regularly won the Qur'an Reading Competition in the town. I have a photograph of the winning team with their banner proclaiming 'Methodist Secondary School Qur'an Reading Competition Winners'. At Chinese New Year the Muslim students took me with them to visit their Chinese friends in their homes. At Eid, the Chinese students took me with them as they visited Muslim friends in their homes in the Malay Kampong. I had left England with no knowledge of Methodism outside England, apart from some mission work in Africa. In Sarawak I had my first experience of American Methodism which I found both challenging and interesting, in particular I liked their hymnbook, both because of its content and the way it was set out.

I left Sarawak, somewhat reluctantly, bound for Singapore where I stayed with the minister in the manse at Wesley Methodist Church before setting off on a week-long coach trip round Malaya. Methodism in Singapore was British. In Sarawak it was American because of the immigration of the Chinese displaced in the Boxer Uprising, most of whom were Methodist.

The coach was overbooked so I ended up touring Malaya by taxi with a young, unmarried, couple. We visited Penang, where the largest reclining Buddha in the world is to be found. In the wall behind the reclining statue were numerous niches. They were intended to house, in a suitable jar, the cremated remains of a deceased person. Once the jar was in place a glass panel with a photograph of the person etched onto it sealed the niche. We also went to the Cameron Highlands, where we visited a Hindu Temple and a Tea Plantation. The Cameron Highlands, which has a temperate climate, was the place where English missionaries often went on furlough. The highlight of the tour, however, was Kuala Lumpur. We saw the only stretch of elevated roadway in South East Asia, the largest War Memorial in S E Asia, the largest, newly built, Mosque in South East Asia – you get the drift. Then it was back to Singapore for my flight back to the UK, laden with all sorts of gifts and souvenirs, among them two large decorated Iban hats and a red and gold tea service. The latter I gave away to a friend in the MYF as there was no way I could carry it on to the plane – my hands were already too full!

When I arrived home, I went with my parents for a week's holiday in Musselburgh, outside Edinburgh. The weather was glorious, but I felt the cold, and everyone commented on my lack of a tan so I was constantly having to explain that the combination of high humidity and avoiding the sun, which was very powerful, meant that people like me just didn't get tanned in that part of the world. Then it was back to Durham, to repack ready to set off to begin my year at Cliff College.

Before leaving for Cliff I was surprised to receive a communication from VSO. They informed me that they had requested, and received, a report from the head teacher at the

Methodist Secondary School in Sibu about my year there. This was their normal practice. What surprised me was that they not only enclosed a copy of the report for me to see, but they also asked me to produce a report of my time there. Keith's main complaint about me was that I spent too much time mixing with the locals! My complaint about him was that he spent too much time never venturing outside the school compound! I learned several years later that when he returned to the UK he resigned from the Methodist Ministry.

I also discovered on my return that I had been sponsored by Christian Aid. Apparently, they covered the cost incurred by VSO when volunteers were sent to Church based projects, so they had paid my airfares since I had had to travel by BOAC as the charter flight to South East Asia had been overbooked. The cost was just over £400.

Cliff College

[1966-1967]

Cliff College traces its roots back to 1883 in Bolton, Lancashire, when the Rev'd Thomas Champness took a number of men into his home in order to train them. Shortly afterwards they all moved to Castleton Hall, Rochdale becoming known as "The Joyful News Training Home and Mission". On the expiration of the lease on Castleton Hall, the work moved to its present site in March 1904 after the premises were purchased by the Wesleyan Methodist Church in 1903, and the name was changed to "Cliff College". In the late 19th Century, many of the college's graduates worked with Hudson Taylor and his China Inland Mission as missionaries.

Essentially Cliff was a lay training College offering an intensive one-year course for students of any age from home or overseas. Its focus was mission and every student took part in a 'Mission' each term. A weekend in the autumn, a week in the spring and a month in the summer. It stood firmly in the Wesleyan evangelical tradition – not to be confused with what has come to be called conservative evangelicalism in the latter part of the 20th century!

Howard Belben, the Principal, was our Old Testament Tutor. He produced his own duplicated notes on every book in the Bible. I still have them, and I have never seen better. Royston Emms was our New Testament Tutor and the commentary we used for Luke's Gospel I discovered later was considered the most radical of the day! Malcom White was our Theology Tutor and he was first rate. I met him decades later when he was minister at Methodist Central Hall Westminster, and he claimed to remember me. It's possible. Certainly, Howard Belben had a prodigious memory. I came across him again some 15 years after I left Cliff when I was teaching in Coalville and he had been invited to address the ordinands at Synod. At lunch he came over to me and not only had he recognised and remembered me, despite the fact I had grown a beard, but told me everything I had been doing since leaving Cliff!

My uncle Ridley had attended Cliff – in the 1940s, I think. Over the years numbers had declined and it was decided to open the College up to women. So, when I went in 1966, the first-year women were admitted, the College was filled to capacity. Perhaps unsurprisingly by the end of the year there were two students who were pregnant!

Every student was expected to help out in the running of the College – six hours a week of 'Manual' work. Some worked in the grounds tending the gardens, others cleaning in the College.

I was assigned to the kitchens where I helped to prepare the cooked breakfasts and when that was done, I prepared pastries and puddings for later in the day. It meant a very early start, but the bonus was that when it came to the two Conventions held in the summer, whilst the rest of the students were required to vacate their rooms for the guests and sleep under canvas in the grounds, I got to stay in my room in the College. After one of the Convention meals a message came back to the kitchen to 'compliment the pastry chef' – that was me!!!

There were four of us candidating for the ministry that year in Cliff. All four of us were eventually accepted for training and went to different Theological Colleges. Alan Ogier, who, as a probationer, ended up in the East Anglia District where I was first stationed. His first year was in Great Yarmouth where the mother of TV celebrity David Frost, a minister's widow, was living. She insisted on passing on David's suits to Alan as they were a similar size and David rarely wore them more than once! Consequently, Alan became the best dressed minister in the District! Alan was moved after just one year and became chaplain at Culford School, which was in the Circuit where I was stationed. He later went into prison chaplaincy.

The other three were John Newbury, who ended up working in Geneva for the World Council of Churches; Paul Burton, who left the ministry after just one year in Theological College; and myself. We received tremendous support from the staff at Cliff. There was a small studio in the College sponsored by the Joseph Rank Foundation. We were each filmed preaching a brief sermon which we watched back with helpful comments from the staff. The sermons were brief because of the length and cost of the film used. With modern technology today such a task would be commonplace and would cost next to nothing. It was a different matter in 1967.

The students who were Local Preachers, and there were several others apart from the ministerial candidates, were regularly planned each Sunday in churches in neighbouring Circuits. Most churches were village churches with small congregations, and I often asked them to move nearer to the front. On only one occasion did they refuse, so I moved from the pulpit and perched in a pew nearer the back of the church. After the service, which was late in the year. they apologised and explained that the only heating was a boiler at the back of the church, and they were loathe to move away from it! I recall on another occasion after the service, I walked back with one of the stewards to his house where he and his wife were providing hospitality. As we approached their dog began barking furiously. They explained that the dog didn't like strangers – I didn't much like dogs! When we went in the dog ceased barking and began wagging its tail. As I sat down the dog came up and made a fuss of me and the cat curled up on my lap. My hosts sat in silence. After a while they explained that they were amazed as the dog usually had to be put out of the room and the cat usually disappeared until visitor had left. They had never known them to take to a visitor before.

Howard Belben had a couple of cars, one of which was a red mini. Preachers who could drive were allowed to use his mini to transport themselves and up to three others to fulfil their preaching appointments. I remember driving back one Sunday night in the dark, it was lashing down with rain. One of the windscreen wipers flew off, driver's side of course. It was quite a journey!

Not only was Howard a generous and humble man, above all he was a gentleman. Howard was also an exceptionally good preacher, and as such was in demand, and was appreciated wherever he went. For a while, after his death, his son published a number of his sermons online, along with his hints on preaching.

Howard had married into wealth but was, apparently, also independently wealthy. One of his ancestors in Tudor times had apparently been a Royal Treasurer – a small painting from that time was casually propped up on the floor against a wall in his study. Rumour had it that he 'owned' a substantial amount of property in Brighton. It was also believed that he had paid for the tennis courts that appeared at Cliff during the time I was there. At Synod, when it was announced that a minister was retiring and had nowhere to live, Howard was seen to raise his hand and the Chairman indicated that the matter was now 'sorted' – this was before the establishment of the Methodist Minister Housing Society.

As I have already indicated very student was sent out 'on mission' in small teams once each term. I can't remember where I was sent on either the Autumn or Spring Missions, although I do recall that one of them was near Leeds. We stayed in quite a grand house. Our host was either a Liberal MP, or a prospective Liberal MP, I can't now recall which. I do recall preaching on one occasion in the open air while standing on top of a bus shelter that was set into the side of a hill. The crowd was small, though attentive. I'm not sure now whether that was on the Autumn or Spring mission. The Summer Mission, however, was a different matter. The team I was in was sent to South Wales where we spent a week in each of four Welsh Valleys. The Rhondda Valley where we visited Ystrad Mynach and Tylorstown; the Bargoed Valley; the Rhymney Valley, and the Taff Valley, where we were based at Merthyr Tydfil. In the Rhymney Valley our supervisor was a Deaconess, Lois Aubrey, who was inspirational.

The highlight was the week we spent in Methyr Tydfil. We were based in a detached house, which the church had bought, on a modern housing estate. The downstairs through lounge was used for worship and meetings. The minister was the Rev'd Irving Penberthy. One of his churches was in Aberfan. The Aberfan disaster had occurred just a month or two earlier. The spoil tip had slipped as a result of torrential rain, burying the village school, killing dozens of children and teachers. We spent a couple of days at the church there running various activities for the children. The Methodist minister didn't get much public recognition but from what we could gather he was incredibly active behind the scenes and his ministry was very much valued and appreciated by the village.

Although I had passed my Local Preacher's exams with sufficiently high marks to become a Fully Accredited Local Preacher, I decided to retake them to see if I could improve my marks, which I did. I also decided to retake my two 'A' levels and this time passed my 'A' level English Literature but again failed 'A' level RE! In addition to the College courses that everyone attended, those of us who were candidating for the ministry were offered the opportunity to study New Testament Greek. We worked our way through 30 chapters of J W Wenham's 'Elements of New Testament Greek' making good progress.

I made good friends with Peter Robinson during the year I was at Cliff. He was a year or two older than me, but we got on really well. He came from Kidderminster and one holiday I went to stay with him and his parents. Since going to Sarawak I had become used to drinking tea without milk or sugar. I remember Peter's mum pouring me a cup that was so black and so strong that I reverted to adding milk and sugar! In the Easter holidays Peter came home with me to Durham. He'd never been further north than Cliff and was amazed at how lovely the countryside was in County Durham – he thought there would be pit heaps everywhere you looked! He had a motorbike, so we went from Cliff to Durham on two wheels. The first and last time I rode pillion.

The week before our trip to Durham we had gone to the cinema in Sheffield to see 'The Bible' which was supposed to be the first of a series of five films covering the whole of the Bible. The other four were never made. The film dealt with the opening chapters of the Bible and was very impressive. While we were in Durham the Palladium were showing a re-run of Cecil B de Mill's 'The Ten Commandments'. The special effects by comparison were rubbish, and we spent the first part of the film making sarcastic comments about them until the woman behind poked us in the back and told us off as she was wanting to watch the film!!!

Peter was a Fully Accredited Local Preacher and he wanted to candidate for the ministry but lacked some of the required educational qualifications. Whilst at Cliff he decided to take the necessary 'O' levels, including RE. To help himself he recorded the whole of Mark's Gospel on tape to learn it for the exam. His endeavours were successful, and he was able to candidate the year after he left Cliff and arrived at Hartley to start his training as I began my second year there. He became very friendly with one of the girls who had come to Cliff that year and in his last year at Hartley they were married.

Although Peter and I were 'best' friends I was also friendly with Richard Machin, who was also a Local Preacher. He came from Wigan and when a couple of years later he married Margaret, his childhood sweetheart, I was invited to be his best man. He proudly showed me his study at the house they had bought in Wigan. All the walls and the ceiling were painted black! He had an eight-volume set of John Wesley's Journal which he gave to me, and which I still have. He joined the Police force, and we were invited to his Passing Out Parade which was held at Catterick Garrison. We kept in touch for several years, but eventually I had a letter in which he informed me that he and Margaret had split up as he had 'come out' as gay and consequently had left the Police as, at that time, gays were not allowed to be serving officers. Although I tried to keep in touch I, sadly, did not hear from him again.

We had two students that year who were disabled. Ian Hurst was spastic but not overly so. He drove an adapted car. I recall once calling to him down a corridor and he promptly fell flat on his face. He instantly got up, none the worse for his fall as if it had never happened. I think I felt worse than he did because I had surprised him the way I had. He was a Local Preacher and after leaving Cliff he candidated for the ministry. He was turned down, which was a shame as, in my opinion, he would have been an excellent minister. He subsequently offered as a candidate for ordination in the Anglican Church, but again he was unsuccessful. What happened to him after that I have no idea. Ron was the other student with a disability. His eyesight was poor, and his left arm was deformed. He regularly told us about the folk on his prayer list, many of whom, sadly, died. If anyone annoyed us, we would threaten to put them on Ron's prayer list! It was, I should add, always said in good humour!

One of the things I did during my year at Cliff was to form a choir. We practiced each week and often sang an anthem in the service on a Sunday. On one occasion when Royston Emms was preaching, he came up to me after the service and began by saying how displeased he was. My anxiety was, however, short-lived as he went on to say that had he known we were going to sing the Te Deum as the anthem he would have come and joined us!

At the end of the year, I not only gained my 'A' level English Literature GCE but I was also awarded The Farndale Old Testament Third Prize. I chose 'The Gospel of Christian Atheism' by Thomas J J Altizer for my book. I guess I was harking back to my study of John T Robinson's 'Honest to God' which I had studied while in Sarawak. No comment was ever made about my choice of book and I have to admit it wasn't a patch on 'Honest to God'!

Alongside everything else that was happening there was the candidating procedure for the Methodist Ministry to go through which included two 'Trial Sermons' and appearances before Circuit Meeting and District Synod to give testimony as to one's commitment to Christ and call to the ministry. The final hurdle was to appear before the Connexional Committee – the so-called 'July Committee which met in June and was an August body'! I recall being asked at the Connexional Committee if I smoked. At that time I didn't, but I refused to answer the question on the grounds that whether I smoked or not was irrelevant when it came to judging my competence to be a minister!

At Conference, which met that year in Middlesbrough, I was accepted for training. After leaving Cliff I duly received a letter to tell me that I was to go to Hartley Victoria College in Manchester to begin training for the ministry. With the closure, a year or two earlier of Headingly College in Leeds, Hartley Victoria College was the northernmost of Methodism's five Theological Colleges which included Handsworth in Birmingham, Wesley House Cambridge, Richmond in Surrey and Wesley College in Bristol.

Hartley Victoria College

[1967-1971]

So, in September 1967 I began four years of training for the Methodist Ministry. Since I didn't have the requisite number of 'A' level GCEs and didn't have an 'O' level GCE in a foreign language, I couldn't apply to do a degree which meant I embarked on the in-College course, part of which led to a Certificate in Biblical Knowledge awarded by Manchester University. I decided to retake my 'A' level RE – again – for the fourth time, and to study for a French 'O' level in the hope that I could embark on a degree course in my second year. Fortunately, one of the fourth-year students was a graduate in Modern Languages and he agreed to tutor me in French.

The Revd Dr Percy Scott, the Principal at Hartley, was our Theology Tutor. He had 'a thing' about names, refusing to call any new student by their Christian name until either he knew them well or was invited to do so. I was the first in my year to be addressed by their Christian name, up to that point I was always Mr. Fisher. Names, he believed were important, choosing his own children's names purposefully – for example his son was called Martin because of Martin Luther, one of Percy's heroes. To know and use a person's name gave power to the user, he cited the story of 'wrestling Jacob' in Genesis. Percy was a fascinating character. He had married a German and was fluent in the language, translating a number of hefty theological tomes from German into English. He was also an ardent Manchester United Supporter – their unofficial chaplain, so it was said. I believe he offered tremendous support to the team after the tragedy of the Munich Air Disaster in 1958.

Owen Evans was the New Testament Tutor. As the name suggests he was a Welshman. He also taught us New Testament Greek using the first thirty chapters of J W Wenham's 'Elements of New Testament Greek' – it was a breeze! In my second year he was replaced by Ivor Jones. It was he who told us that the Commentary on Luke that I had used at Cliff was one of the most radical around at the time. Old Testament Studies were taught by Yeoman Muckle. He was what I would call a 'refined Geordie'. Years earlier, when he was a Circuit minister, he had married my Auntie Ruth and Uncle Ridley. Dick Jones was responsible for Worship and Preaching. He impressed me least and after one of his tutorials I refused to go again as I felt that when it came to the ordering of worship all he was doing was shifting elements around without any sense of logic! Finally, Henry Rack was Church History Tutor and also my Personal Tutor. His widowed mother lived in the North East and several years down the line he would be one of the two minister who officiated when I was married and then, later again, I invited him to assist at my ordination.

The College was full, though not all the students were training for the ministry. We had a cohort of 'non-theologs' – students, usually from a Methodist background, who were studying at the University a whole variety of courses. Some would later candidate for the ministry. At ten o'clock every night we would abandon our studies and gather in one study or another for 'Tea Club'. Duly armed with tea or coffee, and toast or biscuits, groups of six or eight would get together to wind down. Some of the Tea Clubs included non-theologs and ministerial students of different years. One of the good things about Methodist Theological Colleges was that the students were a mix of theological and liturgical persuasions. High Church and Low Church, Conservative and Liberal we learned to get along together – it could lead to lively discussions in Tea Clubs. Some came in and left with the same perspectives, some changed dramatically but all were much more tolerant of opposing views.

One of the fourth-year students, who came from Wales, was a keen musician and he formed a choir during my first term to prepare to put on a performance of Handel's Messiah at Christmas. Through groups like MethSoc at the University we attracted a number of girls, some of whom were keen to find a future husband among the ranks of ministerial students, so we had no trouble recruiting sufficient sopranos and altos to the choir. The production was a success, so much so that Phil arranged for us to perform it again at his home church in Bala in North Wales. That entailed hiring a coach and a fairly lengthy journey. By the time we arrived we were all bursting for the loo. The girls were directed inside where they had to queue for the one toilet. The lads were direct down the side of the church where the church wall served as a much-needed urinal!

In my first year at Hartley Dad decided to buy a new car. After much deliberation he decided not to trade in the Austin A40 which he had bought new in 1959; instead, he gave it to me – my 21st Birthday present! He bought a new Austin 1100 for himself and my mother. The car was a godsend. I still recall the registration: 839 EUP. One of the first things I did after taking possession of the car was to have seat belts fitted. They had just become required in new cars and owners were encouraged to fit them in older vehicles and I was keen to keep my new girlfriend safe!

At home in Durham for Christmas I got myself a job delivering for the Royal Mail. In those days students often took on holiday jobs and the Post Office was a popular choice at Christmas as the number of Christmas cards being posted put huge pressure on Royal Mail. It meant an early start, which was compensated for by an early finish. Most days I was out on a round in an area I knew quite well, south from Neville's Cross. On one occasion I had my ankle nipped by a small terrier. When I reported the incident those in charge took action to have the dog put down as, apparently this wasn't the first time it had happened. I also resolved never to have a letterbox at floor level as having to keep bending down to put mail through floor-level letterboxes really was a real pain! On occasion I remained in the sorting office to sort out the mail into the various rounds. The sorting office was behind the main Post Office on Claypath, and it was there

I had to report to each morning.

> *The third age...*
> And then the lover,
> Sighing like furnace, with a woeful ballad
> Made to his mistress' eyebrow.

At Easter all the students went on campaign to various churches around the country. I was sent, with three other students to Bradwell, near Newcastle-under-Lyme. It was there that I met Kathleen Peers. I am now ashamed to confess that by this time I was no longer either a teetotaller or a non-smoker! I had taken up smoking a pipe but on the day we set off on our campaigns I had helped a colleague to push- start his car and in the process my pipe fell out of my breast pocket and broke. It was Kath who pointed me in the direction of 'The Britannia' pub, across the road from the church. I couldn't buy a replacement pipe from their Off Licence, but I did buy some cigarettes!

We saw quite a bit of each other during the week and on the Good Friday Youth Fellowship Walk, from the church to the Services at Keele on the M6, approximately 11 miles we were inseparable! That evening there was a dance, and we danced together all evening. 'Sitting on the Dock of the Bay' became 'our song'! Kath was in the Sixth form at the Orme Girls School but was hoping to go to St Mary's College in Bangor in North Wales in the September to train as a Secondary School Needlework teacher. There were only two problems with any future relationship and distance wasn't either of them. Kath already had a boyfriend who was in the army, currently serving in the middle east; and Kath's mother thought he was wonderful so from the outset I became something of 'persona non grata'!

There were originally three Methodist Theological Colleges in Manchester. A College was founded in 1881 for training clergy for the Primitive Methodist Church. It was re-named 'Hartley College' in 1906 in recognition of the benefactions of Sir William Pickles Hartley of Hartley's jams. It was nicknamed 'the jam factory' not least because it bore a striking resemblance to the Hartley building in Liverpool. One of its most outstanding tutors was A S Peake, a layman who was a prominent scholar in his day and who lent his name to a one volume commentary of the Bible.

Victoria Park College opened as the training establishment of the United Methodist Free Church in 1877. After union in 1907 and the closure of the Methodist New Connexion's Ranmoor College in Sheffield, Victoria Park became the ministerial training college for the United Methodist Church. In 1934 after Methodist Union, Victoria Park and Hartley College merged, with their students transferring to the Hartley site and the Victoria Park, Manchester site was sold to the Unitarians.

The third College in Manchester, established by the Wesleyan Methodist Church, was in Didsbury. With the merger of Victoria Park and Hartley, Didsbury College was closed and sold. The building became a Teacher Training College. A new Methodist College was established in Bristol and was named Wesley College but was popularly referred to as Didsbury.

Hartley Victoria College was closed in 1972 and the original Hartley College building in Whalley Range was sold to the Northern School of Music, which later sold it to the Kassim Darwich Grammar School for Boys. The NSM graciously retained the Revd Percy Scott as resident chaplain. Unusually for a Methodist College the chapel was cruciform in style, with sanctuary, transepts and two beautiful stained-glass windows, one depicting the New Jerusalem and the other a clean-shaven Ascending Christ.

One of the fourth-year students before beginning his training for the Methodist ministry had previously worked in the pottery industry, coming as he did from 'the Potteries'. He decided to have a plate made commemorating Hartley Victoria Methodist College, depicting John Wesley. It was to be a limited edition. I bought three. One, for my parents, one for Kath's parents and one for myself! Also, that year Westminster Central Hall produced a commemorative beaker, and I bought two. Later that same fourth-year student managed to get Wedgwood to produce a limited edition of framed black relief busts of both John Wesley and Hugh Bourne. I was hooked! So began my interest in collecting Methodist memorabilia. My collection now occupies a couple of cabinets in our lounge and in addition comprises c.30+ plates, most of which fill the delft rail on our landing.

At the end of my first year at Hartley I sat my 'A' level RE and this time I passed! I was entered for my 'O' level French and had my Oral Exam at the nearby Grammar School. When I took my Oral Exam at The Johnston School all I managed to say in French, when the exasperated examiner pointed to a bird outside the window and asked, "Qu'est-ce que c'est", was "Un oiseau"! This time the whole conversation was in French and at the end of it the examiner complimented me and said how refreshing it was to have had such a conversation after so many that, it would seem, had been much like my first attempt. Next, the written paper. Except it didn't happen. The Principal insisted that I took the exam for the Certificate of Biblical Knowledge for which I had been studying all year – the exam dates clashed. As it happened the requirements for University entrance had changed during the year and the need for a foreign language had been dropped. So, with my 'A' level I was able to apply to take a degree and at the start of my second year at Hartley I enrolled on the new BA (Theol) course.

During the summer term of that first year Kath and I had kept in touch. She had failed most of her 'O' levels the previous year and had decided to repeat Year 5 (Year 11 in modern parlance) and then go into the sixth form to take 'A' levels before going off to train as a teacher. As it transpired, she didn't need 'A' levels to go to College so, after successfully passing all her 'O' levels at the second attempt, including two 'new' ones she took after just one year, one of which was RE, she applied to Bangor St Mary's College to train as a Secondary School Needlework teacher. Her application was accepted. To be near her I decided not to go home that summer but got myself a job in Manchester – on the bins!

The money was good, but it did mean an early start each day. Another one of my colleagues from college, whose name I can't now for the life of me remember, had also got a summer job there. We had to clock on at the Wilbraham Road Depot and await to be assigned to a wagon. Mostly we were directed to Jack Ward and his 'flat' wagon. This meant we were assigned tasks, which usually meant clearing the back yard of someone's house or business. Jack was tickled to have two 'vicars' working with him. One thing I recall Jack telling us was that it was often those who were least well off who were often the most generous when it came to tipping. It was true. On one occasion we were sent to dispose of an upright piano from an elderly lady's house. She insisted on giving us a fiver – quite a lot of money in the 1960s. On another occasion we were sent to clear out the back yard of a shop which had been re-fitted. It took a whole morning and we were never even offered a cup of tea! When we got back to the depot the manager asked Jack whether they had given us a generous tip and when Jack told him that we had been given nothing the manager decided to invoice them with the maximum he was allowed to charge for such a yard clearance!

I was only put on a regular bin round on a couple of occasions, each time in Moss Side, a notoriously poor housing area between College and the University made up of Victorian back-to-back terraces. Jack Ward lived in Moss Side. Jack told us that if we were ever put on a regular bin round, we would be better off in Moss Side than the Wilbraham Road area which comprised mostly middle-class folk who lived in large detached houses. The reason – most folk in Moss Side used tinned foods whereas most folk around Wilbraham Road used fresh food, much of which was wasted and ended up in the bin!

On the last occasion I was on a regular bin round I did my back in. Those were the days when the bins were metal and round with a removable lid. You grabbed one of the side handles and hoisted it up onto your shoulder then tipped the contents into the bin lorry. On this occasion someone had filled their bin with rubble disguising it with some regular household waste on top. As I tried to lift it onto my shoulder my back went! I went to the College doctor who prescribed paracetamol! I went to my aunt's doctor in Flixton who prescribed paracetamol! (It transpired that my aunt had lived in Hartley Hall, as it was temporarily known during the war, whilst engaged in war work.) In the end, in desperation I drove back to Durham to see my own doctor who diagnosed a torn muscle, prescribed a stronger painkiller, and called the physiotherapist back to the hospital – she had finished her shift and had gone home for the day – to teach me some exercises to help repair and strengthen the muscle.

That summer there was a General Election. The handful of us who had elected to stay in College for a variety of reasons decided we wanted to cast our vote in the constituency which included Hartley Vic. We were told we couldn't as the College was not our 'permanent residence'. Percy Scott, the principal, supported us. We had to go to court to prove that we had a right to consider Hartley as our permanent residence. We won our case. That is the only occasion I have ever had to go to court. I elected to 'affirm' rather than 'swear' on the Bible.

The summer vacation came to an end, as did my trips to Bradwell to see Kath who started her studies at St Mary's Bangor. For her first year she was in residence in the College itself. I began my first year on the BA (Theol) at Manchester University. It was a new degree course. Previously students in the Theology Faculty were awarded BA degrees by the Arts Faculty. There was one other 'theolog' in my year who began the course and a new 'non-theolog' who had chosen Hartley as his 'Hall of Residence'. His name was David Archer, a Methodist Local Preacher from Edinburgh who was intending to candidate for the ministry after he had completed his degree. He was a vegetarian. We became firm friends during those three years and when it came to eating in the refectory at the University my favourite meal became macaroni cheese with a peeled plum tomato on top!

Much of the Theology Faculty was in a new building. Inevitably graffiti appeared on the wall of one of the toilet cubicles: "Eat more shit – a thousand million flies cannot be wrong." Beneath it appeared a rejoinder: "But have you seen their infant mortality rate." Only in a Theology Faculty! Needless to say, it was quickly removed.

Peter Robinson had candidated during the year after he left Cliff and he was accepted and came to Hartley at the beginning of my second year. Whilst at Cliff he had become friends with Elaine and romance had blossomed, so he was somewhat distracted, and our friendship was never quite as close as it had been when we were at Cliff. Another 'theolog' who arrived that year was Michael Townsend. He was quite a character. He already had a first degree, so he began a BD at Manchester. A confirmed bachelor and a 'high' churchman we became firm friends during my years in Hartley. He came from Barnstable in Devon. During my final year, when Kath and I were married, we had a holiday there, staying with Mike and his parents. His father was into home brewed wine in a big way. Every flat surface was occupied by a demi-john or several! We had home-made wine with every meal. His Saki was to die for!

In the Easter break during my first year on the degree course Peter and I went to Lincoln Theological College for Holy Week. We had an excellent week. Don Cupitt was the guest lecturer. His book "The Sea of Faith" was a radical reinterpretation of Christianity. I recall having quite a lengthy discussion with him after one of his lectures about how we might understand John Wesley's 'strangely warmed heart' at his Aldersgate experience!

One of the students who was in my year training for the ministry confided in me that he was gay. I knew things were not well with him as, whereas many folk chew their finger nails, he had chewed the knuckles of every finger on both of his hands, they were a mess. He had been referred to a clinic by the university but all they could offer was, what today we know of as aversion therapy. What he described was brutal. No wonder he was stressed. He never spoke to me about again. We also had a 'senior candidate' join the student body when I was in my third year. He was a retired army officer so not without funds, in fact he bought my cine camera off me when I was strapped for cash. He was 'camp' and not ashamed of his sexuality at all. Another one of the students who was in my year training for the ministry, Roy Lovatt, was a confirmed bachelor, though there was no hint that he was gay. He was, however, a bit of a character. His Lenten devotional reading each year was J R R

Tolkien's 'Lord of the Rings'! Last I heard he left Methodism and sought ordination in the Church of England. Subsequently. I believe, he was still not happy and became a Roman Catholic priest!

One of our non-theologs was training as a dentist. Like several on his course he had wanted to pursue a career in medicine but was turned down so turned to dentistry instead. He was a nice chap who was keen to recruit as many of us as possible as patients for the dental school. The problem was that his hands constantly shook so the only volunteer he managed to get was me. In fact, once he was working in your mouth his hands were as steady as a rock. I went regularly over a period of months and came away with all new fillings that, because the students were in training, had to be as good as might be expected by a private patient having a gold filling. It meant sitting in the dentist's about twice as long as usual each time, but the result were fillings that lasted several decades.

The BA (Theol) was organised into ten units. Four in the first year, four in the second and two in the final year. In year one I studied "Introduction to Philosophy", "Greek Civilisation", "Introduction to New Testament Greek" – this latter using the first 30 chapters of J W Wenham's 'Introduction to New Testament Greek' – unsurprisingly I failed this unit, probably because I was bored with having to go through the book for the third time. I passed when I retook it the following year, but it meant I couldn't get a 'first' since to do so meant passing every unit first time. The fourth unit was "Comparative Religion". This was taught by Professor S G F Brandon. I bought, and read, several of his books. At the end of my first year he went off to Egypt for the summer. Egyptology was his particular interest and he spent much of his 'free' time in Egypt. Sadly, this visit proved to be his last. On a dig in the upper Nile, far from civilisation, he collapsed with kidney failure, he only had one kidney, and died before he could be flown to a hospital.

One outstanding thing about Hartley was the food, which was excellent. Kay Asplin was the College cook. A single woman in her forties, a little on the large side, with the kind of disposition that was often a feature of such women! When she discovered that David Archer and I were missing Saturday tea to watch 'Doctor Who' she arranged for us to have it on a tray in the kitchen Staff Room, even though it was against the rules! We dreaded the possibility that the Principal would catch us. Inevitably, one Saturday Percy popped his head around the Staff Room door. To our relief he turned to Kay and in his usual gruff voice said, "Glad to see you are looking after my students."

Kay often went, on her own, on coach trips. That summer she met a widower from Preston with whom she became friendly. He was several years older than Kay. He invited her to visit him in the autumn. Much to tour consternation she called Kath and I in to ask our advice. All we could say was "follow your heart". So she did. The visit went well and several visits later Bill proposed, and Kay accepted. Initially Bill's family were both approving and supportive, however, once they were married, they cut all ties with their dad and his new bride. By default, Kath and I became 'family' and they were delighted when our children arrived on the scene and looked forward to our visits.

After many years happily married Bill died, and Kay felt very much alone. In time she met another widower, Ron, and they were married. I was asked to take the wedding ceremony which took place in Fulwood Methodist Church. The sanctuary was a step up from the body of the church and a heating grid ran along the bottom of the step. I stood on the step and Kay and Ron stood below me. As I was blessing the rings one rolled off and I nearly had kittens as I had vision of it disappearing through one of the gaps in the heating grid. Thankfully it didn't and the ceremony proceeded without further incident! We kept in touch with Kay and Ron, and with Kay after Ron died. Kay eventually died some years later.

Each year at Hartley we usually adopted a pop song as an anthem for the year. The one I remember most clearly was the 1968 hit 'Lily the Pink' by the Scaffold. There was a 'top table' in the dining room where the Principal and his wife sat for meals along with students invited in turn. There was a window light high above the table that could be opened by the long cord tethered to the wall behind the table. I recall on one occasion someone had tied a bra to the cord and hoisted it, flag-like, to dangle just below the widow directly above where Percy's wife, Christa, sat. Someone struck up 'Lily the Pink' and all eyes were on the bra. When Christa spotted it she stormed out. She was a lovely woman but, unfortunately, she didn't have much of a sense of humour.

At the end of my second year in Hartley a couple of us decided to have a quick drink at 'The Princess' which was our local before tuning in for the night. When we got there, we found a number of our colleagues had had the same idea. Someone bought us pint and before we could leave another appeared on the table in front of us. We did leave after that drink and walked back to College with Mike Speed who shared a half bottle of whiskey with us along the way. We were very happy! When we got back one of the 'non-theologs', a medic, was standing on the top of the steps that led to the front door clutching his trademark soft-backed floppy Bible! We mumbled 'Good night' avoiding breathing on him as we passed! We decided to see if the Tea Club was meeting and found that it was, and that it was in the process of finishing off the remnants of all the bottles of alcohol that remained before College ended the next day. We felt obliged to help. Eventually I left and made my way to my bedroom, which was quite a way off in the neighbouring block. I passed the same 'non-theolog' medic, again, on the way. I think my 'Good night' was rather more slurred this time.

I hadn't been long in bed before the room began to spin and I felt decidedly queasy. I got up and opened the window thinking that if I was sick, I could be sick out of the window. Fortunately, I remembered in time that the Principal's garage was immediately beneath, so I took myself off to the bathroom at the end of the corridor. I didn't have the sense to put my light on. I found a pair of shoes by feeling the laces. I had two pairs of shoes, one with round laces and one with flat laces. Sure enough I was violently sick. I then made my way back to the study block for some paracetamol passing the same 'non-theolog' medic on the way there and back! I have no idea now who was talking to, but it was obviously a long conversation! Next morning, I was up bright and early and went to the bathroom to wash before going down for breakfast and then departing for Durham. As my fellow student came in, I greeted them with a cheery 'Good Morning'. Each one asked me to tone it down as they had a splitting headache. When asked why I didn't share their condition I explained that I had been sick before finally going to sleep. "Oh, I wish I'd been sick" was their common response!

I think it was during my third year in College, my second year on the degree course, that a Polish Methodist Minister, Gerhard Frohlich, came to spend several months in the College. He was in his forties, married, with a family as I recall, and he had come to pursue his studies. The hidden agenda was to purchase a second-hand VW in Germany on his way home. No way could he have either afforded, or obtained a car in his native Poland which, at that time was under Communist control. We became firm friends during his time in College, even to the point of him coming to Durham with me during one vacation. When he left, he asked me to look after a book about his home region which he had bought on his way to the UK and which if he took it with him would be confiscated when he re-entered Poland. The intention was that, at some future date, he would be able to reclaim it. We kept in touch for a while but, sadly, eventually we lost touch. I have tried several times to track him down without success. I still have the book!

Kath and I got engaged when she went off to Bangor and during the next three years, whenever the opportunity arose either I travelled to Bangor, or Kath travelled to Manchester, or we both went to stay with my parents in Durham. I remember buying the engagement ring at H Samuels on Silver street in Durham. Jack Ward had a caravan in Abergele, not too far from Bangor. He let us use it on a number of occasions as a base when I went to visit Kath in College in Bangor. On one occasion when I was in Bangor and we attended to Methodist Church for a service when the minister was preaching. If I closed my eyes, he sounded like Yeoman Muckle who was the Old Testament Tutor at Hartley. Yeoman's voice was what I would have called, 'cultured Geordie'. As a Circuit minster, many years earlier, he had actually officiated at the wedding of my Auntie Ruth and Uncle Ridley. After the service I plucked up the courage and, as he was shaking hands as we left the church, I asked what part of the North-East he came from. If looks could kill! He informed me, in no uncertain terms that he was born and bred in North Wales. In Manchester Kath stayed with either John Rudge and his wife just across the road from college, (John was Assistant Tutor at Hartley) or with John Hinnels and his wife who lived just down the road in Chorlton. John Hinnels was one of the lecturers on my university course.

When I visited Kath in Bangor it was usually from Friday night until Sunday night. On one of the first occasions I went to see her we visited Beaumaris on Anglesea. It was a Sunday, and our intention was to find a café for lunch. We'd forgotten that this was Wales in the 1960s and nothing was open on a Sunday. We ended up at the end of the pier in Beaumaris where there was a little café, which of course was closed. However, the proprietor and his wife could be seen inside getting ready for the next day's trading. We must have looked somewhat forlorn as he popped his head out of the door and asked if he could help us. When we explained, he invited us in and provided us with a ham sandwich apiece, each with the thickest slice of ham I've ever seen in a sandwich. It was delicious.

Kath's mother was still unwilling to accept me as a prospective son-in-law and on the first occasion, when Kath came to Durham for a couple of weeks, with the intention of spending the rest of the holidays with her parents in Bradwell, the day before she was due to leave, she received a letter from her dad telling her to stay put as her mother was unwilling to have her return home! Needless to say, Kath was very upset. Thereafter we spent most of our vacations in Durham. I got a holiday job driving for the Co-op delivering orders and Kath worked behind the counter on the till at the Co-op at the top of Gilesgate.

It was while delivering orders that I had my first accident when driving. I had left the roundabout at the Cock of the North heading towards Croxdale. I was a tenth of a mile from the roundabout, which was no longer visible in my rear-view mirror because of a slight bend in the road. I was indicating to turn through an opening in the central reservation to deliver to a farm on the other side of the road when an Aston Martin hit me from behind turning me over the central reservation so that I was facing towards Durham. Of his own admission he was doing c. 60 mph in the outside lane but because I had changed lanes I was deemed to be at fault! Result: a fine and three points on my licence! Mr Balfour, the manager of the Co-op in Durham came out and, since the van was undamaged, he made me drive it back to the store; on reflection a wise move to preserve my confidence. When it came to court it was reported in the Durham County Advertiser. It warranted four lines and there was a mistake on each line!

At Christmas, when we were in Durham for the vacation, Kath got a job working in the Co-op store on North Road. The ground floor was taken up with grocery, fruit and veg and butchery. All the other departments were on the first floor. Meanwhile I was asked to be Santa Claus. I was located on the first floor at the end of the store farthest from the stairs. I recall, on one occasion, being visited by a little boy, maybe five or six years old, accompanied by his mam. I did the usual, sat him on my knee, asked him what he wanted for Christmas, promised to do my best then gave him a gift from my sack. As he and his mam walked the length of the store towards the stairs, he began unwrapping his gift. He had it unwrapped by the time he reached the head of the stairs. He stopped, turned round and ran the length of the store and gave me a big hug. 'Thank you, Santa, it's just what I wanted' he declared, and returned to his mam with the biggest grin on his face that I've ever seen! I have no idea now what the gift was that I gave him, but it certainly made his day.

During my third year at Hartley, the second on my degree course, Kath and I decided to offer for overseas service in Asia with the Methodist Church. I had hoped that we might be stationed in Malaysia as I had thoroughly enjoyed my time in Sarawak. Apart from a written application and medicals the process involved a trip to London to 'Mission House' in Marylebone for an interview with Monica Humble. To our delight we were accepted. However, we were required to attend language school for a year in Hong Kong and then to be available for stationing in Asia for a minimum of ten years. After a good deal of heart-searching we decided not to proceed, the principle reason being that my father was due to retire as I finished my training and, as an only child I felt it would be asking too much to be so inaccessible to my parents for at least eleven years after my father retired.

Kath and I married on July 18th, 1970. Kath's mother had refused us permission to marry before Kath reached 21, the age at which one could marry without a parent's permission. However, the law changed, reducing the age to 18 so we decided to marry that summer. I was still required to gain the permission of my Principal as Methodism ruled that ministers in training were not allowed to marry before finishing College. However, with the increasing number of 'senior' candidates being accepted for training, many of whom were already married, some with families, attitudes were changing so it did not prove to be a problem.

Initially we decided to get married in the College Chapel at Hartley and then at a Register Office as the Chapel wasn't registered for weddings. It was 'neutral' territory and mid-way (ish) between the two families. Kath's mother hit the roof, no daughter of hers was going to get married from anywhere apart from her home church! Fine! We asked Henry Rack, my personal tutor, and Peter Kindleysides, one of the 'senior' candidates, and a good friend, to officiate. Peter Robinson was my Best Man; David Archer was my Groomsman and Michael

Townsend played the organ. It was definitely a Hartley 'do' even if we were not in the College Chapel. Kath's minister, the Revd Jim Hardwick, acted as Registrar. On reflection he may have felt a little put out that he wasn't given a more prominent role.

I spent a lot of time preparing the order of service, which included communion for Kath and me. The vows I took from the liturgy of the Church of South India, as whilst the woman promised to 'love honour and obey' the man promised to 'love honour and protect' which seemed appropriate as I was 'under the discipline of conference'! I printed sufficient orders of service for everyone attending, making the covers in red card (red is the traditional colour used in Chinese weddings) with the initials R and K etched in gold ink on the front. It was very time consuming but worth it.

Kath, meanwhile, was busy making Bridesmaids dresses and her own wedding dress. It was stunning. Kath asked her sister Pam, and her best friend at College, Joan Bradley, to be her bridesmaids. Their dresses were a Royal Blue. Kath also had a 'little' bridesmaid, Diane, the daughter of her next-door neighbour. Her dress was white with a blue sash. Kath kept her wedding dress and when our first child arrived, she remade it as a Christening robe and at the same time crocheted a beautiful, very fine, Christening shawl to go with it!

On the Friday night, David, Michael and I travelled to Hartley where we were staying overnight. We went along to The Princess for a couple of drinks – that was my Stag Night taken care of! The next morning, we had arranged for everyone to meet at my Auntie Lila's in Flixton to travel down to Bradwell 'in convoy'. That was fine for all my relatives and friends who were coming down from the North East, but I'd forgotten that Eric and Gwyneth Watchman, who lived in Davyhulme didn't know where to come. Eric and Gwyneth, although a few years older than me had been members of the Youth Fellowship at North Road in Durham. Eric did his degree at Manchester while living in Hartley as a non-theolog. He moved out as I moved in, married and settled in Manchester and was working as a librarian at the University Library. We had renewed our friendship while I had been at College. Since no-one else knew where they lived, I had to go and collect them. When I got back to my Aunt's most of the others had set off. We changed cars, I took Henry Rack in mine and we exceeded the speed limit all the way down the M6!

I parked in the Church car park and dashed into the vestry to change into my wedding suit. I was still putting on my jacket as I entered the church, scattering confetti behind me. Unbeknown to me Peter Kindleysides' children had scattered confetti in my suitcase before I'd left Manchester! Kath was already half-way down the aisle, having been driven round the block several times to delay her arrival. The service began quarter of an hour late! The entrance music was "The Arrival of the Queen of Sheba". While the registers were being signed Michael played "All Kinds of Everything" and "Je t'aime" (at the time banned by all radio stations as 'obscene') and we left the Church to "Crown Imperial". Once the photographs were over, we repaired to the Church Hall for a ham salad meal Kath's mother and the ladies of the church had prepared. I decided to leave the car where it was on the church car park rather than move it to a nearby street. I didn't have either the time or the opportunity and I decided that anyway it was the last place anyone would look for it, 'hidden in plain sight'! Someone, however, found out where it was, so when we set out for our honeymoon in Lindale, near Grange-over-Sands in the Lake District, we had to stop when we were out of sight of the Church to remove the coins from the hub caps and several kippers from the exhaust and engine, and the tin cans attached to the rear bumper bar!

The cottage we had booked from an ad. in the Methodist Recorder was one up and one down. The toilet was, literally, at the bottom of the garden! The folk who owned it had left us a half pint Pyrex measuring jug as a wedding present. Sunday, the only really sunny day of the week was spent cleaning out the car. Removing more kippers, vacuuming out the confetti, cleaning the windows of lipstick etc. Several weeks later we discovered another kipper which we'd missed. Kath's brother had liberally spread confetti throughout all the clothes in Kath's suitcase, so more cleaning up indoors. The rest of the week we spent touring the Lakes, the west coast, Bowness, Kendal, all the usual tourist places, most of which we had never visited before. One of the places we visited was Cartmel. I bought a simple pectoral cross made of beaten stainless steel from the Old Forge. Among other things they made all sorts of church furnishings so later, when I eventually began my Circuit ministry, I purchased a Latin cross, which still sits on my study windowsill along with a small chalice and paten, all made to order. When we returned to Cartmel many years later we sought out the Old Forge only to find it was now an Art Gallery. Apparently, the owner of the

Old Forge had, tragically, blinded himself when a stray spark had entered his eye when beating some steel.

When the honeymoon was over, we moved into a first floor flat at 2 Dartmouth Road in Chorlton-cum-Hardy, just down the road from Hartley. Miss Thornburn, I think that was the lady's name, lived on the ground floor. We had the summer together with a second week's honeymoon in a caravan at Cairn Ryan, near Stranraer. Then it was time for Kath to return to Bangor for her final year at College. Most weekends she came back to Manchester by train so every Friday I would pick her up from the station, dropping her off there again on the Sunday night.

It was also the final year of my degree. Two Units; Hinduism, with John Hinnels and The Doctrine of the Atonement with Fred Kenworthy. I was also expected to do two days a week on 'Circuit Practice'. Mike Townsend and I were assigned to the Ecumenical Team Ministry in Stretford. Mike was to accompany the Methodist minister; I was placed with the Revd James Bentley at All Saints Parish Church. James was quite a character. We often had lunch in one of the local hostelry's, very unMethodist! I got on well with both James and Neil, his curate. I did some visiting in the parish, also preached on occasion, read Evening Prayer quite often, and attended the staff meetings, which were often held at the Lutheran Church, the pastor being a member of the Ecumenical Team. At the end of the year, when both James and Neil were away on holiday I was, in effect, 'in charge'.

During one of our vacations that year Kath and I had a week's holiday in my Uncle Jim's caravan at Beadnell. During the week the weather was poor but, on the Saturday, when we were due to leave, the sun got out, so we headed over the dunes and onto the beach for an hour of sunbathing before we set out to return to my parents in Durham. Although it was sunny there was quite a strong wind coming off the sea. By the evening I was in agony and my parents called the Doctor (those were the days when doctors did house calls!). It transpired that I had severe sunburn and sunstroke. It was the wind 'wot done it'! I just hadn't taken account of the strength of the sun. So lots of cream and lots of water to rehydrate me!

The year finally ended. Both Kath and I graduated, Kath with a Certificate of Education and I got a II(i) in my BA (Theol). My parents came down for my Graduation Ceremony. They had already bought me a Geneva Gown as a preaching gown and it was near enough exactly the same as a Manchester BA gown, so they bought me my hood, trimmed in lilac and ermine. So, I was among the first cohort ever of the Manchester BA (Theol) graduates.

(I also bought for myself a Hartley hood, made entirely in blue and silver. Apparently, all the Methodist Colleges had hoods that minsters could purchase when they finally completed their training; all that is except for Hartley. Someone decided that it was an issue that needed addressing so a Hartley hood was duly designed and registered.)

Some of us were invited to stay on during the summer as delegates to the first ever Congress of Mithraic Studies which was being held in Owens Park, one of the Manchester Halls of Residence. The bonus was that we would be able to attend the second Congress which was scheduled to take place in Tehran the following year. Sadly, because of the political situation, it never happened. Rosemary Orpin, one of my fellow University students, and I were put in charge of the book stall so were excused paying the fees to attend the Congress which proved most instructive. Apart from the lectures we had a coach trip to see the Mithraium on the Roman wall, but the highlight was, undoubtedly, the final meal that was held in an Armenian restaurant in the centre of Manchester. Professor Oikonomedes of Loyola Catholic University in Chicago 'presided'. When we finally got up to leave, he ordered more drinks, of which I had already had far too many! He pulled out his wallet to pay. It was stuffed with Sterling, US Dollars and several other currencies! How I drove back to Chorlton I do not know. We dropped John Hinnels off at his home then drove to Owens Park, which was deserted so we went back to restaurant where 'the party' was still in full swing! I have no idea what time we finally left. I do know I was in no fit state to drive, although I did. When I got home, I spent some time in the loo, although I didn't actually manage to be sick.

During the last term those of us who were leaving to go into Circuit were called, in turn, into Percy Scott's Office and asked where we would like to be 'stationed'. In those days you were not given a choice, you were simply 'stationed' but Percy liked to try and place his students, taking account of their wishes. I opted for 'North', 'Urban'. When the stations came out, I was sent 'South' 'Rural'! So, from 1st September 1971 I was to be a probationer minster in the Bury St. Edmunds and Sudbury Circuit, with a dispensation to administer the Sacrament of Holy Communion.

Peter Robinson and Elaine were getting married at the end of that term and were intending to move into the flat where Kath and I were currently living. Unfortunately, we were not moving into Circuit until late August. James Bentley came to the rescue offering to let us live in the Rectory whilst he and his wife were away in Italy during July and August on condition that we looked after the rabbit and the dog, a dachshund called Pusey. The day after we moved in the rabbit died, and the dog, which was very overweight, we had to put on a diet! Neil was still around for the first few weeks and he buried the rabbit for us. On one memorable occasion we all went to the opening of the new function room in The Melville, the local pub. Kath drank rather too many Cherry Brandies and spent the whole of the next day in bed nursing a hangover! I was fine, well, sort of, I made my way to the kitchen by following the wall with my hand down the stairs, through the hall and dining room into the kitchen never failing to keep contact with the wall! When the time finally came for us to move out Pusey, now much slimmer, tried his hardest to get into our car to come with us as we packed up ready to drive to Bury St Edmunds.

Bury St Edmunds

[1971-1973]

My first appointment as a Circuit minister began on September 1st, 1971. It was a probationer's appointment, so it was only for two years. I was given pastoral charge of five churches. Elmswell, Tostock, Woolpit, and Ashfield were all about ten miles east of Bury St Edmunds. Northumberland Avenue Methodist Church was on a new housing estate about a mile outside Bury St Edmunds. The Manse was on the same estate, not far from the church, a maisonette on the second and third floors of a long block of flats. The ground floor housed several shops, including an off-licence.

The view from the manse window was superb as we overlooked a green the size of several football pitches. One street beyond the top of the green was Northumberland Avenue; halfway up on the right lived Ron Hudson who was one of our Church Stewards. He worked for Calor and he got us a small gas fire and a couple of large gas bottles, at cost price, one of the bottles we still use connected to our bar-b-q. One March morning as I looked out of the front window, I saw Ron on his way to Church. I was planned to preach. It dawned on me that the clocks had gone forward and I had forgotten. I have never washed and dressed as quickly, before or since! It was the only occasion I have ever taken a service without having shaved (except on the three occasions when I grew a beard!).

Northumberland Avenue was a fairly new modern church; I was only their second minister. There was a significant work there with children and young people. The Youth Fellowship met after the Sunday evening service, which members were expected to attend. The Sunday School was oversubscribed so we created a Junior Fellowship which met after the morning service, again members were expected to attend that service. The rest of the Sunday School left for their classes during the second hymn. After six months we asked the Junior Fellowship how they felt about being in for the whole of the morning service. Their only negative comment was that the hymns were unfamiliar. Perhaps always insisting on having 'children's hymns' in Sunday School, and Church when children are present, is not such a good idea if we want our young folk to progress into adult worship? At the end of our first year Kath and I ran a Holiday Club for the children at the Church and in the neighbourhood. It was huge success. The adult helpers wanted a repeat the next year when we were due to leave. No-one was prepared to take responsibility for running it, so sadly it never happened.

Several members of the Youth Fellowship were also members of a guitar group. Guitars were provided by the church although during my time there I managed to negotiate a way for the members to purchase them for themselves at a significant reduction. One lad, John, was not only an exceptional instrumentalist, he was also an accomplished woodworker, making several less popular, but historic, stringed instruments in his spare time. They were beautifully made. He worked as a civilian at the Police Station in the town. One of the fishermen from Great Yarmouth regularly brought fresh fish to the station and John arranged for us to buy some from him. It was great to have a regular supply of fish fresh from the boat. The only trouble was we had to gut them! John married another of the group, Ann Edkins, the eldest daughter of Angus and Margaret ('Ming') Edkins. Angus worked in management for the Water Board. His brother was an Estate Agent in Durham with a shop on Saddler Street. I heard some years later that John and Ann's marriage had sadly not survived very long, and that Ann had subsequently re-married.

The Guitar group, on occasion played at services. They also played at our farewell 'do'. Lindisfarne was the popular group at the time, so Fog on the Tyne was a must. We did try to persuade them not to play the last verse, all to no avail. However, I don't think many who were listening registered the line "we can do a wee wee, we can do a wet up the wall"!

On one occasion we took the Youth Fellowship to a concert at a nearby university, I forget now which one. The headline group was T-Rex, previously known as Tyrannosaurus Rex. It was an interesting experience. The concert was brilliant, and the youngsters thoroughly enjoyed it, actually so did Kath and I.

What was somewhat disconcerting were the number of students openly selling cannabis. Fortunately, none of our group were tempted.

As a 'probationer' minister I was granted the privilege of a dispensation from Methodist Conference to preside at the Lord's Supper. Across all denominations a liturgical revolution was underway. The Methodist Church produced a range of services in modern English, including Holy Communion and Baptism. The booklets were quite large, similar to A5 size (I guess they were probably folded foolscap – this was before our paper sizes went metric). They had matt blue covers. We had used them in College, and I resolved to use them in Circuit. I asked at Northumberland Avenue whether they used the 'blue books'. Receiving a positive response, I then asked how often, "Regularly" came the reply. When I asked, "how often is regularly?" I was told, "A couple of times a year!" My response was clear, "From now on we will use the 'blue books' whenever appropriate". This proved acceptable, except for one elderly lady who after experiencing several 'modern' communions observed that she still preferred the 'old' service. I promised that if she could explain to me what was meant by the phrase "by his one oblation of himself once offered" I would consider using the 'old' service on occasion. Needless to say, she never got back to me and we continued with the 'blue books'!

The prayer, in full, reads: "Almighty God, our heavenly Father, who of thy tender mercy didst give thine only Son Jesus Christ to suffer death upon the cross for our redemption; who made there, by his one oblation of himself once offered, a full, perfect and sufficient sacrifice, oblation and satisfaction for the sins of the whole world; and did institute, and in his holy gospel command us to continue, a perpetual memory of that his precious death, until his coming again. Almighty God, our heavenly Father, who of thy tender mercy didst give thine only Son Jesus Christ to suffer death upon the cross for our redemption; who made there, by his one oblation of himself once offered, a full, perfect and sufficient sacrifice, oblation and satisfaction for the sins of the whole world; and did institute, and in his holy gospel command us to continue, a perpetual memory of that his precious death, until his coming again."

One of the Chemists in town stocked non-alcoholic communion wine. Northumberland Avenue bought their wine there. From time to time, I would get a phone call from one of my rural churches asking me to pick up a bottle to bring out to them next time I was planned there. Another of my rural churches used to stock up on 'Vino Sacro' from the local Off-Licence. This was the alcoholic wine used in the local Anglican Churches. Another of my rural churches used Ribena. The Communion Steward in the smallest of my churches, however, didn't trust any 'bought' communion wines so she brewed her own. Even a sip was enough to blow your socks off!

My rural churches more or less looked after themselves, thankfully! Elmswell was the largest and therefore got more of my time than the other three. Two families were prominent in the church. The Rattenberrys and the Nunns. The Rattenbury family were well known in Methodism, one of whom, the Rev'd J Ernest Rattenbury DD (1870-1963) wrote extensively on Methodism. [When I retired to Crook, I met the Rev'd Matt Turling, vicar of St Paul's Parish Church in Spennymoor. It transpired that he was married to the daughter of the Rattenbury family of Elmswell. Although she was too young to remember me her older brother, who was at university while I was minister in Bury St Edmunds, did remember me!]

Edward Nunn was a prominent farmer in the area. On one occasion, in conversation, I mentioned that while everyone expected the minister to visit them, no-one ever visited the minister. Some weeks later there was a ring on the doorbell at the manse. It was Edward Nunn. When I asked what I could do for him he replied, "Nothing. I was in town for the market and remembered your comment and thought I'd call round to see how you were doing." Thereafter, occasionally, when he was in town for the market, he would call around just to see how I was! His visits were really appreciated.

Woolpit, Tostock and Ashfield were small, long established village Methodist Churches. Like many such causes they were largely reduced to a Sunday service with none of the weekday activities associated with larger city churches. Consequently, it was really just a case of making occasional visits to members. Woolpit and Tostock were sizeable brick and stone buildings. Ashfield, on the other hand, was make of corrugated iron sheets, a simple rectangular building with no land and a frontage straight onto the road.

Kath managed to get a part-time post at St Benedict's Roman Catholic Secondary School as a Needlework teacher. She stuck it for two terms. Some of the girls were really keen but Kath found the girls, who regularly turned up without their equipment, incredibly frustrating. There were three organists at Northumberland Avenue, and you could tell who was playing as you walked up the church path. One was a pianist, Margaret 'Ming' Edkins, had some organ experience, Colin Francis was an organist. Colin, who was also a Local Preacher, was the Head Teacher at Honington Primary School. He happened to mention that he was looking for a teacher for his Reception class. Although Kath was Secondary trained, in her final year exams, she took one look at the Secondary questions and opted to answer the Primary questions instead. She passed, so when Colin mentioned that he was looking for a Reception teacher she jumped at it. She thoroughly enjoyed it even though the classrooms were heated by coal fired stoves in the corner and her classroom overlooked the cemetery, which was used, occasionally, by the nearby USAF base which meant she had to take her class elsewhere when a burial was taking place.

St Benedict's did, however, have a fabulous Staff social life, and although Kath only taught there part-time for two terms we were still expected, and welcomed, at their frequent parties. One of the teachers, Pat Murphy and his wife and family became firm friends. He was an exceptional artist and before we left, we bought one of his paintings. I took up fencing and Pat and I attended classes in Newmarket each week. On one occasion Kath and I were invited to a meal at his home with a Catholic priest who was one of his friends and I found myself assisting in a home Mass. Kath took up trampolining which entailed a trip to Haverhill Sports Centre each week. She did well, obtaining several awards, although she nearly did herself a nasty injury on one occasion when a back somersault went wrong.

Bury St Edmunds was notable in being remarkably ecumenical. The Council of Churches (this was before Churches Together) included all the Churches in the town, including Roman Catholic and Pentecostal, at a time when they were generally excluded from such bodies. All the Churches had abandoned their Church Magazines in favour of a town-wide magazine called The Bridge, named after a bridge which could be found in the Abbey grounds. The original Abbey had been the largest ecclesiastical building in the world in its heyday, now it was mostly in ruins. However, one of its chapels, which had largely escaped destruction, now serves as St Edmundsbury Cathedral. Each Church had an A5 page for Church News and a letter from their minister.

One of the highlights of my time in Bury St Edmunds was an all-night youth vigil attended by young folk from all the town's churches. It was held in the Cathedral, organised by the young Roman Catholic priest and myself. On a less positive note, however, I recall a conversation with an Anglican colleague about the failure of the Methodist Anglican Conversation a few years earlier. He admitted he was one who voted against it because, he said, he believed that that was what the Methodists wanted!

When the Town Council proposed a new Community Centre on the estate on the other side of the town the Council of Churches was invited to have an input. The result was the addition to the plans of an extra room to be used on Sundays as a place of worship with a Roman Catholic Mass followed by an ecumenical service each Sunday. The cost was met by the Council of Churches. Additionally, they agreed to pay for a Church Army Captain to be stationed there to undertake work in the community. Fifty years on and, as far as I know, the post is still maintained.

Whilst we were there the Council of Churches arranged a public meeting in the Athenaeum on Angel Hill, virtually opposite the cathedral, and invited the Revd Lord Dr Donald Soper to come as the speaker. The meeting was very well attended, and it was the first, and last, opportunity I had to listen to such an eminent Methodist. He was well worth listening to.

My probationer's studies were undertaken ecumenically. There were only two probationers in the East Anglia District. Alan Ogier, who was stationed in Great Yarmouth in Norfolk, and me in Suffolk. I was linked with the St Edmundsbury Diocesan deacons, about a dozen of them, to share in their two-year training. It was a first-rate programme. The things I recall most clearly were the 'trust exercises' and the 'time and motion study' we took part in. The outcome of the latter was most enlightening. For two weeks we had to record what we were doing every half hour of the day. The information was then sent off, I think, to the University of Bristol for analysis. Bear in mind that each Anglican deacon was a curate to an incumbent in a single parish whereas I had sole responsibility for five churches. When the results came back what we found was that the bulk of the curates' time was spent in visiting, very little in preparing for or conducting worship, and even less time spent in travelling. In my case the bulk of my time was spent in travelling, a significant amount of time was spent in preparing for and conducting worship, with visiting allocated very little of my time.

One of the stories we were told still makes me smile. It could only have happened in somewhere as rural as East Anglia. When the vicar came to leave his village parish everyone was distraught as they had never had a vicar who was so conscientious when it came to visiting. It transpired however that each week he had a coffee in the little café next to the bus stop where the locals caught the weekly bus to go into town to the market. He noted who got on the bus then set off to drop his visiting card through the doors of those who had gone shopping. 'Sorry I missed you.'!

I was also supposed to be studying for an MA at Lancaster University on the works of

Sarvepalli Radhakrishnan. Eric Sharpe was my supervisor. He had been my 'Hinduism' lecturer at Manchester and had recently been appointed as Professor of Religious Studies at Lancaster. Needless to say, I never did complete the MA. Apart from finding the time to study the fact that Lancaster was 245 miles from Bury St Edmunds, a four-and-a-half-hour drive, made attending seminars and the like nigh well impossible.

In the two years I was in Bury St Edmunds I think I only had four funerals and two weddings. My first wedding was the daughter of Jack Denman, the youth leader at Northumberland Avenue. The second was a lapsed, divorced Anglican and a Buddhist. At that time Anglican clergy were still encouraged not to marry divorced persons in church, and they were very reluctant to extend their welcome to people of other faiths.

There was a problem with Alan Ogier's appointment in Great Yarmouth and finding another at short notice was difficult, so he was moved to Bury St Edmunds. Just outside the town was Culford School one of our Methodist Schools at which I preached on occasion. Alan was appointed as chaplain for one year to complete his probationary period. The Revd Fred King was Superintendent of the Bury St Edmunds and Sudbury Circuit and lived in Bury St Edmunds. Fred and Betty King laid on a Christmas meal for the Circuit Staff and their wives. Alan asked if he could 'bring a bottle' and Fred, a confirmed teetotaller, reluctantly agreed. Fred said he had never darkened the door of a pub and Alan pointed out that pubs sold more than just alcohol. Some weeks later Fred told us that on holiday he and Betty had not been able to find anywhere to get a drink and, recalling, the conversation with Alan, somewhat reluctantly, they went into the nearest pub which provided them with an excellent cup of coffee, and there was no sign of anyone in there who was intoxicated!

As I have already noted travelling took up a lot of my time each week. My section apart, the Circuit was very large. On one Sunday I clocked up 98 miles taking three services with a total congregation, including organists, of 28! My Austin A40 had served my dad and then me very well but it really was getting to the point where I needed a new car. At that time the Methodist Church provided an interest free loan towards the purchase of a new car. So I applied, successfully. My limit was £1,000. There were three possibilities in that price range, a Peugeot, a Renault and a Daf 44. Daf was a Dutch firm that produced three models, imaginatively called 33, 44, and 55! My Auntie Ruth had a Daf 44 and I was very impressed with it. It was a 'variomatic'. Instead of traditional gears it utilized a revolutionary belt system with the belts moving up and down two cones. Given that the other two cars we considered had a lot of bare paintwork inside and the Daf didn't we went for the Daf. The belts needed to be replaced, we were told, after 20,000 miles – I had done 44,000 before mine need to be replaced!

It was slow moving off but very quickly picked up speed as the gears rapidly increased. On occasion, when we went through to Cambridge and had to pass through Newmarket, we would be stopped at lights in the centre of Newmarket, usually next to some racehorse owner, in a Rolls, or a Bentley, or a Jaguar. They would look down their noses at our little Daf and pull away in front of us. I would then take great delight in sailing past them as they were busy changing gear! 'Van der Valk' was a very popular TV detective series, with a very catchy theme tune. It was set in Amsterdam, consequently the car was duly named Arlette after Van der Valk's wife!

While we were in Bury St Edmunds my cousin Paul moved down to London to study medicine. Paul was the youngest son of my Auntie Ruth and Uncle Ridley. We weren't too far away from London so Paul would quite often come up for the weekend. The recently opened M11 meant that we could go down to London for a day visit, which we did, several times, driving as far as Blackhorse Lane and catching the tube there into the city centre. On one such occasion Kath wanted to visit the Needlewoman shop on Regent Street. While she was sorting out what she needed I was browsing. I spotted a booklet with several tapestry kneeler patterns in it. Most were very traditional but one, a very modern design called 'Durham' was rather attractive. When I joined Kath at the till, she was rather surprised when I asked her to add the booklet, and a tapestry stand, canvas and wools to her purchases. I managed to complete about three quarters of the kneeler before it was packed away as we prepared for our next move. It didn't see the light of day for nearly two more decades!

The manse was sparsely furnished. It was actually a Council property rented by the Circuit from the Council and most of the contents were cast offs! Our bed was made up from three old beds and was, literally, tied together with string – I kid you not! The only decent piece of furniture in the manse was a Welsh Dresser and matching dining table and chairs. During the time we were there the Methodist Church transferred manse furnishings to the minister. You paid nothing for furniture over ten years old thereafter the figure increased by 10% per year. All we paid was a tiny percentage of what the circuit had paid to have the dresser, dining table and chairs French polished several years earlier. My parents, on one of their visits brought with them the cottage suit they were replacing, the settee tied precariously to the roof of their car. We bought a fridge freezer on hire purchase. When it came to the end of our time there, and I was about to be ordained we had to fill out a questionnaire about our finances, and the Methodist Church paid off the outstanding balance! No minister began ordained life in debt!

We did have a garage situated a short distance away behind the row of shops. I don't recall ever using it. We also had a 'shed' on the ground floor in a long row behind the 'flats'. Our 'shed' was conveniently positioned just at the foot of our stairs. It quickly filled up with all the things we didn't want in the manse and stayed full until we moved.

I don't now recall why, or how, but on one occasion we signed up for a wine tasting 'at home'. This guy turned up with a whole variety of white wines which we sampled in turn, noting the subtle differences between them. We ended up ordering a case of a dozen. I don't know how he managed to carry his samples up the two flights of stairs to the manse!

My two years as a probationer minister passed quickly and the time came to look for a new appointment. No longer stationed but open to invitation. John Best, who had lived along the street from us in Durham, was now a Circuit Steward in the Ashford Circuit in Kent. They had two appointments coming vacant in the Circuit and he and his wife invited us to stay overnight with them and have a look at one of the appointments. One was rural, and one was based in the town. I quite liked the look of the town appointment, but it turned out that they wanted me for the rural appointment. Reluctantly, I declined their invitation. The next I heard of John he had given up nursing and was rearing sheep on Fair Isle in the Shetland Islands. He was subsequently ordained as a Minister in Local Appointment.

Having declined the appointment in Ashford there weren't many left to choose from. In the end I accepted an invitation to the Ashton-under-Lyme Circuit with two churches, Hurst and Waterloo, both quite large urban churches. It looked very promising.

As we prepared to leave Bury St Edmunds, we reflected on the fact that when we had arrived there, we were told that it was difficult to make friends with 'the natives' – that usually took decades! We felt that we had made quite a number of good friends whilst we had been there, however, when we sat down to reflect on it it quickly became apparent that all of those who had extended the hand of friendship had come from either the North East or, in a couple of instances, from the North West!

Before we left for Ashton I was ordained. Conference that year was in Newcastle-upon-Tyne. It was rather nice that I had been accepted for the ministry at the Middlesbrough Conference and was subsequently ordained at the Newcastle Conference. We stayed with my parents in Durham. Mike Townsend came specially for the occasion, and the night before my ordination he and I went for a drink at the County Hotel in Elvet.

In the morning of Tuesday 3rd July all the ordinands met at Brunswick Methodist Church to be followed by lunch. A photograph of all the ordinands from all four Colleges was taken. (Many years later, when I was Superintendent of the

Blackburn Circuit, for some reason the photo re-appeared in the Methodist Recorder. I recognised myself at the left of the photo. At the right was the Rev'd Terry Young, Superintendent of the neighbouring Darwen Circuit, and a good friend. He had trained at another College, but we had both been ordained at the same Conference and never realised it!).

In the afternoon all the ordinands gathered in City Hall, which was where Conference was being held and we were admitted 'into Full Connexion with the Methodist Conference', a legacy from the days when John Wesley presided over the annual Conference. In the evening the ordination services took place in various churches around the District. Those from Hartley were ordained at Memorial Methodist Church in North Shields. The Rev'd Brian S O'Gorman (Ex-president of the Conference) presided, assisted by the Rev'd Alan O Barbour (Assistant Secretary of the Conference). The Ordination Charge was given by the Rev'd E Gordan Rupp (Ex-President of the Conference). Every Ordinand was able to invite someone to assist at the laying on of hands and I had asked the Rev'd Henry Rack. He had been my Personal Tutor at Hartley and he, along with Peter Kindleysides, had officiated at our wedding. He had connections with the North East; his widowed mother lived there. I bought him a book about Durham Cathedral as a thank-you gift.

Henry was an interesting character. I next came across him when we were living in Kendal and he came to address a meeting of the Cumbria Wesley Historical Society. He had written what many regard as the definitive history of John Wesley. As a tutor at Hartley and lecturer at Manchester University he had lived in

Manchester for years. He went everywhere on his bike and had never driven a car but, he told me, the first thing he did when he retired was to learn to drive!

It was too far for anyone from Bury St Edmunds to travel for my ordination, but a coach load came through from Durham, including the Rev'd R J W Bevan, the Rector of St Oswald's Parish Church. Dad had insurance business with him, and he had always taken an interest in my career, often asking how I was getting on. He had asked if he could come and Dad had said, "of course".

Sadly, the church in which I was ordained closed not many years after my ordination. It was bought by Frankie Wappat, a broadcaster on local BBC radio, who opened it up as an Independent Evangelical Church. It thrived for several years but then closed and the last time I drove past the building stood empty and derelict.

So then it was back to Bury St Edmunds, the round of farewells, and packing up the Manse ready to make the move to Ashton-under-Lyme.

Ashton-under-Lyne

[1973-1974]

The Ashton-under-Lyne manse was a small three-bedroomed semi in a cul-de-sac north east of the town. It had a small sloping garden. It also had a flooded air-raid shelter under the dining room floor; the water was several feet deep and came up to within twelve to eighteen inches of floor level. The Circuit Stewards advised us to lift the trapdoor from time to time and check that the water level hadn't risen significantly. We considered either becoming Baptist and turning it into a Baptistry or putting a light in it with a glass cover and making it into a fish tank! As a manse it was totally inadequate. The kitchen was tiny and there was a small 'morning room' plus two reception rooms on the ground floor.

The fridge/freezer had to reside in the hall, there was no space for it in any other room on the ground floor. The kitchen was tiny with space only for the sink and the cooker, both of which were ancient. We redecorated throughout. The hall, landing and stairs had Lincrusta on the walls, it gave the impression of being panelled in dark wood. The effect was oppressive. The Lincrusta was dreadful to remove.

Initially I turned the small front bedroom into a study. It was too small, so I moved the study into the back bedroom. Kath's younger sister Pam was training as a teacher, although she elected to live at home and go to the Teacher Training College in Alsager to which she could easily commute. When she was placed on teaching practise in our area she came to live with us for a while and had to make do with the little front bedroom. With a three-quarter bed in there it was rather cramped!

Hurst Methodist Church wasn't far from the Manse. It had a good-sized congregation, a decent Sunday School and plenty of activities going on. The senior Society Steward, who was only in his 40s, read the Gospel lesson at my first service, John 14:1-14. Tragically he quite unexpectedly died the following week and I found myself reading the same lesson at his funeral! He left a wife and young daughter.

The first Church Council I chaired at Hurst was scheduled to begin at 7.00 pm. I arrived at 6.45 pm. Just before 7.00 pm there was only the Secretary and a couple of members present. I was told that folk turned up any time between 7.00 pm and 7.30 pm so the meeting usually began at 7.30 pm! What time did it end – "usually between 10.00 pm and 10.30 pm! I explained that we would start at the stated time of 7.00 pm and since most folk could not concentrate for more than one and a half hours, we would end at 8.30 pm. If the business wasn't concluded, then we would re-convene the following evening. We started at 7.00 pm and shortly before 7.30 pm, when most people were finally present, I explained my intention again. We finished at 8.30 pm! It was a pattern I followed throughout my ministry, with addition of a printed agenda with times indicated against each item.

The Church Council Secretary was Fred Cuttle. He was a PA to a female boss, in those days a most unusual role reversal. He was proficient in shorthand and typing and took to helping me out when it came to admin. He was also a Local Preacher. He was not teetotal, and we would often repair to the Oddfellows Arms, his 'local' in one of the backstreets not far from the church, especially after church meetings. It was a small, homely, welcoming local. One of the folk who was a regular was a local chemist whose wife bred, and showed, shelties. When the next litter arrived, Fred took us to see them and bought one for us. She was the best the breeder had ever bred, perfect for showing – except for a white mark on her hindquarters. We called her Nel; her kennel name was Strolca Shanell – the breeder named all her dogs after perfumes!

A constant bone of contention then, and now, in most churches was what to do with the notices and collection. Notices that were read out at some point in the service were usually forgotten. Notices that were printed out were either left in the pew or a coat pocket. I persuaded the folk at Hurst to place all notices on a noticeboard in the church porch. It was divided into sections for 'This Week', 'This Month', and 'Forthcoming Events'. It worked remarkably well. Plates were placed in the porch for people to put their collection in as the entered. The collection could then be brought forward at an appropriate point in the service.

The fourth age

Then a soldier,
Full of strange oaths, and bearded like the pard,
Jealous in honour, sudden and quick in quarrel,
Seeking the bubble reputation
Even in the cannon's mouth.

Virtually around the corner from the manse was the Army Pay Corps HQ and I discovered that I was their chaplain. I led a regular study session using material provided by the Royal Army Chaplains Department. The material was excellent, and the attendance was good. Kath and I were invited to the Christmas dinner. We felt totally underdressed as almost all the men were in Mess Dress and the women in Evening Dress. The food, however, was out of this world. It was the first time I had ever had a 'five bird roast'! The following year when one of the Officers' wives had a baby, I was asked to do the baptism and we were invited to the after-baptism party which was a picnic with unlimited champagne and food to rival the Christmas dinner. The result of my contact with the Pay Corps was an invitation to become a TAVR chaplain. So, duly appointed as a Captain I became chaplain to the Liverpool General Hospital Unit.

I wasn't a very good chaplain. I didn't get across to Liverpool very often, mainly because it was a longish trip which took a huge chunk out of an evening. I was sent on a couple of training courses, one with the Green Howards and the other with the Cheshires. They were training at Warcop before deployment in Northern Ireland which was still in the throes of 'The Troubles'. I spent two weeks with the Cheshires at Warcop. Everything the squaddies were expected to do the padre had to do as well! On the ranges I fared well. I had the highest score using a SLR (Self-loading rifle) even though I had never fired a weapon before in my life! We had three rocket propelled grenades shoulder fired anti-tank weapons. It was decided that two NCOs, who had never fired them before, and the padre were the chosen three. The two NCOs both missed the tank by a mile. I hit it dead centre! The time I failed was on the grenade range. I pulled the pin and lobbed my grenade, as instructed, but it never went off. When that happened the person who had lobbed the grenade was expected to go and look for it. With much trepidation I went searching, but I never found it. To the best of my knowledge it is still out there somewhere.

We had a night exercise where it was decided I would be an IRA suspect being sought for arrest. I was despatched with a couple of privates to hide out in the countryside. Once we were in place a platoon came looking for us. I persuaded the two privates that we should move to a less obvious position which meant being flat against an embankment and standing in a shallow stream. The platoon came over the horizon in clear view and proceeded to look for us. When they couldn't find us – they didn't try very hard – they decided to return to base. At that point we gave ourselves up. On the way back to base we tagged along at the back of the platoon; on a couple of occasions we were separated by a fence when we were forced to take cover because we were being fired on! Back at base the platoon was asked what they had done wrong – no answer. I was asked and I pointed out that when they first appeared they had offered themselves as a perfect target for an armed terrorist and if I had been a real IRA terrorist, they gave me plenty of opportunities to abscond on the way back to base! It was a good couple of weeks. On the last day when prizes and awards were being given out, as the padre I was presented with a four pack of Newcastle Brown Ale – for ensuring good weather during the two week's training!

As a chaplain I had the opportunity to visit the headquarters of the RAChD (Royal Army Chaplains Department) at Bagshot Park near Windsor. The original Bagshot Lodge was built between 1631–33 as one of a series of small lodges designed for King Charles I by Inigo Jones. It was remodelled between 1766 and 1772 according to designs of James Paine for George Keppel, the 3rd Earl of Albemarle, and altered in 1798 by Sir John Soane for the Duke of Clarence (later King William IV), who lived there until 1816. In 1946 King George VI offered the house to the Royal Army Chaplains' Department to be used as a Church House and Chaplains> Depot. The Army Chaplains were in residence from 1947 but relocated to Andover, Hampshire, in April 1996, shortly before the Earl and Countess of Wessex took over the tenancy. It was a very impressive location. Chaplains in the TAVR (Territorial Army and Volunteer Reserve) were not expected to wear Dress Uniform for formal dinners, lounge suits would suffice. However, when it came to the final formal meal I felt distinctly underdressed. Chaplains Dress Uniform was impressive with the predominant colour being purple. I wished I could have afforded one.

Whilst Hurst was a traditional Methodist Church that pre-dated Methodist Union, Waterloo was a very modern building, only a few years old. It was on a side street, built on the site of the old church building with access to the old Schoolrooms behind. The Schoolrooms were accessed from the main road. On the corner was a public house. Unfortunately, the new church was built before chairs became the norm, so it had pews, albeit modern ones. They were not fixed, so allowed some movement, but they were very heavy! Before the building scheme was completed, they ran out of money so couldn't afford an organ, so they had to make do with a piano. I couldn't see the problem as they had no organists, only pianists. However, they were very good. They had an Organ Fund with just £500 in it, only sufficient for a cheap electronic organ. I persuaded them it was better to remain with a piano. If they wanted an organ, they would be better raising more money and buying a 'proper' one. Needless to say, once I left, they bought a cheap electronic organ!

We had a good relationship with the Parish Church along the main road into town. We met together for a Communion Service on regular occasions, in fact, if you included the monthly Sunday Communions, we had a Communion Service, in one form or another once a week, including a regular mid-week Communion at Waterloo. I produced duplicated Order of Service based on a variety of 'modern' Communion Services. On one occasion after using a form, very similar to the

Methodist 'Sunday Service' one couple commented how much they had appreciated it. They were somewhat taken aback when I explained that it was a, very slightly amended version of the new Catholic Mass! All I had done was to omit references to various saints and the Pope.

When it came to Palm Sunday, I arranged for the service to begin in the Schoolroom. As we sang 'All glory Lord and honour...' we processed outside and turned left, past the pub, then left again into the side street, then left again into the Church! Amazingly we were still in time and on note with the piano as we entered the Church. Before we left the Schoolroom, I had invited a lady, I can't now remember who it was, to talk to the children. Appropriately she told a story about donkeys, but the only thing I remember about it now was her obsession with the donkey's droppings!

Waterloo had quite a strong Youth Fellowship made up of several young folk in their late teens and early twenties. One of them, Barry Mackleston, began training as a Local Preacher. He was keen to learn and at times his enthusiasm was wearing. He was also very appreciative of my support to the extent that he bought me a priest's robe as a present. It must have been very expensive, but it has proved very useful, especially when it came to burials in inclement weather! When his grandfather died, he dragged me down to the house. I imagined that the body would by then have been removed but it turned out he hadn't even notified the doctor never mind called the undertakers, so I was taken into the kitchen to see the old man sitting on an upturned bucket having died halfway through having a shave!

When we left Ashton-under-Lyne, we discovered that Barry was an inveterate liar, so it was impossible to know what, if anything, he had told us was true.

By contrast to my previous appointment, I found myself averaging around two funerals a week. One firm, who used me quite often, had a driver who was a keen fan of folk music. When he found out that I was also a fan he persuaded me to buy an LP his group had produced. It proved to be rather good. It just so happened that he kept a stock in the hearse. On one occasion, when I had a burial in the morning and a cremation in the afternoon, he suggested I bring a packed lunch. After the morning burial we sat in the hearse in the cemetery grounds eating our sandwiches. When we finished, he asked me to give him a hand. Puzzled, I got out of the hearse and we went to the back. He opened the door and I had to give him a hand pull the coffin from underneath the platform and place it on top ready for the next funeral!

He was full of macabre tales. He recounted the story of a man who had been drinking in a pub in Mossley which was next to the local cemetery. The man had a hearty meal of pie and chips along with several pints of Guinness. At closing time, he collapsed and died. As it was so late it was decided to simply place the body in the neighbouring cemetery chapel overnight. The next morning the undertakers came to collect the body. When they opened the chapel door the body exploded. No-one had thought to pierce the man's stomach to prevent fermentation! They spent the rest of the day cleaning the chapel!

On one occasion I was phoned and asked if I would take the funeral of a local dignitary, one-time leader of the Council. His only association with the Church was that he had attended a Methodist Sunday School in his childhood. There was to be no Church Service. Would I take the Service in the Crematorium Chapel? I agreed. The undertakers then explained that it was taking place at Rochdale Crematorium and not, as was usually the case, at Dukinfield Crematorium. Also, could I go in my own car as there would be no room in the hearse? It would be a big funeral, so I was to be there for 10.20 am. When I arrived, the cars were queuing up out of the gates and I had to drive half on the road, half on the verge to get to the chapel. When I finally got the end of the long drive the undertakers were pacing up and down and checking their watches. It was only 10.25 am what was the panic? I had assumed that like Dukinfield Crematorium Rochdale was on a half hour turn around, on the hour and the half hour, so although I was a little late it wasn't a problem. What the undertakers had failed to tell me was that Rochdale Crematorium was on a twenty-minute turn around, on the hour, twenty past, and twenty to. When they had said 10.20 am that was when the service was supposed to start. I had assumed 10.20 for 10.30 start. It turned out that the cars queuing down the drive were there for the next funeral at 10.40 am! The poor guy got what was probably the shortest send off in history. Those particular undertakers didn't contact me very often thereafter!

On another occasion I had to make two funeral visits on the same day. The first was to a woman, in her forties, whose husband had died unexpectedly. She explained that she had had the body taken straight to the undertakers and the coffin closed. It would go from there straight to the Chapel for the Service. From there I went to visit man in his seventies whose wife had died. 'Come in', he said, taking me into the sitting room where the open coffin rested on the table, 'Doesn't she look lovely?' A clear indication of how attitudes to death were changing.

Kath had managed to find a teaching post in a local Primary School so during the day I was on my own. When I was out visiting, I had found a couple of local pubs that offered a reasonably priced lunch option. One, near Hurst, offered a selection of plate pies including mince and onion and cheese and onion. They were absolutely delicious. On the bar, to accompany them, there was an unlimited supply of pickled red cabbage. The pub in Stalybridge offered a selection of patés on toast each with a side salad. Again, the paté and toast was delicious.

Nel was a delight. As a pup she managed to chew chunks out of the morning room carpet. When we moved out, I had to put around twenty patches in it. She also chewed a cushion in the bedroom and the arm of the settee in the lounge. Fortunately, since the arm was separate and we had bought the settee from Fraylings, the firm Kath's dad worked for, he was able to replace it for us.

Although there was a lot going on, and much of it was very positive, I was becoming increasingly dissatisfied. Although I did not doubt my call to the ministry, I was seriously questioning whether Circuit ministry was what I was called to. I seemed to spend so much of my time either attending, or chairing, meetings. Little or no time was given over to actually sharing the gospel, let alone sharing it with those outside the church community. Additionally, I missed the kind of support I had received in Bury St Edmunds from my Circuit colleagues. I rarely saw Ken Bounds, the superintendent minister. He was an odd ball who only ever referred to his wife, even in public, as 'Mother Bounds'. My nearest colleague, at Mossley, Brian Skinner, was a Freemason who, whenever we did meet up, spent the time trying to persuade me to join, an offer which I declined. I decided to resign.

I wrote a carefully worded letter which I sent to the President of Conference with a copy to the superintendent minister. I suggested that I continue to the end of the Connexional year so that the circuit wasn't inconvenienced. The response was, I have to say, not what I expected. I received a letter from the superintendent telling me that I was to cease any commitments, especially Sunday services, immediately!

All my services, including the one coming up the next Sunday would be covered. That was it. From that moment on we were, effectively, ostracized. We were forbidden to have contact with anyone in the Circuit and folk in the Circuit were forbidden to have contact with us! Kath had begun training as a Local Preacher being placed 'On Note' with Alan Rose. She had just been placed 'On Trial' but no appointments were forthcoming!

When the President of Conference was on his District visit, he came to see us. That year the President was the Rev'd J Russell

Pope who happened to be a rabid teetotaller. Virtually the first thing he said was to comment on the fact that I was known to visit a couple of local hostelries. "And" he turned to Kath, "I understand you go with him." I was very proud of her when she immediately replied, "Yes, and since I'm teetotal I usually go behind the bar and make myself a cup of coffee." The look on his face was priceless. He admitted that he didn't know what to do with me since the reason for my resignation didn't fit with any category that Methodism acknowledged. I suggested that I was put on the 'President's List', which is what happened.

The minister of the Methodist Church in Gibraltar was about to be replaced. We still had troops stationed there and although it was not a chaplaincy post the minister had a lot of contact with the Garrison. The President, however, made it clear that since I was not a teetotaller, he would make sure that I was not offered the post!

I had to attend a committee in London that dealt with resignations. Like the President they didn't know what to do with me, so I was continued on the 'President's List' into a second year, something, I was told, that was unprecedented. Meanwhile we struggled on in virtual isolation. As well as her teaching Kath took on some casual bar work at the local pub we frequented in Waterloo. She also found me three-week's supply at the Primary School where she was teaching. It was really hard work! I'm not sure it was 'legal', but it helped out financially.

Meanwhile I was approached by Bob Davis, one of our Local Preachers who taught Maths at the Bluecoat School in Oldham.

Was I interested in teaching RE as they were desperate to fill a post at his school and they had had no interest whatsoever? I jumped at the chance. I applied for accreditation and was told that I could be recognised a teacher qualified to teach in Secondary education on the basis that I had graduated with a relevant degree before September 1971. I had graduated in the July of that year with a degree in theology. The only condition was that I would have to complete a two-year, rather than a one-year, probationary period.

We started looking for a house in Oldham and found a new-build three-bedroom semi in Glodwick. My parents loaned us the £500 we needed for the deposit. I say 'new-build' in fact we watched it being built from the foundations up! It wasn't too far from the Bluecoat School. In the meantime, we continued to live in the manse in Ashton-under-Lyne. Eventually the house was finished, and we were able to cut all our ties with the Ashton-under-Lyne Circuit. When we did finally move, we were presented with a ceramic black cat made by one of the folk who was a regular at Fred's local. They also had a whip-round and bought us a large vase. They both have graced the entrance halls of the various houses we have lived in since, right up to the present.

It had been a turbulent time. I was requested, again, to go to London to face the committee that dealt with resignations, again, with no resolution. Kath was pregnant and had resigned from her teaching post and we had taken on a mortgage. Looking back, I don't know how we managed, but we did.

It was around this time that Dad retired. Mam and Dad had always said they wanted to retire to the coast and that is precisely what they did. The sold up in Durham and moved to 98 Plessey Crescent in Whitley Bay. I wasn't sure that this was such a good move. They had lived in Durham for the best part of twenty years. They had spent time and money making the house just how they wanted it. They were well settled into the Church; Dad was preaching quite regularly. Moving just seemed step too far. As it turned out they were right, and I was wrong.

The house they moved to was a three bedroomed semi in need of some TLC. It also had a garden that backed onto the railway line. Bringing the house up to scratch and sorting out the garden took the best part of a couple of years and kept them both out of mischief! They'd never had a garden before and Dad made the best of it by growing, among other things, potatoes. The garden also boasted an apple tree, and a 'kind of greenhouse' at the bottom of the garden. Apples were stored in the legs of old tights with a knot between each fruit. They had perfectly acceptable fruit for months on end, even when the season was over.

Oldham

[1975-1978]

I don't recall now the size of the student body in The Bluecoat
School in 1975 when I began teaching there but it would have
been around 800. Dave Goudie was Head of the RE Department
and proved to be an excellent colleague. My post was full time.
Dave and I had rooms facing each other on the first floor of
the 'new' block behind the original 'old' building. As a Church
of England Secondary School, it was linked to Oldham Parish
Church. The vicar turned out to be the Rev'd James Bentley
who had been my mentor in Stretford when I was in my final
year at Hartley. The vicarage was a modern upside-down house
just down the road from the Bluecoat School. The whole school
attended the Parish Church on Founder's Day. We processed
from the school to the church. The staff were expected to be in
academic dress. That was no problem for me as I had my gown
and hood from when I graduated. Many did not, but there was
a box containing a variety of gowns and hoods from which they
helped themselves. It was amusing to see colleagues dressed in

hoods that bore no resemblance to the degrees they had been awarded; and they often changed from year to year!

Whilst we were living in Oldham James was tasked with refurbishing the Parish Church which occupied a prominent position in the town. Although founded in1280 the present building was completed in 1830 in the Gothic Revival style. The interior was fairly drab. In typical fashion James chose a firm of architects and a design team that had an international reputation for dramatic church redesigns including the cathedral in New Orleans. When the result was unveiled the drab interior had been transformed with the walls brightly painted in pastel colours in panels inspired by medieval designs. The response of those who entered the building was one of either loving or loathing the end result. I thought it was inspired.

Not long after I took up my post there was the usual end-of-term communion service. This was usually taken by the curate, another Neil, and James insisted that, regardless of my current status in Methodism, since I was an ordained minister, I should assist. We used the Conference Room, next to the school hall, as a vestry. Most of the pupils were confirmed so we had 500 plus communicants. When it came to the distribution of the elements Neil stood to one side of the altar and I stood at the other. Next to us stood a server. We gave the wafers and the servers, the chalice. The chalices were large. When we were nearing the end, we ran out of wine. Neil consecrated two new, full, chalices. It turned out that there were only three or four communicants left and Neil and I were left to reverently consume what remained. The wafers were not a problem but a whole, full, chalice of wine! I spent the rest of the day, so my pupils told me, in an amazingly good mood. I felt on cloud nine. Neil and I agreed that if such a thing happened in future, we would cover the elements and consume them in the Conference Room after the service was over.

The school was divided into houses, named after past members of the governing body. I was in Rowntree-Wrigley. Ian Douglas, who taught Science, was Head of House. He had two children in the school, both of whom I taught. Apparently, they had appeared in Coronation Street as the first 'incarnation' of Ken Barlow's children, Peter and Tracey. I also, apparently, missed out teaching the actress who played Deidre by just two years! Dave and I would often send a new pupil down to Ian to asked for a long stand. After keeping them waiting for five minutes he would send them back to us. Many of them still didn't get the point! One of the young women teachers in the Science Department, whose name I confess I cannot now recall, I came across many years later when I was taking a Baptism Service at St Luke's Methodist Church in Newcastle-under-Lyme and she was one of the godparents! During a strike by Firefighters in 1977 a fire broke out in the block where the RE Department was sited. Our two rooms were totally wiped out along with all our stock. Their refurbishment involved new floors as well as fixtures and fittings.

Despite having resolved never to make the same mistake twice I was caught out again, although I waited a couple of years before I put my foot in it this time. The Head of French was a really nice guy. One day, when there were just the two of us in the Staff Room, I plucked up the courage to ask what part of the North East he came from. Quelle surprise – it turned out he was born and bred in North Wales. Needless to say, it is a blunder I have never again repeated.

The RE syllabus across the school was, unsurprisingly, very traditional. Christianity and Biblical studies were at the heart of it. I taught first year (Yr. 7) to fifth year (Yr. 11). I didn't get a look in where the sixth form was concerned. I did manage to persuade Dave to replace the textbooks for the first three years with books that included some work on World Faiths.

At fourth and fifth form level, classes were single sex! I did have one group of girls in the fifth form preparing for a GCE 'O' level in Christian Responsibility. The issue we were considering was 'Race'. I consulted with the girls beforehand and had their agreement. "Should we send the twins home?" I asked (They were African heritage). "Yes" said the class. They were perplexed when I explained that the twins were born in Oldham, so they were home! "What about our Asian heritage student?" The class were a bit hesitant but in fact she had been born in India and immigrated with her parents when she was a toddler, perhaps she should be sent home. "So, What about Julia (Damjanovic)?" Julia was white and spoke with an obvious Oldham accent. The response was a resounding "No!" "But", I pointed out, "Julia, although she was born here, has a Polish father who came here during WW2." The point I was trying to make was well taken.

As far as Methodism was concerned, I continued on the Presidents List. Again, I tendered my resignation and was called to attend the relevant committee in London. Since by then I was teaching they asked why did I not simply apply to go into 'Sector Ministry'? I explained that given the current regulations I would be subject to recall to Circuit Ministry by Conference. That would entail giving notice in my present post and since the last date to give notice was before the Methodist Conference met that would be impossible. Plus, I was in the process of buying a house and there was no reason to believe that it would sell quickly so I would be going into a position which paid half the salary but with an outstanding mortgage still to pay. The committee insisted that they never actually implemented that regulation so it should not be a problem. That being the case, I asked why the regulation was retained. I continued on the President's List. Eventually, sometime later, for the third time, I again tendered my resignation, but this time refused to attend the London Committee. I was allowed to send someone to represent me and the Rev'd Michael Townsend agreed to go for me. This time my resignation was accepted but, when it came to the reason presented to Conference, they created a category especially for me! Whereas the bulk of resignations were reported as 'Loss of Call' my resignation was reported as 'Loss of Call to Circuit Ministry"!

Although initially I continued to appear on the Plan as a Local Preacher and took a number of Services in the Oldham Circuit, I began to explore the possibility of 'taking holy orders' in the Church of England. When I wasn't preaching, we attended St Mark's Parish Church in Glodwick. Robert (jnr) was born on 12th June 1976 in Boundary Park Hospital and he was baptised in St Mark's.

His birth was very long-winded! Kath was in labour over twenty-four hours. I was with her the whole time but all I could do was rub her back with talcum powder to help ease the pain. Eventually they decided to do an emergency caesarean section. I had to sign the consent forms and, as was usual in those days, I was not able to witness the birth. The last I saw of her, she was on a trolley disappearing at high speed on her way to the operating theatre. The next time I saw her she was back on the ward with a baby boy who had weighed in at 9 lbs 4 ozs. The choice of names was no contest because of the pocket watch! Kath spent 14 days in hospital before she was allowed home. One of the nurses who had helped to deliver Robert, Jeanette (for the life of me, to my shame, I cannot recall her surname) attended St Mark's Glodwick so was an obvious choice when it came to choosing godparents. I think the other two were Jeff and Sandra. Sandra had been one of Kath's colleagues at the school she had worked in in Ashton-under-Lyne. Geoff was a journalist. They had become good friends and we still keep in touch at Christmas.

With a view to pursuing the possibility of ordination in the Church of England Kath and I were confirmed at St Lawrence's Church, Stockport Road in Denton. I subsequently met with the Bishop of Manchester at his home and discussed what seeking ordination in the Church of England might entail. I was more than somewhat taken aback by his insistence that I would have to begin from 'square one', first training and qualifying as a Lay Reader, before beginning the process of offering as a candidate for the priesthood. Any qualification or experience gained in Methodism was totally ignored. I politely took my leave and decided that that was a path I no longer wished to pursue!

The mini estate where we were living was in Glodwick and it continued to be built while we were living there. Our house was on the left going up the hill. The gardens behind the houses were not really finished off and sloped not only from front to back but also sloped from side to side! Our immediate neighbours were lovely. Cliff and Iris, adjoining us and Richard and Hilary who shared our drive. I say 'shared' but our drive was a couple of feet higher than theirs. I applied for, and got, planning permission to build a garage and an extra room at the end of our drive and behind our house. I began putting in foundations and building the walls. It gave me the opportunity to reshape the back garden so that it only sloped from front to back.

We bought tons of recycled sewerage – you can't do it today – and barrowed it into the back garden. It didn't smell at all, but it was very fertile. The vegetables we planted were amazing when it came to harvesting them the next year! I coated the fences at the back and sides with sump oil, a trick I had heard of which, like the sewerage was a real money saver. Cliff, when he saw what we'd done with the fences decided it was a good idea. He was a bus driver and brought gallons of the stuff home from the depot. Whereas my fences were a golden brown his turned out black. He had failed to take account of the fact that the oil he was using was from diesel buses! Sadly, before we left Oldham Richard was diagnosed with MS.

Next door to Richard and Hilary was another young couple. I confess I now I no longer remember their names. He impressed the street when he turned up one day driving an Alfa Romeo. It wasn't new, but he had bought it at a bargain price. Not long after the car disappeared. It turned out that it was a 'cut and shunt' – two cars, written off, the front of one welded to the back of another! No wonder it had been a bargain price.

There was a lovely small, homely pub nearby. Turn right at the bottom of our street and go down the hill and you'd find The Dog and Partridge. I used to go in once a week and got know some of the regulars including Alan Baker who was an Anglican Lay Reader. I often got drawn into a game of darts, but I was never any good. Since we now had a young baby and couldn't go out when we wanted, I took to brewing my own beer. We also made some homemade Ginger Beer. We were startled one evening by a very loud explosion. It tuned out that one of the bottles of Ginger Beer in the cupboard under the stairs had exploded. It took a lot of hard work to clean out the cupboard, which also served as a pantry. We caused quite a stir on the street not long after when we had a chip pan fire. There was lots of smoke and the Fire Brigade were called but by the time they arrived I had taken the chip pan outside onto the drive. The most damage was done by one of the firefighters who rush into the smoke-filled kitchen and discharged a full fire extinguisher in the direction of the cooker. Everywhere was covered with a thin white film. Cleaning up took forever.

Kath returned to teaching at Freehold Infant School and that necessitated arranging a child minder for Robert. Kath's TA (Teaching Assistant) was Doreen Carter. It turned out that I was teaching her youngest daughter, Jane, who was in the Third

Form at the Bluecoat School. Kath and Doreen became good friends and we remained friends with the Carters for many years. Sadly, Doreen died of breast cancer several years after we left Oldham and Jane also died of breast cancer, not many years after she had married, leaving a husband and youngster behind. The Carters were members of St Margaret's Parish Church (If I recall correctly). It was very high church, and counted in its congregation, when she was available, the actress Sarah Lancashire.

We decided to take Robert to a photographer to have a professional photograph taken to mark his first Christmas, suitable to send to immediate family. It took an hour. Robert refused to pose. The Jack-in-the-box, which was supposed to make him smile, made him cry! Eventually, when he had calmed down the photographer sat him in a picture bay window with a toy and managed to take a lovely photograph of him. It was the first, and last, time we went to a professional photographer.

1976 saw my dad feeling off colour. Dad being unwell was almost unprecedented. Not many years before he retired, he had had two weeks off work with flu and I had done his insurance round for him. Apart from those two weeks he had hardly ever been ill during the whole of his working life. During the year he visited the doctors, several times, and they could find nothing wrong. Once 1977 arrived Dad perked up. It was only several years later that the penny dropped. His dad had died, aged 67. His eldest brother had died, aged 67. His older sister had died, aged 67. In 1976 Dad was aged 67! Intriguingly his next two younger brothers also died aged 67. Dad lived to be 89 and his youngest brother lived to a similar age.

I successfully completed my 'probationary' period as a teacher. This entailed the Head sitting in on one of my lessons! He perched himself on the waist-high cupboards that lined the back of the room. Not long into the lesson I asked the class to get themselves a Bible. They were stacked next to where the Head was perched. As the class made for the cupboards, he excused himself and left! He was an odd character, and not all that well liked. The school frontage comprised a wide entrance hall opening onto a long corridor with the Head's Office to the left and the Conference Room to the right and beyond it the School Hall. On one occasion I witnessed Ruth, the Head's Secretary, during lessons, walking backwards and forwards along the corridor with a long length of string trailing behind her. Attached to it was a piece of paper with the words "This is my tether, and I am at the end of it!"

At the annual Methodist Conference, the year after I had finally resigned, it was agreed to alter the wording regarding Sector Ministers so that it read that Conference *reserved the right to request* a Sector Minister to return to Circuit Ministry but that the minister had the right to decline. I immediately began the process of applying for re-instatement. This entailed attending a Committee Meeting in London. It was chaired by the Rev'd Lincoln Minshull. He seemed puzzled as to why I hadn't simply asked to be placed in a Methodist School, something that, apparently, could easily have been arranged. He didn't seem to grasp that I wanted to obtain a teaching post on merit and not because I knew the right people! I was successful in my application and was duly re-instated at the next annual Conference.

At the same time that I was applying for re-instatement into the Methodist Ministry I was also applying for a promotion. The most interesting one, that I didn't get (in fact no-one got it as they scrapped the post before making an appointment) was a Secondary School in the midlands who wanted to appoint a Curriculum Co-ordinator who was a specialist in Religious Education. I was, however, successful in my application for the post of Head of Religious and Social Studies at King Edward VII College in Coalville in Leicestershire. There were around a dozen applicants, and half a dozen were shortlisted. I was to start after Easter in 1978. The Head at the Bluecoat School was taken aback when I tendered my resignation as he hadn't been approached for a reference. When I queried this sometime later with the Head at King Edward, he explained that he never requested references because they were always good, either because the candidate was good, or the school wanted rid of them! He found it much better to go by the application letter and the interview.

When I left the Bluecoat School, I was presented with a copy of J R R Tolkien's 'Silmarillion' from the staff. Dave Goudie gave me a red ballpoint pen with the injunction not to make too much use of it!

It really was an incredibly traumatic year. Not only was I successful in my application for re-instatement into the Methodist Ministry, and in my application for a Head of

Department post, but Kath was pregnant. I was expected to start at King Edward VII College at the beginning of the summer term. Kath was due to give birth in the June. We put our house on the market and began looking for a house in Coalville. It all seemed to be coming together nicely when the people from whom we were purchasing found that they were unable to complete on their purchase so wouldn't be able to vacate their house in time for us to move at the Easter.

It proved impossible to find somewhere for me to stay temporarily. However, in the end the people from whom we were purchasing kindly agreed to let me have a room in their house! So, I ended up leaving Kath and Robert behind while I began my new job, living in the house we would eventually be buying. It turned out that it was only for a few weeks. I was back in Oldham for the move, just three weeks before Kath was due. We were watching out for the removal van. Kath was in the bathroom, which was on the front of the house. She decided to look out of the top window light to see if the van had arrived. To do so she stood on the toilet seat – and promptly went through it! Apart from a long scratch on her leg Kath was unhurt although explaining to our purchasers why the toilet lid was broken was a bit embarrassing!

Some time before Kath gave birth, we were visiting Kath's parents and over Sunday lunch the question of the name of the expected baby was raised. We favoured 'Elizabeth' but were reluctant to suggests it. Robert's name was never up for debate but the suggestion for a girl's name was sensitive. My mother's name was Elizabeth although she was always known as 'Betty'.

Kath's mother's name was 'Hilda', which meant 'battle maiden' was a non-starter, not least because it was no longer fashionable. We decide we wanted a Biblical name, possibly Naomi or, or Lois. Imagine our surprise, and relief, when Kath's mother piped up, "Why not call her 'Elizabeth'". So, the matter was settled.

Because Kath was so close to her due date the hospital was not prepared to transfer her to Leicestershire. Also because of the problems she had had with Robert's birth they had decided that Elizabeth would be delivered by caesarean section. When I explained the situation to Bill Hayward, my new Head he was incredibly understanding. I had only been in the school a few weeks and felt bad about asking for time off to take Kath back to Oldham and look after Robert. We stayed with friends nearby for a couple of weeks until Kath was discharged before returning to Coalville. I was quite prepared to take time off without pay, but he insisted that it would be regarded as paid leave.

So we returned to Oldham. Kath was checked into Boundary Park. Robert and I went to stay with Jeff and Sandra in Saddleworth. I went into the hospital to be with Kath before she was taken down to theatre. Jeanette was there and before Kath went down Jeanette wrote on Kath's tummy 'Girl – 7 lbs' and then Kath was gone. About half an hour later Jeanette returned and placed Elizabeth in my arms. She was still covered with Vernix caseosa. Jeanette then took her away to clean her up. Elizabeth was born on 20th June 1978 and weighed in at 7lb 3oz. Kath and Elizabeth stayed in hospital for 10 days as the baby was slightly jaundiced.

I was impressed by the level of security at the hospital. However, it turned out that it wasn't for Kath. The second floor of the hospital was the domain of gynaecologist Dr Patrick Steptoe and he, with scientist Robert Edwards, had begun their pioneering collaboration a decade earlier into IVF (In vitro fertilisation). What we didn't know then was that Lesley Brown was one of his patients and on July 25, 1978, Louise Joy Brown, the world's first baby to be conceived by IVF was born. Naturally once the media learned of the pregnancy, the Browns and the hospital faced intense public scrutiny. Louise's birth made headlines around the world and raised various legal and ethical questions. The high level of security was deemed necessary to keep the media at bay in the weeks leading up to the birth of Louise Brown.

Coalville

[1978 – 1984]

So, finally, we settled down to our new life in 21 Dunbar Road, Coalville, Kath, Robert, Elizabeth and me. When the folk from whom we were buying the house moved out I contacted British Telecom to have the phone line transferred to our name. They insisted that it would have to be physically disconnected at the junction box at the end of the street and then reconnected after the weekend. No amount of protest on my part would get them to simply transfer the line!

Having been re-instated as a Methodist minister I found myself immediately involved in the Coalville Circuit. The superintendent minister had taken seriously ill after the September – November plan had been made so I was asked to cover his appointments. Eventually he retired on health grounds and was not replaced. The Revd Chris Edwards, the second minister, took over as superintendent and I found myself preaching every Sunday so the Circuit, at least from a preaching point of view, didn't notice the difference. The Circuit comprised of a town centre church, Marlborough Square, and a number of smaller suburban and village churches in roughly a ring around the centre, none more than a couple of miles out from the centre. Two churches were quite new, Hall Lane, our nearest, where Kath and the children made their home, and Whitwick, a mile along the road. More about the Circuit later.

One of the nice things about having been re-instated as a Methodist minister was that I was in a position to baptize Elizabeth. Robert had been baptized at St Mark's in Glodwick by the vicar as at the time I was not a minister and we were in the process of becoming Anglicans. Elizabeth's baptism took place at Hall Lane Methodist Church. We invited Michael Townsend to be a godparent as I recalled a late-night conversation at Hartley when Michael had a great deal to say about the role of godparents, so he seemed an obvious choice. In fact, it turned out to be a poor choice since he never once acknowledged Elizabeth at either Christmas or birthdays! He wasn't able to be at the Baptism so someone else acted as proxy. Jeanette and Jane Carter were the other two godparents. Jane was a good choice. I had taught her when I was at the Bluecoat School and Kath was good friends with mum, Doreen. Many years later Jane would have Liz as one of her little bridesmaids when she was married. Sadly not many years later, after Jane and Rob had a young family, Jane died of breast cancer. While we were in Coalville Jeanette also died. She had moved from Oldham to London to take up a senior teaching post in one of the hospitals there. It was quite a promotion. Not long after she took up her post, she had to have a minor operation and tragically died on the operating table.

The Rev'd Peter Kindleysides, who had been in College with me and, with the Rev'd Henry Rack had officiated at our wedding, was superintendent minister of the Wirksworth Circuit which wasn't too far away. He invited me to take the occasional appointment in his Circuit. I was happy to accept and usually gave him a Sunday each quarter. Elsie, Peter's wife usually laid on Sunday lunch in the manse. One Sunday after lunch Kath managed to get herself locked in the loo. We tried everything to release her, all to no avail, ending up by breaking the door in! It never did get repaired.

I was preaching at Wirksworth one Sunday morning. It was a typical Methodist Church with a central pulpit. The pulpit, however, was unusually high with a long staircase to facilitate access. Kath and the children were sitting near the back-left hand corner of the church. Liz would have been about two years old. During the opening prayers she escaped from her mother's arms, walked down the left-hand aisle, across the front of the church and up the staircase into the pulpit. I had no option but to pick her up. She stayed in my arms through the rest of the prayer, the next hymn, the readings, then during the next hymn she wriggled free and made her way back to her mum. She had made no noise at any time during her escapade!

One of the churches in Peter's Circuit, an ex-Primitive Methodist building, was, literally, situated in a farmyard. It was small, with an equally small congregation. They did not have an organist and, Peter warned me before I preached there for the first time, that they still used the Primitive Methodist Hymn Book. Fortunately, I had, and still have, my parents' copies, and they are music editions. It also meant that I had to switch between the pulpit and the organ as I employed my limited abilities to accompany the hymns! Towards the end of my time in Coalville the Methodist Church published 'Hymns and Psalms' to replace the 'Methodist Hymnbook' which dated back to the 1930s. Peter phoned me one Saturday to inform me that the 'farmyard' church, at which I was planned the following day, had obtained new hymnbooks! I was delighted, until he went on to explain that Wirksworth had bought copies of Hymns and Psalms and had passed on their copies of MHB (Methodist Hymn Book) to the 'farmyard' church! Still it was progress, of a sort.

Bill Hayward, the Principal of King Edward VII College, was a real Christian gentleman. He was a member of the United Reformed Church in Loughborough. When I arrived in Coalville they were in an inter-regnum and Bill asked if I would be prepared to take an occasional Communion service for them. I was happy to do so. I recall a conversation in the vestry before one of the services when I asked how they were managing without a minister. The elder who was on duty explained that the experience was a positive one since the members had to take responsibility for routine pastoral work and routine meetings which meant that when a minister came, they were free to pursue their calling. Methodism's insistence that every church had a minster from 1st September meant that incoming ministers were often faced with a full diary before they arrived in their new appointment! When Lent came around at the end of my first year in Coalville Bill suggested that we could run a Lent course in the school as part of their adult evening courses provision. It seemed like a good idea, so it was put into the programme and publicised accordingly. When the first session came around only Bill and I turned up!

There was no 'A' level RE provision in the school when I arrived in the summer term of 1978, but Bill was prepared to timetable 'A' level RE when it came to producing the timetable for the September of that year. Initially the take up was small. Only two in that first year, both girls, and both from Methodist families in the town. It meant quite a bit of preparation on my part. I decided to offer 'Hinduism' and 'Judaism'. Hinduism was not too much of a problem since it had been one of the two subjects I studied in the final year of my degree course and I had kept all of my notes and textbooks. Judaism was a bit more of a stretch since, although my knowledge of Judaism in the biblical period was fairly extensive, post-biblical Jewish history and practice was a whole new ball game! Nevertheless, after two years the girls did well and the number opting for 'A' level RE grew.

The staff were great. There were a number who were Christians, including Clive Caulfield the Head of Rural Science who was a Methodist Local Preacher in a neighbouring Circuit. Margaret Hoskins, who taught Social Studies was an active Anglican, her husband was a lay reader. Intriguingly, most of the Christians were in the Science Departments – and most of those were conservative evangelicals! Interestingly there were three 'Fishers' on the staff. All the staff were designated by two letters of their surname. I was 'Fi', David Fisher, who Head of Music was 'Fs' and … I forget the third Fisher (sorry!). When it came to Ministerial Synod, which was always on a weekday, Bill was very happy to let me attend, on full pay, and my colleagues were quite happy to cover my classes, should that be needed. According to my contract I was allowed to attend any Sunday School activity held during the school day; the clause was interpreted broadly.

A year or so after I started teaching at King Edward VII College, I joined the model railway club in the school. Dave Dickinson, who was Head of Geography, was in charge. I was keen to make a layout of Newcastle Central Station and Gateshead Goods Yard. It would make an ideal layout with Newcastle to north of the Tyne and Gateshead to the south. Dave explained that Ordinance Survey produced maps with squares measuring 10 x 10 each of which was divided into squares of 10 x 10 which meant that I could buy a map comprising two squares that covered the station and the goods yard. He kindly ordered it for me. I still have it. However I still haven't built the layout, but more of that later.

One of the members at Hall Lane, Alan Clarke, worked for Palitoy in nearby Ashby-de-la-Zouche. Palitoy produced all sorts of model railway items under the trade name 'Mainline'. When Alan discovered that I was interested in model railways he would often turn up at the house on a Friday after work with a loco or some item of rolling stock which I could have for an amazingly low price. Basically, they were rejects, bound for scrap. More often than not I couldn't find any fault without extremely careful examination. They were used on the small layout I had built for Robert and Elizabeth. When Palitoy eventually ceased to exist in 1984 Alan set up his own model railways business which traded quite successfully from a small shop in Coalville.

I became good friends with another member of Hall Lane, Alan Buck. He and I got into the habit of going to the Fox and Goose, a lovely little pub on the outskirts of Coalville. We usually went once a week for a couple of pints. He was a member of Moira Male Voice Choir and was also a member of the Adelphic which was a kind of 'poor man's' version of Rotary. It was a national movement for Christian men. They met once a month at the Methodist Church in Swadlincote, the other side of Ashby-de-la-Zouche. At his invitation I joined the Adelphic. The meeting comprised of a substantial meal, usually made by the wives of the members, followed by an after-dinner speaker. I must admit I enjoyed the experience.

Alan had always wanted to run a shop and when the opportunity presented itself, he bought a small 'corner shop' in Shepshed. He managed it for a couple of years, but it didn't prove financially viable and he eventually sold it. He couldn't understand why the Asian family who took it over managed to make it pay. Alan had opened 9.00 am to 5.00 pm six days a week and took a salary out of the business. The family who took over opened 7.00 to 10.00 pm seven days a week and simply took what they needed to live out of the shop! Under their management the business thrived!

Our house was a fairly new semi on a fairly new estate on the outskirts of the town, not far from Hall Lane Methodist Church in one direction and King Edward VII college in the other. It was in the corner of an L-shaped cul-de-sac. Our shared next-door neighbours, Peter and Helen Ufton, both worked for the ambulance service. Our other next-door neighbours were Tony and Maureen Kerry, Tony was a miner. The name of the town should be a give-away. Mining was a major industry. Tony and Maureen had two children, Stephen and Debbie. In fact, there were a number of children in the street, which was great for our two growing up there.

We made quite a few alterations to the house during the time we lived there. The passage went from the front door to the kitchen and we blocked it off to create a hall cupboard on the one side and a kitchen pantry on the other. We also blocked off the dining area to make a proper dining room. The garden was huge and needed a lot of work, first to get into shape and then to maintain it. We never did manage to finish it as we wanted. On one occasion when I was laying slabs in the back garden my back went without warning. I asked Kath to run me a hot bath thinking it would help. I manged to get upstairs, with difficulty, and then realised I couldn't even take my clothes off never mind get into the bath, so I had to shout for Kath to come and turn off the tap before the bath got too full. Rest proved recuperative.

One shocking event that happened in our neighbourhood was a murder/suicide in a house just around the corner. The parents were splitting up and the father suffocated the four young children before taking his own life rather than let the mother have custody. Although it was just a few houses away we didn't know the family.

Not long after we arrived in Coalville Kath managed to get a teaching post at Warren Hills Primary School which, along with King Edward VII College and our feeder Middle School, was one of the three schools on the one campus. It wasn't for from where we lived. It turned out that the Head was a Methodist Local Preacher in a neighbouring Circuit. We were then faced with the task of finding a childminder at relatively short notice. Kath Hall, who lived near Hall Lane Methodist Church, was recommended. She was happy to take Robert, as her youngest son was of a similar age. She reluctantly agreed to take Elizabeth for just a few days until we found someone else. When we went to collect the children at the end of the first day they were with her Kath told us not to bother looking elsewhere for a childminder for Elizabeth as she would take her as well! She was marvellous and we have remained friends with her to this day.

James Bentley, who I first came across when he was my mentor during my final year's Circuit Practice with the Team Ministry in Stretford, and who more recently I had encountered when I was teaching at the Bluecoat School and he was Vicar of Oldham, was appointed as Chaplain at Eton College. He invited me to preach there. So, one weekend in May I drove down to Windsor. I stayed overnight with James and Audrey. I confess I was disappointed not to be preaching in the College Chapel but in one of the assembly Halls. Nevertheless, I did consider it a privilege to have been invited. After the service, while Audrey prepared lunch, James and I went into Windsor to a riverside pub where we sat outside in glorious sunshine, in shirtsleeves, having a pint and listening to a Jazz band who were performing inside.

Just before we sat down for lunch Kath phoned to say not to hang around too long as it was snowing in Coalville and the electricity was off! I was planned to preach at Thringstone that night, a small village about two miles from our house, so I set off straight after lunch and headed home. It was a fairly straight run up the M1 and the weather was fine until I crossed the border into Leicestershire and suddenly it was snowing. As I took the Coalville turn the snow was lying and there were just two tracks left by vehicles that had already travelled along the road. By the time I got into Coalville the snow was quite deep and when I pulled onto the top of the drive it was clear that there was no way I would get off again that evening. Kath greeted me with the message that the service at Thringstone had been cancelled, oh – and the electricity was back on again.

During the time we were living in Coalville I was asked to set up and chair the Circuit Ministries Committee. The first meeting was held at Hall Lane and Chris Edwards turned up; the manse was just next door! Afterwards I tackled him about his presence. I gently pointed out that the whole point of my taking on this role was to give him time to spend with his family – if he wanted to be present then he could take over the Chair and I'd spend time with my family instead! After that he left me to it.

The Committee set about the task of exploring the future of the Circuit. Since all the churches were only a couple of miles or so from the town centre, we came up with three proposals. We could close the town centre church and concentrate our work in the surrounding villages. We could close some of the village churches and concentrate our work in the town centre. We could encourage those churches with good ecumenical links to look to merging with their ecumenical partners and maintain the remaining village churches and the town centre church. We concluded that to do nothing would lead to the closure of several churches, the dropping of a minister and the merging of the Coalville Circuit with the Ashby Circuit within just a few years. We called a Circuit Consultation and invited the two Circuit ministers, who were both due to leave in the September to speak honestly about how they saw the future. We also invited the incoming superintendent to the meeting, however, he declined. When he arrived in the September, at the first Circuit Meeting, he ruled that we maintain the status quo. The consequence was exactly as predicted!

Synod was held in Coalville during the six years we were there. Howard Belben, who had been the principal when I was at Cliff College, had been invited to address the ordinands at the Ordinands Testimony Service in the afternoon session. Synod was held in Marlborough Square, but the lunch was held in the nearby Cinema. As I was eating my lunch Howard came across and spoke to me. I was amazed that he recognised me and knew who I was after fifteen years, but he did! He proceeded then to tell me everything I had been doing in the interim. I should not have been surprised as that was the nature of the man. He kept track of every one of his students when they left Cliff. At the Testimony Service he began his sermon by saying that he had never expected to find 'ambition' associated with being a Christian but in the New English Bible the word appeared six times in the New Testament. He then proceeded to preach a brilliant six-point sermon on 'ambition'; it was typical Howard!

Talking of Marlborough Square, I was preaching there one Sunday when Richard and Margaret Machin were visiting. Richard had been at Cliff when I was there and we were quite good friends, in fact I was his best man when he was married. He lived in Wigan and when we had visited, he showed me his study, the walls and ceiling of which he had painted black! He also gave me a complete eight volume set of Wesley's Journal, which I still have. He joined the police force and we went to his passing out parade. Sometime later he and Margaret split up and he lost his job with the police as he 'came out' as gay. Sadly, we lost touch after that.

Anyway, I digress. I preached on Acts 2:42 "The believers devoted themselves to the apostles' teaching and fellowship, to the breaking of bread and the prayers." – a good four-point sermon! In relation to 'fellowship' I spent some time talking about 'welcome'. After the service, when I was shaking hands with folk, Richard was standing nearby, and I offered him the car keys so he could wait in the car. He declined. As we drove home, I asked him why he didn't want to wait in the car. "I was waiting to see if anyone had listened to what you said in the sermon – not one person spoke to me!" As it happened, I was planned at Marlborough Square the following Sunday, so

I mentioned what had happened the previous week. Everyone looked at one another as if it was the other person's fault!

I was very involved both in the circuit and the community. So much so that at one point I had to cut down on my preaching appointments as I was preaching more often than my circuit colleagues. One community activity I was very involved in was the setting up of the Citizens Advice Bureau in the town. It took a great deal of work, including recruiting volunteers. We were very fortunate to be given space in the Library for the CAB Centre. Being so involved, especially in the circuit, led me to approach the Chair of the Nottingham and Derby District to enquire about the possibility of taking part in an Exchange of Pastorates, even though I was in Sector Ministry. His response was "I don't think it's been done before, but I don't see why not." He referred me to the Connexional Office that dealt with such matters; their response was the same. So, in the Spring of 1981 I applied.

[1981]

The scheme was organised by the World Methodist Council and involved an exchange of ministers, usually between the UK and the USA, though occasionally other countries like Australia, usually for about six weeks during the summer months. It was usual for the exchange families to tack a fortnight's holiday on to the exchange, either at the beginning or at the end. The ministers exchanged homes and cars and took on preaching and pastoral responsibilities, admittedly with a reduced load, made possible because during the summer months a lot of church activities wound down. We were very fortunate in Leicestershire since we had an eight-week summer holiday, the usual six weeks plus 'Leicester fortnight'. We eagerly awaited details of our exchange partner.

We were paired up with the Rev'd Glenn Young in Gaithersburg, Maryland. He was the minister at Fairhaven United Methodist Church. He was married to Siri and they had one daughter, Jenny. There began a period of exchange of correspondence and audio cassettes to enable us to get an idea of what we were going to. His church was a relatively new build; the result of their Conference ordering three small

Churches to amalgamate. Two congregations were black, and one was white. The result was a united church which was about sixty per cent white and forty per cent black. It proved to be almost unique, since most other churches in the area were either black or white, simply because of their historical establishment. Before we went, I was asked to provide and article for the weekly Methodist Newspaper by way of introducing myself. It was a regional publication with space for local church news. I described myself as a 'high church evangelical radical'! Whilst I was there, I had to contribute a pastoral letter each week for Methodist Newspaper.

Not long before the beginning of the exchange, Glenn told us that they had stocked their freezer ready for our arrival. We panicked! We knew that American freezers were enormous, so we hurriedly stocked up our modest freezer, even though we knew we had arranged for them to eat out with our church friends several days each week. We also agreed that it was in order for immediate family to accompany us on our exchange. My parents, and auntie Ruth, would fly out a couple of days after us, returning a couple of days before us. The Young's parents were going to come over for just a couple of weeks part way through the exchange.

Kath and I, with the co-operation of many folk in the circuit in general and Hall Lane in particular prepared a comprehensive programme for the Youngs. Preaching appointments were arranged for Glenn as were a number of weekday meetings. The idea of the exchange was that the minister would have a limited 'church' commitment, no more than two or three days each week, plus some pastoral visiting. The latter was not difficult to arrange as both circuit ministers were on holiday at some point during the period of the Young's visit so they drew up a modest list of folk for Glenn to visit. The rest of the time was free for them to explore the local community and culture. We arranged a number of meals with folk in the local churches, an opportunity to meet folk in their own homes, and experience English food, and the Revd Peter Kindleysides kindly offered to take them around Chatsworth House, which was not too far from Wirksworth. The PE staff at the school were very supportive and arranged passes for the Young family that entitled them to free access to the sports activities that were open during the eight weeks of their visit.

The Youngs arrived a week before term ended. It proved to be a very hectic week as we were trying to pack in readiness to leave as soon as school closed. I had a white Austin Maxi at the time and, no matter how hard I tried, I couldn't get Glenn to drive it before we left. They hardly ventured out of the house, opting instead to watch Wimbledon each day on TV! The first day they were here Jenny deposited a piece of chewing gum on the end of the welsh dresser in the dining room. It was still there when we returned eight weeks later!

Gaithersburg

If the next section of this memoire reads more like a journal than merely my recollections that is because when we were in Gaithersburg, I kept an audio diary which I have used extensively in recalling what we experienced during this Exchange of Pastorates.

The day came, Saturday 4th July. I drove down to Heathrow. Glenn came with us in order to bring the car back to Coalville. We flew by Pan Am from Heathrow to Washington DC. Robert was five and Elizabeth was three. As we settled into our seats Elizabeth managed to spill a whole glass of orange juice over herself. The stewardess helped mop it up and Elizabeth had to sit on a blanket for the rest of the trip. When we disembarked in Washington the first thing we noticed was the heat. Coming out of an air-conditioned plane it was like walking into an oven! We were met by Bill and Sharon Ingleton and we loaded all our luggage into their station wagon. We were driven to the parsonage in Gaithersburg, about an hour from Dulles International Airport. Some of the women from Fairhaven were waiting for us with a meal they had prepared. We met Pearl Campbell who was the Lay Leader (Senior Society Steward) – I should add that Pearl was black, and Bill Phillips, who was white, who was Chair of the Worship Committee.

Bill, we learned much later had a PhD in physics. In 1997 he won the Nobel Prize in Physics together with Claude Cohen-Tannoudji and Steven Chu for his contributions to laser cooling, a technique to slow the movement of gaseous atoms in order to better study them. He worked at the National Institute of Standards and Technology (NIST), and was also a professor of physics, at the University of Maryland College of Computer, Mathematical, and Natural Sciences. He was married to Jane and they had two girls, Katy, later choosing to be known as Caitlin, and Christine, usually called Chrissie. Christine had just been born when we went on our exchange and, had they had the time to arrange it, they had hoped that I would have been able to baptise her. We have kept in touch over the intervening years.

After our meal I suggested to Bill that it would be a good idea to have a look at Fairhaven UMC as I was taking the service the following day, and it was a Communion Service. Fairhaven was about five miles from the parsonage, so I suggested I drive in one of Glenn's cars. I can still see the look on Bill's face when I observed that wasn't used to driving on the wrong side of the road, nor was I used to driving at two o'clock in the morning! (I hadn't at that point changed my watch). When I got back to the parsonage Kath and I explored. Apart from the dining room and living room it was filthy. There were chicken bones lying on the windowsill in the kitchen, and balls of fluff and a pair of dirty nickers under the bed in the main bedroom and the massive freezer in the basement was empty apart from a couple of part-used loaves of bread and a couple of part-used tubs of ice-cream!

On the Sunday the service went well, and we were made very welcome. After the service they always had refreshments, which always included home-made cake. On this, our first Sunday at Fairhaven someone had made a birthday cake as it was my birthday on the Monday. They sang 'Happy Birthday' both in the service and in the Fellowship Room afterwards. Not only was their welcome amazing so too was the Offertory, c.£360! We were told to go back to the parsonage and get some sleep as, they assumed, we would no doubt be suffering from jetlag! Pearl said she would call around on Monday to make sure we knew how to operate the appliances. When we got back to the parsonage, we didn't know what to do about a meal as we had no food in the house, so we went to the nearby McDonald's. In 1981 McDonald's was virtually unknown outside London so it was a new experience for us. After lunch we decided to drive into Washington to see the White House, it was only about 25 miles, 40 minutes, and we had nothing else to do. When we finally decided to stop and ask directions from a Policeman, we found we were only one block away. Not bad!

On the Monday morning (6th July) just as Pearl arrived so too did Glenn's dad who had come around to show us around the neighbourhood, so our meeting with Pearl was delayed. When we got back Virginia Blair, who lived nearby arrived to make sure we knew how to use the appliances! She was shocked when she found out what we'd done on the Sunday afternoon. "We don't ever drive into Washington!" she told us.

When we did finally meet up with Pearl she apologised for the state of the parsonage, but despite all their efforts the women from the church hadn't managed to get the key from Glenn until the day they left and the first chance they'd had to get into the parsonage was the day we arrived. They spent most of their time cleaning the two main rooms but had then run out of time. One of the conditions of an exchange was that the US church had to make a payment to the UK of several hundred pounds to cover the difference in the cost of living. I tentatively approached the matter with Pearl, and it transpired that Glenn had told them that the money was for the US minister to take with him 'on holiday'! It quickly became clear that Glenn had told his church very little about the purpose of the exchange. I shouldn't have been surprised since I'd had to badger him to give me a list of folk who might need visits and he'd only just scribbled a short list on a scrap of paper as we were leaving Coalville on the Saturday morning.

In the first week I began my visiting with a visit to an eighty-four-year-old lady, who was in Suburban Hospital near DC. She had had a leg amputated and was awaiting the amputation of the other. Her attitude was so positive. As I began to visit those on the list Glenn had given me, I began to be suspicious. The welcome I received at each home was amazing, "It's so good to see the pastor."! Later in the Exchange I talked to Pearl about it since it became clear that everyone on the list was black. I explained that I was not going to continue working down the list since to do so would probably make things difficult for Glenn on his return. Pearl was in agreement with my decision. It transpired that Glenn was racist – hardly the right choice of pastor for such a church!

At the beginning of that first week we had to work out how we were going to meet my parents and aunt from the plane when they arrived on the Wednesday. They flew from Newcastle to Toronto and then from Toronto to Washington. We managed to meet them without too much drama although we had a bit of a problem finding parking at Silver Springs Metro Station. I could only find a two-hour parking spot but a guy in a nine-hour parking spot offered me his and opted to find street parking near his office! So, all was well, and we got to Arrivals just as they came through from reclaiming their baggage. We brought them back to the parsonage for them to get settled in. My parents took over the second bedroom. Ruth was relegated to the basement! Robert slept on the floor in Jenny's room where Liz slept in Jenny's bed. The next few days were spent exploring the Shopping Mall, where most shops were open until 9.30 pm, some until 11.00 pm, and the Giant food store was open 24 hours!

On Friday (10th July) we had a trip into Washington to visit the Cathedral. It was a fascinating building, recently started, and still unfinished, built in 14th century gothic style. What was remarkable was that when you went in It was warm, unlike many churches and cathedrals in the UK where, no matter what the temperature was outside it always felt cool when you stepped

ROBERT FISHER

through the church door. The outside temperature, most of the time we were there was around 90 degrees Fahrenheit / 32 degrees Celsius. That evening we went to John and Donna Bowers for a Potluck Supper. It was one of many we enjoyed whilst we were there. The food was always excellent and there was always more than we could eat!

On the second Sunday (July 12th) the congregation was larger, so too was the offertory – $1171 (c.£585). Our first Sunday had been a holiday weekend, the day we had arrived was the annual celebration of Independence Day. At refreshments after the service, we met Robert and Linda Kelly. They offered to take us to Colonial Williamsburg, which is a 'living museum'. They were hoping that we would be able to stay with Linda's parents who lived nearby. On the Monday Kath drove the family to Seneca State Park while I visited Mrs Holman again at Suburban Hospital and did some work in the Church Office.

On the Tuesday (14th July) we had our first real trip out, to Harper's Ferry, of John Brown's body fame. It was here where, arguably, the American Civil War began. The issue that provoked it was that of slavery. In the evening Kath linked up with the Quilting Group and I had a wedding to prepare for. Glen had arranged the wedding before he left for the UK. It would take place in the bride's garden. There were none of the complicated restrictions that apply in the UK. The only requirement was that the officiant was an ordained minister of a recognised religious denomination.

On Wednesday (15th July) we all went to Annapolis which

193

was about an hour and a quarter away. It meant using the Beltway, a multi-laned motorway that circles Washington. It was, predictably, busy and also somewhat confusing as far as signposting was concerned! In Annapolis I found a discount Bookshop where I bought several very cheap books. We had a harbour boat trip which gave us a remarkable view of the famous Naval Academy and the Bay Bridge. The bridge is c.17 miles long linking several small islands and is reckoned to be one of 7 wonders of the modern world. We also visited the Statehouse, which is the oldest in the US, and is still in use. In the evening we went to Pearl's for an evening Bar-b-q. She had invited the Prasads, the Hendersons, and another couple of families. A pleasant evening all round.

On the Thursday (16th July) Kath and I with the children went to Baltimore. The minister of Mount Vernon UMC, the Revd Ken Jones had invited us to spend the day with him. It took us about an hour and a quarter to drive there. Ken then took us in his car on a tour of the oldest part of the town. It comprised of run-down terraced houses. The city had sold them off at $1 each, on condition they were renovated within a year! Now that's what I call an incentive to regenerate an area! As we drove back into the city centre, he pointed out the church where the Evangelical United Brethren had been established. Baltimore had had a large German speaking population. In the early days of Methodism in the US the large number of German speaking immigrants resulted in separate congregations. In the end the German speaking congregations formed their own denomination, the EUB. It was only in 1968 that they united with the Methodist Church to form the United Methodist Church.

We ended up by the harbour. The USS Constellation, one of the two oldest sailing ships of the US Navy, is moored there. It has never been out of service. Nearby is the Aquarium and two Shopping Malls. One is exclusively devoted to gifts and the other to food. In the food Mall we each went off and bought one item and brought them back together to share what proved to be a very satisfying and very inexpensive meal. After we had eaten Ken took us first to the Railway Museum, which was a little disappointing, and then to Lovely Lane UMC. Methodism in the US began in a society that met in Lovely Lane. In fact, it is arguably the first Methodist Church in the world since many in the UK that date back to the time of John Wesley were founded when the Methodist movement had not yet split from the Church of England. The building is the fifth on the site and was now in need of refurbishment. Seating around 1,000 its current membership was only around 100. We then returned to Ken's church and parsonage. The latter, which was attached to the church was once the German Consulate and was a spacious and impressive building. Much to the children's delight Ken showed us his extensive model railway. What is it with clergy and model railways both here and in the US?

On Friday (17th July) I spent the morning in the church office. After lunch we went into Washington. I called into Suburban Hospital to visit Mrs Holman who had had her other leg amputated. I didn't stay long as she wasn't really up to receiving visitors. We went on to visit the Washington Mormon Temple. We weren't able to go in of course but it was well worth the visit. The building is incredible, and the grounds were spectacular. In the evening Pearl and Bill, with some of their friends from

Church took us to the Chesapeake Crab House to celebrate our Wedding Anniversary which was the next day. Kath and I had a seafood platter which comprised flounder, oyster, shrimps, and crab cakes with French fries! It was delicious. I didn't eat all of my food, so I had the opportunity to ask for a doggy bag! Towards the end of the meal the waiter arrived with champagne for everyone and a dessert for Kath and me – "on the house".

The next day we went to visit Siri's parents in their RV (Recreational Vehicle) in the Virginia Hills. We had a Bar-b-q for lunch then spent some time in the swimming pool before heading back to Gaithersburg for a Church picnic. As always, the food was fabulous and, again, as always, there was far too much to eat. Whenever folk got together for a Church meal there were always two items we looked forward to. One was a Watergate Salad, sweet but always eaten with savoury items. The other was Miss Emma's homemade bread buns. I've never tasted bread buns as good either before or since! Elizabeth was reluctant to leave Pearl, insisting on going home with her in her car so we all ended up at the Campbells before finally managing to get Elizabeth into our car and back to the parsonage.

Sunday (19th July) – again the Church Service was well attended, the offertory seemed to have settled down to around c. £350, I think the second Sunday was excessive because the previous Sunday had been a holiday Sunday and quite a few folk had been away. During the previous week there had been a number of TV news items about race riots in the UK. American TV gave little background to what was happening, and I was asked to spend a few minutes in the service to give some context to the TV news reports. We went for Sunday Lunch at McDonald's; a pattern was beginning to emerge. After lunch Mam and Dad and Auntie Ruth decided to stay in the parsonage while Pearl took the rest of us into Washington. We parked near the Tidal Basin which gave us an opportunity to visit various sites including the Washington Monument. We went to the top. The view was fabulous. The colour of the stone with which it was built changes part way up, the result of its erection having been halted by the Civil War and only completed when the war was over.

On Monday (20th July) I met with Jay Sterling who was on placement at Fairhaven with a particular responsibility for youth and children's work. Afterwards Kath and I went shopping for shoes for Kath. After lunch Tom Starnes, the District Superintendent, arrived to take us out for the afternoon and evening. After we collected his wife, we went to visit Wesley Theological Seminary. We then went to the Methodist Centre, which is situated near to the Supreme Court, both of which we went into. Then on to the Capitol. We went in and explored the Rotunda and then Tom took us into the House of Representatives. We had cocktails in The American Café before visiting the Air and Space Museum. The Starnes then drove us into Virginia to a traditional Inn where the staff were dressed in period costume. Unsurprisingly the meal was fabulous.

On Wednesday (22nd July) we went to Williamsburg with Bob and Linda Kelly. It was a three-hour drive. When we got there, we had lunch outdoors at one of the Taverns and in the afternoon, we explored some of the houses. We checked my mam and dad and Auntie Ruth into a Motel that Bob had booked, and we went on to Linda's parents' home where we were staying. In the evening we went for a meal in Norfolk which was on the other side of Norfolk Bay; the biggest natural harbour in the world.

On Thursday (23rd July) we collected Mam and Dad and Auntie Ruth from their hotel at 8.00 am. We went for breakfast at Sambos. Most of us, including my Dad had a 'Full English' priced at 99cents! The food was excellent, but the service was slow, and we were booked on a tour of the Governor's Palace at 9.45 am. We just made it! From there we went on to the Capitol Building and then to the Bindery and Printing House. I bought a print of the Game of Life and a rejected, marbled, end paper as souvenirs. At home they were framed and have hung in the hallways of every house we've lived in. Later in the afternoon we drove to Jamestown, further down coast. The drive there was beautiful. The site was a reconstruction of the first permanent British settlement established in 1609. The original settlement was now several hundred yards offshore, beneath the waves. Coastal erosion is nothing new! Then it was back to Gaithersburg.

On Friday (24th July) we were taken into Washington and explored the Air and Space Museum and the Museum of American History. In the evening I had the wedding rehearsal. Kath was supposed to come with me, but she cried off with a headache.

The couple were disappointed as they had arranged, in typical

American fashion, a meal after the rehearsal and had intended to take us with them as their guests!

On Friday evening I had a conversation with Pearl regarding what were supposed to be my responsibilities during the exchange of pastorates. I had a similar conversation with Bill Phillips after the service on the Sunday morning.

Saturday (25th July) was the day of the wedding which took place at 3.00 pm in the bride's garden. Maggie and Larry made a lovely couple. We spent the evening with the Ingleton's at their home in Poolsville, which was just a few miles down the road from Gaithersburg.

On Sunday the church was full. We had a quiet afternoon then it was off to Terry Cremens at 5.30 for a bar-b-q.

Monday (27th July) we all went to Baltimore. We parked near the harbour and had lunch in the food hall where we had eaten when we had visited the city with the Revd Ken Jones. After lunch we toured the USS Constellation. In the evening I had a meeting about the upcoming Vacation Bible School since no one knew what they were doing. Jay Stirling took the meeting. Interestingly all these years later I have come across Jay Stirling again, this time through his regular posts on Facebook!

On Tuesday (July 28th) Thurman Davis took us into Washington to visit the Capital which is where he worked. He was about six feet six, well-built and black. Somewhere I have a wonderful photo of him with three-year-old Elizabeth on his shoulders!

We visited the offices of one of the Congressman. What was particularly striking was that one whole wall showed a map of the world but instead of the usual projection with the United Kingdom in the centre it showed the Pacific Ocean in the centre which meant that the USA and the USSR were almost touching at the top centre! A whole new and different perspective! Back in the UK I produced a similar map which I often used in class to encourage my students to see the world differently.

We travelled into the Capitol via an underground train which ferried employees around the Capitol and associated buildings. After lunch we went to the Bureau of Engraving and Printing where US banknotes were printed. There wasn't a lot to see on the tour, apart from millions and millions of dollars in every denomination. Strange to us was the fact that all US bills are the same size and colour irrespective of denomination, only the images printed on them are different. Sometimes appropriately called 'greenbacks' the average life of a single bill is only around eighteen months. We spent some time in the shop and I bought several prints of historic buildings as they appear on various denominations of dollar bills. They were suitable for framing. From there we went across to the Museum of American History where Thurman was meeting us to take us home. We didn't have much time before he arrived as we'd taken longer than intended in the Bureau of Engraving and Printing.

On Wednesday morning (July 29th) Dick Henderson, accompanied by Pearl Campbell, took us out to Gettysburg for the day. Kath had got up at 4.30 am to watch the Royal Wedding of Charles and Diana live, I slept on! Gettysburg should never have happened, but it became the turning point of the Civil War. The year was 1863. The Confederate South was winning. Their troops, some 75,000 soldiers were camped to the south of the town, 90,000 troops of the Unionist North were camped to the north of the town. Some Confederate soldiers went into the town to buy shoes. They met some Unionist soldiers, and a fight broke out which sparked an all-out battle. The result was that the North won, and the tide was turned. However, the northern commander did not press his advantage and the war dragged on for another two years. What was fascinating was that the last surviving soldiers on both sides, aged 109 and 117 years old respectively, had died in my lifetime, in the 1950s!

From Gettysburg we drove on into Pennsylvania Dutch country where the Amish live.

The Amish are a group of Anabaptist Christians with Swiss German and Alsatian origins. They are closely related to the Mennonites who are an Anabaptist denomination named after Menno Simons (1496–1561) of Friesland. Through his writings, Simons set out the teachings of earlier Swiss founders. The Mennonites were founded on the belief in both the mission and ministry of Jesus, which the original Anabaptist followers held to with great conviction, despite persecution by various Roman Catholic and Protestant states. Rather than fight, the majority of the early Mennonite followers survived by fleeing to neighbouring states where ruling families were tolerant of their belief in believer's baptism.

The Amish are known for simple living, plain dress, Christian pacifism, and slowness to adopt many conveniences of modern technology, with a view to not interrupt family time, nor replace face-to-face conversations whenever possible. Consequently, they still ride about in horse and buggies. They do not use electricity and avoid luxuries, for example windows have blinds to keep sun out, but no curtains. The history of the Amish began with a schism in Switzerland within a group of Swiss and Alsatian Mennonite Anabaptists in 1693 led by Jakob Ammann. Those who followed Ammann became known as Amish. In the early 18th century, many Amish and Mennonites immigrated to Pennsylvania for a variety of reasons. In the second half of the 19th century, the Amish divided into Old Order Amish and Amish Mennonites. The latter have assimilated into modern American life.

There were nine of us in Dick's car! He bought a tape tour that we followed which took us around Amish country, beginning at a Pretzel factory. When we finished the tour, he took us for a typical Amish meal. Then we were off again to visit Hersey's chocolate factory where we went on a tour that took us through the whole process of chocolate production. We got home that night at around 10 pm!

On Friday (31st July) We went to visit a relative of Auntie Ruth's who lived in Wilmington in Delaware. The Revd Ronnie Nevin was the vicar in a parish there. I think, if I have worked out the relationship correctly, he was my second cousin, but I could be wrong. He began in the UK as a Methodist minister. He then became a priest in the Church of England and came to America on a Parish Exchange. He then moved over to the

US permanently. He lived in the vicarage which had been transferred to him about ten years earlier. While we were in the US the UMC was in the process of doing the same sort of thing with their parsonages. It was the last denomination to do so apparently. The journey to Wilmington took us across the Bay Bridge, the views were stunning. We had lunch in a Howard Johnsons and arrived at 3.00 pm, as arranged. In my conversation with Ronnie, he agreed with our observation that, in general, prices were half those in the UK and salaries were about twice those in the UK which made living in the US very attractive.

On Saturday (1st August) Thurman took us into Washington again. We visited the Jefferson Memorial, the Lincoln Memorial and then went on to Arlington. There we made use of the tour-mobile to visit the graves of John F Kennedy and his brother Bobby, then the grave of the unknown soldier, where we saw the changing of the guard, ending up at the House of General Robert E Lee. Lee was married to the daughter of George Washington's brother. In the Civil War he began supporting the North but then switched his allegiance and served in the Confederate army. When he switched sides, he forfeited his home in Arlington and after the war the grounds, which are vast, became a cemetery. Technically, although it is usually thought of as part of Washington DC, Arlington is on the south of the Potomac River, in North Carolina which was a Confederate State. The intention was to go on to visit Mount Vernon, George Washington's home, but we ran out of time, so we went back to Thurman's for a late lunch before going on to Carolyn and Harry Ridenours for a meal around 7.30ish!

Sunday (2nd August) I went to the prayer breakfast where Dick led a study on 'the role of women in the church'. The morning service was a service of Holy Communion which I had prepared on the basis of 'The Sunday Service' which I would have used in the UK. The church was full. Although the choir were not actively involved in the service, they sat in the choir stalls which was just as well as there would have been no room for them in the body of the church. After the service, at refreshments, Bill enquired what we were intending to do after our final service the next Sunday. I explained that we hoped to visit various cities on our way north taking my mam and dad and aunt to catch their flight home from Toronto, staying in motels along the way. Bill said, enigmatically, that he would see what he could do!

After the morning service Alma Ridgely invited us to go with her to her home church in the afternoon for their Homecoming Service. Alma thought we would appreciate the opportunity to visit an all-black congregation. We were supposed to be visiting Glenn's parents for a picnic at 4.00 but we agreed to go as long as we could sit at the back in order to slip out early to get to the Young's senior for the picnic.

Kath and I went off with Alma at 2.30 pm and drove the half hour to her home church. They wanted us to sit on the platform with the dignitaries. We explained the situation and a compromise was reached – we sat on the front row! The church was packed, and the service was long, but it was well worth the visit. It finally finished at 5.30 pm! We were late for the picnic. Glenn's dad couldn't understand why we would want to attend a black church service!

Monday (3rd August) saw the start of Vacation Bible School. It would meet every morning from Monday to Friday. Kath was involved with crafts, but I had a 'roaming brief' which gave me the opportunity to spend some time in the church office. It was just as well as I received a phone call from the Department of Energy which demanded an immediate response. Fortunately, there was a meeting of COPA that night, so I was able to respond within their very tight timescale.

At 1.30 pm Alma picked up Kath and me up to take us to an Elementary school where Alma was employed as an ancillary. We spent a very useful hour in conversation with the Head as we toured the school. Later in the afternoon we did some visits, including Mrs Holman, and then on to the Mall and an opticians for me to have an eye test and order new glasses – much cheaper than in the UK! While I was at the COPA meeting Kath was at the quilting group which was meeting at the Phillips' house. I picked her up from there after my meeting.

Tuesday (4th August) Tom Starnes picked me up to take me to a meeting of ministers. On the way we collected another exchange minister from the UK. We expected to simply be observers but found that most of the meeting we were answering questions about what Methodism was like in the UK! Tom then took us to lunch in a nearby Mall.

In the afternoon Bill and Sharon Ingleton took us to visit Mount Vernon, the home of the Washington family. It was about an hour's drive away and it was very hot. We toured the house but found that some rooms were closed as they were being redecorated. We did see the graves of George Washington and his wife Martha, which were in the grounds, a little distance from the house. In the evening the United Methodist Women had arranged a meal at the Golden Bull. Kath was to be the honoured guest, however I managed to persuade them that the minister should also be invited. As usual the meal was fabulous, and we finished off with cocktails – we've still got glasses which came included in the price of the drinks. In the parking lot Marge Mapother and Judy Ferris sang 'what a friend we have in Robert" to the tune of 'What a friend we have in Jesus'! We got home around 9.45 pm.

On Thursday (6th August) afternoon we took my mother and Auntie Ruth to the Shopping Mall. Dad stayed at the parsonage with Robert and Elizabeth. We then went over to the Phillips' where Jane was busy organising somewhere for us to stay in New York and Boston when we were travelling to Toronto the next week. In the evening we went to the Prasads. The Hendersons, the Campbells, the Ingletons, Marge Mapother and Jay Sterling were also invited.

Friday (7th August) was the last day of Vacation Bible School. In the afternoon Dad and I went into Washington to visit the Roman Catholic Basilica. Well worth a visit. However, we did get caught up in traffic; we should have anticipated that on a Friday afternoon. When we got back to the parsonage, we collected the rest of the family and we went to Pearl's for tea. In the evening there was a VBS meeting.

On Saturday morning I took Mam and Dad into Washington so

they could visit the White House. We managed to get tickets for the 10.30 am tour. We filled in time at the Museum of American History. Then it was back to the White House for their tour while I waited around until they had finished.

In the afternoon Terry Cremens took Kath and the children to Cabin John Recreational Park, near Bethesda. Robert and Elizabeth had a whale of a time ending up with a ride on a little train, then a drink and an ice cream. Then it was back to the parsonage and into the bath, then off to bed. Kath and I then went shopping at Lake Forest Mall. We bought sheets, a tablecloth, and a bag to put them in since our suitcases were already full! The quality was so good and the prices, compared to the UK, were so cheap we just couldn't let the opportunity pass. Then it was back to the parsonage to change and off to Marge Mapother's for a choir evening. The choir sang for us, The Cat Song and then the Doxology to the tune of Hernando's Hideaway, which worked remarkably well! The meal was superb. I had a steak that Marge's husband had cooked on the bar-b-q. It was 'rare' but I have never had such a tender steak! He explained it was all to do with the quality of the meat.

Sunday (9th August) was my last service at Fairhaven. For Children's Time I told the story of the camels:

The Camels

A rich man died and left his 17 camels to his three sons. The eldest was to have half, the middle son, a third, and the youngest a ninth. The camels were not to be shared or divided. At the end of the will the man had written "whatever is given in love will always return". The sons found it impossible to fulfill their father's wishes. Half of 17 is eight and a half; a third is five and two thirds and a ninth is one and eight ninths! In the end they consulted their uncle, who was poor. He only had one camel. He puzzled over his brother's will and in the end offered his nephews his one camel if it would help. 18 divided by two is 9; 18 divided by 3 is 6; 18 divided by 9 is 2 – 9+6+2=17! So, they returned their uncle's camel and realised then that the final phrase in their father's will made sense.

I co-opted members of the congregation to be the father, the uncle, the sons and the camels! It went down well! Kath and I sang Colours of Day, and we finished the service with 'Blest be the tie that binds'. For the congregational response to the benediction we sang two verses of 'All praise to our redeeming Lord' then the choir sang 'God be with you till we meet again'. It was very emotional. The Offertory that Sunday was $1311.71 (c.£650)!

For refreshments after the service, they had made three cakes, one for 'Robert and Kath and Bob and Betty and Ruth, with a picture of Fairhaven UMC on it, and one with the Washington Monument on it for Robert and Elizabeth, which Robert cut, and one with 'God be with you' and Ichthus on it. We never did get around to cutting into that one. During the service we presented the church with a John Wesley plate we had brought with us. Now Pearl Campbell presented us with a book, made by Billy of sugar paper, with various Bible texts written on the pages. The last page had $350 in various denominations, pinned to it in the form of two crosses! Bill Phillips then gave us details of the accommodations he had arranged for us and was very apologetic that he had failed to arrange anywhere for us to stay in either Philadelphia or Toronto!

Since we had been to Macdonald's for our first Sunday lunch, we went to MacDonald's for our last Sunday Lunch. We then dropped Mam and Dad and Auntie Ruth back at the parsonage before we went to the Holman family picnic. Mrs Holman had been brought from her nursing home for the day, though she was not too well. Then it was back to the parsonage to pack everything we wouldn't need the following week. We took our cases to the Campbell's where we left them as we were staying there when we returned from our trip to take Mam and Dad and Auntie Ruth to Toronto the next week. Thurman Davis had given me various maps from AAA to help plan our trip and after studying them I found that we needed a 'letter of authorisation' to take the car into Canada. Glenn's dad arrived with that, and the international insurance card that we also needed.

We spent the morning of Monday (10th August) cleaning and clearing up at the parsonage. Dad and I went to church to drop off some of the things I still had at the parsonage and then did some shopping to leave some food for the Youngs when they returned. The ladies remained behind to finish the cleaning, washing, ironing and making up the beds. We finally left at mid-day. We left the keys with Glenn's parents, then went to Macdonald's for lunch. After lunch we drove to the Beltway heading north towards Philadelphia. On a fairly uneventful drive we worked out which Motel we would stay in that night on the outskirts of Philadelphia.

The next day we drove into the centre of Philadelphia to explore. The journey in was a nightmare, not sure why, perhaps because of a lack of signposting, but eventually we succeeded and parked up. The highlight was a visit to the Mint, one of four in the US that produced all the coins in circulation. The other three are to be found in Denver, San Francisco and West Point. Apart from occasional special editions the US only uses four coins. A one cent (a penny), a five cent (a nickel), a ten cent (a dime), and a twenty-five cent (a quarter). Half dollar and one-dollar coins were tried but proved unpopular and tend now to be reserved for special editions. The tour of the mint was really interesting, much more so than the tour of the Bureau of Engraving and Printing in Washington.

From Philadelphia we drove to Boston. Bill had studied at the Massachusetts Institute of Technology (MIT) which is situated in Cambridge, adjacent to Boston, and he arranged for us to stay with one of his old lecturers. He could only accommodate Kath and I and our children, but he had arranged for my Mam and Dad and Auntie Ruth to stay with friends nearby. Baltimore was famous for Paul Revere (21st December 1734 – 10th May 1818). He was an American silversmith, engraver, early industrialist, and Patriot in the American Revolution. He is best known for his midnight ride in April 1775 to alert the colonial militia to the approach of British forces before the battles of Lexington and Concord. His action is immortalised in Henry Wadsworth Longfellow's poem, "Paul Revere's Ride" (1861). We made a point of visiting Paul Revere's house. We also visited the harbour, site of the 'Boston Tea Party".

The Boston Tea Party was an American political and mercantile protest by the Sons of Liberty in Boston, Massachusetts, on December 16, 1773. The target was the Tea Act of 10th May, 1773, which allowed the British East India Company to sell tea from China in American colonies without paying taxes apart from those imposed by the Townshend Acts. American Patriots strongly opposed the taxes in the Townshend Act as a violation of their rights. Demonstrators, some disguised as American Indians, destroyed an entire shipment of tea sent by the East India Company. They boarded the ships and threw the chests of tea into Boston Harbour. The British government responded harshly, and the episode escalated into the American Revolution. There was a replica ship moored in the harbour and we were able to go on board and throw 'tea chests' overboard by way of re-enactment. The chests were then fished out to be used again by the next group of revolutionaries' aka tourists.

From Boston we drove on to New York. Bill Phillips had arranged for us to stay in his sister's apartment in the centre of Manhattan, on 34th Street. She was away so left the key with a neighbour. We had two nights there. It was easy to drive around New York which is mostly built on a grid pattern. I missed the turn at first and ended up driving through Harlem. Harlem was predominantly black and poor. Lots of folk were simply sitting on their steps watching the world go by. My passengers felt very uncomfortable and couldn't wait for me to get back to the centre of Manhattan and find the apartment.

I had to park on the street outside the apartment block. It was not unusual to 'double park' since the street cleaners came around early each morning which meant getting up and moving the car to the other side of the street then moving it back again when the cleaners had been. When we went down in the morning, we had to step over a young girl asleep in the entrance hall. She was clearly a rough sleeper.

We travelled around by Metro and visited most of the usual tourist places. Wall Street and the financial district. Broadway and the theatre district. Fifth Avenue and St Patrick (RC) Cathedral. Times Square. Battery Park and the Statue of Liberty. We went up inside the Statue. It took ages as the queue was very long. Halfway up the last flight of steps, which would have led us to the viewing platform outside on the crown, Robert decided he was desperate for the toilet, so we had to descend. We never did get to the top. We did however get to the top of the Empire State Building; the views were amazing. We shopped in nearby Macey's.

From New York we headed west to Syracuse where we had an overnight stay to break our journey on the way to the Canadian border at Niagara. Bill had arranged for us to stay in a house owned by his old University Chaplain. The family was Asian Indian, and they laid on a full meal for us in their own home when we arrived. It was absolutely fabulous. The women of the family waited on us hand and foot. After the meal we were taken to the Caretaker's House where we were to spend the night. There we found they had set out a fantastic breakfast ready for us to eat in the morning before we left to move on towards to border.

We stopped at Niagara and visited the Falls. We didn't have time to take the boat trip which goes under the falls. I have a fabulous picture of Elizabeth eating a chocolate ice cream most of which seems to be on her face! Then it was on to Toronto where we found a motel for the night. We did manage to go up The CN Tower 1,815.3 ft high. It held the record for the world's tallest free-standing structure for 32 years until 2007 when it was surpassed by the Burj Khalifa. It is currently the ninth tallest free-standing structure in the world and remains the tallest free-standing structure on land in the Western Hemisphere. The floor of the viewing deck was glass. As you stepped out it was as if you were stepping out into nothing, scary!

At their insistence we didn't stay to see my parents and aunt onto their plane home, so we said our farewells at the motel, and we headed south, back to the border and on to Buffalo where Bill had arranged for us to stay with an aunt of his. Her husband worked for Kodak which was based in the town.

The next day we set off to return to Gaithersburg. Given that we were driving down the west side of New York State, and that there were no particular places on route that we wanted to visit, we decided to press on to Gaithersburg, so we arrived back at the Campbells a little earlier than we had intended.

On Thursday (20th August) Pearl Green took us around National Geographic headquarters where she used to work. She had only recently retired. There was not a lot to see but we did visit the computer room. It was an odd feeling that my details were there on file; I had taken National Geographic for years. We had lunch there in the staff dining room. Both the building and its grounds were beautiful. Inevitably I bought some books from their bookshop. Pearl insisted on paying for the books on the World's Religions and the Bible Lands. In the afternoon we did some last-minute shopping, including picture frames for some of the prints we had collected. They were so cheap compared to the UK. Then we washed and cleaned the Youngs' car to return it to them.

In the evening the church had arranged a social evening at Fairhaven. The Youngs were there of course, since they had arrived home while we had been away the previous week. They sat with us and we assumed that it was to be a 'welcome home' for them. There was a special cake for the occasion with the US on one side and the UK on the other. The evening began with a 'Potluck' supper.

After the meal it became clear this was a 'farewell' for the Fishers. Bill Phillips began by reading a passage from his favourite book, 'The Little Prince'. We were then called to the front to receive a 'going away' present and a large (washing machine size) cardboard box was brought in! We opened and unpacked it to find, in the centre a silver Paul Revere bowl, apparently a traditional gift for departing friends, and some Lego for Robert and a soft toy for Elizabeth.

We thought that that was it, but no, Alma Ridgeley and Bonnie Tyler came up to the front. They both worked in schools and because they knew that we did they presented us with a 'whereinthehellisgaitherburgmd' t-shirt for me and a green and yellow Seneca Valley High t-shirt for Kath (it proved to be too big for Kath so I got that one too!) and a Screaming Eagles t-shirt for me and t-shirt each for Robert and Elizabeth. It didn't end there we were also given a set of textbooks that contained the entire school syllabus, and a handful of pencils with the name of the school on them. Since we had said how much we enjoyed it someone then gave us a recipe for 'Watergate Salad'. Finally, Sharon Ingleton presented us with a beautiful, framed, blackwork picture which she and Donna Bowers had done on holiday the previous week. It showed four of the buildings in Colonial Williamsburg. They had done it because they knew how impressed we had been when we had visited there with the Kellys. It was an amazing evening. At the end of the evening Bill Phillips came across and gave me his treasured copy of The Little Prince. I'm not often lost for words, but I was on that occasion. We were both very emotional.

On Friday (21st August) Jane Phillips looked after Robert and Elizabeth while Kath and I borrowed one of Bill Campbell's cars, a big Dodge, and we drove into Washington in a final attempt to visit the White House. We ended up parking at exactly the same spot on 23rd Street where I'd parked when I took Mam and Dad in for their White House Tour. We managed to get tickets and we then went to Bureau of Engraving and Printing where we bought some more prints to take home as presents. We had something to eat at the Washington Monument and then returned to the White House for our tour which began on time and was really excellent and well worth the visit. It was about midday when we got back to the car and we then drove to Wheaton where there was a Jewish Bookshop I wanted to visit. We went first to the eating place which I had visited when I had met up with Glenn's minister friends. We then visited the bookshop where I bought a couple of books I wanted.

Then it was back to Gaithersburg. On the way we searched out Mary Graham's house. I had visited her in hospital, but she wasn't able to be at my final service and I wanted to see her before we left. We stayed with her for a little while. We then did some final shopping and picked up the children from Bill and Jane's at about 5.00 pm. Then back to the Campbells where Pearl laid on a final farewell 'do'! The Ingletons, the Greens, Bernice Joppy, and Miss Emma (I never did discover her surname) were all invited. Bill Phillips came around with a box and tape and string as we still couldn't get everything into our luggage. We were then shunted off into the corner and we were given a variety of gifts including a brass Maryland crab and more t-shirts for the children.

On the Saturday morning we finished our packing and despite acquiring additional boxes and bags we still ended up having to borrow a suitcase from Pearl. Then we went to the parsonage to say our farewell to the Youngs. Back to the Campbells. About half past two Bill went off and brought a 'crab and chips' take away for me as I was reluctant to leave without one final crab meal. It was delicious. Finally, we set off for the airport accompanied by Pearl and Bill and Billy. We saw our plane arrive, offload and refuel, then we said our farewells and went on board by which time it was getting dark. There was some turbulence at the beginning of the flight. The meal was served but Robert and Elizabeth didn't eat much of theirs as they were falling asleep. Kath and I watched the movie. The children were still half asleep when we landed and deplaned. Maurice Fennel met us when we cleared customs and we transferred all our baggage into his car for the journey home. Kath and the children slept in the car. We dropped all our luggage at home then went to the Fennels for lunch. When we got back home Robert and Elizabeth took themselves off to bed and slept – again!

Once we were home, we began to learn about Glenn's visit to Coalville. Lisa welcomed us home and when Kath mentioned how clean the house was Lisa looked a little sheepish. She then confessed that she had come in to check that all was ready for our return and was appalled at the state they had left the house in. She told us she had used up all the dusters we kept under the sink to get it as clean as it was.

We were somewhat prepared for what awaited us as Glenn had told us, before our return that he had left our car in a garage in Huddersfield with a gearbox problem. When the stories began to be told someone commented that they didn't think Glenn ever drove beyond second gear! Apparently, he had never driven a geared car before. That would explain his reluctance to drive the car during the week they were with us before we went to Gaithersburg. Alan Buck, one of our friends from Hall Lane MC offered to go and collect my car. The bill was in excess of

£250. Glenn made no contribution! Two weeks later the car was still playing up, so I bought a 'new' Austin Maxi from Maurice Perry, and ex-Methodist minister turned car mechanic / salesman who lived in Shepshed. Maurice took my Maxi off to a car auction. A couple of weeks later I had a phone call from the guy who bought it wanting his money back as the car had died as he drove it back from the auction. I had to explain, as sensitively as I could, that it was no longer my responsibility. When I came off the phone, I breathed a sigh of relief that I had got rid of it when I did.

The children's slide in our back garden had been in one piece when we left. It was in three pieces when we returned. The passes my colleagues at school had given them so that they had unlimited, free, access to the activities that were available during the holiday period lay, unused, on top of the rubbish in the bin.

We had left a diary for the Youngs with all the various things we had arranged for them listed along with the appropriate dates and addresses. When we returned, we learned that they simply ignored it when it suited them. Several people had meals prepared ready to serve up and the Youngs simply didn't turn up having made other arrangements. One family who owned a small Garden Centre had closed it for the day and arranged for a tour of their rose garden followed by afternoon tea. When the Youngs got there Glenn decided he'd rather go to the cinema and promptly turned around to drive back home. Fortunately, Glenn's mother was visiting and was with them. She decided to stay so the situation was rescued somewhat. They did turn up in Wirksworth, at the Kindleysides who took them to visit Chatsworth House. Peter was less than impressed when Glenn completed his tour of the house in less than half an hour. Peter took his time, keeping Glenn waiting outside for an age!

Apparently, his services generally left much to be desired. On more than one occasion he announced the hymn 'Stand up, stand up for Jesus' with the direction, "We will remain seated for this hymn"! I had planned him to preach at Hall Lane one Sunday morning and Whitwick that same Sunday evening. I had warned him not to use the same service/sermon as many of the morning congregation went to the evening service. Hall Lane and Whitwick were only a mile apart on the same road. He took the same service and sermon at both churches!

We discovered later that on his return to Gaithersburg Glenn was called before the Worship Committee and thereafter at the conclusion of each service he had to meet with them to review the service. It was very flattering and rather humbling to discover that the services I had taken had been so much appreciated.

Back to Coalville

I'm not sure when we began, each Christmas, to send out a 'round robin' (whatever that actually means) with our Christmas cards. The first one I kept, which is undated, clearly recounts what we were up to as a family during 1982. It does mean, that, with the exception of two years (the Christmas letters for 1986 and 1993 are missing) I now have a very helpful aide memoire when it comes to completing these 'recollections'.

[1982]

The highlight of the year 1982 was undoubtedly the visit of the Campbells during the summer. We met them off their flight from Washington and drove them from Gatwick to Coalville. They were amazed at how much countryside we drove through. They had expected one continuous conurbation. They also confessed, when they left, that they had been amazed at how well they had been welcomed everywhere. They had expected racism to be rife, especially after seeing the TV reports of race riots which they had seen the previous year. It took us a while to work out what to arrange for them to see. Each time we suggested somewhere Pearl would reply "I don't care". Fortunately, we soon realised that what she meant was "I don't mind". It would have been easy to be offended if we hadn't been sensitive to the subtle differences between English English and American English!

In fact, we had a great three weeks with Bill, Pearl and Billy; we wished that it could have been three months. The Campbells wanted to visit London so twice we went by train from Leicester. The first time we took a tour bus in order to see all the sights of interest, and then a boat trip with the same intention. I explained that it would be impossible to see everything on foot even if we spent a couple of weeks in the capital. On the second visit we visited the two or three places they particularly wanted to see.

On the train down on our second visit, we were separated as the coaches were full. Pearl, Bill and Billy were at one end of the carriage, and Robert and I were sitting opposite a young couple at the other end of the carriage. (Kath and Elizabeth had decided to stay at home.) The woman kept staring at me, which was quite embarrassing until I realised that she was actually staring was not me but the T-shirt I was wearing. It was the one that I was given when we left Fairhaven. It read: 'whereinthehellisgaithersburgmd'. Eventually the woman spoke, "I used to live there"! Later that day, when we went to see Buckingham Palace, the Campbells went over to the Palace gates and Robert and I stayed in the shadow of the wall on the other side of the roundabout. As one couple were passing, they stopped, looked at my T-shirt, and said "I used to work there"! Before the Campbells left, we bought Bill a T-shirt with 'Coalville' boldly emblazoned on the front.

The second week they were here we went to stay with my parents in Whitley Bay. From there were took them to see various places of interest in the North East from Lindisfarne to Durham. Looking back, I'm amazed how much we fitted in. I suspect when the Campbells returned to the States, they were ready for a holiday! We even managed a day trip to Boulogne on the Wednesday before they left. We also managed to fit in a bar-b-q to say farewell. In the UK a bar-b-q was still relatively rare. When the Youngs were here the previous year, Glenn had picked up a small portable bar-b-q, a freebee gift with engine oil when he had filled up with fuel. It had been gathering dust in the garage, so we decided this was a good opportunity to make use of it. Folk from church and neighbours gathered – and it rained – heavy and persistent! We were all crammed into the house. We put Bill in charge of the bar-b-q and I still have a photo of him sitting alone under next door's car port tending the bar-b-q with a glass of whiskey in his hand!

Their final departure is something we shall never forget. We certainly weren't looking forward to seeing them off, but Saturday finally arrived, and we set off for Gatwick, in the car, in good time. We left Tony, our next-door neighbour, to look after Nel. When we got to London, we debated whether to drive straight through the centre or take the North/South Circular. We chose the latter – and crawled! We arrived before their flight was due to depart but, whereas it was possible to check them in, it was too late to check in their luggage, so they were unable to fly. They were offered a flight the next day and given a free upgrade, so they weren't too disappointed, except what to do about an overnight stay.

They refused to let us return to Coalville insisting we stay with them in a motel. We phoned Tony, our next doors neighbour, who agreed to look after Nel and then went in search of a motel room. They booked a 'family room' thinking that, as in the States, it would contain two double beds and two singles. What we got was one double bed and bunk beds! We took the mattress off the double bed and put it on the floor between the double bed and the bunks. Kath and I slept on that, Pearl and Bill slept on the bed base. Robert and Elizabeth slept, top to toe, on the bottom bunk and Billy had the top bunk to himself. So, we spent an evening in Brighton, which wasn't too far away. The next day we made sure we were in good time for their flight and finally saw them on their way.

All in all, it was an interesting year. Elizabeth was very thankful to reach the age of four that year. She had spent the first six months feeling very disgruntled about the fact that she was only three! Her vocabulary grew enormously and during the second half of the year she was very eager to learn to read and write. She wasn't due to start school until the next August. Fortunately, however, she was able to go to Play School three mornings each week and she thoroughly enjoyed it. Christmas saw her practising to be an angel in the Sunday School Nativity Play — Liz a little angel?

Robert (jnr.) made a poor start to the academic year in September. He was reluctant to do much work and finished little of what he began. At Parent's Evening we were told that he was quite bright but...! Eventually he seemed to settle down and, with a little incentive, began to do quite well, He made a beautiful book cover for the end of term competition at school and looked forward to being a shepherd in the School Nativity Play. In fact, he was so excited about it that he learned his lines in a single night.

Kath, as usual, was doing far too much! She had an interesting year in school, though, not unsurprisingly, a hectic one. During the summer term, along with several other members of staff, she went with a group of children on a week-long canal trip, and later in the same term a week-long visit to France. Both of these, though exhausting, she enjoyed immensely, especially the visit to France as it was her first visit to that country. In the Autumn Term she changed from teaching Upper Juniors to teaching Lower Juniors and found it most refreshing. She also took responsibility for teaching both guitar and recorder groups in the school. At the end of the year she was fully involved as prompter in the school's production of "Charlie and the Chocolate Factory" which they put on in the theatre at King Edward VII College.

One of the Fifth Form girls approached me to ask if, in my capacity as a Methodist minister, I would visit her gran. She explained that her gran was mentally disturbed, and no prescribed medication seemed to have any effect. I confess that I was somewhat hesitant, but eventually agreed. She took me to her gran's, and it was obvious from the outset that she was very disturbed. I spent some time talking to her and praying with her before we left. It was an experience I have never forgotten. It was the nearest I have ever come to meeting someone who, although I have difficulty with the idea, was demon-possessed.

I was looking for promotion and had applied, unsuccessfully, for three posts during the year. The first one I applied for was the position of minister in an Anglican/Methodist/Presbyterian Church in Nairobi. I'm not sure I would have been a good fit theologically as they were clearly very conservative. The second, which resulted in an interview, was for the post of Chaplain at a Methodist School in the South-West of England. The third was for the post of Tutor/Chaplain at Bath Technical College. In the case of the first and the last no-one was appointed, which was perhaps even more frustrating than to have a successful candidate, other than oneself, appointed to the post.

My timetable that year was fairly light since I had no sixth form teaching of any description, but an excellent fourth year option set for Religious Studies which was some compensation. As a consequence, I had a lot more free periods than most members of staff and ended up doing a lot of substitutions for absent colleagues. In Circuit I gave up my Chairmanship of the Ministries Committee, though I continued as Local Preachers Tutor. I also managed to reduce my preaching commitments so that I was sure of having at least every other Sunday free to be able to sit in the pew with the family, a much appreciated and refreshing change.

We did consider purchasing the circuit manse since that had become vacant when the circuit decided to build a new manse in the town centre. After due consideration, we decided to extend our present house instead and had thought to make a start during the summer. However, that didn't happen as we were waiting for one of my colleagues to finish drawing up the plans. We were given some pallets which we set about sorting out to make fencing for the garden. Progress was slow as by the time we got home from school it was dark so that any work we wanted to do outdoors had to wait until the weekend, providing it wasn't raining!

Some months after the Campbells had returned home, we had a phone call from the States to tell us that Sharon and Bill Ingelton's eldest son, Dean, had been killed in a car crash. A young girl had gone through a red light straight into Dean's car, he died instantly. Dean was much loved by everyone. He was the iconic young American, handsome, academically clever and into sport. It was a real blow to the family.

[1983]

So, when the Ingleton's asked if they could visit the next summer we were looking forward to their coming with a certain amount of trepidation. Our experiences with the Campbells in the summer of 1982 served us in good stead. One thing we had learned – the hard way – was that we needed to take account of the fact that in the UK, even at the peak of the tourist season, unlike in the US where most places remained open until late, often sunset, here they are closed by 5.30 pm at the latest. Consequently, we were able to ensure that we actually toured the places we took them to visit. As we had with the Campbells, we took the Ingletons to stay with my parents in Whitley Bay. One evening Scott decided he would like to visit a local pub, so we went to the one nearest my parents'. It just so happened that that evening was a folk evening when people turned up and played their instruments and sang folk songs. This all took place in 'the Snug' which didn't have a bar; for drinks you had to purchase them in the Lounge. The Snug was packed. We couldn't get Scott out until closing time!

We also took the Ingletons to visit Kath's mum and dad. Several years earlier Kath's dad had built a boat in the back garden earning him the nickname Noah! He built it with the aim of using it on the fairly extensive network of canals in the area. This wasn't a traditional barge but a cabin cruiser. It was powered by an old ford car engine with one forward and one reverse gear. Getting it from the back garden to the front drive proved a bit of a task but it was achieved and duly transported to the canal system and launched. It was named Hilden (a contraction of Kath's parents given names – Hilda and Dennis). We had a number of very enjoyable holidays on it. Anyway, Kath's parents took the Ingletons for a trip on their boat and I can still see Bill's facing lighting up when Kath's dad offered him the chance to 'drive' it!

Bill was keen to visit Ingleton in Yorkshire. Apparently, Ingleton is an uncommon surname and Bill had been unable to trace its origins. We were happy to oblige. We also discovered, but didn't let on until we arrived there, that there was another Ingleton, in County Durham. Bill was delighted to have the opportunity to visit both. Whilst we had eaten everything that was put before us in the States, here Bill drew the line at Black Pudding! The only thing that marred the fortnight was the fact that the car decided to play up. However, rapid repairs kept us mobile. When they left Sharon presented me with a plate – a Round Tuit – that still graces my bookshelves.

Autumn saw the return of the car's problems and, although we had hoped to keep the Maxi on the road for at least another eighteen months, we were forced to conclude that enough was enough, so we exchanged it for a newer Renault 20. It was certainly more comfortable; we could only hope that it would prove to be more reliable.

Talking of cars – Kath finally decided to take her driving test. After holding a provisional license for about 12 years when she realised that in another 10 years Robert (Jnr) could well have passed his test she decided that 'the time had come!' She had begun driving when we had the Daf, which was classed as an automatic, and she was reluctant to drive in a geared car. She drove with me whenever possible and had a number of lessons in the Driving School's car. When the time came, she took her test at the test centre in Loughborough. She failed, twice! The first time because on a one-way street she passed a bollard on the left instead of the right and the second time because she was just too nervous! After the second time she was offered a cancellation and when the driving instructor came around, Kath asked if, instead of using the Driving School's car she could take it in ours? His was a small car ours was a Renault 20. He took her out for a lesson in ours the night before the test and he agreed to let her take the test in it. She passed with flying colours!

At school Kath was promoted from a Scale 1 to a Scale 2 and found that the demands on her time increased quite dramatically. She was given the responsibility of organising the Christmas Service at her school, utilising the talents of both the guitar group and the recorder group both of which she had responsibility for. For relaxation she took up swimming and gained her bronze medallion for personal survival which involved, among other things, swimming twenty lengths. Not content with that achievement she began preparing for her silver medallion which required her to swim forty-four lengths!

Bill Hayward, the principal of King Edward VII College, retired and a new principal was appointed. Bill was not a well man;

he was developing Parkinson's Disease and had recently been widowed. Richard Holdsworth could not have been a bigger contrast to his predecessor if he tried. He began to initiate change as soon as he took over in the role. The admin part of the building was reorganised. The principal's office was abolished, and he and his deputies took over the 'Conference' room. School uniform was abolished, or as one colleague observed was 'changed'! Now students arrived wearing denim jeans and denim jackets or gilets – still a uniform, just different. When it came to parents' evenings, he wanted everyone to wear badges with their Christian names on them. I was union rep for the NASUWT. Many of my members objected since, some, who were of foreign origin had unusual names which the students could well use to taunt them. Then he started in on the curriculum. More of that in a moment.

Robert (Jnr) seemed to be more settled having moved from the Primary to the Juniors at School. That move meant that he had a six-week swimming course early in the term and it was that that set Kath off, and even resulted in several visits to Loughborough Leisure Centre's pool and persuaded me to venture into the water after twenty year's abstention. However, to return to Robert (Jnr) he decided to learn to play the recorder, and on occasion could even be heard practising in his bedroom after the official curfew – such enthusiasm was not to be discouraged! Part of the attraction was undoubtedly the fact that his Mum was the one who taught the recorder at school. He also began attending a gymnastics club in the spring with erratic enthusiasm and, although he chose not to continue with the club in the autumn, he looked forward eagerly to the weekly gymnastics club that was held on Thursday evenings. He was in the 'chorus' of the Sunday School's production of "Kid's Praise" earlier in the year and with Christmas on the horizon he could be found rehearsing his lines as a shepherd for the school Nativity Play. He suddenly decided that he really did enjoy reading and could be caught doing just that after 'lights out'! Even more encouragingly, he, not infrequently, wrote stories for his teacher – twelve months previously writing was definitely his most 'unfavourite' pastime.

Elizabeth achieved stardom in the spring when she sang a two-line solo in the Sunday School's production of "Kid's Praise". To our delight Bill Phillips, from Gaithersburg, was in Loughborough visiting a colleague and he came to spend the day with us so was able to be present. In the summer she was a bridesmaid for one of my colleagues from school. I had the privilege of having been asked to officiate at the wedding, a rare privilege since becoming a 'Minister in Other Appointments'. Elizabeth really looked the part – long dress, apron and mop cap. With her brother she joined the gymnastics club in the spring and continued to attend with great enthusiasm. In September being moved up a class only served to encourage her eagerness. September also saw her begin school. For the previous six months she had longed for the day. When meeting Mum one day after school in the summer Robert's teacher asked her if she was looking forward to starting school in the autumn. "Yes", said Elizabeth, then after a pause continued, with hands on hips and a somewhat disgruntled expression, "everyone keeps asking me that question and I have to keep answering, 'Yes, yes, yes, yes.'" She had a habit of being quite disconcerting at times, for example, she was overheard describing the 10p she had been given for her collection at Sunday School as "I can't remember what it's called, let's call it a tip"! She eagerly awaited the school trip to see 'Winnie the Pooh', their Christmas 'treat'!

At school my timetable went from the sublime to the ridiculous. The previous academic year I had had a very light teaching commitment, now, partly because 'A' level time had not been allowed for and a number of students had decided that they wanted to do the course. As a consequence, I had to give up free periods and a couple of lunch hours. My teaching commitment consequently became quite demanding. Another factor was the introduction of 'Integrated Humanities' as a core course, despite the objection of a large number of those who ended up teaching the subject, myself included.

My peaching commitments were not significantly reduced during the year, although I did tend to preach further afield than previously. I thoroughly enjoyed my second year as Study Supervisor for one of the Probationers in the District and I continued as Circuit Local Preachers' Tutor and Chairman of the local Council of Churches.

In the autumn my free time was taken up making some useful alterations to the house – blocking off the dining room from the kitchen and turning it into a study which had the benefit of enlarging the kitchen and clearing the bedroom of books, desk and filing cabinet to make way for Kath's sewing and knitting! It sounds simple when it is put down in words, but it took a lot of time and effort though it proved to be most worthwhile.

Extending the house was postponed for another twelve months or so, time being the main problem.

[1984]

The first part of the year was fairly uneventful. All that changed, however, when in May I was successful in my application for the post of Head of Religious and Social Studies at the Lakes School in Windermere. The house was valued and sold immediately, but more of that shortly.

I took my leave of king Edward VII at the end of the summer term. The vice-Principal and Margaret Hoskins and several other of my colleagues took me out for a meal at a restaurant in one of the villages near Leicester. I was presented with a vase, fashioned in the shape of a gravestone the top of which was removable to allow for it's intended use. It had a cross on the front along with a butterfly and on the side a caterpillar – good theology! On the bottom it read: From all your friends at King Edward VII. It was made by John Macauly, who taught pottery at the school. When I was asked what I wanted as a leaving present, I said that I'd like a piece of John's pottery but I never expecting a piece specially designed for me. I was also presented with a framed print of Mount St Bernard Abbey, a Roman Catholic Cistercian monastery founded in 1835, situated between Coalville and Shepshed. The abbey was the first permanent monastery to be founded in England since the Reformation and is the only Trappist house in England. It has an excellent bookshop which I often visited.

to the USA - again

We had planned a visit to the States during July and August. This time it was not on an Exchange of Pastorates. The friends we had made on our first visit insisted that they host us for the whole summer, so this really was a holiday. Our departure, however, had to be delayed by a few days since I had been invited to share in the ordination of the Revd Ken Kilby, the minister whose studies I had been supervising during the previous two years. I considered this to be a great privilege.

Like the first time we visited the States in 1981 I again kept a tape cassette journal of our visit in the summer of 1984. What follows therefore, will read more like a Journal than simply a collection of memories. My mam and dad came with us again, but this time without auntie Ruth.

We set off on Thursday 5th July. Maurice Fennel, our friend from Hall Lane MC, took us to Leicester where we caught the early 7.06 am train for London, then we went by tube to Victoria where we caught the 'Gatwick Express'. We arrived c.9.45 am and met up with Mam and Dad who had arrived just a few minutes earlier having travelled by bus to Victoria Coach Station then by bus to Gatwick. We had some refreshments and then killed time until it was time to board our plane. We were flying by People's Express, a new no-frills airline. The plane was a new Boeing 747. We arrived in Newark on time, sailed through immigration and customs and caught a bus into the main terminal in Manhattan, then a taxi to the YMCA where Bill Phillips had booked us two rooms for four nights.

We were on the eighth floor. We were in room 803A and Mam and Dad were in room 828, on the other side of the building. They were double rooms but, unlike most American Hotels they had two single beds rather than two doubles. We had to make up a shakedown for the children on the floor between the beds. There was no air conditioner, so the night was rather hot and sticky! The next day, Friday 6th July, we had breakfast in the 'Y' dining room then set off to walk up 5th Avenue. The YMCA was very central, on same street as May's and the Empire State Building. We went into Central Park then headed down towards Broadway. We took a bus tour which took around four and a half hours. It was rather expensive, $15 each for the adults and $11.50 for the children. It was, however, an excellent tour. In Upper Manhattan we stopped off to visit St John's Anglican Cathedral, reckoned to be the largest Gothic Cathedral in the world. It was still unfinished. In Lower Manhattan we stopped off and, having visited Liberty Island last time, we took a trip out to visit Ellis Island. In days gone by all immigrants passed through the facility there. We then had a stroll through Chinatown. It was c.6.30 pm when we arrived back at the bus stop from which we began our tour.

Saturday (7th July) we breakfasted in MacDonald's as the 'Y' dining room was closed. It was raining and I bought a collapsible umbrella from a street vendor. We decided to visit the Museum of Natural History which meant using the Subway. Amazingly cheap; 90c each to travel anywhere. The children thoroughly enjoyed the dinosaur exhibition. We had something to eat in the café and from there we went, by taxi, to the United Nations building. Dad and I had a tour, the rest of the family stayed outside. We then walked back to the 'Y' via 42nd Street and Grand Central Station, which was a magnificent building.

On Sunday 8th July we had breakfast in MacDonald's again! Afterwards we caught a taxi down to the financial district where we saw NatWest USA. We then went to visit John Street UMC, built on the site of the oldest Methodist Church in the US which was founded on 12th October 1766. The congregation was quite small, only c.35. We had a look in their museum where I spotted a plate that was produced for Hartley Victoria College when I was there as a student. When they were produced, I had bought three, one for me, and one each for my parents and Kath's. After refreshments we headed to Pier 83 on West 42nd Street to catch a Circle Line boat trip which took us around Manhattan and lasted about three hours. We went past the 'Little Red Lighthouse', subject of a popular children's story. Dad paid $10 each for all of us, a birthday treat for me and the children! We walked back to the 'Y' for our usual pizza supper. On the way we called into Penn station to see if it was worth taking an Amtrak train to Washington. Tickets were $37 each but with discounts proved a very economical $74 in total for all of us. So, we booked our tickets, ready to travel the following day.

Next day we had breakfast in a little diner down the street. I'd hurt my back on our second day, so we then went to Woolworths and Macy's and another shop, looking for a luggage trolley. In the end we found one for $12.99. It was then a dash back to the 'Y' to check out by 12 noon. We had time to kill in the station while we waited for our train which was due to depart at 2.15

pm. When we found out which platform it was arriving at, we discovered we would have to carry our luggage down three flights of stairs. The train was very comfortable with aircraft-style seats, all facing forwards. We got into Washington Union Station at c.5.45 pm and phoned Pearl Campbell to tell her we had arrived. We caught the Metro to Silver Springs where Bill and Cheryl met us. Cheryl was the Campbell's daughter, quite a bit older than her brother Billy. Pearl had a meal ready for us when we arrived. Later Bill and Sharon Ingleton come over to collect Mam and Dad as they were staying with the Ingletons while we were staying at the Campbells.

On Tuesday, 10th July we did very little beyond working out what we wanted to do during our visit. In the evening we went around to the Phillips's. The next day, Wednesday 11th July, Bill Campbell left me the keys for the Jeep, so we went off to Lake Forest Mall. In the evening Pearl and Kath went off to Rockville to buy a Care Bears pool for the children. In the evening Kath and I went to Dart Drugs to buy audio cassette tapes to use for my audio journal. When we set off Bill warned me that the lights on the Jeep were playing up, although Sharon had used it and had had no trouble. Unfortunately, I did.

Thursday 12th July. Sharon dropped Mam and Dad off at the Campbells on her way to work. She did this each day. The children were playing in the pool. Kath and I went into Gaithersburg to buy stamps at the Post Office. I also bought a set of the Olympic stamps that had been issued that year. At lunchtime Jane Phillips called around and took us off to the swimming pool at the Washingtonion where Janice Henderson worked. I sat out in the sun and got sunburnt.!

On Friday (13thJuly) both Bill and Pearl had taken the day off work to take us to the National Zoo. Alma Ridgeley came over to take some of us in her car. We had taken a picnic and so once we were in the Zoo, we found a picnic table and Mam and Dad elected to stay there and reserve it for us. It was hot. We went off to see the lions, tigers, reptiles, and small mammals, before returning to the picnic table. After lunch we went off again to see the elephants and hippos and zebras and the birds! The thermometer at the Zoo read 98 degrees Fahrenheit. Alma stayed with Mam and Dad. In the evening we went to the Phillips's. Bill took Mam and Dad back to the Ingletons and we drove back to the Campbells.

Saturday (14th July) Loretta Davis came over to take us into Washington to visit the RC Shrine of the Immaculate Conception where we had a guided tour. The mosaic work was amazing. From there we went to the Franciscan Monastery which is laid out to replicate the geography of the Holy Land. The church is typically cruciform in design. In the crypt there was a Nazareth Shrine and a Bethlehem Shrine separated by 'mock' catacombs. At ground level in one of the transepts, there is a Calvary and Rock Tomb with heights and distances replicating those in Jerusalem.

On our way back to Gaithersburg we were going to call at a play park at Wheaton but in the end went to Cabin John where there was a miniature railway, and an amazing playground set out as a Cavalry Fort and an Indian Encampment! The children had a whale of a time. From there we went back to the Davis's for a meal. Thurman was as tall as ever! The meal, burgers, corn, fresh fruit salad, was superb. Bob Kelly called to take me to collect the Pontiac 6000 which I was to be driving the following day.

Sunday (15th July) we went with Kellys to the Eastern Shore on the far side of the Chesapeake Bay via the Bay Bridge, beyond Annapolis, then down to Oxford. After eating sandwiches which Linda had prepared, the like of which I've never seen before, we had a look in the Museum and the Custom House, then caught the ferry to St Michael's where there was a Maritime Museum and a lighthouse which had been moved there from its original location. James A Michener, the novelist who wrote 'Chesapeake', which is a brilliant novel encompassing the history of the region, lived in St Michael. From there we went down to Toman Island where we ate at an hotel. I had a crab meal, no surprises there! The return home was a bit hairy as we hit heavy traffic, some of which was the result of roadworks. I returned the hire car then went home.

Monday (16th July) was the first of our days out with Bill Ingleton. We went to Sugar Loaf Mountain. The views were fabulous, despite the haze. When we returned, we went to a softball game, the church team, the Fairhaven Fouls lost, apparently par for the course! Tuesday 17th July, we set off early, first going to Front Royal where, first of all we cashed some travellers' cheques then bought some film for Kath's camera. We then set off down what's known as the Skyline Drive. We stopped to have some lunch at c.2,500 ft., then drove on to the highest point, 3,600 ft. Finally, about halfway, 60 of the c.120 miles, we stopped just outside Charlottesville to visit Monticello, the home of Thomas Jefferson. We caught the shuttle to the top of the hill (that's what the name of the house actually means) then had a guided tour of the house which was full of quirky innovations. We left c 6.00 pm and got back to the Campbells c.9.00 pm.

On Wednesday (18th July), our 14th Wedding Anniversary, we didn't do much in the morning. At around mid-day we went off to Lake Forest Mall. In the evening Pearl had organised a 'party'. A lot of old friends turned up, and with the food they brought, and the food Pearl had prepared, we had a veritable feast! We had a number of cards, several with promises of crab suppers!

Thursday (19th July). Pearl and Bill had the day off and we went to Baltimore. There was a Greek Naval Ship moored in the port and Kath and the children had a look around on board. I spent some time in the Cokesbury bookstore. The next day I went down to visit Kensington UMC, membership c.1,500, to have a look around as I was taking the service there the next Sunday.

After lunch we met up with the Ingletons. Mam and Dad stayed with Scott while Bill and Sharon took the rest of us with them. We set off, with a bushel of crabs, for the West Virginia mountains to visit a camp owned by Jim, the husband of Bill's sister, Lorraine. It wasn't used as a camp any longer though the cabins were still in situ, each named after a famous hotel. We were in 'Lord Baltimore'. The loos were at the far end of the camp. The men's toilets were named 'Egypt' and the ladies were named 'Siberia' and when you went in there were three loos in a row, no cubicles! On the Saturday evening, we ate the crabs that we had brought with us. Robert was intrigued by our sitting down to a meal with a wooden hammer, rather than a knife and fork, as one of the essential items of cutlery! Afterwards we sat on the porch watching the lightening, like regular Hill Billies!

Next morning was beautiful. We made a picnic lunch and set off for Blackwater Falls then into the Canaan Valley. We walked the Club Run Trail, at the end of which was a beaver's dam. We saw the dam, but, sadly, no beavers. The children enjoyed the Information Centre. We had a beefburger bar-b-q at the camp that evening.

Sunday: we woke to rain which finally eased mid-morning allowing us to go onto the Potomac in one of Jim's boats. Kath and the children went swimming when we got back. Had a lunch of pork chops and baked potatoes. Then we visited a nearby graveyard with c.20 graves, the oldest dating back to the 1728. We then packed up and returned to Gaithersburg.

On Monday (23rd July) went to see Phyllis, the local Travel Agent to find out about making a trip to Florida. Then Bill drove us down towards Washington to visit the Great Falls. First, we went to the Virginian side which gave us the best view. Quite impressive. We then came back to the Maryland side where we saw the Chesapeake and Ohio canal, no longer used, surprisingly not even for leisure craft. Back to Bill and Sharon's for 'tea' then we went to watch another softball game. This time Fairhaven Fouls' won! Glenn and Siri were at the ball game. Siri ignored us and Glenn spoke to Kath in passing.

On Tuesday (24th July) Bill took us to Baltimore to visit Fort MacHenry. It was built in 1798. It saw service in the war of 1812 keeping the British fleet at bay. One of the women in the town had made a Star-Spangled Banner measuring 30 ft. by 24 ft., ironically of British Wool. On the morning of 14th September 1814, it was draped on the fort to signal American victory over the British in the Battle of Baltimore. The sight of the ensign inspired Francis Scott Key to write the poem "Defence of Fort M'Henry" that was later set to the tune "To Anacreon in Heaven" and became known as "The Star Spangled Banner", the national anthem of the United States. We went into the Visitor Centre then on a guided tour around the fort. During World War I the fort was used as a massive military hospital. We picnicked in the grounds then afterwards I asked Bill to take us to Lovely Lane calling at the Cokesbury book shop on the way. The day before I had received a letter from Alan Buck to say that the Adelphic wanted me to buy myself a book from them for my services to the Adelphic! Having bought myself volume 1 of a two-volume work on Wesley I decided to take this opportunity to buy volume 2. This gave Mam and Dad the chance to actually see inside Lovely Lane. Another superb meal at Bill and Sharon's then we watched some of the slides Bill had taken when they were in England.

Wednesday (25th July) we had the day with Pearl. We went to Wheaton Country Park where we had a picnic then to the

National Tram Museum which was interesting though not up to the standard of Crich. Most American trams are single deck. It was Cheryl's birthday and when we got back to the Campbells Bill took us all down to Rockville to a smorgasbord Restaurant – help yourself to what you want, as much as you want – the food was fantastic! Bill paid, $5 a head!

Thursday (26th July I) was going down to Kensington St Paul's UMC to have a dry run through of the slides on "My Methodism" that I was going to be showing at the Sunday morning service. Bill Ingleton was bringing Mam and Dad from Poolesville and he picked us up and ran us down to St Paul's then after I'd run through my slides, we drove to Silver Springs to catch the Metro into Washington where we spent the afternoon in the Air and Space Museum while Bill took Mam and Dad to see the Library of Congress and the Supreme Court. We met them there and caught the Metro back to Silver Springs. The children had an early night. We got changed and went to the Ingletons where we met up with the Bowers and Tom and Barbara Taylor and we all went out for a seafood meal, a 'crab fest', another one of those eat as much as you want kind of places! Glenn and Siri were supposed to be going, it was to be a treat for Glenn's birthday and our wedding anniversary, but they cried off, babysitter problems and a previous commitment, apparently!

(Friday 27th July). I sorted the final order of slides for Sunday. Kath sorted out the washing, then we had a snack lunch of leftovers. Bill and Sharon arrived to take us to stay overnight with Sharon's brother, Buddy, and family in St Mary's County.

We drove down the western shore of the Chesapeake, stopping off at Calvert Cliffs, a nuclear power station. When we arrived, we had a meal then watched some of Buddy's slides of a trip down the Colorado River. We slept in the basement and the children slept in Joshua's room. Joshua was Buddy and Candy's son.

We were awakened by the children at 5.15 am to discover breakfast was underway.

I spent most of the morning, with Buddy, unblocking the downstairs loo! It was nearly lunchtime by the time we got underway. We went down to St Mary's, to the pier. We had a picnic of bagels and cream cheese then sat down to some serious crabbing. A piece of chicken on a line dropped into the water. Robert caught the first one. Those less than five inches had to be thrown back. Those that were kept had to be put in the cool box, which was filled with water to keep them alive. Crabs are cooked alive by dropping them into boiling water. You never cook dead crabs! In all we went home with about fourteen decent sized crabs. When we got back to Buddy's he and I cooked them but only Robert and I ate them, the others couldn't bring themselves to eat crabs that had been boiled alive! We watched a little bit of the Olympic Games opening ceremony before we set off back to Gaithersburg.

On the Sunday morning Pearl came with us to St Paul's, where the children went into Sunday School. There were about four hundred in the congregation and the service seemed to go well and the slides were appreciated. We had the usual refreshments then went back to Pearl's for bacon and eggs for Sunday lunch – we'd missed breakfast! Mam and Dad stayed with the Ingletons. We spent the afternoon wandering around Lake Forest Mall.

On Monday (30th July), Sharon dropped Mam and Dad off, as usual, and we all went down into Washington. We parked at the Tidal basin and then walked across to the Museum of American History. We went back to the Campbells and got ready to go over to Jean and Ed Williams' for dessert. Mam and Dad stayed at Pearl's to babysit.

Dessert was 'Melt in the mouth Blueberry Cake', and it did!

Tuesday (31st July), we went up to Poolesville in the Jeep to collect Mam and Dad from the Ingletons. We then went to Quince Orchard Plaza to have a look around Crown Books. Lunch at MacDonald's then to Lake Forest Shopping Mall. At about 4.30 pm we went to the Phillips's so the children could have some time to play together. The Phillips' gave us dinner. We ate outside and the children caught fireflies. They showed Mam and Dad around the house as they would be staying there after our return from Florida.

Wednesday 1st August, we made another trip into Washington and again parked at the Tidal Basin. We had a picnic lunch there before visiting the Natural History Museum which was, we felt, better than the one in New York. Afterwards Mam and Dad went into the Art Gallery while we made a return visit to the Air and Space Museum. Robert and Elizabeth took to wandering off on their own. We stopped to watch them when they realised we were nowhere in sight. Robert took Elizabeth's hand and they started to look for us. He was being very protective of his little sister! Pearl and Bill met up with us at Air and Space and we all then went down to Hains Point. Basically, we were killing time in order to see Washington by night.

Hains Point is named in memory of Peter Conover Hains, Major General, United States Army, who is buried in Arlington National Cemetery. He designed the Tidal Basin in Washington, D.C., thus solving the drainage problems and foul smell of most of the Washington area marshlands. He was born in 1840 and died in 1921. He attended the United States Military Academy at West Point. Hains Point is located at the southern tip of East Potomac Park between the main branch of the Potomac River and the Washington Channel in southwest Washington, D.C. Hains Point was famously known as the location of a sculpture called *The Awakening*, which was installed at the Point in 1980. (The sculpture was moved to the National Harbour, Maryland development on 19th February 2008.) It portrays a man struggling to emerge from the ground.

Back to the Tidal Basin and had some frankfurters then to F Street to have a look at some shopping which we'd not seen in Washington before. In a small Mall we found a Thornton's toffee cabin! By then it was dark enough to go down the Mall and see

The Capitol, The Washington Monument, The Jefferson Memorial and The Lincoln Memorial all floodlit.

Thursday (2nd August) dawned dull. We had intended to go to a beach near Frederick but decided to go to Washington to visit the National Children's Museum which was experiential! They displayed the traditional Chinese proverb "I hear, and I forget. I see and I remember. I do and I understand." (Confucius) Every display was interactive. The biggest 'exhibit' dealt with communication. The children thoroughly enjoyed the visit, so too did the adults! We intended then to visit the National Geographic Explorers Hall which was next door to the B'nai B'rith Museum which I wanted to visit but time was against us and we went back to the Campbells. The weather really deteriorated, the thunder and lightning, and rain were spectacular.

We got changed when we got back as Kath and I were going over to Marge and John Mapother's. First, we ran Mam and Dad back to Poolesville. The meal at the Mapother's was superb. We had steak. I've never had steak cooked so incredibly rare yet so incredibly tender. "It all depends on the cut of the meat", John told us. There was a Kentucky-style sauce to go with it along with stuffed egg plant followed by a fresh fruit salad. An excellent meal, as always.

Friday (3rd August) Robert and Elizabeth and I went to collect Mam and Dad from Poolesville while Kath finished off the ironing and packing ready to leave the next day to drive down to Florida. We had something to eat in Lake Forest Mall and bought one or two things. The children had an early night and Kath and I went over to the Phillips's where we had something to eat and Jane gave Kath a quilted sewing tidy to hang over an armchair.

On this visit to the States, we planned to visit Disney World. Pearl and Bill, along with Billy, arranged to go with us. Today, Saturday (4th August), was the day we would set off to drive south to Florida. I was up by 6.00 am to collect Mam and Dad from the Ingletons then it was down to National Airport to collect the rental car, an Oldsmobile Cutlass, white with a blue interior, new that June, only 9,000 miles on the clock! The first part of the journey was slow because of traffic and road works, but eventually we got up to speed and drove south through Virginia, North Carolina, into South Carolina where eventually we stopped at a motel called Thunderbird near Lake Marion. The next day we made an early start. I was up at c.6.00 am. We had breakfast then set off again to drive on south through Georgia and into Florida where we were booked into a Days Inn. It had a pool and after we had eaten Kath took the children for a swim.

Monday (6th August) we got up early to make sure we made it to the Magic Kingdom for 9.00 am. We queued for tickets, which didn't take too long, $42 for each adult and $34 for each child. We then caught the monorail to take us to the Magic Kingdom itself. As we entered the Magic Kingdom we were met by Mickey and Minnie and Snow White and one of the Dwarves along with Chip and Dale. Liz was petrified when she saw Mickey. Dad had his photo taken with Snow White. Since Billy was a bit older than our two and wouldn't want to visit some of the rides that ours would want to visit, we decided that the Campbells would do their own thing and we'd meet up again at lunchtime. Bill was wearing the 'Coalville' tee-shirt we given him when they visited us in England. When we met up again, he told us he'd been stopped by someone who had seen his tee-shirt. He told Bill that he used to live in Coalville!

After we split up, we then had a ride on the train that goes right around the park. In Tomorrowland we had a trip around on the people-mover. We had a look in the 'Carousel of Progress' which showed a typical American house in four different periods of history. From there we went by Skyway, a cable car, to Fantasyland. First, we visited 'It's A Small World' which you travel around by boat. Then on to 'Peter Pan's Flight', a kind of flying pirate ship, a small suspended 'gondola', which took us over London by night into Never Never Land. We had hot dogs at one of the eating places then briefly went into Liberty Square in Frontierland to visit 'The Haunted House' before going on several more rides including 'Snow White's Adventure', which was disappointing, and 'Twenty Thousand Leagues Under the Sea', which Elizabeth wasn't keen on. We saw a bit of Donald's birthday Parade in the late afternoon and visited the 'Hall of Presidents'. In the evening we watched the Electric Parade before heading for the monorail and the exit. Dad was most impressed by the efficient way entrance and exit from the park was managed. We got lost driving back to the motel, so it was around midnight before we got to bed.

Next morning, we made it to Epcot by c.10.00 am. The queues were quite long but moved quite quickly. We began in 'Spaceship Earth', which was a fabulous ride that took you through the history of communication, lasting, like most of the rides in Epcot, about thirty minutes. We then visited the 'Universe of Energy' which was a kind of theatre where the cars moved eventually taking you into Brontosaurus Land. Then we went into 'Horizons' which looked into the possibilities of living beneath the oceans and in space. Next the 'World of Motion', which was sponsored by General Motors and looked at the development of transport. Although it was quite good it was, I thought, the poorest of the pavilions.

We had lunch in the Odyssey Restaurant on the border of Future World and World Showcase. We then visited World Showcase starting with a water ride in Mexico before going on to China which featured the Temple of Heaven from the Forbidden City. Then c. 3.30 pm it started to rain. We waited to see if it would ease up but eventually gave up and walked through Germany and Italy to the American Adventure in the rain. Then, after watching the film we walked on, still in the rain, through Japan, France, the UK and Canada back into Future World to meet up with Pearl and Bill and Billy at 7.00 pm to head for the motel and a reasonably early night.

On the Wednesday (8th August) we managed to get up early and made it to Epcot by 9.00 am. We got into the Land Pavilion straight away where we saw something of how food production has developed. It was very interesting. From there we went to the 'Journey of Imagination' where we met Professor Dream Finder and his impish companion Figment, which was a little purple dragon! From there we went to the World Showcase beginning with Canada and their 360-degree cinema presentation. Then to UK, where like in each 'land' we marvelled at the faithful reproduction of authentic details, well mostly – the American phone in the red British phone box was a little out of place! I passed on having a beer in the Rose and Crown, I thought $3.75 a pint was just a bit too much. We had look at Japan before we left Epcot to head over to the Magic Kingdom.

We got there about 2.00 pm and first of all had a hot dog on Main Street USA. We then briefly went into Adventureland to visit the 'Swiss Family Robinson Tree House', before finding a place in the circle outside the Enchanted Castle to watch the afternoon parade properly. It was 102 degrees F! The parade was fabulous. Once it was over, we went back into Adventureland to visit the 'Pirates of the Caribbean' then into Frontierland to visit 'Tom Sawyer's Island'. Kath, Robert, Elizabeth and Billy then went off to Big Thunder Mountain Railroad. I went with Mam and Dad to have a ride on the Paddle Boat. We met up with the others in Liberty Square and then Kath took the children into Tomorrowland as Billy wanted to go to Space Mountain. We agreed to meet back in Main Street at no later than 7.00 pm. In fact it was 10.15 pm by the time we finally met up. Robert had not enjoyed Space Mountain, so Kath took them to the racing car circuit. They finally got back by c.8.15 pm but missed us so Mam and Dad and I stayed put and had a grandstand view of the Electric Parade and the Fireworks. When we did meet up, we found we'd been standing on opposite sides of the street for the Parade! We got onto the monorail to go back to the Car Park. That was interesting as there were no lights inside the compartments.

Next day we breakfasted in our rooms while Bill took the children down to breakfast in the restaurant as we were entitled to a free breakfast as part of the deal! We then set off first of all to find Windermere Among the Lakes which took a bit of finding. I bought myself a t-shirt. We then headed east to the Kennedy Space Centre and Cape Canaveral. We got there at c.2.00 pm. We would have liked to take a conducted tour which lasted around two hours but since the next one wasn't until 4.00 pm, we simply had a look around on our own. We had a picnic lunch and set off at c. 2,45 pm and headed north through Florida, Georgia and into South Carolina stopping at a MacDonald's to eat at c.10.00 pm. We got to the Motel, the same one we had stayed in on the way south, at about midnight.

On the Friday, (10th August) we left after breakfast at c. 9.00 am. The weather was poor. We stopped for a picnic lunch before pressing on to Gaithersburg. We arrived

at about 8.00 pm. After we unpacked, I returned the car to National Airport. Bill followed to bring me back. We then took Mam and Dad around to Bill and Jane's. They were packing to go off on holiday so we said our farewells as they wouldn't be back before we left to return to the UK.

Saturday (11th August) Kath caught up on the washing. We then went around to the Phillips's where we made ourselves something to eat, leaving Pearl and Bill to have a bit of peace and quiet. In the evening we all went back to the Campbells. I finally got in touch with Oaks Chapel where I was due to preach on the Sunday. It had a membership of c.140 and an average congregation of c.40. The offertory was $580! The service went well, and the folk were lovely. Back to Pearl's and on to the Holman family picnic which turned out to be the Rich family picnic. Again, the food was fabulous and plentiful. In the evening we went to see Cheryl's new house in Montgomery Village. In the process of clearing out her room at her mum and dad's she had bagged up a load of soft toys for our two to take home with them!

On Monday (13th August), we woke reasonably early, went around to pick up Mam and Dad, and went out to find a Christian bookshop for Kath to buy a copy of Kid's Praise. We had a hotdog lunch then to Lake Forest Mall for some last-minute shopping.

On Tuesday we took the children to the Phillips. Kath and Pearl went off to K Mart and Sears. Kath bought a pillow to embroider. They got back about 4.00 pm. We had been intending to go out with Scott, but the weather was threatening so we postponed our trip until the Wednesday. He took us down into Washington where we visited the National Geographic Explorers Hall which proved to be very interesting. I finished, as usual, ahead of the others so went one block up the street to visit the B'nai B'rith Museum which was well worth the visit. There was an exhibit on Danish Jews during World War II. From there we went to Ford's Theatre where Abraham Lincoln was assassinated. While the others went back to the car, I briefly went into the Museum of Natural History bookshop to buy a book on the Holocaust.

Scott returned us to the Campbells. We then went around to the Phillips's where we had a salad tea. Back at the Campbells we put the children to bed, and I went around to the Crown

Bookstore where I bought a book on Judaism which I had put off buying until I had visited the B'nai B'rith Museum.

Thursday (16th August) Scott called for us at 9.00 am and took us to Frederick, an historic little town not too far away. We followed the town trail, which was interesting though lacking in actual buildings, so it was mostly "the site of..."! What was most fascinating was the Opera House where the town fathers had signed a ransom during the Civil War. The building had been demolished and turned into a parking lot, but a sign had been erected explaining its significance! We then went to see the home of Barbara Fritchie (1766–1862), a central figure in the history of Frederick, Maryland. A Unionist during the Civil War, she is best known for her folkloric defiance in the face of Confederate troops. As the occupying rebel forces were marching out of Frederick in September 1862, Dame Fritchie, then 95, was said to have waved a Union flag from her upstairs window. Her fabled act of heroism was immortalized in an 1863 poem by John Greenleaf Whittier.

We had lunch in a pizza place in the Frederick Mall, which was a little way out of the town. Scott had a whole pizza, all six slices. We shared a pizza, six slices, one slice each! We then drove to the other side of the town to a visit a mansion that was being turned into a Children's Museum. It was very good. The children had the opportunity to comb out and spin wool, to sew part of a quilt and do some weaving on a loom. Outside, in the garden, they were introduced to various herbs and visited a replica pioneer wood cabin. Then it was back to the Ingletons for a 'Thanksgiving' dinner with ham rather than turkey. Another fabulous meal. The rest of the evening was spent looking at some of the slides Bill had taken when he was in England.

Friday (17th August) Kath had a laundry morning at the Campbells while I took the children round to the Phillips's. We came back to the Campbells for lunch, Spaghetti Bolognese. We left the children playing with the Ridenour children. The Ridenours lived just down the road from the Phillips'. We returned to the Phillips's and were joined a little later by Pearl and Bill then we all went to Carolyn and Harry Ridenours for our evening meal. Thoroughly good evening.

Saturday (18th August) Pearl was back at work on Friday and Saturday. We went around to the Phillip's and Paul Ridenour came to play with our two, stayed for lunch then took Robert and Elizabeth back to his house, so Carolyn had them for the rest of the afternoon. Mam and Dad had a walk while Kath went to collect our two and stayed awhile talking to Carolyn. We had some tea then it was back to the Campbells where we watched the video Bill had taken when we were in Disney World.

Sunday (19th August) Dad phoned to say they were not going to church as Mam's foot was playing up. We went and heard Glenn preach on 'The Joy of the Kingdom' though it would probably have been better entitled 'The Call to Commitment'! Mam stayed at the Phillip's as she had a bit of an upset tummy, but Dad came back with me to the Campbells for lunch. Kath made us a salad sandwich for lunch. Billy then took our two down to the park while Kath and Pearl went off to do a bit of shopping, including buying some Kool Aid to take home with us. Collected Mam and brought her back for our evening meal.

Monday (20th August) Kath was up early to go to work at the Montgomery County Fair. (She brought me some crab cakes back with her. Bless her!) We went around to the Phillip's where we had lunch. I came back to meet with Kath and Pearl, and we went shopping. I went to collect the children, but they insisted on staying so I came back alone to have dinner and collected them later.

Tuesday (21st August) we all went to the Fair. We each took an exhibitor's pass to get us in free, otherwise it would have cost us $2 for parking and $3 per person. We began by looking around the livestock exhibits, then on to the arts and crafts exhibits in three halls, before we went to have lunch in the Fairhaven Booth – I had a crab cake! Kath went in to work for a bit and the rest of us went to look around the Fairground attractions for the children. We set off to return to the Fairhaven Booth. Meanwhile Kath and Pearl had left to find us. They had stopped off at the Ladies when a call came over the tannoy asking them to return to the Fairhaven Booth. When they got there Glenn rushed in and asked to search Kath's bag where he found a plastic carrier bag stuffed with money which we later heard was c.$1,200! Whoever was looking after it had stuffed it into Kath's bag by mistake. The bag it should have been put in was identical! After the Fair we went back to the Campbells, took Mam and Dad back to the Phillips's and then went around to the Kelly's. More crab cakes! After the meal Bob showed us some slides at a rapid pace, accompanied by a commentary from Linda comprising mainly of the phrase "Move it, Bob"! It was a good evening.

Wednesday (22nd August) we went round to the Phillips's as usual and Robert went off to the Ridenours to play with Paul. We spent the afternoon there, then it was back the Campbells for dinner.

Thursday (23rd August) Scott took us to lunch at MacDonald's before he went off to help at the Fair. We spent the afternoon at the Campbells until Sharon called to take us to Poolesville for a 'cook-out'! Scott ran us back to the Campbells. Before we left the Ingletons gave us gifts, a book on lap quilting for Kath, a book on the National Parks of the West Coast, and a book on Washington for Mam and Dad.

Friday (24th August) First to the Phillip's where we had lunch then we ran down to Bethesda Naval Hospital, where Pearl Campbell worked. She was just coming off duty, so she showed us around. In the evening we went off to the Prasad's where I had four helpings of Vicky's chicken curry! As well as the Campbells and the Fishers we were joined by Betty and Richard Rudisill. Another pleasant evening.

Saturday (25th August) we went off to visit Greenbriar National Park, taking a picnic lunch. In the centre is a lake around which is an artificially created sandy beach and in the surrounding trees are dozens of picnic tables and grills. The children had a whale of a time. I was sent to find them when lunch was ready. At first, I couldn't see them anywhere. It was only when I reminded myself that I was looking for a white girl and boy and a black boy that I spotted them! After lunch the children went into the lake to swim. We left c.4.00 pm and I took Mam and Dad to the Phillip's then took the children down to the play park for a good hour.

On Sunday (26th August) I preached at Fairhaven, sharing the service with Glenn. A super service. A lot of people turned up, much to Glenn's amazement! The church was virtually full. The Gospel Choir sang, 'The Lord is my light', at my request, and I told the children the story of 'the hare on the moon' and preached on Acts 2:42 where the early church is described as a community that "devoted themselves to the apostles' teaching and fellowship, to the breaking of bread and the prayers."

The Hare on the Moon

In the west children are told about the 'man in the moon' but in the east they are told the story of 'the hare on the moon'

There were four friends who lived together in the forest. A hare, a monkey, a jackal and an otter. Together they resolved on the next holy day to perform an act of selfless generosity. The otter found seven red fishes abandoned on the bank of the river. The jackal helped himself to a lizard and a pot of yoghurt from somebody's apparently abandoned house. The monkey brought a bunch of mangoes. All these three were willing to offer their gifts to some beggar as act of charity. But the hare, failing to find anything appropriate decided to offer himself.

When they came across a wandering beggar, in turn they, reluctantly offered the food they had acquired, and each offer was declined. When it was the hare's turn. His offer was accepted. The beggar collected wood and kindled a fire. The hare leapt into the flames. However, the flames did not burn him and as he looked out from the fire the beggar seemed to grow and grow and grow until he was able to break off the top of a nearby mountain. With it he reached into the heavens and drew on the face of the moon an image of the hare to acknowledge the amazing generosity of his self-sacrifice.

[A Buddhist story from the Jataka Tales]

After the service we had 'brunch' back at the Campbells. Quite a number of the Gospel Choir came, and other friends turned up. I had quite a chat with Geoff Kaiser who was born in Hartlepool and had spent a year in Durham. He was a Methodist Local Preacher when he lived in the UK and still preached occasionally.

When everyone had finally gone Kath and Pearl and I went shopping. They bought Elizabeth a pair of pink slippers. They'd bought Robert some earlier, with a bear's head at each toe end. At c.6.00 pm, after we had taken Mam and Dad back to the Phillips's, Pearl and Bill took us to the Harlequin Dinner Theatre. We had drinks before the show. They came in glass Texan boots that you could take away with you when you left, which we did. The show, which began at 8.30 pm, 'The

Best Little Whorehouse in Texas', was a musical based on the 'Chicken Ranch' which was closed down only about a year earlier. The food, buffet style, was served during an extended interval. It was a wonderful evening.

Monday (27th August) I took Robert around to play with Paul Ridenour while Kath and Elizabeth went off swimming with Terry Cremens. And that was it. It had been a fabulous summer vacation. One we would look back on fondly. But 'all good things come to an end'. It was time to go home. One of Elizabeth's tee shirts proclaimed, "Maryland is for Crabs" and Maryland's crabs we would long remember – on this trip we not only ate them (the recollection of several crab dinners we would long savour) but caught them and cooked them as well!

Disney World was everything people had told us it would be. I would often recall how my shoulders aching from carrying Elizabeth so she had a grandstand view of the Electric Parade, bouncing up and down shouting "Mickey Mouse, Mickey Mouse." with such innocent enthusiasm that our eyes would fill up at the recollection. As for the dinosaurs in one of the Epcot features, if he 'd seen nothing else, that would have sufficed for Robert. What is it about prehistory that so fascinates the young? Perhaps Disney World is for kids but given how much my parents enjoyed themselves there it is possible that there is such a thing as 'second childhood'!

We left Newark on the Tuesday (8th August). Finally settled back in Coalville Robert (Jnr.) began with a rash on his legs on the Thursday. The following Tuesday Elizabeth's rash began to develop, and Robert's had blistered and burst. Visits to the doctors caused them consternation but a phone call to the States and a visit to the hospital confirmed it – Poison Ivy – unknown in the U.K. Fortunately, it did not take too long to clear up although it was one souvenir we could well have done without. Robert's discomfort was more than compensated for by the attention he received at the hospital, with all and sundry being called in to see what a Poison Ivy rash looked like, and having his legs photographed from all angles!

Kendal

[1984-2001]

I took up my new post as Head of Religious Studies at the Lakes School in Windermere in September 1984. The school was quite a contrast to King Edward VII College. The pupils wore uniform, there was good discipline and Religious Studies had a fair share of the timetable, in fact it was compulsory up to the end of the fifth form (Year 11). Everyone was expected to take it as an exam subject, three periods a week, leading to either a GCE or a CSE. There were also two good Sixth Form 'A t level groups. Sixteen students had chosen 'A' level RE that year! At 'A' level they studied Hinduism and Philosophy of Religion. The department was big enough to warrant a full-time assistant. It was also nice to be in an eleven to eighteen school again.

The sale of our house in Coalville had fallen through and we hadn't yet purchased anything in the Lakes. It meant I had to find temporary accommodation. I ended up living in the home of Colin and Jean Tolson. They ran a 'Bed and Breakfast' establishment in Windermere. Colin was the organist at Windermere Methodist Church. He was a very accomplished organist but quickly made it clear that he was an atheist and had no interest in religion whatsoever! I stayed there from Monday to Thursday, returning to Coalville on Friday after school, setting out to return to the Lakes early on Monday morning, a commute of 165 miles each way.

I had no problem with taking on the Hinduism course, which I had taught previously in Coalville, and Hinduism had been one of my final year's units in my degree course. Philosophy of Religion, however, was never one of my favourite subjects, especially the teaching of it. That was one reason why I opted to introduce Judaism at 'A' level at King Edward VII. Anyway, there was a series on TV, late on a Sunday night, that had a relevance to the Philosophy of Religion course. One programme in particular, dealing with re-incarnation, looked very promising so I set the timer to record it. On the Monday I retrieved the video tape before I left very early to drive back to the Lakes. My first lesson was an 'A' level Philosophy of Religion group and the material on the tape was directly relevant. Imagine my dismay when the programme stopped part way through – I hadn't set the timer to end at the correct time!

When Peter Kindleysides heard that I was taking up a post at the Lakes School he invited me to call on his eldest daughter, Angela, who was training as a doctor and who was currently on placement at Barrow-in-Furness General Hospital. So, on two or three occasions during my first term, living as I was in Bed and Breakfast accommodation, I took the opportunity to drive down to Barrow after school to visit Angela and have a meal with her in the small terraced house where she was living.

Ken Oldfield, my predecessor at the Lakes School tried to persuade me to buy their house, a bungalow on the outskirts of Kendal. Financially, however, it was more than we could afford. He was a Methodist Local Preacher. Before I started at the Lakes School, I asked him how many of the staff were Christians. He thought for a moment, and then told me there were no more than three. Within the first two weeks no less than a dozen had spoken to me and told me about the churches they regularly attended! Ken had been on VSO in India which was why he taught Hinduism at 'A' level. Because of his contacts he had been able to arrange to take a group of 'A' level students to visit India every couple of years. He was moving on to a lecturing post in a College in the south of England. Everyone was shocked when, only a couple of years after he left, we received the news that he had taken his own life.

After I was appointed, I discovered that Kendal was the thirty-ninth most expensive place in the UK for house prices. The first thirty-eight were in and around London, and the fortieth was Aberdeen! That first term much of my spare time was spent house hunting. We didn't want to buy in the Lakes itself both because of the cost, and the hassle of driving in, or out, every time you wanted to go anywhere, especially during the tourist season. Eventually I found a house on the riverside, on the southern edge the town centre. Kath wasn't keen at first. She was put off by the several inches of pigeon shit on the top front step! The house was a three-story end-of-terrace with two basements, in one of which was an old fruit machine. In short it was in a shocking state. It was empty and had been for some time. There was neither wash basin nor sink unit. It had been owned by an Irish builder (sorry about the implied stereotype, but...) He had stripped out all of the period features and removed various internal walls so that when you went through the front door you could see right through to the back of the kitchen, with the stairs going straight up from the resulting 'through lounge'. It also had a leaky roof. But potentially it was fantastic.

The most important factor, however, was that we could afford it! The sale was in the hands of the Courts as part of a divorce settlement because the husband had proved to be untraceable. We appointed Tom Bailey of Bailey, Wain and Curzon, in Fenton, as our solicitor. I'm not sure now how I came to get in touch with him, but I think he had met my dad at a meeting of the Regnal League at my parent's church in Cullercoats. The vendors kept trying to up the price, but Tom was determined we should avoid paying Stamp Duty so in the end we paid £250 for the TV ariel which satisfied the vendors and kept us within the limit for avoiding Stamp Duty. We had anticipated a completion by the second week in December but, sadly, our purchasers had been let down and we had to put our Coalville house back on the market. To complicate matters further we had to complete on the purchase of the Kendal house quickly or risk losing it. A bridging loan was inevitable, although the cost was, in part, met by my not having to pay for Bed and Breakfast.

Kath had tendered her resignation in the light of a likely December move. Fortunately, she was offered her old job back on a temporary contract, at least until Easter. Since September she was kept busy packing up, so efficiently that the Christmas decorations had been boxed-up and taken by me to the Lakes on one of my weekend 'mini removal of boxes' to the attic room of the manse in Ambleside. The Rev'd Bob White, superintendent minister of the Ambleside and Windermere Circuit, had kindly offered his empty attic rooms for temporary storage and one of my students, Ian Thompson, known as Cleo for some reason, helped carrying them up, and later, down the stairs. Kath also had the added responsibility of a lodger, Lisa Davis, one of my Sixth Formers from Coalville, whose parents, sadly, had split up. In the end Lisa's presence proved a godsend since we were able to leave her to look after the Coalville house, and the dog, when we began camping out in the Kendal house.

Elizabeth had continued with her gymnastics and ballet during the year before the family moved. She was so enthusiastic about ballet that she would not let matters rest until she had all the gear. At school she made good progress again and was looking forward to her part in the Nativity play. Her reading had come on apace and she left me standing on some computer adventure games.

Robert finally found something to be enthusiastic about! He joined the Cubs. He was proud of his uniform and was always ready long before it was time to go. He even polished his shoes without being told to do so. He was delighted when he was invested and couldn't wait for his Mum to sew on all his badges. At school he also continued to progress well and enthusiastically rehearsed for his lead role as Hansel in the school pantomime production of Hansel and Gretel.

When I first arrived in the Cumbria District, I had a conversation with the Rev'd Norman Pickering who was the Chair of the Cumbria District and who, as it happened, lived in Windermere. The normal pattern in Methodism was for 'Ministers in Other Appointments' (I'm not sure now why or when the designation was changed from 'Sector Minister') to be stationed in the Circuit in which they resided. Since we were going to be moving into Kendal that would have been the Kendal Circuit. However, that Circuit had 11 churches with 3 ministers plus c.10 supernumerary ministers, many of whom were still preaching, and c.28 Local Preachers, most of whom were active. By contrast the Ambleside and Windermere Circuit, had five churches, just one minister, one retired deaconess and three active Local Preachers. So, I asked Norman if, instead of being stationed in the Kendal Circuit where I would be residing, I could be stationed in the Ambleside and Windermere Circuit, where I would be working. He agreed.

Given that my appointment was in the education sector Norman asked me to serve as the District representative on the Connexional Schools Committee. This entailed one trip each year to London for the Committee meeting, travel expenses paid. Kath and the children often came with me. We went by train and we made a day of it. What was also nice about it was the fact that I met up again with John Kidd, Joe Kidd's eldest son, who was the representative from the Darlington District.

[1985]

We began 'camping out' in our new house in the middle of January. The main bedroom on the first floor served as lounge, dining room and kitchen, water being carried by the bucketful from the top bathroom wherein resided an ancient Victorian cast iron bath. At night the room also doubled-up as a bedroom far Kath and I, the children 'camping' in the next-door bedroom! Yes, camping is the right word; we slept on camp beds for nearly three months until the completion of the sale of our house in Coalville allowed us to move our furniture here at the end of March. For cooking and heating we relied on calor gas camping stoves, although to be fair we found a good plumber who managed to get the central heating working fairly soon after we moved in.

We set to work with a vengeance. The first weekend after we moved, we began demolishing walls on the top floor to create a smaller bathroom and a larger bedroom by moving one wall about a metre. Then we almost doubled the size of the little bedroom on that floor by moving the landing wall and incorporating a large landing cupboard to make a good-sized study for me.

It was the ground floor to which we next turned our attention. The previous owner had pulled down all the walls to make a huge, and somewhat strangely shaped, lounge. We put the walls back up to make a passage, lounge and dining room, not quite on the original wall lines, but very much to suit ourselves. Then it was back up to the first floor and the large front bedroom which we divided into two and a bit to make a bedroom for Elizabeth, a bedroom for Robert, and a toilet.

I was very fortunate to have a lot of help from a couple of colleagues from school. Alf Henderson, who taught woodwork, came over more times than I care to count to help erect stud walls both upstairs and down. Each stud wall we put in was filled with fibreglass for insulation and soundproofing. We found a superb plasterer who was happy to come when needed. He spent many, many hours plastering the walls we had erected. Hugh Wright, who was the drama teacher, and into woodworking as his hobby, turned several newel post knobs to replace those that were missing on the staircases.

One Saturday, early on, I was off at Synod and Alf had come over to carry on with the work of erecting walls. The doorbell rang and Kath went to answer. On the doorstep stood a big burly Irishman who was clearly very angry. Kath persuaded Alf to go to the door. Alf was barely five feet tall and very wiry! The man at the door demanded to know why he couldn't get into 'his' house. Virtually the first thing we had done after we moved in was to change all the door locks. Alf explained that it was no longer his house, the courts having been unable to trace him had sold it to us. He grudgingly accepted Alf's explanation, but insisted that he collect his fruit machine from the back cellar, which was fine by us as we wanted to see the back of it.

Whilst all this was going on the plumber came, from time to time, first to plumb in a new bathroom suite in the top bathroom, and then vanity units in the children's bedrooms and then to supply and re-site new radiators for the central heating system to match the size to the rooms. As well as a Victorian bath in the top bathroom there was a new blue loo and matching washbasin, although this latter was lying in the back cellar. We couldn't get a bath to match the loo and washbasin. We managed to purchase the necessary bathroom fittings from a factory outlet at Carnforth: a corner bath, washbasin and toilet, for the top bathroom and the basins for the vanity units. In the corner of the bathroom the old tanks were removed, and I set about fitting the alcove out as a shower unit, tiling it out and fitting a glass door. Between the bathroom and what was to become our bedroom we fitted a sliding door, making the bathroom accessible from both the landing and our bedroom.

For a house that was supposedly rewired there was an amazing lack of plug sockets and light fittings. With help from an electrician friend from church, I was often to be found scabbling about under floorboards and behind walls, effectively rewiring the whole house from top to bottom. Only one plug socket in the kitchen – I ask you? By the end of 1985 only the ground floor ring main was left to do. I don't pretend to understand much about electricity, but the system was clearly inadequate. It transpired that instead of one, or more, ring mains, our Irish builder had wired everything in sequence (I think that is the correct term) which meant that as more things were switched on the lights would gradually dim! As the electrician observed it might be suitable for a brothel but not a family home!

We were duly wood-wormed in March, fortunately, just before all the furniture arrived and in June the whole of the front elevation of the roof was replaced at considerable expense. Once these jobs were finished it was possible to begin to make the house habitable, at last. The study was decorated, fitted out with shelves and study furniture, and boxes of books began, thankfully, to disappear. I had gradually been bringing over the boxes I had temporarily stored in the attics of the manse in Ambleside. Then the top bedroom was tackled, a new bedroom suite purchased, from M.F.I. – over a period of many weeks because of items not being in stock, or damaged. We then moved down to Robert's bedroom. Once that was finished, we began in Elizabeth's bedroom. The large front bedroom on the first floor, where we had 'camped' when we first moved in, had two windows so we were able to erect a stud wall and divide it in two for the children's bedrooms. In fact, the only room we didn't alter was the back bedroom on the first floor which the children used as their bedroom until their new rooms were finished.

When we came down from our top floor bedroom we were faced with the doors to the children's rooms. Eventually we got so fed up with Robert leaving his door open so we could see into the tip he called a bedroom that I changed the position of his door. We utilised the 'blue loo' from the top bathroom to create a toilet on the first floor between the back bedroom and Elizabeth's front bedroom. The blue washbasin we fitted in the back bedroom. Instead of facing the stairs Robert's door now faced the first-floor toilet with the doorway to Elizabeth's room on the right!

Having put up walls downstairs to create a passage, lounge and dining room, we then began the task or renewing the skirting board, putting up dado and picture rails and cornice. We also built cupboards into the alcoves and put in a new fire surround. The modern 4 inch skirting the previous owner had used looked totally out of place given the height of a Victorian room. It had to be replaced! The chimney wall had to be replastered as it ran out of true by about two inches from bottom left to top right!

We made good progress during that first year, but the kitchen remained to be tackled, although with a sink unit, cooker, fridge and some units fitted it was a considerable improvement on the four bare plaster walls and two free-standing taps, almost at ground level, which greeted us on our arrival. The kitchen units were given to us by a church member who was having a new kitchen fitted. They weren't brilliant but would serve until we could afford a new kitchen of our own. The downstairs bathroom, basements, and garage were virtually untouched. But then 'Rome wasn't built in a day'!

Not least, because of the amount of work being done on the house, I had two 'dos' with my back. The first beginning just before Easter resulting in five weeks off work at the end of the summer term. This meant I missed out on my first School Activity Week when, with several other colleagues I should have been accompanying a group to visit Wuppertal in Germany. The second 'do' was in the autumn term, though this time I had the sense to stay off school and stay flat on my back so I was only off work for a couple of weeks. I should have known better. When I tore the muscle in my back when I was working on the bins during a summer vacation at Hartley, I was warned that it would always be a weakness and that it could recur again, as indeed it did when we were living in Coalville.

Kath' s year had its frustrations. Just a matter of days before the Spring term began, she was fortunate enough to obtain a two-term temporary teaching post at St Mark's Church of England Primary School in Natland, a village just outside Kendal. Robert and Elizabeth were duly enrolled there, and Kath and the children settled down to two very happy terms. Sadly, her contract was not made permanent so whilst the children continued to attend St Mark's Kath re-joined the ranks of the unemployed with occasional supply teaching thrown in to relieve the tedium. She applied for, and was interviewed for, a number of posts but with no success.

The children settled in well to their new environment. Robert immediately joined a local Cub pack and obtained his one-year star and his bronze arrow, much to his delight. He also stayed after school one evening each week to take part in a gymnastics class. Elizabeth quickly found a ballet class to attend although, sadly, this came to an end with the marriage of the ballet teacher. Like Robert she too remained at school one evening each week to attend a gymnastics class; this she thoroughly enjoyed. Her lack of ballet lessons was more than compensated for by the fact that in the autumn she joined the Brownies and to her delight was soon enrolled and therefore allowed to, officially, wear her uniform.

Since my predecessor at the Lakes School had regularly taken his 'A' level students to visit India I felt the need to do something similar. India was out since I didn't have the contacts Ken had had. So, since I had replaced the Philosophy of Religion course with a course on Judaism, I decided to arrange a trip to Israel. There were several Tour Operators offering to organise trips to Israel, and I chose one that was headed up by an Anglican priest based in Bristol. I did not want to organise a traditional Christian Pilgrimage since the main focus was Judaism, although we clearly could not visit Israel without visiting the main Christian sites. The Tour Operator offered one free place for every ten booked so I opened it up anyone who might be interested. The result was a party made up of some sixth-form students, some colleagues and ex-colleagues, my Auntie Ruth and her friend (who was my cousin John's mother-in-law), along with others the Tour Operator had added, including a Roman Catholic priest and a Pentecostal couple. The whole party worked together superbly. Since we had more than 20 people in total Kath came with me and we left Robert and Elizabeth in my parents' capable hands.

The weather was predictably fantastic, 90-1000F, and brilliant sunshine. That resulted in one or two of us suffering quite nasty sunburn! We stayed in a two-star hotel on the Mount of Olives. It was very basic. In our room we had one bed that had a mattress like a hammock and one that had a mattress like a board! In the evenings we walked along to the nearby five-star hotel to enjoy a drink in their lounge. This, our first trip to Israel, impressed us, despite the fact that it was occasionally spoiled because of the country's, understandable, desire to cater for large numbers of pilgrims/tourists! We swam in the Dead Sea on our day trip to Masada. Masada itself was very impressive, needless to say we chose to ascend via the cable car rather than walk up the snake path! Kath and I attended the Sunday morning service at the Garden Tomb. The service was only marred by what we considered to be a most unexciting choice of hymns, our least favourite ones, but that was quite insignificant compared to the experience of worshipping there.

The Garden Tomb was unearthed in 1867 and is considered by some Protestants to be the site of the burial and resurrection of Jesus. The tomb has been dated by Israeli archaeologist Gabriel Barkay to the 8th–7th centuries BCE. The organisation maintaining the Garden Tomb refrains from claiming that this is the authentic tomb of Jesus, while pointing out the similarities with the site described in the Bible. It is adjacent to a rocky escarpment which since the mid-nineteenth century has been proposed by some scholars to be Golgotha. It has since been known as Skull Hill or Gordon's Calvary after Major-General Charles Gordon visited Jerusalem in 1883 and became an enthusiastic supporter of the site as being the site of the Easter events. It is not difficult to see why. Since at least the fourth century CE the traditional site where the death and resurrection of Christ are believed to have occurred is within the Church of the Holy Sepulchre. That may well be true, but centuries of building over that site make it difficult to envisage it as being where the events took place. Whereas in The Garden Tomb it is easy to see how the events of that first Easter may have unfolded. The only distraction being the siting of Jerusalem's Bus Station at the foot of Skull Hill!

When we visited the Dormition Abbey near the supposed site

of the Last Supper the Pentecostal couple refused to enter as the floor was made up of a magnificent mosaic showing the signs of the zodiac! I'm not sure that my auntie Ruth's friendship with cousin John's mother-in-law survived the visit to Israel. Apart from the fact that she nearly set fire to their room by placing one of those heating elements used for making cups of tea on a newspaper whilst it was still switched on, setting the paper alight, she also almost caused us to miss our flight home. She was determined to get all the duty free to which she was entitled, and by the time she had finished our flight had boarded and was ready for take-off while Kath and I were still in the Departure Lounge trying to hurry her along!

All in all, the visit to Israel was a success. It also proved to be the highlight of the children's year since the fact that Mum and Dad went away on holiday without them meant that they spent ten days at my parents at Whitley Bay and thoroughly enjoyed themselves. No doubt they were spoiled rotten!

When we first moved to Kendal, we made a point of visiting Stricklandgate Methodist Church which was at the other end of the main street to our house. It was around Easter time and Alan and Freda Buck, friends from Coalville, had come to visit. We were made welcome. The minister was preaching, and it proved to be a most unhelpful service and sermon during which he asserted that "If I got into a spaceship and was fired off into space, I would eventually arrive in a place called heaven"! It thoroughly depressed Freda and we resolved that it was not the church for us. It turned out that the minister was relatively new. However, he applied for a curtailment that same year.

Thankfully his successor, the Revd Ian Mason, was a very different character altogether. Meanwhile we finally settled on the local evangelical Anglican Church, St Thomas's, which was just across the road from Sticklandgate Methodist Church. Trailing the family into the Ambleside Circuit when I was preaching there most Sundays was alright during the summer when we could take a picnic with us, but the children were missing out on having a fixed base. Elizabeth joined Explorers at St. Thomas's and Robert initially hovered between going out with his sister and staying in with his mum. Eventually he chose the former.

[1986 – This letter is missing!]

The absence of the 1986 letter as my aide memoire provides the opportunity to recall a couple of school matters that involved me almost from the outset. My predecessor at the Lakes School, Ken Oldfield, had been a member of SACRE and the two Examination boards the school used for CSE and GCE 'O' and 'A' level RE – NEAB and JMB.

SACRE, the Standing Advisory Council on Religious Education, was well-established in Cumbria long before I arrived on the scene. It was charged with overseeing the provision of religious education in the Local Authority, including the revision of the locally Agreed Syllabus. Many Local Authorities did not have SACREs until, with the advent of new legislation in 1988 regarding the establishment of a National Curriculum, SACREs became mandatory since RE, although it was part of the Basic

Curriculum, was subject to locally Agreed Syllabuses. SACRE usually met three or four times a year and, in Cumbria, was made up of RE enthusiasts. We often had a guest speaker; on one occasion we were addressed by Rabbi Hugo Grin, who as a child, had survived Auschwitz. It was a real privilege to meet him. With the requirements of the 1988 Act the structure of the Cumbria SACRE changed as it had to meet the requirement of having four, representative, groups. I felt that the tenor of our meetings changed for the worse, as we were more formally meeting as a Committee! During my time we oversaw two new Agreed Syllabuses, including a Syllabus for Years 12 and 13. I contributed to the final product in each case. We also tried, unsuccessfully, to produce a new 'A' level syllabus.

When I arrived at the Lakes School, we were still in the days of CSEs (Certificate of Secondary Education) and 'O' and 'A' level GCEs (General Certificate of Education). It would not be many years before the exams set at Fifth Form level would be merged into GCSEs! Ken had set up a 'Mode 3' CSE, which was a school-based syllabus and exam. This entailed him being a member of NEAB (Northern Examinations and Assessment Board) which met at Westerhope, just outside Newcastle. I inherited his place. We met each year to consider the questions set for that year's exams. It was strange driving to a meeting past a cemetery where my grandparents were buried and a shop which my father, as manager, had opened as a new Co-op in the 1930s!

JMB (Joint Matriculation Board) was based in Manchester. I served on the panel that met each year to consider the questions set for that year's 'A' level exams. It usually met over a couple of days as we had questions for around ten syllabuses to consider, including each major world faith as well as those relating to the Philosophy of Religion, Ethics as well as the traditional Old Testament and New Testament papers. My particular interest, of course, was in Hinduism and Judaism. The two days at JMB were always interesting. Sometimes a question was accepted without debate, at other times it could take up to half an hour to be satisfied that we had the correct wording to elicit the kind of answer the examiner was looking for. 'Context' and 'Modern Relevance' were our watchwords. On one occasion I recall having a heated debate with the newly appointed Judaism examiner who insisted on beginning his question with reference to "foot festivals". It was a phrase I had never come across and one I knew would defeat my students. Eventually he agreed to replace it with the term "pilgrim festivals"! It was never easy to complete the syllabus knowing what questions were going to appear on the exam paper!

I think this was probably the year when Kath was successful in obtaining a teaching post at Heversham C of E Primary School. Transport was a potential problem. If I recall correctly my dad 'loaned' his Ford Escort to Kath to initially resolve the problem. Sometime later he bought an FSO, a Polish version of a Fiat and the Escort became Kath's, by default.

The house still took up a significant portion of our 'free' time. Shortly after we had finished putting up the various stud walls, when I was out, a guy called at the house offering several rolls of carpets for sale, the kind used in exhibitions. It was a cash only deal and Kath eventually agreed to be taken to the nearest cash till to withdraw the necessary funds. I arrived home to find several rolls of this carpet cluttering up the hallway! Cut up and joined together they served quite well as floor coverings until we could afford something better. We did eventually find a carpet fitter who was good at obtaining roll ends of top-quality carpets at incredibly reduced prices. He was able to 'invisibly' join together the pieces he obtained enabling us eventually to have fitted carpets in every room in the house.

The garage doors were, literally, falling off so one of the first things we did, when we had managed to get a semblance of order in the house by erecting stud walls, was to replace them with an up-and-over garage door. Cleo, and Robert, helped to lay slabs on the short drive. Cleo's Dad, who, apart from running an antique shop in Bowness, was a talented woodworker set about sorting out the bay windows on the front of the house. 'New' windows had been fitted by the previous owner – badly! Calvin, Cleo's Dad set about fitting sills, sorting out the bottom panels with the addition of architrave, and making and replacing various dentils around the top of the bay. He then re-fitted the cellar windows and made covers faced with Perspex to fit the wells.

1986 was the year when I arranged a second trip to Israel. I shopped around to find a suitable Tour Operator. This time I used an Operator headed by a Pentecostal Pastor based in Manchester. He agreed to the usual terms: one free place for every ten places purchased. I had no problem finding ten people from my sixth-form students plus a colleague but ended up paying for Kath's place as the Tour Operator decided to use the second free place for himself! My main objective was to introduce my students to Jewish sites, whilst not neglecting the obvious Christian ones. The Pastor saw himself as leading a Christian Pilgrimage. Our Guide was a young Israeli woman, Sara, a Jew who was very sympathetic to my remit. As a result, the bus effectively divided into two, my group at the rear, the Pastor's group at the front! It wasn't long before a couple from his party, Ivor and Judy Jenkins, defected and joined ours!

We got talking, as you do, and discovered that they were from Stretford, and that they were Anglicans who attended All Saint's Parish Church. When I explained that I had done my 'Circuit Practice' there with the Revd James Bentley...well, that was it. Of course, they knew James, and Neil Handley, his curate. Although I didn't remember them, and they didn't remember me it was clear that they were there when I was there. We became firm friends and later, when I had to attend JMB meetings, I would often stay overnight with them.

Sara's husband worked for the Israeli government as an archaeologist. I had wanted to take my group through Hezekiah's tunnel. Access was very limited, but Sara managed to arrange it. The tunnel only permitted single file and we followed a Catholic group who were singing 'Ave Maria'. My group thought it was a good idea and promptly began with a rendition of 'O Sir Jasper do not touch me'. I was at the back, so no-one could see my blushes! We were in Galilee on the Friday. Sara sent one of my group off to find a Hallah loaf and arranged to welcome the sabbath in traditional fashion. It was a memorable occasion. Most evenings while we were in the Galilee we would walk down to the Lakeside. On one of our visits one of our party had a birthday and so we bought them a massive ice cream which came complete with sparklers.

[1987]

1987 was one of those 'Milestone Years'. I reached the age of 40! We bought a new car! The Renault 20 was proving to be increasingly expensive to keep on the road, so we bought a Lada estate, and, as the adverts promised, it proved to be good value for money. Two of my dad's brothers, who lived next door to each other and always changed their identical cars for identical cars had bought Ladas and couldn't fault them. When we were visiting Kath's parents on one occasion, we called at the Lada dealers in Stoke-on-Trent and I got talking to a customer who was there to buy his fifth Lada! Ladas were Russian, based on a design by Fiat. They were the cheapest new car on the market and the butt of jokes by a number of comedians, most notably Jasper Carrot! However, everyone I came across who had bought a Lada swore by them, so we took a chance. We never regretted it. They proved to be reliable and remarkably nippy. On one occasion I caught myself doing 95 mph on the M6 driving home from Manchester. I was totally unaware of my speed creeping up to that kind of level.

In the house we, reluctantly, turned our attention to the hall, landings and stairs. I say 'reluctantly', because it was a mammoth task, however it was next in line; almost all the rooms were done, and we were getting fed up of coming out of nicely decorated rooms into bare plaster walls and bare floorboards in the passage, on the landings and staircases. Burning paint and varnish off stair rails in a three-storey house was no fun and we were grateful to those of our family and friends who, on various visits, willingly accepted the paint stripper and set to with a will. With the preparations done we turned our thoughts to choosing the wallpaper. We saw just the one we wanted – but at nearly £11 a roll we decided we had better think again. The first drop from the second floor to the first floor was one whole roll in itself! It turned out that we needed 15 rolls by the time we had finished measuring up. Fortune smiled on us. Our local wallpaper shop told us that they were opening a new shop in Morecambe and they had 500 rolls on special offer supplied by various firms. A phone call confirmed that the one we wanted was among them, 11 rolls at just over £3 a roll. The difference we made up with Anaglypta painted with a cream emulsion. It looked very elegant.

Next the stair carpet. We worked out the size and reckoned up the likely cost and gulped. We went to our local carpet shop where we discovered one of our near neighbours was one of the salesmen. First of all, we had a look at the carpets and discovered that, for an even moderately good stair carpet, we would have to double the number we first thought of. We then plucked up the courage to ask our neighbour, whose house is similar to ours just how many square yards he thought we might need, yes, you've guessed right, it was double what we'd worked out. Still, thanks to help from my parents, we were duly carpeted, and it really looked good.

By the Easter we were ready for a rest, from decorating at least. We were visited by our first set of friends seeking refuge from the winter in the delights of the Lake District. And they kept coming in various combinations until the end of October. I joked that we should have set up in the Bed and Breakfast business! But it was good to see so many folk. One of the advantages of living where we did was the fact that people did actually come to visit.

It was then time to turn our attention to the outside of the house. We finally lifted all the tarmac at the front, laid concrete slabs to the front door to complement the drive, then we laid a small lawn and began planting the borders. Now the neighbours were beginning to worry about the fact that we were in danger of showing them up.

Summer half-term saw us bound for Paris for a week. The Phillips family from America were over there for several weeks. Bill was doing some research and giving some lectures, they had an apartment at their disposal. "Would we like to visit?" Silly question really. All we had to do was get there. We did. It was great, seeing our friends again, and the sights of Paris. On one day we visited Sacre Coeur and I managed to drop a roll of film down a drainage grid. It was quite deep, but it was dry. No way could we easily reach it. Robert offered to be lowered into the hole, so we removed the grid and lowered him down and he successfully retrieved it.

On another day we visited the Orangerie Museum to view Monet's paintings. It was most impressive. We also visited the

Louvre. We made a bee line for the most famous objects to show them to our children. Jane insisted on taking her two girls around at a much slower rate, painting by painting. Katy and Chrissie quickly became bored! When we visited Notre Dame, we stopped briefly in the garden outside. It had been raining and there was a surfeit of puddles. Chrissie decided it would be a good idea to jump into the middle of the biggest one. I can still hear Jane, at the top of her voice, shouting, "Christine Phillips". We weren't all that bothered, even though we were splattered with mud. Actually it was difficult to keep a straight face while Jane told her off! We had a wonderful week.

We were able to return the hospitality a few weeks later when Jane and the girls came to stay for all too short a time whilst Bill was lecturing in Sweden. Jane began working on a pair of patchwork bedspreads (a quilt-in-a-day) for the single beds in the guest bedroom. The materials used were in a variety of pastel colours intended to match the wallpaper. When I first wrote this in our Christmas letter for 1987, I concluded with the phrase, "Kath still has to finish them, either that or else Jane will have to make a return visit." I am writing this just after Easter in 2021 and Kath still has to finish them; in fact, Kath thinks we now only have one of them, and that Jane took the other one back to the States to finish it there!

Meanwhile holidays in Europe again – there was a small catch though – it was the Lakes School Activity Week, which took place each year late in the summer term. Although we went free, and in term time, it was to supervise 45 youngsters. I should add that there were three other adults there as well. Holland by barge; Amsterdam, Gouda, Delft, Haarlem . . . even with 45 school children, it was great week. Robert and Elizabeth came with us and had a whale of a time since the captain had his two children on board who were of a similar age. In Amsterdam we visited Anne Frank's house, which really was worth the visit. Some of the students discovered the Sex Museum, which, off course, we had to check out! We visited the model village at Madurodam, which is an extensive working model village, and a beach nearby where most of the women went topless! In Delft we visited the factory that produces the famous Delftware.

The barge, which was very large, was entirely self-sufficient. The crew comprised, the Captain, his wife (with their two children), and one young woman deckhand. The two women did all the cooking, and we were well fed! They were amazing when it came to avoiding food waste. The first morning there were bowls of hard-boiled eggs for breakfast, most of which went uneaten. The next evening, they turned up in an egg curry which was quickly demolished by the students.

The summer break finally came, and went, with various visitors arriving and leaving. Robert went on his first ever one-week Scout Camp – he thought it was wonderful, a whole week without a wash! He also spent a week attending the Y.M.C.A. day camp, which was held at the foot of Lake Windermere. Coming home each night meant getting washed that week! In between, and despite visitors, I went ahead working on the kitchen. Units were assembled and fitted, the ceiling tiled and the floor carpeted. For Kath this was bliss after three years of having to make do. Mind, the units didn't have doors fitted yet but then you can 't have everything.

Through all this Kath was kept busy making three bridesmaids dresses for Elizabeth's godmother's wedding which was held in the August. It was to be a 1920 's style occasion and Elizabeth was, of course, one of the bridesmaids and looked lovely, feathers and all!

Robert began his secondary education at the Lakes School in the September of 1987. He settled in well, and clearly enjoyed it much better than he had his primary school years. I don't think he'd ever worked as hard in all his life.

Homework, however, was not his most favourite evening pastime. Still, at the Parents' Evening he received some glowing comments, and none that were bad, even Maths was quite encouraging. The First Form (Year 7) operated as a self-contained unit to help the youngsters to find their feet, some had come from very small village Primary Schools. One activity they arranged was an evening adventure searching for the 'Treasure of Matke' organised by the First-Year staff, out on Coniston Old Man, cold and dark. Robert thoroughly enjoyed it though by the end he was absolutely shattered.

Elizabeth transferred from St Mark's C of E Primary School in Natland to the school in Heversham where Kath was now teaching. With Robert at secondary school and the other children, with whose parents we had shared lifts also at secondary school, this proved to be a much more convenient arrangement. Elizabeth settled in well, made lots of friends and began working harder than ever before. Near Christmas she was kept busy rehearsing for the school's Nativity play in which she was one of the main singers. They were performing Psalty's Christmas Calamity; Psalty being a song book, with Kath playing Psalty, the main part! Kath wore a very fetching cardboard fridge box, suitably painted as a Songbook.

Basically, Elizabeth did well with her piano lessons and actually took her First-Grade exam. She had missed out on it earlier in the year because we were in Holland. Robert continued with his violin with a little more enthusiasm now that he, like his sister, was into playing 'proper' tunes. Elizabeth also gained a number of Brownie Interest badges and Kath had become a Brownie helper. Elizabeth also did well in both her swimming and gymnastics during the year.

The autumn saw the top bathroom finally decorated, leaving only the dining room and bottom bathroom still to complete. We had a bit of an 'extension' added to the garage, simply by roofing over the bit of yard behind it. The intention being that it should enable us to clear the cellars ready to start making them habitable in the next spring. Before the year was out, I was in the throes of organising our next proposed visit to Israel for August the next year.

I think 1987 was the year we ended up with a second Lada. We had sold the Escort and, for just a few hundred pounds bought a Triumph, not sure of the model – possibly a 1300. We only had it a few weeks when there was a special offer on Lada saloons at the Lada dealers in Whitley Bay, near to where my parents were living. The deposit needed was more than we had paid for the Triumph and they were prepared to accept the Triumph as the deposit. It was too good an offer to miss so I drove over to Whitley Bay on August the first in the Triumph and returned in a brand-new Lada saloon. Well, almost. At Hexham I had to pull off the main road as there was clearly a problem. I called the breakdown service and they relayed me to Kendal. The driver of the low-loader warned me that we might be pulled over by the Police as a newly registered car on a low-loader might be considered to have been stolen. Thankfully we weren't stopped. Next day the Lada dealers in Morecambe collected the car, repaired the, minor, fault, and returned it – all at no cost! It never gave us any further problem.

[1988]

In 1988 the house continued to be a 'work in progress' although we did finally manage to complete the dining room and make a start on the bottom back bathroom and porch. In the autumn we did a bit of moving around on the first floor, making the guest room more permanent, and creating more space in the children's rooms. In addition, we managed to complete the workshop behind the garage which we had begun before the previous Christmas.

The cellars we still hadn't touched at all, so I still hadn't managed to get started on the model railway. It had always been my intention to use the back cellar as a model railway room. I had plenty of locos and rolling stock from the time we lived in Coalville where a couple of members of Hall Lane Methodist Church worked at Palitoy in Ashby-de-la-Zouche. Palitoy produced a large range of 'OO' gauge locos and rolling stock under the brand name 'Mainline' and employees were offered 'seconds' for next to nothing. I had also joined the staff of the model railway club at the Lakes School. Dave Dickinson, Head of Geography, was in charge. When I had explained that I was planning to make a layout based on Newcastle Central Station and Gateshead Goods Yards he had ordered a detailed plan from Ordinance Survey for me.

The main problem was lack of time! Much of the summer holidays were taken up moving my parents from their three-bedroom house in Whitley Bay to a one-bedroom apartment in sheltered accommodation in Kendal (some of their excess furniture helped to fill our already overflowing cellars!) They settled in quite quickly and it was nice to be able to call and see them frequently as they were now only 5 minutes' walk away instead of about 120 miles drive away. They had decided that they were now of an age that they needed to be closer to us. They had looked at two sheltered accommodation developments, one right in the centre of the town and the other near us on the south of the town. The former was slightly better but by the time they'd made up their minds the apartment had gone. I don't think they were too disappointed as the other one, the one they moved into, was so much closer to us.

Before we got caught up in that move, we had a couple of weeks visiting Kath's sister and family in Northern Ireland. It rained everyday but that didn't stop us from enjoying ourselves.

We managed to cover the whole coastline from Londonderry in the north west to the Mountains of Mourne in the south east. Remarkably whenever we got to where we were going the rain went away and the sun shone. It really is one of the most beautiful parts of the United Kingdom we've ever visited. We were, however, disappointed when we sampled one of the local delicacies – seaweed! It was awful!

Apart from our visit to Whitley Bay to supervise the move of the Fishers (senior) Northern Ireland was our only major excursion during 1988. Our proposed trip to Israel we had to cancel. The unrest on the West Bank proved to be a deterrent to many who had initially shown interest. I decided that I wouldn't organise another trip, but so many colleagues and friends asked if I would organise one in 1989 that I finally capitulated and began arranging a visit for the October half term week the next year.

Elizabeth was now into her final year of primary education. She settled in well at Heversham School where Kath was teaching. She made lots of new friends and her work improved no end. She continued to play the piano, albeit a little reluctantly at times. Earlier in the year she took her Grade One Theory Examination, scoring 99 out of 99 – not bad really! Brownies were now a thing of the past – she was into Guides in a big way. She had become rather fed up with her Brownie pack and insisted that when the move was made, she wanted to transfer to the Guide troop at Saint Thomas's. It proved to be a good move, and she found that she knew one or two of the Guides already from the Explorers Group she attended at church on Sunday mornings. The menagerie continued to grow. Once

Robert finally got the gerbils he had been longing for for ages, Elizabeth insisted on having a Guinea pig – she ended up with two, Blackberry and Apple! BlackBerry kept going lame and Elizabeth kept nursing him back to health.

As for Robert he acquitted himself well during his first year in secondary school. He was awarded House First Year Prize for 'Effort'. The summer term ended with all the first-year pupils going on a 'self-reliant' journey. Robert's group was made up of five girls and himself! They hiked to Hawkshead where they met up with another group of six girls. The two groups spent the night in the Youth Hostel with a female member of staff – all in the girls' dormitory! Undoubtedly an opportunity to make great capital out of the experience when he reached the senior end of the school! He continued to play the violin and, at last, began to enjoy Junior Strings at school now that they are preparing for the Christmas Carol service. The flute was his latest interest. This he enjoyed playing it and he made good progress. In the summer he finally refused point blank to go to Scouts. 4th Kendal was a big troop, rather rough and not at all interested in badgework which Robert enjoyed. After a little persuasion he finally agreed to try the Phoenix troop which had been recently formed out of the remains of Saint Thomas's, the Methodist and RC troups. Once he settled in, he seemed to be enjoying Scouts again.

For Kath 1988 was marked by more than her usual share of headaches. The doctor finally agreed to refer her to a specialist. Eventually it was decided that she was dairy intolerant. She was still teaching at Heversham – Tuesday through to Friday morning, with occasional supply work on Mondays and Friday afternoons. Each year we held our breath as the end of the year approached and it looked like numbers in the school would mean a reduction in staffing, and each year it worked out. This year was a bit complicated as Kath had to change classes and take on a group of 32 which, shared as it was with another part-time teacher, was far from easy.

This was the first year of GCSE and 99 candidates were entered for Religious Studies from the Lakes School. Only one failed and the rest achieved grades in exact relation to the national average. I was both relieved and pleased. The 'A' level results were excellent, the best of any subject in the school, and this year there were 31 students studying Religious Studies at 'A' level.

As for preaching, for the first time ever I missed a couple of services through ill health. The problem turned out to be kidney stones. On the 1st occasion the pain hit late on a Saturday night, resulting in an early morning visit (4:00 am) to the Accident and Emergency Unit of the local hospital. On the second occasion, again on a Saturday night, the doctor was called, and a shot of pethidine later I knew nothing more until the Sunday lunchtime! When it flared up again a few days later, the doctor decided to have me admitted to the Royal Lancaster Infirmary – my first time in hospital as an in-patient! Several X-rays and blood tests later and after another agonising night of pain, I was condemned, on each visit to the loo to carry a bottle, the contents of which were tested and showed traces of gravel and blood. After five days I was finally discharged although I did have to have some more X-rays and another visit to the specialist before Christmas. Once the pain had gone, I never had such a relaxing and hilarious time in years. With the two guys in the neighbouring beds, we prowled the corridors. When stopped we explained that we were the escape committee doing a recce! The hospital food was excellent and in that respect I was sorry to leave when I was eventually discharged.

[1989]

This year work on the house definitely took a very low priority in our schedule. We finally finished the back porch and back bathroom, and one or two little bits outstanding in the rest of the house but sadly we didn't really get down to the task of converting the cellars as we had hoped.

As a family we managed to get about quite bit during the year. In June, when the Lakes School has its biennial Activity Week Kath and I, with Robert went with three other staff and 50 pupils to Northern France. Not what one might call a 'holiday'! Elizabeth stayed home and was looked after by Kath's parents. Since my parents moved to Kendal just over a year previously my mam had been waiting to have a cataract operation. She finally got an appointment – the week we were going to be in France of course – and the operation was scheduled to take place in Barrow-in-Furness. It was as well that Kath's parents were around to help get Dad to Barrow to visit because, although it is only about thirty miles from Kendal, to travel by bus took several hours and necessitated several changes and meant that he arrived late for visiting and had to leave early. Mam quickly recovered from the operation, with much improved vision; and we all had an excellent time in France.

The summer holidays were fraught with problems. Fortunately, we had decided to spend some time in Kath's parents' caravan and on Kath's parents' canal boat because it meant that we could be fairly fluid where dates were concerned. First of all, Kath was called into hospital to have a varicose vein operation which she had been waiting for for some time. Then I was called into hospital for more tests on my kidneys. Neither of these proved to be a problem apart from curtailing our time in the caravan and on the boat, Kath's operation was a success though it took some time for her to get over it, and my kidneys were, to quote the consultant, 'most curious' more tests were to follow.

The 'big' holiday in 1989 was our visit to Israel in October. This time, unlike the previous two visits, we took both Robert and Elizabeth, along with 22 other folk; some pupils from the Lakes School, some from Settlebeck School, some of my colleagues, some friends from Manchester (Ivor and Judy were keen to go again), and some folk from Kendal Churches who are now friends! The ages ranged from 11 to 71! I think it was on this trip that, when we stopped at a Services on the way to the airport, Robert disappeared and reappeared having bought me a baseball cap with two peaks one pointing to the right and the other to the left with the legend "I am their leader, which way did they go"! We had a fabulous time in Israel, once we had sacked our guide on the second day and been supplied with a new one! The guide that was supplied, Haggai, took it on himself to alter the itinerary I had prepared and refused to go back to my original. He also tried it on with one of the Year 13 girls. Eventually the contact in Jerusalem agreed to replace him and the guide we were given, Shabbtai, was superb. He was a retired archaeologist who had served as a tank commander during the Israeli war of Independence.

One of the first places we visited this time, out of sequence, was the synagogue in the Hadassah Medical Centre. It was a square building with three beautiful stained-glass windows set quite high up on each side. They had been designed by Chagall. The Centre shop sold printed tapestry canvases of the windows. We had seen them on our last visit and Judy decided that she wanted to buy one. I decided to do the same. Judy bought 'Judah'. I was undecided as I wasn't sure whether the windows represented the 'twelve tribes' or the 'twelve sons of Israel'. If the former I would have a problem, if the latter no contest. The windows turned out to be of the twelve sons of Israel, so I bought the canvas of 'Levi' which became the 'tribe' that was not one of the twelve, so had no land, but assisted the priesthood in the worship in the Temple. (Neither Joseph nor Levi were counted among the 'tribes' with Joseph's sons Ephraim and Manasseh, making up the numbers.) So began my renewed interest in tapestry and after finishing Levi I rooted out my unfinished Durham Cathedral kneeler to complete. The visit, in the end, proved so successful that I was prevailed upon to arrange another visit at some point during the next two years!

For Elizabeth 1989 was the big year. In September she began secondary school and, like her brother before her, she chose to go to the Lakes School. She settled in very quickly and thoroughly enjoyed it. One of the things she insisted on doing when she started in Secondary School was to begin learning a second musical instrument, so she had a clarinet as an early Christmas present. She continued to play the piano with much more dedication than before, and during the year was successful in passing her Grade 2 examination. The highlight of hweek was Guides on a Monday evening. Shortly after moving up from Brownies she went with the Guides on a week's camp near Loch Lomond in Scotland. Not only did she enjoy it, she won the award for the best 'first-time camper'!

Robert continued in his own 'sweet way'. Work, especially homework, was something he tackled reluctantly and at his own pace! Nevertheless, he made good progress at school in all his subjects and did especially well in both French and German oral and written tests at the end of his second year. He was still playing the violin and was given his pieces for his Grade 3 examination. The flute he enjoyed, although he was not too keen to practise. He was, however, successful in passing his Grade 1 examination earlier in the year. At Scouts he was promoted to Patrol Leader and began working for a life-saving award for swimming. Both he and Elizabeth were involved in the School's forthcoming production of a play written by one of the students about 'Green' issues; Robert was to play a fridge – ozone unfriendly, and Elizabeth, a politician – Eggwina Curry (so named after Edwina Curry MP who was a Junior Health Minister for two years, resigning in 1988 during the salmonella-in-eggs controversy). We eagerly awaited the performance!

The drama bug seemed to be catching in the family. Kath, earlier in the year joined Kendal Amateur Dramatics and appeared in their production of 'Bonaventure', as Nurse Phillips. It was a commendable performance! At School her teaching time was reduced from 7 tenths to 5 tenths in the autumn term because of falling rolls and she moved from teaching older junior children to teaching infants. From January, however, she was to be full-time as the infant teacher in the school. It would be the first time for a number of years that she had had a full-time post, and it would make a difference to our income. She wasn't slow planning how to spend the extra money – top of her list for Christmas – a dishwasher! With two of us working I could hardly complain, it was either that or paper plates!

As far as the Lakes School was concerned, it seemed to be ever more time consuming as new initiatives worked their way into the system. I found myself co-ordinating the efforts of several Cumbria R. E. teachers who were trying to produce a new 'A' level G.C.E examination in Ethics. It proved to be a somewhat formidable task. The third revision had finally been drafted and we were all hoping that it really would be 'third time lucky'. My students 'A' level results that summer were extremely gratifying, with 6 of the 15 candidates gaining a Grade A. The GCSE results were, sadly, not so good, though not terribly bad either.

Interestingly I was 'discovered' by the Kendal Methodist Circuit during the year and so had been invited to preach in number local Methodist Churches. In August we finally bought the car we really wanted, quite by chance. Since my parents moved to Kendal my father's F.S.O. had occupied the drive, keeping our Lada Estate and Lada Saloon company. We decided that one car had to go and, to Kath' s chagrin, it would have to be the Lada Saloon. We spotted a Renault 21 Savanna Estate for sale, and the Garage was prepared to take both Ladas in part exchange! So, Kath took on driving the F.S.O. and the rest of the family went off to school in the Renault!

The end of the year saw us travelling to Manchester to see Kath's parents off on their way to visit Kath's brother in Australia for three months, a trip which their three children paid for between them as a retirement present. They were so excited since neither had ever flown before, or even been abroad before.

It was around this time that David Tipping announced his decision to resign as Head Teacher of the Lakes School. He had been accepted by VSO to go on a two-year contract to work on curriculum development in Nepal (or was it Bhutan?). Before he left, he signed up for a course on experiential RE that was being held over several days at St Martin's College in Lancaster. It was a course that I had earlier signed up for. Over coffee, one day, I asked why he had appointed me to my post. His response was typical of the calibre of the man. He explained that he wanted a person who was identifiably a member of a faith community. It did not matter which faith community, Christian, Muslim, Jew, Hindu, Buddhist or Sikh. What mattered was that they were practicing members of their community. He openly admitted that he was an agnostic. He had, by choice, obtained a BA, a BSc and a BEd, which was an indication of his commitment to his chosen vocation. He was a man of great insight, who had always been supportive of me and my department. I knew I would miss him greatly.

Initially I had great hopes when his successor was announced. Arthur Capstick, who succeeded David Tipping, turned out to be an evangelical Anglican and he linked up with St Thomas' Church in Kendal. However, I never felt that I had his support in the way I had had with David Tipping. Whether it was because he didn't want to be seen, as a practising Christian, to be supporting the RE department in case he was accused of favouritism, or he was unhappy with the trend in RE to teach all world faiths, I never discovered.

[1990]

In 1990 we actually managed to start work on the cellars, sorry basements! Robert moved himself down there at the Easter. We began to think he had troglodyte tendencies, as we had to drag him out in the summer so we could begin putting up false walls and putting in some wiring for lights and plug sockets. By the end of the year the front cellar was almost finished, and we were ready to start on the back cellar. Fortunately, there was a DIY shop in Kendal, just up the road, at the south end of the High Street. You could buy nails or screws or any hardware in whatever quantities you wanted, and they would cut anything, wood, contiboard, or plywood, to your measurements – at no extra cost. That proved very useful as I had to build in a bookcase by the window in the front basement. Sadly, the shop closed when a DIY Superstore was opened on the newly developed retail outlet on the south of the town. Thereafter everything had to be bought in packs or full sheets!

Kath's constant frustration with having no doors on the kitchen units finally persuaded me to turn to the task of refurnishing the kitchen. The basic units were, after all, someone else's cast offs which, gratefully received when we had nothing, had seen six years good service. The other, door-less, units could be re-used in the back-basement room – which was planned to be the railway room. A trip to MFI saw a new kitchen purchased, and a lot of work, and several weeks of total disorganisation saw it installed, well, almost – there were still a few bits to finish off.

We had hoped to visit the Phillips's in France during the summer half-term holiday, but for various reasons this had to be cancelled, and the summer break loomed large with no arrangements made. We were delighted when a phone call from Paris came suggesting a visit in August before their return to the States. We had an absolutely fabulous time visiting with them and visiting the places we'd never visited before. Versailles was spectacular! The Catacombs were macabre! – six million skeletons buried in winding passages. The sewers were smelly! The Père Lachaise Cemetery was fascinating. We saw the graves of Jim Morison, Édith Piaf and Oscar Wilde, among others. We rounded off our visit by staying for a few days in London with our god-daughter and used our English Heritage cards to visit all the places there we 'd never visited before. We thought France was expensive until we got back to London. Our cards proved invaluable and saved us pounds.

My life went on much as before. I was kept quite busy during the early summer when the Revd Bob White, Superintendent Minister of the Ambleside and Windermere Circuit, took a three-month sabbatical. Fortunately, the lay folk were so well organised that apart from a wedding, some mid-week morning communions and an increase in the number of preaching appointments I took, it didn't cause any undue additional work. The head, at school, was happy to accommodate any additional commitments Bob's sabbatical might cause.

In the end the only event that encroached on my school activities was a funeral that I had to take at Grasmere. The deceased was a prominent person in the community, and the church, which was quite small, was packed with many gathering outside on the road with the church doors open so that they could hear what was going on. After the service we set out for the crematorium at Lancaster, some 40 miles and an hour's drive away. Quite a lot of cars followed the hearse and the funeral party. We managed to keep together fairly well on the motorway but, inevitably, we lost the last three cars as we neared Lancaster. We waited as long as we could. Eventually we had to proceed with the committal, which is only a few minutes long, as the next funeral party was waiting to enter the chapel. As we left the chapel the last three cars arrived, and I had to apologise that they had travelled so far and missed the committal. Thankfully they were very understanding.

At school I was pleased with the significant improvement in the GCSE results this year, at last reaching the kind of standards I had hoped to see achieved. The 'A' level results were good and bad, those expected to do well did so; those expected to fail did so, sadly there were more than usual of the latter.

1990 was the only 'Christmas letter' when I managed to get the children to write their own bit. I have decided not to try and summarise what they said but rather to let them speak for themselves:

"Hello, Elizabeth here. I am still enjoying school. This year, because of the new National Curriculum I am in Year 8 – last year I was in the First Year! At the moment we are rehearsing for the School Christmas Play, "The Skulls of Calgarth", based on a

local legend, a bit of a ghost story. I am acting the part of a school child, except in one part, where I play a Jester. Earlier in the year I took my Grade 3 Theory and Grade 3 Piano exams and passed both. In Guides I have just had my new uniform which I think is really nice. During the year I have been helping in Brownies and for that I have received my Service Flash."

"Hi, Robert here. I am going to tell you about the past year. I am now in Year 10 (the old 4th Year) and am working on my GCSEs. Last year I had to make my Option choices and I chose to do French, History, Art and Design. I very much enjoy Design and at the moment am making a prototype Walkman in the shape of an initial 'R. I have my Dad to teach me for Religious Studies, so far it has been alright. Like Elizabeth I am in the School Christmas Play. I am still going to Scouts and for the past few months have been helping in Beavers which counts towards my Explorer and Chief Scout Awards. Earlier this year I took on a paper round for one of our local 'Free' papers. I do this after school every Wednesday night. During the year I have taken my Grades 1 and 2 Music Theory exams. The first I passed with 94 marks out of 99, the second I am still waiting to hear about."

Kath's year was a busy one. Since the January she was employed full-time at Heversham Primary School as an infant teacher. Under the new National Curriculum that meant teaching Years 1 and 2. It necessitated a great deal of work since whole sections of the National Curriculum had to be introduced in these years. Unlike Secondary colleagues who had to grapple with just one subject area, the Primary teacher had to contend with them all as they came on stream! She survived – only just, and administration apart, thoroughly enjoyed her class even though it was large, with 32 children, and covered four age groups! At Church she was very much involved in Pathfinders and thoroughly enjoyed her Sunday mornings. Her one regret this year was that she hadn't really had time to do much in the way of needlework.

[1991]

At Easter 1991 the Lakes School began running its own Roller-Skating sessions in the Sports Hall during the holiday period. Kath and our two, plus an assortment of friends went off to try their skill, I had more sense and did some photocopying! Just before the end of the session Kath fell and broke her left wrist, quite badly. The nurse at Kendal Hospital had little sympathy! It was Kath's first time in plaster. Not to be outdone, at the beginning of the summer holidays, off trouped the youngsters plus friends, Kath refused to go (I 'm sure I don't know why), to give the Roller Skating another go and just before the end of the session Robert fell and broke his left wrist! His first time in plaster. Thankfully those were the only accidents, of that nature, during this year!

I say 'of that nature' because, in the summer holidays we borrowed Kath's parents' caravan, and lost it! We had had a splendid week at Loch Lomond and after a few days at home, during which time both Robert and Elizabeth went off to camp, Kath and I set off, with the caravan, for a few days on our own – bliss! Only a mile out of Kendal the van unhitched itself and disappeared into a hedge. Amazingly we knew the farmer in whose field it had decided to come to rest (a few yards earlier and we would not have been so fortunate). He towed it out of the hedge with a tractor, and to our astonishment, apart from one broken glass, a broken skylight and a dent on the top corner, the caravan had survived unscathed. So, a day later we set off again and grabbed a couple of days to ourselves before the gruesome twosome – do teenagers ever stop arguing? returned to the fold! No big holidays this year but I was planning another visit to Israel for the next October.

The house renovation progressed – we finished – well almost. We completed the renovation of the cellars and finally installed Robert in the front one, it was the biggest room in the house! (Robert: "Honest Dad, when I get a bigger room, I promise I'll keep it tidy!" No comment!) The back one was intended to be a railway room but since we finished putting up walls, fitting electric lights and sockets, decorating and carpeting it, we kept finding the floor wet! For seven years whilst it had been a dump it had been dry, now it was finished – wet! and could we find out where the water was coming from? Obviously, we did, eventually!

My parents were still doing well and enjoying their sojourn in Kendal. Kath's parents were off 'down under' again at the beginning of December for four months! What it must be like to be retired!

My intention to pursue the possibility of doing a second degree this year came to naught. Instead, I was asked to take on responsibility for a Post Graduate Certificate of Education course in RE being set up by Charlotte Mason College in nearby Ambleside but, unique – in the sense that it was designed to be school, rather than College, based. As Director of Studies (School-based) I was relieved of half my teaching timetable to enable me to organise and/or take the 'taught' elements of the course in school. This year I had just four PG's (including one with a PhD and one who was a Benedictine priest) next year it was anticipated that there would be twenty, covering three other subjects, and three other schools would be involved. It proved hectic, time-consuming and very exciting. I thoroughly enjoyed it! It was the first SCITT (School Centred Initial Teacher Training) course in the country. Many others would follow in subsequent years.

I was also in the process of 'moving' from the Ambleside & Windermere Circuit to the Kendal Circuit. When we first moved to the Lakes, I had asked the Chair to be stationed in the Circuit in which I worked, primarily because it was so short of preachers, however, over the years more and more active, retired preachers had moved into the Circuit so that it now made more sense to be in the Circuit in which we were living. Bob White was moving on to take over the Superintendency of the Alston Circuit, so it seemed an opportune moment for me to move on as well. We went to Bob's farewell 'do'. I had slipped into the Circuit quietly and had hoped to slip out just as quietly. To my surprise when the speeches and presentation for Bob were over, they then turned to me and I was duly thanked for my contributions to the life of the Circuit and presented with a cheque even though I would be continuing to work within the Circuit and make occasional appearances on the Circuit Plan.

Bob's successor was another Bob and he immediately launched into a Circuit Review. The result was a decision to refurbish Bowness Methodist Church. The cost, if my memory serves me, was in the region of c.£50,000. The scheme involved creating a new entrance from the main street removing the pews and refurbishing the flat beneath the main worship area. The result was stunning. A team of four young people were employed for a year to work with young people in the hospitality industry. They also came into school on a number of occasions to take assemblies and lessons. I could not fault the intention, but I was sceptical of the likely result as the church membership was small and elderly. Sadly, I was proved right When Bob, in turn, moved on into retirement, Bowness MC 'ceased to meet and the building was sold to 'The Lakes Christian Fellowship'.

The Pastor's son attended the Lakes School and I taught

him in Yrs. 10 and 11. He had clearly inherited his father's fundamentalist attitudes when it came to the Christian Responsibility paper and as far as the Islam paper was concerned, he was a rabid Islamophobe! He is the only student, in all the time I was at the Lakes School, to withdraw from the GCSE in Religious Studies. I was not surprised when we were in Bowness this August (2021) to see that the Church building was again up for sale!

As she reflected on 1991 Kath said that all she seemed to do was go to work at school and come home to work at home, and that was usually for school! She seemed to have been busier than ever this year, certainly during the spring and summer terms when many of her class were involved in SATs (Standard Attainment Tests).

For both Robert and Elizabeth, the highlight of their year was their visits to summer camps. Elizabeth, with a friend from Church, went for nearly two weeks to a Pathfinders camp at Ledbury, not far from Hereford. Robert, with several other members of the Youth Fellowship, went for a week at a CYFA camp at Denstone, near Alton Towers.

Elizabeth was very keen on the clarinet, and piano lessons were temporarily abandoned. It was her intention to begin them again after Christmas. Robert abandoned his music this year as he prepared for his Year 11 GCSE exams the next summer. However, he took on a morning paper round to earn himself some money; he probably spent more time on that than ever he did on his music! As to preparing for his exams he worked when we sat over him, how much he did otherwise is questionable. He thoroughly enjoyed his week of work experience with a friend who was a dental technician, and he was keen to go on to Higher Education and was looking to a career in modelmaking. The first hurdle, however, was his GCSE's and they could be good / could be bad we would just have to wait and see,

[1992]

1992 was the year that we felt that we had, at last, finished the house. Of course, it would now be a case, next year, of beginning again – the outside was in need a good coat of paint and one or two rooms were starting to look in need of redecoration – where houses are concerned – you simply cannot win!

This was Robert's big year. The summer saw him taking his GCSEs. It was hard work – on his Mum that is – trying to get him to revise! Well it paid off. He got Grades A for Art, B for CDT, Cs for Religious Studies, Science, History and English, and Ds for Maths and French. He really needed a C in Maths so, because he did so well in his coursework, he re-took the Maths in November but did no real revision! We weren't holding our breath.

in September he began a BTEC National Diploma Course in General Art and Design at Lancaster and Morecambe College. He thoroughly enjoyed the course, though he was thrown a little when on his very first session he was given the task of sketching a 40-year-old female nude! In September he also began working part-time at the newly opened Morrisons Supermarket as a checkout operator. He worked three evenings a week and most of Saturday, also plenty of overtime on the occasional Sunday. It did his bank balance the world of good. At the weekends all the produce that was unsold, or time-limited, was sold off, for coppers, to the staff. He brought so much home that we had to invest in an upright freezer! We found a second-hand one at Barbon. We bought it and installed it in the back basement.

Elizabeth began her GCSE courses in September. As well as English, Maths, Science and Religious Studies, she chose to study Geography, French, Food Studies, and Information Technology. Whereas Robert had dropped his musical instruments Elizabeth continued to play the clarinet and took up the piano again after quite a long break. She enjoyed it immensely and did very well. She continued to attend Guides and Pathfinders at Church.

In the summer Elizabeth went again to a Pathfinders camp while Robert attended a CYFA camp. Both had a marvellous time. Kath and I meanwhile had a week to ourselves in the caravan the family had been given earlier in the summer. We also had a marvellous time, the first time on holiday on their own since the family arrived!

We didn't keep the caravan long as I wasn't all that keen on towing. Also, the previous year we had bought a week of timeshare at Burnside Park in Bowness-on-Windermere. We bought, off plan, Week 34 – Cottage 35. The Cottage slept 4 and the week we bought was the last week in August which was the most popular week in the year. We paid a monthly maintenance fee. We had no intention of using it whilst we were living in Kendal, but instead exchanged it for holidays abroad.

Kath received a well-deserved, though at the time temporary, promotion in September with the retirement of the Deputy Head Teacher at her school. Since the school was too small at that time to warrant the position of a Deputy Head Teacher the next most senior teacher was given the responsibility, though without the title or the salary, only an 'A' allowance. Still, it was better than nothing!

At my School the PGCE course was expanded into other subject areas and the number training for RE was reduced by 50%. Therefore, I no longer had overall responsibility for the course and was actually quite relieved to be rid of it. It had been a very successful year but amazingly time-consuming, made worse by staff changes in the department, including tragically, a suicide. This year I began to feel I had regained my sanity somewhat!

The 'big' family holiday was taken during the Autumn half-term week when Kath and I took the junior Fishers and twenty-five others on a visit to Israel. Some were old friends and previous Israel visitors; others were from among my Year 13 students and others from various Churches in Cumbria and elsewhere. They were a marvellous group who mixed together well. Four were particularly pleased to be asked by the tour Company to fly out two days early at their expense because of overbooked flights. Robert was one of the lucky four. Everyone thoroughly enjoyed the visit, made better because we managed to secure the guide we had had last time who was excellent. The only hiccup was when we were given a decrepit Service bus instead of the promised luxury Coach on the day we visited Masada. Air-conditioning was by way of missing windows, the consequent noise making it impossible for the guide to be heard, even over the intercom. We were duly compensated by being taken to sites not on our original itinerary so in the end all turned out well.

As on previous visits when we were in the north of the country, we visited Mount Tabor, the mount of transfiguration. Coaches parked at the foot of Mount Tabor and visitors were taken up by taxi, no other vehicles were allowed. We were early and when we arrived at the summit, we found that the church was closed for lunch, so our guide gave us a fascinating talk, not only tracing the history of the site but referencing the biblical accounts of Jesus' transfiguration. He concluded by telling us that whilst Mount Tabor was the traditional site of Jesus' transfiguration, he didn't believe that it was. Mount Hermon, further to the north, was a more likely candidate!

After visiting the Church the descent was scary. The road was steep and comprised a series of hairpin bends. The Mercedes Taxi drivers drove fast and on each outside bend had a habit of taking their hands off the wheel – "Look, no hands". Nevertheless, we did arrive at the bottom safely.

[1993 – this letter is missing!]

I have no idea why I didn't keep a copy of the Christmas letter for this year, especially as it was the year we went on our second Exchange of Pastorates. I didn't keep an audio diary of the exchange this time, instead I kept a video diary. However, that has not proved to be as helpful as an audio diary would have been since it was not always clear where we were, or when we were! I did keep a very brief written note of what we did each day on the Exchange which helped when there were gaps in the video record.

One thing I do recall when listening to a conversation I was having that was recorded on video, was that before the exchange took place Robert and I were involved in the school Activity Week. This time we went to Salou in Spain. We went by coach. We left late at night and drove down through England to the south coast where we caught a ferry across the channel. We then drove non-stop through France into Spain, and on to Salou, just south of Barcelona. It was a long 24 hours. Once we were settled, unknown to the staff, some of the older lads went off and found a bar where they had far too much Sangria! I remember I was sharing a room with Ed Blood, one of our Art teachers who moved himself to another room after the first night as, apparently, I snored!

We had a day in Barcelona which was very enjoyable. The coach took us around the city so that we saw quite a bit of Gaudi's architecture, in particular Sagrada Familia. We also visited a folk museum and the Olympic Stadium. My lasting recollection, however, was when the driver found himself in the wrong lane, twice. He had just pointed out Barcelona's Bull Ring, missed his lane and had to drive around again. As we came past again, he pointed out Barcelona's 'second' Bull Ring! The kids accepted what he said until, when, having missed his lane again we were driven past Barcelona's – he didn't get to say 'third' Bull Ring. They weren't that stupid!

The missing letter gives me an opportunity to say a few words about the Sixth Form at the Lakes School. John Luker was Head of Sixth Form. He was a popular teacher, a valued colleague, and a gracious gentleman. He would regularly ask me to take the weekly Sixth Form Assembly. I recall on one occasion talking about how I might have invented the video recorder based on my tape-recording (sound only of course) various TV programmes in my youth. Each year, when the President of the Methodist Conference visited the Cumbria District, like my predecessor, I arranged for him to take one of the Sixth Form Assemblies. It was always appreciated. After a few years the President's schedule was changed so it became impossible to continue with such visits.

I was also responsible for Full School Assemblies and used to regularly invite local clergy to take them. They were usually very accommodating. On one occasion I contacted the newly appointed Vicar of Ambleside. He had come from Jamaica and, on the phone, spoke with a broad Jamaican accent. I was surprised when he turned up and turned out to be white. When he addressed the school the look on the students faces was priceless as they clearly were baffled by a white man with such a broad Jamaican accent.

I also had responsibility for the annual School Carol Concert. I took it out of school and made it a Carol Service. We went to each of the churches in our catchment area that were big enough to host us. Ambleside Parish Church, Windermere Parish Church, The Roman Catholic Church and Bowness Parish Church. I think we did use Ambleside Methodists on one occasion and the URC in Bowness on one occasion. I usually invited the minister of the previous year's host church to preach, although I did preach on a couple of occasions. I produced the Order of Service with readings and Carols and included musical items provided by the Music Department.

In my early years at the Lakes School, we had a Head of Music who was singularly unhelpful. Under him the Music Department deteriorated significantly. His only interest was in choirs and, to be fair, he developed the school choir to such a standard that it was invited to appear on Harry Secombe's Sunday programme on ITV. However, he had little interest in instrumental music and the various instrumental groups went into decline. At one point I spotted an advert in the Times Educational Supplement for a peripatetic music teacher in the Shetland Islands – boat supplied. I couldn't resist the temptation to cut it out and put it in his pigeonhole in the staff room.

Over the years I was at the Lakes School I gave a lift to a number of pupils from Kendal who had chosen to go to the Lakes School, apart from my own two. Marco Tremble was one, he's still single, living in Kendal and working for Virgin Money, and Melody and, in turn, her younger brother was another. Melody took 'A' level Music and told me on one occasion that she had asked the Head of Music why they couldn't have a choir for those who simply enjoyed singing. She was immediately put down with the comment, "Choirs are there to win competitions, not to enjoy singing!"

Once the 'A' level exams were over the Head Boy and Head Girl usually organised a leavers event. This was in the days before the Prom made its appearance in the UK. Usually, it was simply a dance and a buffet. The teachers who had taught 'A' level subjects were invited to attend. One year they decided to be more adventurous and booked a lake diner cruise with buffet and band! It was amazing, and, as one might expect, was never topped!

Arthur Capstick's daughter, Nichola, decided, after beginning the Sixth Form, to change from Maths to RE, much, I think, to her father's disappointment. She did well. So too did Kishore. His parents owned what was then the only Indian Restaurant in Bowness. The family regularly went to visit family in India. Kishore spoke only English and had no knowledge of the family's cultural background, consequently his parents insisted he take 'A' level RE to get a grounding in Indian tradition. He was a keen student. In the weeks leading up to their final exams I used to give my students my home phone number so if they were stuck with their revision, they could contact me. Kishore was the only one who ever did. He went on to study for a degree in Sports Studies at Loughborough. One of my other 'star' pupils, Rachel (Wiggy) Woollett, went on to take a degree in Religious Studies, then into teaching RE and the last I heard she was a Head of RE at a school in Hong Kong.

Anyway, back to the Exchange. It wasn't as easy to organise as the first one since we were limited to the School's summer holiday, without the advantage we had enjoyed in Leicestershire where the Authority tagged 'Leicester Fortnight' onto the summer break, giving us a good eight-week break. Before we went, I explained to the Head that I had, in error, not allowed for the time difference for our return flight. The first day back was a Training Day so there were no children in school. He was adamant that if I wasn't there my pay would be docked. I asked him if my colleague, Inda Kaur, phoned in on that first morning to say that she was sick, even if she wasn't, would he dock her pay? He said he wouldn't. So being honest clearly didn't pay! When we landed back in Manchester after the Exchange it was a mad dash up the M6, dropping off the family in Kendal and straight on School in time for lunch. I was docked a half day's pay. Inda, in fact, did phone in sick, even though she wasn't, and did not have any pay docked!

This time we were paired with the Revd Bert Clayton from Highland Terrace UMC in San Antonio, Texas. After our experience last time with Glenn, who had clearly had problems with a geared car, we decided that we would insure Kath's car, a Volvo 345 for Bert. Although my Renault was bigger it was, what Americans called, a stick shift. Kath's Volvo was smaller, but it was automatic. The irony was that Burt was over six feet tall and drove a shift stick regularly!

A friend of Arthur Capstick's was setting up a Garden centre and to help him get established he asked Arthur to offer the staff the opportunity to have hanging baskets filled with flowers at a very reasonable cost, all we had to do was supply the baskets. I jumped at the chance so when Bert and Janice arrived, they were greeted by the most magnificent hanging baskets at the front door and in the back yard.

Having read James A Michener's 'Chesapeake' before our visit to Gaithersburg, and found it very instructive, I made a point of reading Michener's 'Texas' before we went to San Antonio. All Michener's books are hefty tomes, but they are so instructive. Having taken my parents with us to Gaithersburg this time we took Kath's parents with us to San Antonio. Because we were going to be in the States, Jane insisted we visit in Gaithersburg, so we booked an 'open jaws' ticket – London to Atlanta, Atlanta to San Antonio, San Antonio to Washington, Washington to Atlanta then Atlanta to London.

San Antonio

We flew from Manchester to Atlanta and then on to San Antonio. We all arrived safely, all that is except for Liz's suitcase which, when it came around on the carousel. was virtually demolished. Liz was upset as it was well-travelled and had labels on it from all the places she had visited. The luggage folk were very apologetic and said that if we returned just before we were due to leave, we could collect a replacement from those unclaimed in their store. We did as we were asked and Liz ended up with a bigger, better, expandable, case. She was delighted.

San Antonio (Spanish for "Saint Anthony"), is the seventh most populated city in the United States of America and the second most populated city in the state of Texas, with a population of 1,409,019. It was the fastest growing of the top 10 largest cities in the United States from 2000 to 2010. The city is located in the south–central part of Texas and is the seat of Bexar County.

San Antonio was named for Saint Anthony of Padua, whose feast day is on June 13, by a 1691 Spanish expedition in the area. It is notable for several Spanish colonial missions, the Alamo, the River Walk, the Tower of the Americas, and the Alamo Bowl. Commercial entertainment includes SeaWorld and Six Flags Fiesta Texas theme parks. According to the San Antonio Convention and Visitors Bureau, the city is visited by around 26 million tourists a year.

The US armed forces have several facilities in San Antonio: Fort Sam Houston, Lackland Air Force Base, Randolph Air Force Base, with Lackland AFB/Kelly Field Annex, with Camp Bullis and Camp Stanley located outside the city.

(Friday 23rd July) Once we were settled into the parsonage, the first thing Kath did was to phone Pearl Campbell in Gaithersburg to let her know we had arrived safely Stateside – we had our instructions! Then it was into work almost immediately. I took the service on the Sunday and Monday saw us immediately caught up in Vacation Bible School. We were all involved in the various activities that took place that week. It was a chance to get to know some of the congregation.

Claire Overton was the choir director who, with her husband Earl took us out for a Mexican meal on our first Sunday evening. The meal was excellent, if a little bland, and avocado is something I have still never grown to like! Marilyn Wienk was the Nursery Attendant. She was married to Dennis who was the Custodian (Caretaker in UK parlance). It turned out that he was Native American, his tribal name was Crazy Horse. His grandfather, Crazy Horse, was leader of the Lakota division of the Sioux who led the defeat of the American soldiers at the Battle of Little Bighorn. Dennis' mother had remarried a German, hence his name. He told us that when he was drafted and his superiors discovered that he was Native American, he was sent to join the black draftees, despite the fact that he was as 'white' as his superiors! It wasn't to be the first time we would encounter racism in Texas. We were also introduced to Novelle Lucas, who was in charge of the Foodbank, but more of that later.

Quite early on in our exchange we set out to explore San Antonio itself. The road system was fantastic and very well designed. Driving around the outside of the city on a multi lane highway took us past a number of significant sites.

The Alamodome, a 64,000-seat domed indoor multi-purpose stadium located on the south-eastern fringe of downtown San Antonio. The facility was only opened on 15th May 1993, having been constructed at a cost of $186 million. It has the largest suspended dome in the US.

The Tower of the Americas, a 750-feet high observation tower-restaurant located in the Hemisfair district on the south-eastern portion of Downtown San Antonio. The Tower was designed by San Antonio architect O'Neil Ford and was built as the centrepiece of the 1968 World's Fair, HemisFair '68. One of the members of Highland Terrace took us for a meal there before we left. It was an excellent meal and an interesting experience.

Then there was the famous River Walk which is a city park one level down from the street. The River Walk winds and loops under bridges as two parallel sidewalks lined with restaurants and shops, connecting the major tourist draws from the Shops at Rivercenter, to the Arneson River Theatre, to Marriage Island, to La Villita, to HemisFair Park, to the Tower Life Building, to the San Antonio Museum of Art, to the Pearl and the city's five Spanish colonial missions, which have been named a World Heritage Site, which includes the Alamo. During the annual springtime Fiesta San Antonio, the River Parade features flowery floats that float down the river. Some of these sites I will return to later, suffice it to say we visited the Shops at Rivercenter on several occasions!

On Tuesday 27th July, we had a picnic trip to The Natural Bridge Caverns. They are the largest known commercial caverns in Texas. The name is derived from the 60 ft natural limestone slab bridge that spans the amphitheatre setting of the cavern's entrance. The span was left suspended when a sinkhole collapsed below it.

On Wednesday 28th July Claire Overton took us out for lunch at North Star Mall. The next day we were introduced to the

Quilting Group and the Food Bank.

On Friday 30th July we had a trip into the Hill Country to visit the historic town of Fredericksburgh. Claire had been raving about it, so we felt that we ought to make the effort at the first opportunity. It was a good 70 miles and an hour and a half drive from San Antonio. On the way we passed several roadside stalls selling peaches, not entirely surprising since this was 'peach country'. The journey through the Hill Country was fairly unexceptional, not much hillier than the Cheshire Plain! When we arrived, we found a very small town comprising just two streets that intersected at a crossroads. Most of the buildings were single story. There wasn't much of interest. There was a Christmas Shop, but it was closed! The only other building of interest was a small museum commemorating Admiral Nimitz whose hometown this was. On the Sunday, after the service, Claire was eager to know what we thought of our visit to Fredericksburg and the Hill Country. 'Nice' said I, she wanted more, 'Very nice' said I, she still wasn't satisfied. In the end I suggested that when Bert returned from Kendal, she should ask him about historic towns in 'the hill country' of Cumbria!

There was a perception that everything in Texas was bigger and better than anything elsewhere in the world. Claire also pointed us in the direction of a particular shopping mall. Now admittedly the pair of cowboy boots that framed the entrance were two stories high, but you could have fitted the Mall into the Metro Centre at Gateshead four or five times over! She was amazed when I told her this and explained that it was the largest shopping Centre in Europe.

On Saturday 31st July between 9.30 and 12.00 we joined in with Funtime. We discovered that each Saturday morning there were activities arranged for the children. In the afternoon we went to a Flea Market.

(Sunday 1st August) At this point I ought to say something about the pattern of Sunday. The day began early with Sunday School at 9.00 am. There were classes covering the whole age range from pre-school to adult. Everyone attended. Parents came with their children. Grandparents came. There was then a brief break before the Morning Service which began at 10.10 am. Usually, refreshments followed the morning service.

I have nothing recorded for Monday 2nd August, so it is possible that that was the day we visited the Alamo. The Alamo Mission in San Antonio, commonly called simply the Alamo, was originally known as the *Misión San Antonio de Valero*. It is a former Roman Catholic mission and fortress compound, and the site of the Battle of the Alamo in 1836. The Alamo is now a museum in the Alamo Plaza Historic District of downtown San Antonio. Built by the Spanish Franciscan priest, Antonio de Olivares and Payaya Indians in 1718, it is the origin of the present city of San Antonio, along with the Presidio San Antonio de Bexar and the Acequia Madre de Valero.

The compound, which originally consisted of a sanctuary and surrounding buildings, was built by the Spanish Empire in the 18th century for the education of Native Americans after their conversion to Christianity. In 1793, the mission was secularized and then abandoned. Ten years later, it became a fortress housing a Spanish Army unit, the Second Flying Company of San Carlos de Parras, who likely gave the mission the name Alamo. This was early in the period of the Mexican War of Independence.

After independence from Spain was achieved in 1821, Mexican soldiers held the mission until December 1835, when General Martin Perfecto de Cos surrendered it to the Texian Army following the siege of Bexar. A relatively small number of Texian soldiers then occupied the compound. General Sam Houston believed the Texians did not have the manpower to hold the fort and ordered Colonel James Bowie to destroy it. However, he gave Bowie leeway to make his own logistical decision. Bowie decided to work with Colonel James C. Neill to fortify the mission (in part because there were not enough oxen available to move the cannons from the area). On February 23, 1836, Mexican General Antonio Lopez de Santa Anna led a large force of soldiers into San Antonio de Bexar and promptly initiated a siege. The siege ended on March 6, when the Mexican army overran the compound; by the end of the Battle of the Alamo nearly all of the defenders had been killed. Of the 212 men that fought and died at the Alamo, 29 are known to have been from the United Kingdom. Famous names of men who died defending the Alamo include James Bowie, William B. Travis, and Davey Crockett. When the Mexican army retreated from Texas at the end of the Texas Revolution, several weeks later, they tore down many of the Alamo walls and burned some of the buildings.

During the Republic of Texas period, which overlapped a

period of civil war in Mexico, the Alamo was used off and on to garrison soldiers, either Texian or Mexican, but it was ultimately abandoned. In 1849, a few years after Texas was annexed to the United States, the US Army began renting the facility for use as a quartermaster's depot. During the Civil War, the Confederate Army took over the site. The U.S. Army regained possession after the war and used the facility until 1876, when nearby Fort Sam Houston was established. The Alamo chapel was sold to the state government of Texas, which conducted occasional tours but made no effort to restore it. The other buildings were sold to a mercantile company which operated them as a wholesale grocery store.

After forming in 1892, the Daughters of the Republic of Texas (DRT) began trying to preserve the Alamo. In 1905, Adina Emilia De Zavala and Clara Driscoll successfully convinced the state legislature to purchase the remaining buildings and to name the DRT as the permanent custodian of the site.

Given the heat it is not surprising that we spent quite a bit of time in swimming pools. On Tuesday (3rd August) we went to visit Bert Clayton's mother. In the complex where she lived there was a swimming pool and our family made the most of it. Unsurprisingly eating, and eating well, was a feature of this Exchange, as it had been of our first Exchange and on Wednesday 4th August, we attended a UMW (United Methodist Women) lunch at Church where we were joined by members of Aldersgate UMW.

Talking of eating on Thursday (5th August) we were taken

out for an Italian meal at 'The Olive Garden'. We were quite a large group and we had to sit and wait for quite some time for sufficient table space to become available. The waiters kept bringing bread sticks and other nibbles to keep us going. Not surprisingly when the meal arrived, and it was a fabulous meal, we were already well filled. As a consequence, we all asked for 'doggy bags'. They came in the form of a printed box into which we placed what we hadn't eaten, sufficient for another meal – even without having eaten so many breadsticks the meals were so big we would inevitably have asked for 'doggy bags', the fact they were printed boxes suggested they were used to such a request!

During the next couple of days, we found ourselves having to look for cowboy boots for Robert as he was determined to be kitted out properly for the Line Dance evening which was coming up. On Friday (6th August) we drove out to the Hill Country again to visit Braunfels, Gruene and San Marco. We visited a fabulous RV site where the parents of one of the church members kept their RV. It is impossible to compare British Camper Vans to American Recreational Vehicles. The latter are palatial! It was not unusual to see smaller RVs towing the family car! There was, of course a swimming pool that the children made good use of.

On Saturday (7th August) we went to Storytime from 9.30-11.00. Afterwards we visited the County Fair. Like the one we previously visited in Gaithersburg it bore no comparison to British County Shows, catering for far more than merely agricultural matters. There was even a British Pub complete with a British Pub sign! From 4.00-7.00 pm we went to a Country and Western Dance event which was held at Highland Terrace. Robert looked the part, resplendent in cowboy boots and hat. Kath's Mum and Dad thoroughly enjoyed themselves. Kath was really good, Robert and Liz not so much. Me – I was cameraman! Of course, there was food!

Sunday (8th August) followed the usual pattern with Sunday School and Morning Service. In the afternoon from 4.00-6.00 pmwe went to a Pool Party at Dan an Billye Laxon's. The children had a whale of a time, the adults watched, occasionally helping themselves to the buffet the Laxons had laid on. While we were in San Antonio, I was driving Bert's very large, luxurious Chevrolet. Robert noted that the car's license plate was most appropriate – BKF 82Y (Bob and Kath Fisher)!

It was on either the Sunday afternoon or the Monday that we visited the San Antonio Missions National Historical Park which preserves four of the five Spanish frontier missions in San Antonio. These outposts were established by Roman Catholic religious orders to spread Christianity among the local natives. These missions formed part of a colonization system that stretched across the Spanish Southwest in the 17th, 18th, and 19th centuries.

In geographic order from north (upstream of the San Antonio River) to south (downstream) the missions are located as follows: Mission Concepcion, Mission San Jose, Mission San Juan, and Mission Espada. The Espada Aqueduct, also part of the Park, is due east of Mission San Juan, across the river. The fifth (and best known) mission in San Antonio, the Alamo, is not part of the Park. It is owned by the State of Texas, and operated by the Daughters of the Republic of Texas; it is upstream from Mission Concepcion in Downtown San Antonio. The Alamo we had already visited.

Misión Nuestra Señora de la Purísima Concepción de Acuña was established in 1716 as Nuestra Señora de la Purísima Concepción de los Hainais in East Texas. The mission was moved in 1731 to San Antonio. Founded by Franciscan friars, this is the best preserved of the Texas missions.

Misión San Francisco de la Espada was established in 1690 as San Francisco de los Tejas near present-day Augusta. and renamed San Francisco de los Neches in 1721. The mission was moved in 1731 to San Antonio and given its current name.

Misión San José y San Miguel de Aguayo was established in 1720. The church, which is still standing, was constructed in 1768. Mission San Jose was founded by Father Fran Felan. It is made from limestone.

Misión San Juan Capistrano was established in 1716 as Misión San Jose de los Nazonis in East Texas. The mission was renamed and moved in 1731 to San Antonio.

Some friends of Bert and Janice were going to stay with them in Kendal and they invited Kath and I for an evening meal in a very classy restaurant to discuss their impending visit. They came armed with maps. They wanted to travel from Kendal to Fort William, to Edinburgh, to York and back to Kendal in just three days. No matter how much we explained that there was so much to see between those towns, never mind within them, they were immovable. The problem was that in Texas everywhere was a three-hour drive with nothing in between. They just couldn't conceive the possibility that that was not the case in the UK. When they returned, we discovered they had done as they had intended. They missed so much, but they'd had a fabulous time they told us!

On Tuesday (10th August) Ruby and Roland Arnold took us all out for breakfast at the Guenther House, home of the founder of the Pioneer Flour Mills. The meal was sufficient to keep us going all day! We toured the house, well worth the visit, and the nearby Steves Homestead. Highland Terrace UMC is situated on Steves Avenue.

We decided to visit Austin, the State capital on Wednesday (11th August), typically a three-hour drive with nothing in between the two cities! We took a picnic and once we were parked up, we got out of the car to eat it. It was so hot we promptly got back in the car and turned up the air-conditioning and ate in! After lunch we visited the Capitol building. It's strange how most, if not all State Capitol Building feature a central dome. The grounds, as usual were well tended and prominently displayed was a large standing memorial-style tablet with the Ten Commandments engraved on it. It seemed odd in a nation where Church and State are so clearly distinct, mind you the same could be said of its money which often proclaims, "In God We Trust"! Turning our back on the Capitol we were facing

First Methodist Church a huge building looking not unlike Westminster Central Hall in London.

Kath and I were invited to lunch with the Lions Club by Charlie Grimes on Thursday (12th August). The next day, (Friday 13th August), we went with Larry Oefinger to the south west of San Antonio where we ate at Britschs' Restaurant. It was the first time I had ever been asked to say grace in a public restaurant! It was a lovely setting. The drive, through cattle country, reminded me of the Texas joke: 'The Texan asks the Vermont farmer, "How big is your farm?" The Vermont farmer points to a big bush and says, "Well that there is one end, and it goes over to that barn, then back up to that road you can see there, and we're sitting right on the fourth corner." The Texan ponders this for a moment before the Vermont farmer asks, "Well how big is your farm?" The Texan explains, "Well say I get in my car at about 6.00 am and leave one end of my farm. If I drive all day, I should reach the other end by about dinner time". The Vermont farmer looks up and replies, "Yeah. I had a car like that once."'

Barbed wire enabled the establishment of such huge cattle ranches and some folk maintain that it was invented in Texas, but in fact the first patent in the United States for barbed wire was issued in 1867 to Lucien B. Smith of Kent, Ohio, who is regarded as the inventor. There are some 800 unique barbed-wire patents, and many more unpatented variations, a total of perhaps 2,000 types of barbed wire. We saw several plaques displaying a variety of styles of barbed wire being sold as souvenirs and I did buy a resin paperweight in the form of a map of Texas with a piece of barbed wire embedded in it.

From Britschs' Restaurant we went on to visit the site of some ancient dinosaur tracks. We then visited Camp Verde General Store and Post Office. It was in the middle of nowhere and seemed to me to be a cross between a craft shop and a living museum looking much like it must have looked when it was first opened in 1857. It became a Post Office in 1887. We were intrigued, however, to discover that it sold bottled Welsh water and English crisps.

Six Flags Fiesta Texas was our destination on Saturday (14th August). The name refers to the flags of the six different nations that have governed Texas: Spain, France, Mexico, the Republic of Texas, the United States of America, and the Confederate States of America. The original park was (and still is) split into separate regions, such as the *Spain and Mexico* section which featured Spanish-themed rides, attractions, and buildings. We had a fabulous day out.

On Sunday (15th August) after the usual morning Sunday School and Morning Service we drove out to Kerrville and Boerne to visit a series of caverns there. Next day we went with Novelle to the distribution centre where the Supermarkets brought their foodstuffs that were surplus to requirements. They came in by the truckload, in some instances by the articulated truckload. We gathered, with vans from other San Antonio churches, to be loaded up and sent off to stock the foodbanks which operated from the churches, providing essentials for those who were needy in the neighbourhood. It was all very well organised.

Only people with the necessary credentials could collect a food parcel on the days when the food bank was open. Liz had to do a Personal Study for her GCSE RE exam when we got home, and she chose Novelle Lucas as her subject. In the afternoon we were taken some distance out of San Antonio to a farm where Robert had the opportunity to practice his archery skills.

We did another one of those – "it's only a three-hour drive" days on Tuesday (17th August). This time to the Gulf Coast, to Corpus Christi. We were impressed by the US aircraft carrier that was moored there and surprised to find, moored nearby the replicas of the Santa Maria, the Nina and the Pinta. La Santa María (The Saint Mary), was the largest of the three Spanish ships used by Christopher Columbus in his first voyage across the Atlantic Ocean in 1492, the others being the Niña and the Pinta. The last time we saw them was on our first Exchange visit when we visited Boston where they were moored in Boston harbour. We visited the nearby Aquarium then drove over the bridge onto Padre Island with its white sands. Most of the family took the opportunity to swim in the Gulf of Mexico.

On the Wednesday (18th August) Kath and her Mum were guests at a UMW Lunch. In the evening we were all invited to dinner by Don and Betty Hand. At this point in the video diary, we tour Highland Terrace UMC building. It stands on a corner site with a Mom-and-Pop store on the opposite corner, in the UK it would have been a Spar shop! The building was both substantial and impressive. The church itself was very impressive with pews, sanctuary with pulpit and lectern and altar table, stained glass windows and some banners. The ancillary premises were arranged around a quadrangle and contained a number of rooms, both large and small, including the pastor's office and a church office. There was also a basement that was used to house the Food Bank. Although the present building only dated back to the early 1970s the society was first established in 1942. The membership peaked in 1967 with 1230 members and 608 scholars in the Sunday School. Although declining, Sunday attendance was still significant with the church comfortably filled whilst we were there. We were saddened when I began this memoire in 2021 to discover that the building had just been sold for development for just short of one million dollars!

Thursday (19th August) began, as was usually the case on a Thursday, with me in the church office putting the finishing touches to my service for the bulletin for Sunday. In the afternoon we drove out to Bracketville where, north of the town was to found a tourist attraction called 'Alamo Village' built in the 1950s as the set of John Wayne's movie *The Alamo*. Scenes from James A Michener's *Texas* were also shot there. (As of July 2009, Alamo Village has been closed to the public.)

I'll mention here two other events that I can't now place in either my very brief notes or the video diary. One place we visited in San Antonio was the Lone Star Brewery.

The Lone Star Brewery, built in 1884, was the first large mechanized brewery in Texas. Adolphus Busch of Anheuser-Busch, founded it along with a group of San Antonio businessmen. The castle-like building which was once its brewery now houses the San Antonio Museum of Art. Lone Star beer was the company's main brand. One-third of the Texas flag is blue containing a single centred white star. The remainder is divided horizontally into a white and red bar.

Despite the fact that there was a significant Hispanic population in San Antonio, not surprising given its proximity to the Mexican border, there were only a couple of Hispanics in the congregation at Highland Terrace. As I noted above the US armed forces have numerous facilities in San Antonio. This meant that there were a significant number of African Americans among the troops stationed on one or other of theses bases. Towards the end of our visit a couple of the Church members, Eugene and Margaret Bishop, he was a retired US Army Colonel, asked if they could take Robert on a tour of one of the bases. We agreed. When he was returned, despite the fact that he had thoroughly enjoyed the trip, Robert was somewhat perturbed by the fact that the Bishops had been very dismissive of the African Americans they had passed referring to them in very pejorative terms. Having said that, the Bishops were a lovely couple. He 'whittled', often producing a figure of a Circuit Rider, complete with horse, usually around twelve inches high. He told me that he would have liked to produce one for me, but time was against him. Instead, he gave me a figure he had already made of a 'typical' Texan. His wife painted in oils and gave us a very small framed painting of a field of Texas Bluebonnets.

On another occasion when we were out as a family having an evening drink the discussion turned to our respective education systems and syllabus contents. One of the folk, talking of her own youngster who was around Robert's age, expressed her disappointment that her son was unable to identify more than half a dozen Native American nations, whereupon Robert immediately reeled of the names of twenty or more!

Our last trip – one of those "it's only a three-hour drive" days – was on Friday (20th August) when we drove to Laredo which was on the US side of the Rio Grande which despite its name it was not much more than shallow stream! Across the bridge was Mexico. We parked in Laredo and walked across into Nuevo Laredo, Mexico. Laredo has the distinction of flying seven flags (the Flag of the Republic of the Rio Grande, which is now the flag of the city, in addition to the Six Flags of Texas). Founded in 1755, Laredo grew from a village to the capital of the brief Republic of the Rio Grande to the largest inland port on the Mexican border. Laredo's economy is based on international trade with Mexico. We bought a typical multi-coloured, striped Mexican blanket as a souvenir. We didn't spend much time in Nuevo Laredo before returning to the north. But it did mean we had crossed both the north and south borders of the US!

On our last Saturday (21st August) we went to Storytime from 9.30-11.00 am as usual, then in the afternoon at 4.00 pm we went to a bar-b-q at Dennis and Marilyn's. Their son, Jimmy kept us entertained with his iguana and we distributed gifts to various folk who had shown us hospitality during our visit, mostly in the form of unframed prints from the Lake District. We'd never have managed anything bulkier in our luggage flying over.

Sunday (22nd August) was my final service at Highland Terrace. Robert videoed some of it. We had taught the choir 'Shine, Jesus, shine' and, with the choir, we taught it to the congregation. I presented the church with an oil painting of Mow Cop that my Dad had painted and explained its significance and proximity to where Kath's Mum and Dad lived. For Children's Time I told the story of the 'Biggest Cabbage in the World'.

In the afternoon, starting at 4.00 pm, there was an Ice Cream Social – what a way to end our visit!

On Monday (23rd August) we finished packing at the parsonage. Before we closed the last suitcase, we had a phone call from one of the church members asking us to call round as they had a gift for us. Panic. We did go round and came back with a lidded mesquite bowl which he had turned – I confess that sadly I don't now recall the name of the person who gave it to us! Eventually we were then taken to the airport to catch our flight to Washington DC for what would be a busy week before we returned to the UK. Mostly we were covering territory we'd visited before, but it was all new to Kath's Mum and Dad and we were quite pleased to re-visit places we fondly remembered from previous trips to the US.

On Tuesday (24th August) the Phillips family took us to Gaithersburg County Fair. The highlights, apart from visiting the Quilt barns, were the pig races and the duck races! That evening we had a meal at the Phillips'. On Wednesday (25th August) we went into Washington. We saw the usual sights, the Jefferson Memorial, the Lincoln Memorial and the Reflecting

Pool, The White House, the Washington Monument and the Capitol. We spent some time in the Air and Space Museum. We had our evening meal at the Campbells and afterwards Scott and Robert monopolised the pool table in the basement.

Thursday (27th August) saw us driven by Jane into Amish Country. We visited the usual places like Intercourse and because we had Kath's Dad with us, we drove on to Strasburg to visit the Railroad there. First, we visited the model railway which really was very impressive, then we had short railroad ride in carriages pulled by a vintage steam train. Kath's Dad was in his element.

On Friday (28th August) Pearl and Bill took us to lunch on board the Spirit of Washington on the Potomac. Lunch and a scenic cruise, oh, and some line dancing thrown in for good measure. A fabulous experience. Then we went to Poolesville for our evening meal with the Ingletons. Before the meal the youngsters spent some time on the playground on the green outside the Ingleton's house.

Saturday (28th August) was the Campbells day and Bill 'borrowed' the Rolls Royce he looked after for a wealthy client to take us to Harpers Ferry. I never did discover what Bill really did beyond the fact that he was a mechanic and worked in a garage. At Harpers Ferry where the Shenandoah and the Potomac meet, we had the opportunity to paddle in the Shenandoah. Then we had a picnic on the station platform before exploring the town and climbing up to the Overlook to take in the spectacular views. In the evening there was a meal at Fairhaven. On the Sunday, (28th August) I took the morning service at Fairhaven. Robert again videoed parts of it including me telling the story of the Stonecutter:

The Stonecutter

A stonecutter, up to his knees in the river, was chipping away at a huge boulder to create a monument that would survive for centuries. On the road that ran alongside the river a Maharajah was passing by. Everyone who saw him bowed low in homage. "Ah," thought the stonecutter, "Now that's power and influence for you, I wish I was a Maharajah!"

In the blink of an eye, he found himself in the howdah on the back of the elephant, and all who saw him bowed low in homage. As he was enjoying the attention, he felt a stinging sensation on the back of his neck. At first, he thought it was an insect, but no matter how much he swatted at it, it didn't go away. He realised, eventually, that it was the rays of the sun shining through a tiny hole on the fringe of the canopy on the howdah. "Ah," he thought, "Now that's power and influence for you, "I wish I was the sun!"

In the blink of an eye, he found himself high in the sky shining for all he was worth on the people beneath him. He was enjoying himself, the people on whom he shone, were having to take off various bits of clothing because they were so hot, then they were getting sunburned, or were breaking out into a sweat. He had a real sense of power until this little cloud kept

337

getting in the way. "Ah," he thought, "Now that's power and influence for you, "I wish I was the cloud!"

In the blink of an eye, he found himself between the sun and the earth stopping the sun from annoying people with its powerful rays. All was well until he came to a huge hill, and as everyone knows when a cloud comes to a hill it goes up as a cloud on one side but comes down as rain on the other! Still, it wasn't so bad because the rain helped to swell the stream and turn it into a raging torrent that cut into the banks on either side as it rushed down the hillside. It gave him a real sense of power until, that is, the river broadened out in the valley below as meandered its way towards the sea. Then he came to this enormous boulder sitting in the middle of the river. He tried to shift it, but it remained firm. "Ah," he thought, "Now that's power and influence for you, "I wish I was the boulder!"

In the blink of an eye, he found himself to be a huge boulder, firmly planted in the middle of the river, immovable, despite the river's attempt to topple it. All was well until he felt this stinging sensation on his back. He realised, after a while, that it was the chisel that the stonecutter was using to care the boulder into a monument that would survive for centuries. "Ah," he thought, "Now that's power and influence for you, "I wish I was the stonecutter!"

In the blink of an eye, he found himself up to his knees in the river with a hammer in one hand and a chisel in the other carving this enormous boulder into a memorial that would last for centuries!

And the moral of the story: "I have learned how to be content in any circumstance." (Philippians 4:11)

We had refreshments after the service then it was back to Pearl and Bill's for lunch then a last trip into Washington to the Tidal Basin. In the evening Jane took us to see the Prasad's new house – very large and very impressive! It had a very sophisticated entry and alarm system. On one wall was my Dad's painting of Windsor Castle that he had given them on an earlier visit.

back to Kendal

Then it was time to catch our flight back to the UK. First our flight to Atlanta where we had to wait for around four hours to catch our connecting flight to Manchester. We flew up the east coast before crossing the Atlantic. By now it was getting dark. All would have been well had the pilot not announced that, "if you look out of the window you can see the lights of Washington DC." Kath's mother nearly burst a blood vessel. She hadn't realised we were having to travel the same route in reverse to complete our 'open jaws' flight and couldn't believe we'd spent hours flying down to Atlanta only to retrace our steps! It was an overnight flight, so dawn was breaking when we eventually landed in Manchester. Once we cleared Customs, we got a taxi out to Ivor and Judy's in Stretford to pick up the car and drive back to Kendal. I dropped everyone off at home and rushed into school just in time for lunch and the afternoon session of the Training Day!

Although these next two incidents didn't appear in any of my Christmas letters, they are worth the telling so, although I don't recall exactly when they took place, I thought this was as good a place as any to include them.

I regularly took my 'A' level groups to both Lancaster University and Durham University when they laid on a Religious Studies day for 'A' level students. Those study days were always really worthwhile. On one such occasion we went to Durham where we heard the then bishop, the Right Revd David Jenkins deliver the afternoon lecture in the Students Union building in Elvet. He was bishop between 1986 and 1994 and had gained a reputation for being controversial because of his radical views, often, it has to said, misrepresented in the media. The lecture was excellent and much appreciated by my students.

After the morning session we went, as we usually did, for a 'Businessman's Lunch' at the Kwai Lam Chinese Restaurant on the corner in Saddler Street. After lunch and before the afternoon lecture I had a wander along to the House of Andrews bookshop where, outside, I bumped into Tom Greener, my old RE teacher who I had not seen since I failed my 'A' level Religious Studies exam at the end of my sixth form studies at the Johnston School. I took great delight in telling him that not only had I finally passed my 'A' level GCE in RE but had gone on to gain a BA(Theol), successfully candidated for the Methodist ministry, and was now Head of the RE department at the Lakes School and was in Durham with some of my 30 plus 'A' level students. He was most gracious, as always, and commended me on my success!

I regularly took the midnight Christmas Eve Communion at Windermere Methodist Church. On one such occasion a drunken man stumbled in just as the service was about to begin and sat himself down at the back. He interrupted the sermon a couple of times, not rudely, but to agree with what I said, and to commend me for taking the midnight service. When it came to the administration, he staggered down the aisle. There was no communion rail in the church and the folk either side of him had to help him stand straight when he received the elements. I wondered what I was going to say to him when I was shaking hands after the service, however, I needn't have worried as he was off before I had walked down the aisle. A couple of weeks into the spring term we had our 6th Form (Year 13) Parent's evening. One of my 'A' level students came with her father. He was charming and articulate and clearly had no recollection of having been in my Midnight Communion service at Windermere Methodist Church just a few weeks earlier. How I kept a straight face I'll never know!

[1994]

1994 was a year of quite significant changes. For both Robert and Elizabeth, the summer brought the onset of final examinations. Actually, for Robert it wasn't exams, as his course has been continuously assessed throughout. His final project, however, was crucial to obtaining his BTEC qualification. He chose to produce a model of a full-size dinosaur though thankfully he restricted himself to modelling only the head of a raptor which would have stood some 8 feet high and was about the same length!

Robert finally obtained a Grade C in his Maths – third time lucky! And in the Spring, he also passed his driving test. When I learned to drive my dad took me out with him to drive whenever he used the car. When he felt I was competent he paid for half a dozen lessons with a driving school before I took my test. I had resolved to do the same with our children. They had the advantage of Morrisons car park. In the year before their seventeenth birthday, I would take them to the car park when it was deserted and get them used to gears so that when their birthday arrived, and they had their licence they could begin driving on the road with some confidence.

In anticipation of Robert successfully completing his course, the Spring was spent looking at possible courses for him in the Autumn. A visit to Middlesbrough led us, quite by chance, to the College of Art and Design at Hartlepool which was offering an HND course in Craft Design and Production for the Entertainment Industries just what he wanted! A similar course at Rochester in Kent seemed a sensible alternative. He applied for both, was interviewed for both and obtained a place on neither. Still the return rail trip to Rochester was a pleasant experience.

Hartlepool told us that there had been 60 applicants for their 15 places, and 45 of those had wanted one of the 5 places allocated to Special Effects. Guess what Robert had wanted to do? They put him on their reserve list, and we arranged for him to do a 'fill-in' year on an Arts Foundation Course at the local

Technical College. Two weeks before the end of the summer holidays he received a phone call from Hartlepool to say that someone had dropped out of the course and there was a place for him if he wanted it. He did. He started at the beginning of September and thoroughly enjoyed himself. He was looking after himself, sharing a house with three girls! He also linked up with the local Methodist Church and joined their youth group, becoming involved in their production of 'Burning Questions'. We went to see it just before the half-term break – we were most impressed.

For Liz it was exams, exams, exams. This was the year of her GCSEs. They seemed to go on interminably. Eventually they were over, and it was a case of waiting for the results. When they came we were delighted. She obtained 8 Grade C passes and 2 Grade D passes. So, the autumn saw Liz beginning her course at Kendal Technical College. She decided to take a BTEC in Nursery Nursing, and she thoroughly enjoyed it. Providing she was successful this qualification would be accepted instead of the traditional 'A' level GCEs allowing her to go on to University to take a degree. She was hoping to go into teaching.

Before the summer holidays Liz applied for a part-time job at Morrisons supermarket where her brother had been working part-time for the previous two years. She heard nothing until the autumn when she was taken on as a checkout operator on Thursday and Friday evenings and all-day Saturday. She wasn't too keen at first but eventually settled into the job and enjoyed it. She soon gained the reputation as being the fastest checkout operator in the store!

Half-way through the Summer term the Head Teacher at Kath's school decided to take early retirement and his job was advertised. There were only a few applicants and none that the school governors felt were suitable. Kath was asked to take on the post as Acting Head for the autumn term. This she reluctantly agreed to do. When the term began, although she found it very demanding, she also found that she enjoyed both the challenge and the responsibility. The post was re-advertised, and she applied, rather reluctantly it has to be said. She was shortlisted against a Head and two Deputy Heads. After the interviews, and two hours of deliberations on the part of the school governors, she was offered the job!

My life went on much as always. At school the department survived some serious staffing problems which took some time to be resolved. At Church we began an 'alternative' service on the first Sunday evening of each month. Although they did not attract a significant number of young people, as we had hoped they would, they seemed to have been warmly welcomed by those who did come. It was also sometime around 1994 that I was asked to take on the role of Chairman of Coniston Youth Centre. It was part of the Carlisle Diocese and the previous Chairman had been in place for years. It was felt that a change was needed, and I met their requirements. It meant regular, if infrequent trips to Coniston. The biggest issue was the absence of anyone prepared to be a Treasurer, so I persuaded them to employ a finance company based in Kendal. It worked well. It proved to be an interesting experience.

We had no adventurous holidays abroad in this year, but we did have a very enjoyable week in the north of Scotland. We even managed a visit to John O' Groats. Next year would be rather different as in February Kath and I would be taking our fifth trip to Israel, only two more and I could actually become an Israeli Government registered guide! In June we had a family holiday in Wales, a chance to visit old haunts from Kath's time at College there.

In July I was in Denmark for my birthday, taking a school trip there for our Activity Week. The idea was to visit Legoland, largely to satisfy Robert's obsession with Lego. In the end numbers were small and we ended up hiring a mini-bus – it had to have a tachograph – and a female member of staff and I shared the driving. Liz came with us.

We went by overnight ferry from Newcastle. The food was superb, a proper smorgasbord, and Robert was sea-sick! We had a fabulous day in Legoland and also visited a Viking Museum and a 'Beamish-like' folk Museum. We ended up in Copenhagen. We saw the famous mermaid statue, which was fine, but spoiled by its location in the docks, and the Tivoli Gardens which were excellent. As a souvenir of our visit I bought three Royal Copenhagen Christmas Plates. One each for Robert and Elizabeth to commemorate the year of their birth, and one for Kath to commemorate the year of our marriage. That evening I realised that the one I had bought for Kath was for the year after we were married so it was a quick dash into Copenhagen the next day to change it for the right year. We stayed in Youth Hostels which proved very comfortable. Parking in Copenhagen was interesting and very fair. You paid by the minute. So even though you were in the centre, where charges were higher, you only paid for the time you actually parked, unlike in the UK where you paid by the hour even if you stayed only ten minutes.

[1995]

1995 was another year of milestones. My parents celebrated their Diamond Wedding Anniversary on 1st January with a 'bit of a do' at Kent Court, the sheltered housing complex where they were living. Then it was my mother's 90th birthday on 28th March. Finally, Kath and I celebrated our Silver Wedding Anniversary on 18th July.

One way or another it was a year of re-decorating. The trouble was that we had never before lived anywhere long enough to get around to re-decorating. However, after nearly 12 years in Kendal we decided we needed to tackle some of the bigger jobs that summer. We began gently by redecorating the back bedroom, traditionally the guest room, and moving Liz into it, at her request for a bigger room than the one she had. Then we turned our attention to the outside. We'd made a start the previous year and then stopped because we were undecided on the colour scheme. From brown and cream we'd decided to change to blue and gold. The garage looked great with a blue frame and gold door but on the front door . . . we weren't so sure. In the end we went blue and cream. Once the painting was underway, I left Robert to it and turned my attention to the inside once again.

Hall, landing and stairs were next in line, no mean feat in a three-storey house, but we managed it. Only the bannister rail remained to be painted. We were aiming to finish before Christmas. The long hot summer was a real bonus. The eaves were too high – they had not been painted last time! We were fortunate to get the guy who had been doing the painting at Kath's school to paint the eaves, he made it look so simple! There were still a few little bits to finish off, but they would have to wait for the next spring. Meanwhile there was the study, and the front bedroom, more than enough to keep my mind of our impending OFSTED Inspection at school during the penultimate week of term – happy Christmas! I would be glad when it was all over, I seemed to have spent so much time writing up all the department's documentation! My increasing involvement with the Young People's group at Stricklandgate Methodist Church provided a blessed relief from the pressure at school.

Kath's first full year as Head had been both busy and successful. She was rarely home before 6.30 pm any weekday evening, was often in school at a weekend, and during the summer holidays was in school every single day supervising various alterations and decorations. The only days Kath didn't go into school in the summer were the few days we were away visiting friends. Numbers at the school had increased during the year, an extra part-time member of staff had been appointed and Kath's office hours had been increased from two to three half days. In the lead up to Christmas she was kept busy rehearsing the lead in the school's Christmas production of 'Psalty's Christmas Calamity'. They did do it several years ago and it looked set to be as good, if not better, than last time. At Church she continued to fulfil her duties as a Church Steward and enjoyed the responsibility,

Kath and I took a trip to Israel during February half-term and had a wonderful time. It was good to see the land in springtime when even the desert had a touch of green and there were lots of flowers about. On most of our trips to Israel we had one or other of my colleagues decide to come along. If my memory serves me correctly on this occasion it was Kevin Wall, one of our Biology teachers. Like others who went before him he found it enjoyable, interesting, and challenging.

We always made a point of visiting Yad Vashem, Established in 1953 by an act of the Knesset (Israeli Parliament). Yad Vashem, the World Holocaust Remembrance Centre, is entrusted with the task of commemorating, documenting, researching and educating about the Holocaust: remembering the six million Jews murdered by the German Nazis and their collaborators, the destroyed Jewish communities, and the ghetto and resistance fighters; and honouring the Righteous Among the Nations who risked their lives to rescue Jews during the Holocaust. Yad Vashem encompasses 45 acres on the Mount of Remembrance in Jerusalem and is comprised of various museums, research and education centres, monuments and memorials. Among these are the Museum Complex, the Hall of Remembrance, the Valley of the Communities and the Children's Memorial.

The Children's Memorial is hollowed out from an underground cavern and is a tribute to the approximately 1.5 million Jewish children who were murdered during the Holocaust. Memorial candles, a customary Jewish tradition to remember the dead, are reflected infinitely in a dark and sombre space, creating the impression of millions of stars shining in the firmament. The names of murdered children, their ages and countries of origin can be heard in the background as you walk through the cavern. It was built with the generous donation of Abe and Edita Spiegel, whose son Uziel was murdered in Auschwitz at the age of two and a half. I defy anyone to walk though without being moved to tears.

Kevin told me after the trip that he was a lapsed Catholic who had become a practising Jew after his visit to Israel. His mother was Jewish (being Jewish is determined by a mother's faith). She had married a Roman Catholic and Kevin had been brought in his father's faith. As a biologist he also told us quite a bit about the medical experiments that had happened in the concentration camps. Apparently much of what is now commonplace in plastic surgery owes a great deal to those experiments. Another member of the party that year was Gladney, a member of Stricklandgate Methodist Church. He began to open up for the first time since he returned from the War. It transpired that he was among the first troops to liberate Belsen and enter the camp, something he had not talked about before.

After a visit to Israel in the Spring we came back feeling really refreshed. In the summer half-term week, we went to St. David's in Wales. Robert and Liz elected to stay at home and give us a week by ourselves. We thoroughly enjoyed the week visiting a part of Britain we had not been to before. In the summer we celebrated our Silver Wedding Anniversary and were both surprised and delighted by the number of folk who sent gifts and greetings.

Robert completed his first year at Hartlepool in fine style. He was the youngest member of the course and was up against some stiff opposition from his more experienced classmates. At the beginning of the course, he was managing 'passes' with the occasional 'merit'. The final first year project was a group effort. All 21 members of the class were asked to produce a plan for an Elizabethan scene for Taming of the Shrew. Robert's was the plan selected and he made most of the baseboard. Everyone, including Robert, produced various buildings that went onto it along with the various figures that made it into a fantastic display. It covered the area of an average room. It had to be accurate in every detail such that it could be used as a film set, if required. We were most impressed when we saw it, but even more impressed when we learned that he was one of only two in the group to be awarded a 'distinction'!

We all went to the MAYC London Weekend in May and had a wonderful time, though I have to say that Church floors don't get any softer as the years go by. Robert came back with a girlfriend! His dress sense and hairstyle improved remarkably over the following few months, by contrast our phone bill deteriorated alarmingly! Unfortunately, the relationship didn't last long.

Like Robert, Liz was into the second year of her course though she was much less settled. The adult / young person mix in her classes has led to all sorts of friction and her results were very mixed. This year she was also doing an 'A' level in English. Although she was quite keen to go off to Manchester University to do a B.A. (Hons.) in Early Childhood she was talking about taking a year out first and staying at home, and Robert was threatening the same for next year before getting himself a full time job just when Kath and I thought we were going to have a quiet life at last! Liz continued playing the piano though she was avoiding exams which we thought was a pity and something she was likely to regret later. She also did quite well earning, and saving, her pocket by babysitting and working at Morrisons supermarket on three evenings and all day on Saturday. Liz also helped run the Traidcraft Stall with the young people at Church on a Sunday morning.

[1996]

February half-term saw Kath and I taking ten Year12 students to Brighton where we stayed with Colin Lawlor in his Vicarage (Colin was one of my PGCE students who, having successfully graduated decided instead of going into teaching to go into the Church). From there we visited two Jewish Museums, a Hindu Temple and the British Museum in London, ending the week by attending a Synagogue service in Brighton itself. We all had a terrific time.

Robert (Jnr) successfully completed the second, and final year of his HND course at Hartlepool. Sadly, he did not enjoy it as much as his first year and finished without any real idea of what to do next. As a result, he got himself a job at Morrisons supermarket, working on the Deli counter. He also got himself a girlfriend, Rebecca, and there was talk of an engagement at Christmas. She'd been married before and had a two-and-a-half-year-old youngster called Luke who was really cute. Getting engaged gave us some cause for concern, but they seemed to know what they wanted to do. Robert also bought himself a car – and a week after he bought it it had to go back into the garage, so he borrowed our Volvo 340, Kath's car, and wrote it off! Thankfully neither he nor Rebecca was hurt. We were on the point of replacing the Renault, which was showing distinct signs of age; as it was, we ended up replacing both cars!

Elizabeth successfully completed the second, and final year of her BTEC course at Kendal. Like Robert, she didn't much enjoy it and finished without any real idea of what to do next, so she decided to spend the next twelve months working at Morrisons supermarket on check-outs! She bought herself her own car, a red VW Polo. She was tickled to bits with it. It suited her down to the ground. She also applied to Manchester University with a view to doing a degree there, starting the next September.

Kath continued to come to terms with being Head Teacher in an increasingly popular village Primary School. They were booking youngsters in for the year 2000 already! She was in the process of launching an appeal to raise money to build a School Hall, a desperately needed facility. Hopefully they would manage to raise sufficient money, around £100,000, with a similar sum coming from the Funding Agency, quickly enough to enable the building to go ahead the next summer.

I applied to take 'early' retirement from teaching with a view to returning to Circuit ministry the following September. By a happy chance of circumstance, the Arnside section of the Kendal Circuit became vacant in September 1996; since they were unable to find anyone to replace him, the minister, who was retiring, agreed to stay for a further year; and I was invited to fill that appointment from September 1997. This would mean that Kath could continue in her post as head Teacher at Heversham for the foreseeable future which suited us both extremely well. The niggling worry was that the Government had just announced changes to the premature retirement scheme in an attempt to retain experienced teachers. This could mean that my application might be unsuccessful. The Circuit might then be left short of a minister, although if they were unable to fill the appointment last year, because of shortages, it was unlikely they would be able to fill it this year. That would not, however, make me feel much better about matters if they turned out that way.

As part of my application to return to Circuit ministry I had to have a full medical which resulted in identifying the fact that I had diabetes type 2! Fortunately, this was relatively easily controlled by diet, or by diet and pills if that proved necessary. The first thing was to lose some weight.

We didn't venture far on holiday during the year. In the summer Kath and I had a week in Scotland near Oban. It gave us a chance to visit Mull, twice, and Iona, briefly, in the rain, before going on, by boat, to Staffa and Fingal's Cave – by the time we got there the weather was so bad we couldn't land and Kath, after grabbing an excellent photograph of Fingal's Cave, spent the next hour in the loo being thoroughly seasick! It was a great week although the weather was not brilliant.

Later in the summer we returned to Brighton to visit Colin Lawlor again. We had a fabulous few days, with glorious weather. Apart from Brighton itself we indulged ourselves and had a day in Legoland at Windsor. It compares very favourably with Legoland in Denmark which I had visited a couple of years previously. On the Sunday I preached in Colin's Church then we set out to spend a few days visiting old friends in the Midlands. Another great week.

The senior Fishers continued in good health, despite advancing age. So too did Kath's parents despite the shock of having had their car stolen and crashed. Thankfully it was restored to good working order, although not before making certain security arrangements at their house!

The end of the year saw me putting the final touches to our Israel trip which was planned for February half-term week the next year. This time we were also planning to visit Jordan, including a day trip to Petra. This would be our sixth trip and we thought this would definitely be our last one as it just takes so much organising!

On Christmas Eve, I received a letter from Cumbria County Council to say that my application to take early retirement had been refused. In the light of Government proposals to change the Pension scheme Cumbria had decided to allow no early retirements after Easter 1997! As it turned out the Government shelved its plans in the Spring, but by then I had had to withdraw my acceptance of the invitation to the Arnside section of the Circuit.

[1997]

Robert and Rebecca did get engaged on New Year's Day 1997, and a few weeks later announced that Rebecca was pregnant! So, on October 8th we were duly presented with our first 'official' grandchild – Robert Karl, weighing in at 5lbs 5oz. He was the most contented baby we'd ever come across, so much so that Luke complained that all his new brother did was sleep!

Elizabeth's first application to University, in the Spring, was unsuccessful. That appeared to be that. No way was she going to try again. Then, just before the 'A' level results were published, she announced that she was going to re-apply to University with a view to becoming a teacher. Her first contact, University of York at Scarborough, on the eve of the publication of results, offered her an interview the next week. The morning after, her first phone call, to the University of Durham at Stockton, resulted in an unconditional offer. So just a couple of weeks later saw us delivering her to Stockton, ironically only about 12 miles south of Hartlepool, which Robert had left only twelve months earlier. So, she began her first term of a three-year B.Sc. (Hons.) degree in Science and Childhood in Society, to be followed by a further year studying for a PGCE.

Kath and I had several really good breaks during the year. February half-term saw us taking our sixth (and definitely our last) trip to Israel. This time we began with three days in Jordan including a visit to Petra. At the beginning of our visit, as we crossed from Israel into Jordan one of our party was taken away by security and was away for ages. Just as we feared the worst, he re-joined us. We never did discover the reason he was taken off for additional questioning. Petra was amazing, spoiled only by the fact that Kath lost her camera. She had it when she went to the loo, but when she realised that she'd left it there and went back it had disappeared. In Jordan the weather was glorious, and the scenery was out of this world. Unfortunately, the last couple of days, in Jerusalem, it did nothing but rain but even that didn't spoil what was probably our best trip ever.

In August we went, for the first time, to Gran Canaria, taking Kath's Mum and Dad with us. The weather was fantastic, as was the apartment. As indeed was the scenery. We had one day driving right round the island and a couple of days driving into the interior. On one of those trips, we drove to the top of the highest point on the island, the views were magnificent. It really was a relaxing week.

We also had a few days in Brighton during the summer again this year, and we visited friends in Manchester for a few days on a couple of occasions. Neither place was as exotic as either Israel or Gran Canaria, but nevertheless the visits were just as enjoyable. Then it was back to school.

At the beginning of September, the day we returned to school, my dad was rushed into hospital with heart failure. He was very poorly for several weeks and was still very confused when he was discharged home. Mam couldn't cope with him, so he was transferred to a Residential Home after just a week. Four days later he was back in hospital with heart failure once again. After four weeks Social Services recommended that he be placed in a home for the elderly mentally infirm. The day after he was assessed, his confusion disappeared and he began to recover, going from strength to strength. Four weeks later, he was discharged home once again, and he seemed to be managing well. So, providing he took things easy it was anticipated that he would be around a while longer.

Kath was still enjoying her post as Head, well most of the time. The amount of administration did not ease and, under a new Labour Government, the School's status was under threat, with no clear indication as to how precisely this would be changed. Most importantly the scrapping of the Funding Agency meant the new School Hall project was under a shadow. Providing they got their act together they might just get away with it, as some funds were still around for Grant Maintained and Voluntary Aided Schools, but these would soon disappear. She finally heard that the School would be inspected by Ofsted during the last week of the Spring term the next year. I would be relieved when Ofsted had come and gone, although I had no doubt but that they would 'pass' with flying colours.

At Church, because of changes among other Stewards, Kath became Senior Church Steward two years early. This involved her in the search for a new Minister to replace the current one who would leave the next September. The position was filled, and we were looking forward to welcoming a minister from Peterborough in September 1998.

I was still enjoying my continuing involvement in education – in other words I was stuck where I was, whether I liked it or not! I was trying to persuade the local Churches to make a real financial commitment to RE by buying several computers for the RE Department, as well as trying to get some folk to come into the classroom on a regular basis. If successful it would certainly help raise the status of RE and perhaps begin a trend. I wrote to every church in the 'catchment area', as far as Kendal. Apart from a donation from Stricklandgate Methodist Church and an offer from two people in one of the evangelical churches to come into school I received no positive response. I confess I was disappointed.

[1998]

Dad died at the end of March, peacefully, in his sleep. He was just a month past his 89th Birthday. He had never really fully recovered from his illness the previous September. He was in hospital for about four weeks before he died. Thankfully he had lived long enough to see his great-grandson and he had been able to spend Christmas with us as usual. Mam, who would be 94 the next March was still coping on her own. She was, however, increasingly frail but managed remarkably well.

Dad died the night before Kath's Ofsted inspection began. It was a very traumatic week for her. They did offer to postpone but she decided that it should go ahead. The inspection went well, and the school received a glowing report. This was on top of gaining the highest SATs results of any primary school in Cumbria. The result of all this was that Kath's school featured in the 'Sunday Times' supplement listing the best schools in the country. Hers was 87th in the top 200! To cap all that the school was successful in its bid for funding for the building of the new school hall. The school was a Church of England Voluntary Aided School and the local Church was very generous in giving substantial funds to the school, the result of the sale of some property and land, which added to what the school had raised, was doubled by the Funding Agency. The £240,000 project was now well under way and should be completed by the spring of next year. So Kath turned her attention to finding more funds, a mere £5,000, to extend a classroom by incorporating the soon-to-be-redundant servery! That, she insisted, would complete the building work she wanted done at the school.

Liz was now well into her second year at University. She surprised herself by passing everything at the end of year one, even her Maths which were now way beyond anything Kath or I could attempt! She wasn't too happy at Easter, in part because of Grandpa's death, in part because she had helped her mum out during Ofsted week and found it very stressful, making her think twice about going on with the degree with a view to teaching at the end of it. However, the main reason was that she wasn't terribly happy in the flat she shared in the Hall of Residence. Some of her 'flatmates' were incredibly inconsiderate; the kitchen was considered a health hazard by the

University and they were all fined. When Liz and another of her flatmates, contacted the authorities to explain that they were not responsible, the two of them were let off the fine. In September, with her two best friends, she moved into a house. During the summer the landlord, who had only recently purchased the property, had had the house completely refurbished. New central heating system, carpets, decoration, and some furniture. It was really lovely. So, she was much happier, and the social life was great!

Robert and Rebecca, Luke and 'little' Robert seemed to be doing well. They had their ups and downs over the previous year mainly because Robert hadn't been able to find a job. However, things improved when they became agents for Kleeneze. It was taking a while to build up their business, but they were beginning to, and at least they were enjoying it. They still ran the Traidcraft stall at Church each Sunday morning. Luke was knocked down by a car when he ran out between two parked vehicles. He broke his leg and had it in plaster for six weeks! His timing was impeccable, just a couple of weeks after he had started school, so he missed most of the first half-term.

Kath and I went to Malta for a week during the summer half term. We took Kath's Mum and Dad with us. We had a wonderful time. The weather was glorious though there was quite a wind most days. We had a hire car and we toured a lot. We also went on a coach trip to visit the nearby island of Gozo which was really lovely. We went that week as it was the first opportunity to get away after Ofsted, but it meant we didn't have a holiday during the summer. We did, however, enjoy the opportunity to visit friends, ending up in Brighton once again. During those few days we managed a day trip to France – via the Channel Tunnel – an interesting non-experience!

Shortly after we returned from Malta Kath's dad was found to have an 'aneurysm' and urgently needed surgery – or he would be unlikely to survive until Christmas. The earliest date that could be arranged was at the beginning of September. Kath's brother, Raymond came over from Australia, the first time he had been back since the family emigrated there eighteen years ago. Diane, his eldest, came with him. Kath's sister and her husband and family came over from Northern Ireland and we ended up hosting a family reunion the weekend before Kath's dad went into hospital! The operation went well, although her dad's heart rate took some time settle so he spent ten days in intensive care. He made a good recovery, though complained of lack of energy. At 74 he was doing remarkably well!

I had the privilege of marrying two of my colleagues at Easter. The service took place in the chapel at Damson Dene Methodist Hotel. Our minister was moving on in the summer so, when it became known that we were not going on holiday, I had another two weddings to take in August. It was just as well that we were not going on holiday, and not just because of the weddings! In July, when the central heating boiler was serviced, we were advised that it needed replacing. The engineer didn't add as he had for the past five years, that it would probably last another year, so we decided we had better do something about it. British Gas carne up with the best quotation so they were given the job which they came to do in August. It took two days, cost a fortune and was a disaster from start to finish. So much so that I wrote a lengthy letter of complaint – something I had never done before. This resulted in all sorts of apologies, additional work and refunds! During the month of August, we experienced the wettest summer we could remember in Kendal and the kitchen roof, which was a flat roof, began to leak – badly! As a result, we had to have a new roof put on at the beginning of September – more expense!

[1999]

My mam didn't make her 94th birthday. She died in early February, quite unexpectedly. Following Dad's death, the previous March she had coped remarkably well, but just before Christmas she became depressed. The tablets the doctor prescribed didn't help and she came off them on Christmas Eve. Christmas Day was difficult but by New Year she was more like herself. At the beginning of February, she began to fail quite quickly. She was admitted to hospital and a week later died in her sleep. I think she had simply decided that her time had come.

During the next few months we were faced with the task of clearing the flat and selling it. Neither proved to be too difficult a task. Most of the furniture was distributed between the family, and a Rental Agency were very keen to buy the flat as they already had a prospective tenant. By the end of the summer holidays everything was sorted – except for some of the bits and pieces which were stored in our back basement.

Easter saw the opening of Kath's school hall. The job was completed ahead of schedule, just, and within budget. The Bishop performed the official opening which was a very impressive occasion. In the summer Kath had her way, funds were found, and the redundant servery was incorporated into the next-door, rather small, classroom. So much for this being her last building venture – she was now planning a cloakroom and toilet extension to the 'top' classroom! She continued to enjoy her job – with some reservations! The paperwork seems to increase with each new government initiative so, most evenings, she didn't get home until six and by half past seven was wading through paperwork, often until midnight!

During the summer half-term break Kath and Liz and I had a week on the Costa del Sol, in Spain. The weather was lovely, the mosquitoes were not! Apart from touring locally we had a trip to Granada where we visited the Alhambra, which was quite magnificent. We also visited Seville, which was fascinating.

The beginning of the summer holidays was hectic. Kath spent several days in school whilst I got on with the task of clearing Mam's flat. At the beginning of August, we went for a weeks holiday in the Isle of Man taking Liz with us as well as Kath's mum and dad. I made a start on a tapestry cushion based on a Celtic design I had copied from a series of cross-stitch patterns I had borrowed from a friend of Kath's mum. It was an enjoyable holiday, but the weather was changeable with alternate days of steady rain! After we had been back a week Kath and I decided that we really needed some sun before we faced a long Autumn term so on the next Monday we phoned for a 'late break' and the Friday saw us bound for Tenerife! It was wonderful, and just what we needed. Our apartment was superb and perfectly located. The weather was brilliant, and the scenery was breath-taking.

Liz was none too pleased at missing out on this particular trip, but she was busy working. The long summer break was a chance for her to earn some money before beginning the final year of her degree. She passed everything again in her second year and seemed to be coping well with her final years work. She decided to apply for a PGCE course so that she could go into teaching. Ironically, even though she was studying a BSc (Hons) at Durham University they turned down her application to do a PGCE course with them. She was, however offered a place at Lancaster, who had previously turned down her application to study for a degree with them three years earlier. It meant that for her PGCE she could live at home. I don't think that Kath and I were the attraction but rather the young man she had met during the summer when she was working, once again, at Morrisons supermarket. His name was Gareth and he seemed very nice and clearly thought the world of Liz.

Kath and I went on a computer course earlier in the year, and we got certificates to prove it! Despite that I was not convinced that either of us was any more proficient, but we kept hammering away! That, however, was not the highlight of Kath's year. When her school hall was being built, she casually commented that it would be completed in time for her to have her 50th Birthday party in it, a comment she immediately forgot about. We didn't however, and so on the weekend of her birthday when her parents were visiting us and, by pure coincidence, her sister and her husband were going to join us, we arranged a 'surprise' party. Apart from colleagues her school and friends from church, we had invited friends from Coalville and Manchester and Southport. We convinced Kath that we were taking her out for an early meal, just her Mum and Dad, the two of us and Pam and David who were meeting us at Kath's school because they had taken their youngest son Martin back to University at Lancaster. Imagine her surprise when she took Pam and David to show them the school hall to find it full of balloons and banners, food and drink, and friends from near and far. Robert and Rebecca, and Liz and Gareth had put up most of the decorations, and after everyone had eaten Robert organised party games. Everyone seemed to enjoy themselves.

Robert and Rebecca seemed to survive. Neither had a steady job. Rebecca had a part-time cleaning job and the pair of them got a succession of casual jobs, mostly delivering things – telephone directories and umbrellas! Luke settled well into school and 'little' Robert had begun toddling about pointing at everything and telling us what it was!

My fifteenth year at the Lakes School. A new head was appointed earlier in the year and she took up her post in September. I was a little apprehensive when she was appointed as it turned out that she had started her career as a teacher of Religious Education. However, initially she proved to be very supportive, and seemed to be a delightful person. We were informed that the school was to have an OFSTED inspection during the first week of February, so the next few weeks proved to be hectic, ensuring that all the paperwork was in place. In addition, there was all the preparation needed to get the new 'A' level course in place following the governments reorganisation of post-16 education. It never seemed to end! I was also expected, by the Methodist Church, to complete my accompanied self-appraisal during the current year! I was also informed by the Methodist Church that I was due to take a sabbatical – I wouldn't have minded one, but I didn't think the Education Department would approve it!

Christmas 2000 – the last Christmas of the 20th century!

In the July Kath and I went to Stockton to see Liz graduate from the University of Durham with a B.Sc. (Hons.). She gained a II(i)! We were, justifiably, proud of her. The PGCE course she embarked on was a SCITT (School Centred Initial Teacher Training) course based at Workington in the north of Cumbria. It was ironic that the first University she had applied to for her first degree, that had turned her down, would be the University that would validate the PGCE course!

Next to her graduation, the highlight of the year for Liz was her engagement to Gareth during August. She celebrated by joining Kath and I on the second week of our holiday in Lanzarote, leaving Gareth behind, working! They planned to marry in December 2001, and all being well I would have the privilege of conducting the wedding. Well, I baptised her and confirmed her, so it seemed fitting that I should officiate at her wedding.

In the summer half-term week Kath and I went to Austria ending up at Oberammergau for a performance of the Passion Play. We went by coach, which rather put us off coaching holidays – two days there and two days back with hardly a break! The Passion Play, however, made up for all the discomfort. We had to be in our seats by 9.15 in the morning. We broke for lunch at 12.00 and had to be back in our seats for the second part of the performance at 2.45 p.m. The play finished at 6.30 p.m. The stage was huge and was open to the elements. The audience of 4,000, however, was under cover. Nearly everyone in the village was involved in the production, c.2,000 people, plus birds, sheep and goats, when Jesus 'cleansed' the Temple, and a live horse for the centurion at the crucifixion. The whole thing was in German although we all had transcripts in English. The music, singing and acting were absolutely brilliant. It was a really moving experience, and we were so glad that we went.

Kath and I also had a week in Spain during the spring and autumn half-term weeks, courtesy of timeshare promotions! We didn't want to buy the timeshare, but we were quite happy to accept the holiday weeks they offered for attending. Each week only cost us one airfare, the other airfare and accommodation being free! Cheap holidays in the sun – bliss! Mind you the autumn half-term we left Manchester in the rain and for the first four days it rained in Spain (and we weren't on the plain!). Still, it was warm rain and the last three days were glorious and hot. Because of the rain we attended Spanish classes though how long we would remember what we learned was debatable.

Kath still plodded on, at times somewhat wearily, in her post.

That, in part, was the reason behind our frequent holidays in the sun that year. Generally, she was still, by and large, enjoying her job but it was becoming increasingly pressurised. The next hurdle she had to face was setting her head teacher's performance objectives for the next year!

She bought herself a lap-top computer earlier in the year and was spending an increasing amount of time in front of it producing a growing number of forms for all sorts of record keeping, from test scores to lesson plans. When the computer became popular it was claimed that it would reduce workloads. I quickly came to the conclusion that the opposite was true. Because computers could be used to produce all sorts of records, all sorts of records now needed to be produced it seemed! And preferably, yesterday!

The RE Department at the Lakes School had always had two full-time members of staff with several other colleagues taking the 'odd' lesson to ensure that the subject was taught across the board. Marjorie Crombie twice served as my second-in-department. She was excellent. When she left, the first time, she was replaced with a woman who gave up after only a few weeks and who then, sadly, took her own life. One good thing she did do was to introduce 'Here I Am' by Russel Stannard as a novel to read to our Year 8s. Ken Oldfield had introduced the reading of a chapter of an appropriate novel at the end of the lesson in Years 8 and 9. Inda Kaur was my second-in-department for quite some time, as was Marilyn Mason.

At one point, when the post was vacant, Arthur Capstick

appointed Rod Champion as a part-time second-in-department. Rod was friend of his, a one-time Head of RE and Ofsted Inspector. I was not consulted. Rod's main interests were Philosophy of Religion and Hinduism. As a consequence, the 'A' level Hinduism course was taken off me and given to Rod. Because he was only part-time it also meant more colleagues were expected to pick up the slack. By and large we rubbed along OK until the Government rationalised the Exam Boards and changed the syllabuses making it no longer possible to teach two World Faiths at 'A' level. I proposed to take over the Hinduism and give Rod the task of introducing Philosophy of Religion. Rod refused to give up the Hinduism course, and the newly appointed head supported him. That left me with the Philosophy of Religion course. I was not happy teaching a course with which I was unfamiliar, a course I had abandoned for just that reason when I was first appointed to the school. In the end the head took it on; she had been an RE teacher and Philosophy of Religion was her forte. It seemed that the time had come to consider leaving Sector ministry and returning to Circuit ministry.

In some respects, I knew I would leave reluctantly as there was much about teaching, I still enjoyed. For example, as I came to that decision, I had to write a reference for one of my students who left a couple of years previously and who now wanted to take a degree in Religious Studies and go on to teach Secondary Religious Education. She wasn't the first, so I must have been doing something right!

I had always anticipated such a move at some point in my

career. So, God willing, and with the approval of the Methodist Church's Stationing Committee, it seemed quite likely that from the next September we would be living elsewhere than 2 South Road, Kendal. We had hoped to be sufficiently nearby for Kath to continue in her post for the next few years. However, it became clear that that was unlikely to happen. Kath felt that she was quite ready to leave her present post. In fact, she saw it as a good excuse to go!

The next year, then, promised to be busy, exciting and, no doubt, traumatic. We'd got out of the habit of moving to a new house since moving to Kendal, but that trauma would, I believed, be more than compensated for by the excitement of having a pastoral charge once again, though no doubt that would bring traumas of its own!

Robert and Rebecca continued much as always, only occasionally in work, and going from one mini crisis to another! The children were doing well. Luke enjoyed school, as much as most six-year olds enjoy school, and little Robert was more talkative than ever! There was talk of a house exchange with someone in Leicester the next summer, but then there had earlier been talk of a house exchange with someone in Derbyshire that came to nothing.

[2001]

As we anticipated, 2001 was, without doubt, a particularly traumatic and exciting year. Early in the year I was invited to consider a post as minister of a church in Greenock, linked with a smaller church some distance away. We drove north to have a look. Both churches looked promising. After a look around the manse and the church in Greenock we were taken out to lunch. Our host, it transpired was a fairly wealthy member of the church, the owner of the local football team! We drove from there to the other church, I can't now recall its name, where after a look around we were entertained to tea at the home of one of the Stewards. We were disappointed when, some days later, we received the phone call from the Senior Circuit Steward to say that I was not invited. In keeping with protocol no reason was given. My superintendent minister and my District Chair were amazed. They made some enquiries and it transpired that the 'big noise' at Greenock was holding out for a husband-and-wife team – two for the price of one! The Revds Trevor and Janet Capstick were due to move from the Kendal Circuit that September. Arthur Capstick, recently my Head Teacher, was Trevor's cousin. Arthur was a member of Rotary, as was the 'big noise' as Greenock – you do the Maths! My Chair spoke to the Chair of the Scotland District, the result – no minister would be appointed to Greenock that year!

The Chair then suggested that I might be considered to replace the Capsticks, only my name was put forward too late as it turned out, an appointment had already been made. He phoned from Stationing Committee to ask if I would consider an appointment as superintendent of a Welsh speaking Circuit . . . er, not really. In the end I was offered the post of Superintendent Minister of the Blackburn Circuit. We were very encouraged by our visit to the Circuit, and we were delighted when they invited me to take up the post.

Kath and I had a week in Tenerife at half term in the February and once we returned it was 'all systems go'! Both of us had to tender our resignations from our respective teaching posts. My successor was quickly appointed, and I spent the next few months at school sorting out the RE Department Office and the Resources Room so as not to leave my successor with the task of wading through all the things I had collected 'just in case'. It wasn't so easy for Kath as she didn't have the benefit of a summer timetable freed up by pupils on 'exam leave' so she had to go into school during the summer holidays to complete the handover to her successor.

In the last week of term Kath's school had arranged a 'surprise' farewell party for her when she was presented with some pottery and a substantial cheque. I had a 'farewell do' at the end of that week, but it was a fairly subdued affair as there were a lot of staff leaving and the school was in 'Special Measures' after a disastrous Ofsted, only my department had been deemed 'good'! At Church, after my final Service we were presented with a beautiful watercolour painting of Kendal and another cheque! As we finished school on the Friday it was Liz's wedding on the Saturday, and we then flew to the States on the Wednesday!

In addition to getting sorted out at school we had to get sorted out at home. The house went up 'for sale', just before Easter so it was 'all hands on deck' as we finally got around to all the cleaning and repair jobs that we'd kept putting off! We had a steady stream of folk looking around. Most wanted a garden, something we didn't have, and had never claimed to have. The couple of days in mid-August when we were in the process of moving, we finally sold it – twice, and both sales fell though within twenty-four hours as the sales of the prospective purchasers fell through! We did, however, finally sell it – ironically to one of the first families to look around the house just after Easter, one of those who had made an offer in August.

Then we had to turn our minds to preparing for Liz's wedding. Liz and Gareth had decided to bring the date of their wedding forward from the December to the July so that I could officiate at the wedding before moving on to Blackburn. It was all very much a 'home grown' affair – at Liz's own insistence, although she bought her own wedding dress – Kath simply didn't have time to make one! We made the invitations and produced the printed the Orders of Service. Kath arranged for one of her mums at school to decorate the cake that Kath's mum had made. Another of Kath's mums, who worked at a florist's was given the task of sorting out the bouquets and the floral displays for the Church. Still another, who ran a catering business, was given the task of providing the buffet for the evening 'do' – which was held in the hall at Kath's School! Liz wanted to arrive at the church in a white Smart car. We had first come across them in Spain. They were not yet too popular in the UK and a white one could not be found. In the end Gareth arranged for a white limousine to transport her to the church.

The wedding itself took place at Sticklandgate Methodist Church, our church, and I had the privilege of officiating. That meant, of course, that I couldn't give Liz away! In Year 10, in a Religious Studies lesson, when we were dealing with marriage,

Liz had shocked her fellow students when I was making the point that women were not the possession of their fathers to be 'given away'. Her classmates turned to Liz, "So what will you do, who will walk you down the aisle?" Liz confidently answered that she was perfectly capable of walking down the aisle on her own! And that is precisely what she did.

The service, and indeed the whole day, went without a hitch. The previous minister, who was invited with his wife to return as a guest for the occasion, took the photographs! The reception was held in the Church Hall and the meal was prepared by some of the ladies of the church with some male help! Given that they had originally intended to marry in December they stuck to their original menu. Choice of starters, full turkey dinner, choice of sweet, cheese and biscuits – it was absolutely superb. We had plenty of non-alcoholic wine on hand – we were on Methodist premises. Many of Gareth's family, who were not tee-total, never even realised, and complimented us on our choice of wines! In an hotel it would have cost a fortune!

We had the evening 'do' in the hall at Kath's school. Robert and Rebecca had decorated it and they manned the bar. We provided an amazing assortment of buffet foods and we had a DJ. It was an wonderful evening, enjoyed by everyone. Liz and Gareth had one night away in an hotel near Ambleside, courtesy of Helen, one of her bridesmaids, who worked there. Next day they came back to South Road to pack as they had decided that for their honeymoon they would 'tag along' with Kath and I when we went on our summer holiday the Wednesday after the wedding.

We flew to Florida and had a week 'doing' Disney. It was hectic, but thoroughly enjoyable, even doing 'The Animal Kingdom' in torrential rain! Before we embarked on Disney, however, we visited 'The Holy Land Experience', which was quite an experience in itself! The site was 'compact', so it was a little strange to turn the corner by the Qumran caves and come face to face with the Jerusalem Temple, just next to Calvary!

From Orlando we flew to Washington to spend a few days with friends in Gaithersburg, where we had been on our 'Exchange of Pastorates' some twenty years before. I preached at Fairhaven United Methodist Church, and it was as if we had never been away! The last five days were spent with the Ingletons, friends from Gaithersburg who now lived in Venice, Florida but had a 'summer retreat' in a cabin in West Virginia. Those were days of relaxation that we badly needed after the busy weeks that had preceded them, before we returned to the UK to begin packing up the house ready to move to Blackburn.

The Fifth age

And then the justice,
In fair round belly with good capon lin'd,
With eyes severe and beard of formal cut,
Full of wise saws and modern instances;
And so he plays his part.

Although the beard bit belonged to an earlier 'age' the "wise saw and modern instances" seemed to resonate with the change of direction my life was about to undergo as I left "Sector" for "Circuit" ministry, so I include the quote here despite its obscure language.

Blackburn

[2001-2005]

When we returned from the USA, we had just a week to pack up the house. We moved into our new home in Blackburn on 22nd August, and Liz and Gareth moved in with us! Liz had tried to find a teaching post somewhere between Kendal, where Gareth's parents lived, and Blackburn. There were few posts advertised in South Lakes or North Lancs., and the interviews she was invited to took her nearer and nearer to Blackburn. The first post she applied for in Blackburn itself was the one she got! Gareth, who was a department manager at Morrisons was able to get a transfer, so they began looking for houses in Blackburn during the last couple of weeks of the summer term, found one, and began the process of applying for a mortgage.

After being turned down by the first company they had applied to, because Liz was on a 'temporary contract' (something they had known from the outset!), they finally received confirmation of a mortgage offer and hoped to have completion on their purchase before the end of the November. Meanwhile we had left most of their belongings and furniture at 2 South Road in Kendal, anticipating that they would have bought before we had sold. In the end they had to bring all their things down to the manse during half-term as our sale was to be completed before their purchase (Unfortunately Kath and I were not able to help them move as we were on holiday in Madeira). Consequently, we were only able to settle into part of the manse. The garage, the loft (which was substantial), one bedroom and the dining room became storage areas for Liz and Gareth's belongings! We hoped to have reclaimed them in time for Christmas!

We were all made very welcome in Blackburn. My Welcome Service was packed with folk from all the churches in the Circuit as well as other local churches. The local Anglican priest, Catholic priest, the Superintendent minister of the neighbouring Darwen Circuit, the Revd Terry Young, and the Dean of the Cathedral were all in attendance, as were the mayor of Blackburn and his wife. Terry's wife, Cathryn, taught at Queen Elizabeth School, a private school in Blackburn. It turned out that Kath could have had a job there, but the position had just been filled!

I had three excellent ministerial colleagues and some first-rate Circuit Stewards. I had intended to do little and listen a lot during my first three months but that didn't happen. Everyone was very keen to know what I wanted to see happening in the Circuit. I still did a lot of listening, but things began to happen quite quickly. My youngest colleague, Phil Gough, was invited to extend his stay by two years in order to develop work among children and young people. So, at my first staff meeting, just two weeks after arriving, I found myself changing the pastoral charge, relinquishing Mellor Methodist Church and taking on Wesley Hall in order to 'free' up Phil to extend his youth and children's work. Similarly, on the computer front things moved quickly. We began computerising all church records and accounts and looked into using PowerPoint, with the Circuit projector, which stood idle most of the time, to enhance the opening of worship. I also produced my first Circuit Plan, with acceptably few mistakes! At my main church I persuaded the Church Council to purchase copies of the Methodist Worship Book and they arrived in time for my first Baptism – twins!

When I was appointed to the Blackburn Circuit, we did consider several possibilities where Kath's job was concerned. She could have commuted each day from Blackburn to Heversham but felt that that would be just too much. It would entail an hour driving each way, and she often had meetings after the end of school. We couldn't afford to keep the house in Kendal, but we did think about possibly buying a flat nearer to her school where she could live during the week, coming back to Blackburn for the weekend. In the end, truth be told, she was ready for a change anyway, so resigning was the only real option. However, shortly after we moved a Primary Headship became vacant in a Methodist Primary School near Blackburn, similar in size to the one she had left, so she applied. She was unsuccessful. It was the usual story; someone was already lined up for the post!

So, in the end Kath spent the first few weeks filling in forms to do 'Supply' teaching. First there was Lancashire County

Council, then, because Blackburn with Darwin was a Unitary Authority, there was Blackburn with Darwin, and then, because it would take some time to get known, there was Key Stage, a teaching Agency. She had two or three days on Supply for Blackburn with Darwin, the same for the Agency and then she was asked to go into QEGS, Queen Elizabeth's Grammar School, into the Junior Department where Cathryn Young taught. That was two weeks before half term and she was given a contract until August 31st the next year!

At some point early during our time in Blackburn I changed my car. Daewoo, a Korean company, were offering a leasing scheme for their cars. At the time such schemes were virtually unknown. It was a good deal, so I opted for a Daewoo Tacuma. It was an elegant design, automatic, and very spacious. We were delighted with it, so much so that when the lease expired, I exchanged it for another, shortly before we moved on.

The North Lancashire Methodist District, with the Rochdale District, offered a 'Reading Week' for their ministers at the Gladstone Library at Hawarden in North Wales. It was heavily subsidised so was quite affordable. I took the opportunity each year whilst we were in Blackburn to go on the 'Reading Week'. The accommodation was good, the food was excellent, as was the actual library, although, for the most part, like many of those who went, I took books from my own shelves that I'd not yet got around to reading.

[2002]

Elizabeth and Gareth were still living with us at Christmas 2001 as they were still waiting for completion on the purchase of the house they were buying in Blackburn. In the end it was February before contracts were finally exchanged and we got our dining room back! During 2001-2002 Elizabeth was teaching at St Peter's RC Primary School in the south of Blackburn. It was only a one-year contract because of re-organisation within the school, the post disappeared by the end of the academic year, so the summer term was spent looking for a new position. She was successful and from September she found herself teaching at Rishton Methodist Primary School, just a few miles to the north of Blackburn. It was in a socially deprived area and the children were quite difficult; she did not enjoy it very much. Gareth continued working at Morrison's Supermarket. The temporary departmental manager's job he was given when Morrison's transferred him to Blackburn from Kendal was made permanent.

Robert and Rebecca were still in Kendal, so we didn't see as much of them and the grandchildren as we used to, or as we would have liked. They moved into the caretaker's house at Stricklandgate Methodist Church and Robert took on the part-time caretaking role, just six hours a week. However, in the October, he was asked to take over the full-time job when the present caretaker became ill. As he said he would rather have taken over the role in different circumstances. During the previous year Rebecca had discovered relatives she didn't know that she had, so the family made two visits to the Isle of Wight.

Luke continued to work steadily at school though I'm not sure he actually enjoyed it. Swimming and Football were his real interests and in both he excelled! Little Robert started school in September and was bored! Basically, he was just too bright for his own good. He was moved up twice in his reading group, and when we visited just before the end of term, he was busy writing out his Christmas cards to his classmates!

Kath's job at QEGS came to an end at the end of the summer term with no prospect of employment at the beginning of September. Under the circumstances this proved to be fortuitous as her father had had a stroke in June. She had a few days off school when he was first taken into hospital, then until term ended, she was going down to stay at her mum and dad's every weekend, to help her mum out and visit her dad in hospital, and she also went down for the evening each Wednesday. In the July Kath's dad was transferred to a rehabilitation unit but then had a setback and was transferred back to hospital. He was eventually discharged home on 15th October, just before the beginning of half term. He made slow, but steady progress. His legs had been severely affected so a bed had to be put up downstairs and he was confined to a wheelchair, something that he was slow to come to terms with.

We did quite a bit of travelling during the 2002. The February half-term week we spent in Morocco, at Marrakech, which was every bit as exotic as we imagined. Although the middle bit was wonderful the beginning and end left much to be desired! When we booked our flight, we were told that we couldn't get a flight to Marrakech, so we booked to Casablanca and arranged to pick up a hire car at the airport for the three-hour drive to Marrakech. When we got to Heathrow, not our airport of choice, we were told that the flight we were booked on was to Marrakech, stopping first at Casablanca! We were not too impressed.

We picked up the hire car and set off for Marrakech. The first part of the journey was on a dual carriageway. By now it was dark and there was an absence of street lighting. When we got to the toll booth, the attendant told us, mostly by sign language (he had no English, and our French was rudimentary) that we were going in the wrong direction. There was no way of crossing over to the other carriageway. No problem, just turn around and go back a couple of miles and we'd find a place to cross. It was a hairy journey driving the wrong way down a motorway in the pitch black in a foreign country! Fortunately, we did not meet another vehicle! It was in the early hours when we arrived in our hotel. We were given our key and went to our room. There was a problem, there was no electricity. Anyway, we were too tired, so we just turned in. Next morning, we woke to find that our apartment which was on the ground floor, had no outlook, making it feel very claustrophobic. At the welcome meeting on the roof terrace, Kath complained. We were given a smaller apartment, several stories up, but it did have a balcony.

Our problems didn't end there as I discovered that I had left all my tablets at home! We had to phone Liz, who phoned the doctors. She was then able to give me a list of my medications over the phone. We found an all-night pharmacy where, fortunately the pharmacist spoke English and was able to supply most of my tablets – at a price!

Nevertheless, we had a wonderful week. Marrakech was fascinating. We made a point of having a meal one evening in the famous Market Square, the Jemaa el-Fna. In Marrakech we made several trips into the souk, which was fascinating, and we visited the Jardin Majorelle and the Bahia Palace, both of which were very impressive. We had a day trip to the coast, by coach. We passed through some magnificent scenery. At one point the driver stopped so we could photograph the goats that stood on the branches of a roadside tree. When we arrived at Essaouira we had a fabulous fish meal at a stall in the harbour.

On the last night, there was a bar-b-q on the roof terrace, complete with belly dancers. We left early as Kath was feeling unwell. Back in our apartment she was sick. Next day we packed the car and drove the three hours to Casablanca to fly home. She spent the whole journey home feeling very unwell. I was fine until after the in-flight meal. Once we had disembarked at Heathrow, I was violently sick! So, all in all it was a holiday to remember!

We stayed closer to home in the summer half term. We had a week's break in Norfolk. Elizabeth and Gareth came with us. This was an opportunity for us to visit London, which Gareth had never visited before. The weather was mixed, and we spent our sightseeing day in London on the top deck of an open top bus sheltering under an umbrella! For Kath and me it was a chance to visit old haunts since we were staying not too far from Bury St. Edmunds where we had lived for two years when I finished my training for the Methodist ministry. On the Sunday we went to Northumberland Avenue, my first church, for the morning Service. It was further than we thought from where we were staying so we were a few minutes late. The preacher had not turned up, so I found myself having to take a part in the Service, which the Church Stewards had already started. It was also the weekend of the Queen's Golden Jubilee celebrations so on the Monday we had tea at Sandringham – the Queen was in London – still you couldn't have it all.

Our summer holiday was spent in Tenerife – relaxing, lots of sun, just what we needed. The autumn half term we spent in Portugal, which was just what Kath needed after spending all those weeks at her mum and dad's.

One of our best breaks in 2002, however, was spent visiting the Phillips, our friends from the States who were in Oxford for a year. Bill was the visiting Eastman Professor. It rained almost all the time! When we arrived, Jane was still unpacking various items they had had sent over from the States, including two table-lamps, each housing space for a couple of dozen thimbles. They had been made by Jane's dad who, in retirement, had taken up woodworking. Kath wondered why Jane had bothered having them sent over for just a year, then Jane told her that they were for her. When last we were in the States and Kath had seen Jane's lamps, she had said she wished she had something like that. Jane had taken her at her word.

We went to sung Evensong at Magdalene College on the Saturday night. It really was superb, and we had a Wesley hymn sung to a good Welsh tune! On the Monday night we went to sung Evensong at Christ Church Cathedral and then Bill and I went for dinner in the College hall. Christ Church is the College John Wesley attended and the famous Romney portrait hangs in the hall there! George Romney was a Lake District artist, born in Barrow-in-Furness and died in Kendal. The hall was also the inspiration for the hall in Hogwarts in the Harry Potter movies. Although the staircase was used in the film, the hall was reconstructed, and slightly altered, in the studios used for the filming, adding and extra row of tables making four instead of three.

My work in the Circuit kept me extremely busy. Thankfully my Church at Lammack could largely look after itself. Wesley Hall, however, was a different matter. A town centre Church but with a small, elderly, though very committed congregation. This year was their 40th Anniversary so we arranged a series of concerts through the spring and summer and refurbished the kitchen during August. One of the concerts was by a United Methodist Church choir from the USA who were touring the country. We also had some commemorative china mugs made by a firm near Blackpool

Two other Churches in the Circuit decided to close. Hoghton, a small village Church, over two hundred years old closed at the end of the year. The congregation was very small and elderly, and the building had not been well maintained over the years. There was no running water and to bring it anywhere near modern standards would have cost in excess of £70,000! It did have a pulpit from which, it was claimed, John Wesley had preached on occasion. It also had a small graveyard. The other church, Bentham Road was a small suburban Church, again with an aging congregation. Although it had been well maintained their finances were not sufficient to face the future with any confidence.

One of my colleagues, the Revd Colin Anderton, was due to retire in September 2003 and we began looking creatively at ways of replacing him. What was clear was that we would not be able to appoint another presbyter. (I forget now when, and why, we ceased being ministers and became presbyters!) The shortages continued across the Connexion. So, we were hoping to appoint a deacon with a rather different role. They would be based at Wesley Hall with part of their time spent in developing community links and part of their time having pastoral care for the housebound, those in homes and in hospital. The churches that Colin had responsibility for would be shared between one of my other colleagues and myself.

Kath and I decided to apply to do a third 'Exchange of Pastorates' in 2003. So we were anticipating that we would be off to the USA for about eight weeks, probably during July and August. When we went on the two previous 'Exchanges', twenty-one years ago, in Maryland, and eight years ago in Texas, I was a Sector minister. We expected that this time it might be a little different since I was now a Circuit minister.

[2003]

Just before Christmas 2002 we received the letter telling us that for our Exchange of Pastorates we were paired with the Rev'd Samuel Velez and his wife Diane and their two children Lindsay and Jennifer who were at East Prospect United Methodist Church in Pennsylvania. East Prospect, it turned out, was a small township about fifteen miles north of York, about the same distance west of Lancaster and about thirty miles north east of Manchester! A bit like 'home from home' really!

Over the next few months, we exchanged numerous e-mails as we tried to agree a date for the exchange. We were hoping to begin the exchange at the beginning of July so that we could have a couple of weeks holiday at the end of August before we came back to the UK. However, Samuel was adamant that he didn't want to begin the exchange before the middle of July as he wanted to fulfil all his commitments before leaving East Prospect! No matter how much I tried to explain that this was an exchange of pastoral responsibilities he didn't seem to understand. In the end we took our two weeks holiday at the beginning of July, arriving in East Prospect mid-July, returning to the UK at the end of August.

We managed to book a couple of weeks in Cape Cod, at a Resort in Hyannis, just around the corner from the Kennedy compound! We had a great time; the weather was warm and sunny, and we explored every corner of the Cape including a visit to several of the lighthouses there. In one of the museums that we visited I spotted a footstool with a tapestry covering.

The design is best described as a windmill pattern. A centre circle with four 'sails', each motif locked in to the next. It was an ideal pattern to use up all the extra wools I had collected over the years. I quickly drew it on a piece of paper I found, and, over the years, I've made several cushions using that pattern. All in all, it was a fabulous fortnight and, of course, the weather was beautiful.

We then drove across to Pennsylvania, straight through New York City to East Prospect. We broke the journey spending a night in a motel just outside Bethlehem – actually I've seen better stables! We asked at a tourist point for details of an inexpensive motel for the night. Instead of booking into a known chain Kath chose the cheapest independent motel – big mistake. We were given the only room they had left. When we got in, we immediately knew why it was so cheap! There was a patterned carpet on the floor, except the pattern was no longer discernible as it was so worn and had had so much spilled on it over the years. Everywhere was thick with dust and the window was missing! Air conditioning? We went round to the Office and the proprietor, resplendent in a sting vest, assure us he would get it fixed while we went off to find somewhere to eat. When we returned the window was still missing! Eventually someone came to fix it and discovered that actually it had slipped down into the cavity, so in the end the issue was easily resolved. At least the bed linen was clean! We woke early, packed up, dropped the key through the letter box in the Office door and hastily set off on the last leg of our journey!

We arrived in East Prospect on the Sunday in time for the

Church family picnic and apart from two folk from the Church, who called in to the parsonage during the week, one to take us to visit the 'shut-ins', we saw nothing of the Church family until the following Sunday when I had my first service. One couple took us out for lunch at the beginning of our second week. We had a bit of a welcome after my second Sunday's service and on the Friday of the third week we had our first invite to someone's house for a meal!

Liz joined us at the beginning of our second week and when we went to collect her from Baltimore airport, we took the opportunity to visit friends in Gaithersburg where we had been on the exchange twenty-two years before. Liz stayed with us for the rest of the exchange. Her husband, Gareth, came over at the beginning of our third week for his two weeks summer holiday. We took the opportunity to spend three days in New York during the first week he was with us. The brother of one of the members at the East Prospect church kindly loaned us his apartment. We had a fabulous time. We parked the car in a Parking Lot just around the corner from the apartment. It was one of those vertical car parks where the cars were stored on 'shelves' accessed by a car lift.

Being the pastor there was interesting. For health and safety / safeguarding reasons pastors didn't visit alone. Each church had a pastoral assistant who arranged the visits and accompanied the pastor. My pastoral assistant turned up one day and we all piled into his car as we drove around the corner to make our first visit. We could have walked there in the time it took to get into the car. We drove to our next visit, just around the next corner! Samuel actually lived about forty miles away and only came up to the parsonage a couple of days each week.

With little to do apart from a service each Sunday morning and visiting the 'shut ins' we took the opportunity to visit friends in Maryland and West Virginia as well as visiting places of interest in Pennsylvania itself. Apart from York and Lancaster, the home of the Amish, we visited places like Hershey, the home of American chocolate, and Gettysburg, the site of one of the critical battles of the Civil War and Lincoln's famous Address. By the end of the six weeks exchange the church had finally woken up to what the exchange was all about but by then it was too late. Our last Sunday came round all too soon, and the next day we were winging our way back to the UK.

Earlier in the year when it became apparent that we would not be able to get a minister for the three Churches at Wilpshire, Langho and Mellor to replace the minister who was retiring, we had applied for, and got, a deacon. However, since we were not supposed to give a deacon pastoral charge of a Church, we based her at Wesley Hall, in the town centre, to develop the work there and to have a pastoral role caring for the housebound and homebound across the Circuit. This meant a rearrangement of the pastoral organisation in the Circuit. I still, nominally, had pastoral charge of Wesley Hall. Lammack, I was going to share with my colleague Joan, who had two Churches of her own. Joan and I were also going to share Mellor and I would have sole charge of Wilpshire and Langho. It made little sense to have the deacon in the manse at Wilpshire, which was about as far away as you could get from Wesley Hall. It was decided, therefore, that since I was taking on pastoral charge of Wilpshire and Langho, the deacon would move into our manse at Lammack and we would move into the Wilpshire manse.

We arrived home from our Exchange of Pastorates on the Tuesday, spent Wednesday packing up the manse and on the Thursday and Friday, with help from Robert and Rebecca, we moved to our 'new' manse at Wilpshire! When we had first visited that manse, while Colin was living there, we noticed that on a shelf in the toilet underneath the stairs there were three African American 'models', one of a preacher at his lectern, and two pews, one with a young family and the other with an elderly couple. When we had visited Amish country with Jane Phillips during our Exchange of Pastorates with East Prospect, we called in at a roadside Market Barn and on one stall found the same, or similar, models. We bought them and installed them in the toilet under the stairs at the manse in Wilpshire when we moved in!

Two of our Ministers would be moving in September 2004. One appointment we reduced to 0.5 and that we managed to fill. The other, we were unable to fill. We hoped that it might be possible to appoint an American minister when it came to the last round of 'stationing' in January. If not this would mean that in the space of three years, we would have reduced the staff from four full-time Ministers to one and a half, plus a Deacon!

Kath managed to be gainfully employed for the whole of that year. In the spring term, and for most of the summer term, she was working every morning at St. John's C of E Primary School in Great Harwood, just a few miles away. She was covering a Year 4/5 class while the class teacher was giving additional help to those who were preparing for SAT's. The second week of the Autumn term, having just moved to our 'new' manse, found her working at Deepdale County Primary School in Preston covering a maternity leave, at least until Easter and probably until the end of the Summer term. She had a Year 1 class, all of whom, except three, were of Asian Heritage, and it proved hard going. Because the class was so difficult the school found the funding to have Kath in to work with the teacher who wasn't beginning her maternity leave until half term. The three white children were the worst, and several of the Asian children had minimal English.

Kath's mum and dad had their ups and downs. Because her dad was now permanently in a wheelchair, getting about was not easy. Kath went down to visit them most Saturdays so she could take her mum out shopping, and generally keep an eye on things. They came to spend Christmas with us, and we were looking forward to them coming up again later in the year. For them it was a welcome change of scenery.

Liz was much happier this year as she had a smaller, and much nicer class than the one she had previously. Gareth seemed to be more settled although he still occasionally hankered after changing his job if he could find something similar, although that was not so easy to do. Liz decided to transfer her membership from Lammack to Wesley Hall and in September became a Church Steward and, temporarily, Church Council Secretary. As well as the pair of them joining us for our exchange during the summer they also came with us for a week's holiday to London in May. Gareth's only visit to London had been on the day trip we had made the previous year, and I had been saying for years that I wanted a week there to visit all the places we'd never got around to seeing because whenever we'd been in the past it had always been on 'business' or to show visitors the popular sights. The weather was good, and we all had a great time visiting places like the Bank of England Museum, sadly no free gifts, and St. Paul's Cathedral for the London Methodist Districts' Wesley Tercentenary celebration.

Robert and Rebecca, Luke and little Robert were still living in Kendal and we didn't see as much of them as we would have liked, although we had the boys, on their own, for a weekend just before Christmas so we were able to take them to the Christmas Tree Festival we were holding at Wesley Hall. They had one or two good holidays during the year, camping on the North East coast and visiting relatives of Rebecca's on the Isle of Wight.

The Christmas Tree Festival was a 'trial run' but proved to be a fantastic success with thirty-one trees decorated according to different themes, some of which were incredibly ingenious. The overwhelming response was that we simply must do it again next year! Folk were already coming up with ideas for themes for their trees in 2004!

[2004]

At the beginning of 2004 we were still 'settling in' at the manse. There were boxes that still remained to be unpacked, some of which hadn't been opened since we had moved from Kendal over three years earlier. Little by little, however, we were getting through them, and the charity shops were the beneficiaries!

The Circuit had erected a new porch on the front of the Manse over a year previously, but it was still leaking like a sieve when it rained. The kitchen and the living room were decorated early in the year and looked very smart. There were still quite a few things that needed to be done in the manse. Neglected over recent years minor things had now become urgent and were likely to prove expensive. We hoped that some of them would be addressed in the near future, but we didn't press the matter as the Circuit had been faced with selling a manse, which was well below the required standard, and purchasing a new manse that met the requirements, during the previous few months and that had to be a priority.

The reason for the sale and purchase of manses was because we were able, very much at the last minute, to find a minister willing to come to Blackburn so we were able to maintain our staffing level in the circuit at 2.5 presbyters and 1 deacon. This meant that, since September, I had pastoral charge of (only!) 4 churches, in addition to being Superintendent Minister of the circuit, with our new minister taking over what had been my main church at Lammack, along with 2 other small churches.

We had a black family arrive at Wesley Hall. It transpired that they were refugees from the Congo. French was their native language. He was a journalist and a university lecturer who had been forced to flee after criticising the government. He fled with his wife and two young daughters. In the Congo he was also a Methodist Local Preacher. He had had to leave his father and young son behind. Trying to discover their whereabouts proved difficult. After about eighteen months we learned via a Pentecostal pastor that his father and young son had died after being tortured in an attempt to discover the family's whereabouts. The Local Authority arranged a day-long meeting for everyone who might have an input regarding the settling of refugees in the area. Everyone was present, representing business and commerce, education and leisure, sadly I was the only person present from the churches! Very disappointing.

With Terry Young, my neighbouring Superintendent, we set up a 'drop-in' centre at Wesley Hall for Asylum Seekers who found themselves living in Blackburn and Darwen. It proved successful and to the best of my knowledge still continues to serve the two communities even though Wesley Hall is no longer used for worship. I wonder what happened to the Triptych Robert painted for the worship centre. It was massive. The first panel depicted Jesus' birth, the second, his crucifixion and resurrection, and the third Pentecost. Talking of Easter reminds me that one of the Stewards at Wesley Hall, Ann Saville, used to paint Easter eggs. She was in her eighties then, a widow, her late husband had been Polish and that had been her inspiration. She had lost an arm to cancer, yet she managed to paint hard-boiled eggs with the kind of intricate designs that she had learned about from her husband. I still have one of her eggs.

Kath finished the academic year at Deepdale Primary School in Preston and in the last weeks of the summer term was asked if she could go to St Ignatius' R C Primary School in Preston for the first couple of weeks in September, mornings only. She turned up on the first day of term to be told that it was actually full time and would be there until, at least, the end of November! She's remained there, on contract until the end of the spring term! She had a Year 4 class every morning, which she enjoyed, then a mixed Year 4 / Year 5 class every afternoon, which drove her to distraction, although it did improve. The staff, however, were very friendly and supportive.

We had a weeks holiday in Scotland in the late Spring. Liz and Gareth came with us and the weather was wonderful. It was a really good break. In early August we went to Malta for two weeks, again accompanied by Liz and Gareth. It was a wonderful break. The weather was glorious, wall-to-wall sunshine every day! We had a hire car and did a lot of exploring including visits to a number of pre-historic remains, now designated as World Heritage Sites. Since we were last there, a few years ago, the roads had not improved at all! No doubt it kept car mechanics in business. By the end of the two weeks, I think we had seen everything of interest on the island, including the landfill site! Kath was navigating and had a penchant for exploring 'white' roads! Needless to say, when the two weeks were up none of us wanted to come home.

Later in August Kath and Liz took Kath's mum and dad for a

week's holiday in Lincolnshire where they had found a cottage adapted for the disabled. The weather was kind, and they had a good week. However, in early September Kath's dad was taken into hospital with an infection and, sadly, died in October. It was a very difficult few weeks as the family were constantly being given conflicting stories. 'It's only a matter of time', said one Doctor, 'He'll be out in a couple of weeks', said another!

A week and a half before half-term Kath was phoned by the hospital and told she had better go down. That was on the Tuesday. On the Wednesday they were told to send for Kath's sister, Pam, from Northern Ireland, so they did. Then they were told, they needn't have bothered as there was no immediate problem, but Pam was already on the way. Kath and her sister ended up staying for the next two and a half weeks.

Kath and I were due to go on holiday to Portugal for the Autumn half-term. Given the circumstances we delayed making a decision about whether or not to cancel until the last possible moment and then decided to transfer the flights to Liz and Gareth who both happened to be on holiday but had made no other plans. Kath then phoned on the Thursday morning to say that if I could get a flight, I should go with them. So, when I phoned to transfer the flights, I managed to get a single seat on another flight for myself. On the Friday evening Liz and I went down to Stoke to see Kath's Dad and the family before we left on the Saturday morning. We stayed for about an hour and a half then set out to come home. I hadn't been in more than about five minutes when Kath phoned to say her dad had died about half an hour after we had left.

Liz and Gareth took my luggage with them, so I didn't have anything to check in and didn't have the hassle at the other end of waiting by the carrousel for my luggage to appear. Because of the lateness of our arrival, we had a bit of a bother collecting the keys for our apartment. Eventually we managed and settled in to what proved to be an excellent week's holiday. I had the bedroom and Liz and Gareth had the sofa bed in the lounge – age has to have some privileges! We had hoped that Kath's dad's funeral would be in the week after our return but, as it turned out it was scheduled for the Friday, so Liz and I missed the funeral although we were able to go down, with Kath, for the burial of the ashes on the Thursday after half-term.

Thankfully Kath's mum seemed to be coping well, although in the space of just a few weeks she'd had to replace the freezer, the washer, the vacuum cleaner, the cooker and the living room fire! We brought her up to Blackburn for Gareth's birthday, and also for the last weekend of the Christmas Tree Festival at Wesley Hall. The Christmas Tree Festival was, again, a great success and with the money raised from the Festival and Circuit Christmas Celebration we were able to send £487.00 to Christian Aid! Kath's mum went to spend Christmas with Pam and her family in Northern Ireland and then came to Blackburn for New Year.

We looked forward to seeing Robert and Rebecca and the grandchildren at some point over Christmas. Luke was now in his final year in Primary School and 'little' Robert in Year 1. Both seemed to be doing well at school and 'little' Robert was well ahead of his peers academically. Earlier in the year Rebecca took over Robert's role as caretaker at Stricklandgate Methodist Church and Robert landed himself a job valeting at the Porsche Dealers in Kendal. He was in his element, on occasion getting the opportunity to drive the vehicles he had to valet!

Liz seemed to be much more settled at School. She and Kath enjoyed going to tap dancing lessons on a Monday evening, held at Wesley Hall Methodist Church in the centre of Blackburn. They found it great fun and a good way of keeping fit! Both thoroughly enjoyed the classes, but neither of them thought they would ever move into the advanced class, although Liz did win an award at the end of the year for, I think it was, 'the most improved student' in the whole of the Dance School. The trophy took pride of place in her living room!

As the minister at Wilpshire I was approached by a young woman who wanted her four-year-old daughter baptised. It transpired that she was a 'lapsed' Methodist who had once spent a year at Cliff College. She was currently working for Monsignor John Devine who was the Regional Ecumenical Officer. She was single and her daughter, who had a terminal illness, was adopted. She wanted her to attend a Rainbows group that was associated with a church. The one at Wilpshire was the only one at Blackburn. She also wanted to have her daughter baptised and wanted John Devine to be a 'godparent' and have some part in the service. I was happy to accommodate her. The Sunday we chose was one when I was planned for a service of Holy Communion. I asked John Devine if he would read a lesson and explained that as it was Communion I wouldn't be offended if he chose not to come forward or chose just to come forward for a blessing. He was, of course, welcome to come forward and receive the elements. He chose to come forward and receive both elements! After the service, our next-door neighbour came up and interrupted us as John and I were in conversation to say how well he had read the lesson. I took perverse delight in introducing him to her as Monsignor John Devine. Her embarrassment had to be seen to be believed!

One of my churches was in Mellor, a village on the edge of Blackburn. It was a small, relatively new building and was really attractive both inside and out. It was built on half of the footprint of the previous building, a Primitive Methodist Church, which had been built to be higher than the nearby Parish Church! The other half of the footprint was turned into a car park. There was a small graveyard which was always well tended by one of the members of the church. There was an area set aside for the burial of cremated remains and I said, depending when I died, I would have my remains buried there. One of my predecessors, the Rev'd James Thomas East was buried in the graveyard. He wrote the Epiphany hymn, "Wise men seeking Jesus", sadly omitted from our latest hymnbook. Apparently, he had saved throughout his ministry, to afford a visit to the Holy Land. However, his wife (or it might have been his sister) fell ill and he used his savings to meet her medical bills. His hymn reflected his situation:

1   Wise men seeking Jesus
     travelled from afar,
     guided on their journey
     by a beauteous star.

2   But if we desire him,
       he is close at hand;
       for our native country
       is our Holy Land.

3   Prayerful souls may find him
       by our quiet lakes,
       meet him on our hillsides
       when the morning breaks.

4   In our fertile cornfields
       while the sheaves are bound,
       in our busy markets,
       Jesus may be found.

5   Fishermen talk with him
       by the great North Sea,
       as the first disciples
       did in Galilee.

6   Every town and village
       in our land might be
       made by Jesus' presence
       like sweet Bethany.

7   He is more than near us,
       if we love him well;
       for he seeks us, ever
       in our hearts to dwell.

James Thomas East (1860-1937)

Gareth was still working at Morrisons supermarket, managing the Home and Leisure department, and he seemed more settled, though at times he was frustrated when his staffing was reduced! We saw them both each Sunday when they came for lunch and we went to their house for Christmas lunch, the first time since we were married that we had not spent Christmas day at home.

I wrote our Christmas letter, as usual, during Advent, once a time of fasting and reflection. As I went off to my fourth Christmas dinner, I was conscious that in our time it has become a time of feasting and activity as everyone prepares for Christmas. We ended the year conscious that during the next few months Kath and I would have to decide whether we wanted to remain in Blackburn or start looking for a new appointment commencing September 2006. It wouldn't be an easy decision, as I would then have six years left in the ministry before I was due to retire. Do we extend by one year, leaving the possibility of a five-year appointment before retirement? There were some in the Circuit who were talking of extending my invitation by a further six years. We'd have to wait and see.

[2005]

February half-term came around and Kath and I decided to seek the sun! Since Ibiza was out of season and, we were advised, would be quiet, we decided it looked like a good option. Now there's quiet and then there's quiet. Ibiza in February isn't quiet, it's dead! Even the resort we were booked into was closed and when we arrived, we found a notice on the hotel door saying 'Closed'! Fortunately, another notice below advised that we had been transferred to the hotel next door! From the resort to the town centre was about two and a half miles of continuous shops. However, there was only one gift shop, one supermarket, and one pharmacy open along the whole stretch! To make matters worse I developed a chest infection on the Monday and for the next three days we didn't venture outside the apartment. It was another ten days after our return to England before I shook off the infection! But it was sunny!

After Easter we had a few days in Craster on the North East coast. Kippers to die for! The weather wasn't brilliant, but we enjoyed the break, and it gave us a chance to visit some of my relatives in the area who I hadn't seen for a few years.

In May Robert announced that he and Rebecca had decided to separate after nine years together. So, we were then into helping to him to find, and finance, a flat in Kendal so he could stay near to the boys. The flat we eventually found was small (the bedroom was, literally, a hole in the wall off the lounge), and expensive, but the only other properties available were even more expensive so he moved in on a six-month lease. Thankfully, the boys both seem to have coped with the split very well. We saw them for a weekend every month when Robert came to visit. Luke had started Secondary School and seemed to be enjoying it. 'Little' Robert continued to do well in Primary School. He was definitely the more academic of the two. Luke enjoyed sport more than academic work whereas

Robert was just the opposite!

After the move into his flat Robert changed jobs, from valeting for Porsche to serving coffee in Costa. He enjoyed his new job far more than he did the old one. He also linked up with St Thomas' Church, again, and became very involved with the youth work there. He went with the youth group to 'Soul Survivor', a Christian youth camp near Shepton Mallet, for a week in August. The Youth Workers at St. Thomas' encouraged him to consider the possibility of doing a Youth Work degree with a view to becoming a full time Youth Worker himself. The lease on his flat was up in October. Not having managed to find another flat he ended up 'lodging' with one of the folk from St Thomas's.

Since we were anticipating a move in either 2006 or 2007, and since there was no sign of Elizabeth and Gareth producing a grandchild for us, we decided to go for a 'big' holiday this summer. We anticipated that on our return we would set about the task of clearing out the attic and outhouses in anticipation of having to downsize ready for a move twelve months or two years down the line.

Liz and Gareth announced that they would like to come with us. They had for several years been hankering after visiting Egypt, so Egypt, we decided, it would be – one week cruising down the Nile followed by three days in Cairo and four days in Luxor. We booked and looked forward with eager anticipation to our Egyptian holiday in July. Then Liz discovered she was pregnant, with the baby due on 5th January. No panic, she was still allowed to travel but wasn't able to have any vaccinations. Fortunately, this didn't prove to be a problem.

Then, in early June, the Chair of District phoned. It was the phone call every minister dreaded receiving. Would I consider moving a year early? He handed me over to the President of Conference, who 'just happened' to be with him at the time! He explained that there was a 'priority' appointment that had to be filled and they felt that I was just the person they were looking for. Where? Newcastle-under-Lyme: only a couple of miles from where Kath's mum lived! Talk about carrot and stick!! In a year or two, when we finally came to move from Blackburn, we would have been asking for an appointment somewhere in that area, so at the very least we had to consider it.

They wanted a Superintendent minister for a Circuit of ten churches. The person appointed would have pastoral responsibility for two of the ten churches. One of them, Newcastle Methodist Church, in many ways a typical town centre church, with well-used premises, much like Wesley Hall, the other, St Peter's Methodist Church, was the Methodist half of a Local Ecumenical Project, the other half being Anglican, St Andrew's, just across the road. The Circuit had been without a Superintendent minister for nine months and there had been other problems.

We decided to go for it. Kath's mum was obviously delighted. She celebrated her eightieth birthday this year and was managing remarkably well but missed having family nearby. However, it wasn't an easy decision because it meant that

Blackburn would then be without a Superintendent minister for the next twelve months. In addition, we were at a critical stage in reshaping the Circuit, involving possible mergers with neighbouring Circuits. It would also mean moving house in less than two months, not the twelve or even twenty-four months we had been anticipating!

The manse we would be moving into was uninhabitable when we saw it in the June. It had been let, but since January had been empty. There was a new bathroom suite to go in and it was to be re-carpeted and redecorated throughout before we would arrive in mid-August. Amazingly it was, but only just! It took them three days to reclaim the garden. It was also one room less than the Manse we were leaving in Blackburn, and all rooms were smaller. It also lacked the outhouses that we had used for storage. We managed to dispose of several items of furniture before we moved, but much of the 'stuff' we'd intended to sort through had to come with us to be sorted out and disposed of as we unpacked it.

Egypt was amazing, hot and sunny. The cruise ship was quite small (not an ocean-going liner! We were on the River Nile after all). On the very first day we visited the Valley of the Kings, including the tomb of Tutankhamun. Thereafter it was a blur of incredible sights including the Temples at Karnak, the island of Philae, the Temples of Abu Simbel, then on to Cairo and the Pyramids. Liz and Gareth and Kath all picked up the expected 'tummy bug' but quickly shrugged it off after a couple of days. I escaped – until the day we left Cairo, and I didn't shake it off so easily. I had a really severe case of 'the curse of the Pharaohs'. It lasted for the remaining four days of the holiday, the whole of the next week, while Kath and her mum packed up the manse, and virtually the whole of the following week while we moved and began unpacking. I should have seen a doctor while we were in Egypt and been prescribed the usual cocktail of drugs they dished out when someone contracted the virus. But I didn't and when I visited the doctor when we got back to Blackburn, he wouldn't prescribed anything at all. All my subsequent medical problems with chest infections I can trace back to Egypt!

Newcastle-under-Lyme

[2005-2012]
[September 2005]

My welcome Service, at St Peter's Methodist Church in the Westlands, was held on 31st August. And we were made very welcome. In the congregation were a couple we knew from Stricklandgate Methodist Church in Kendal. He occasionally lectured at nearby Keele University and they had a flat not far from the manse. The manse took a bit of settling into because, as we had anticipated, we had far too much 'stuff' however, we gradually thinned things out as we unpacked. The garden shed we were promised was erected during the October half term, while we were away for a few days in Cornwall. So we had no excuse for not sorting out the garage – except the weather!

One of the first people I was introduced to was Michelle Bradbury. She was secretary to the Church in the Westlands, based in St Peter's. She was a tremendous asset. She set about putting the membership records of my churches onto the computer using a programme developed in a neighbouring circuit. Eventually we appointed her as the Circuit Secretary and based her in an office in the Newcastle church where we bought and installed a fabulous printer that simply did everything including folding and stapling booklets. When I came to leave seven years later and move to a circuit where few of the churches had copies of the Methodist Worship Book Michelle produced booklets for all of the main services. They proved invaluable.

Kath had been asked to stay on at the school in Preston where she was teaching until the end of the autumn term. It was likely that she would then have continued there into 2006 as at Christmas one of the staff was going off on maternity leave. Instead, because of the move, it was back to 'Supply' teaching. She ended up registering with two Local Authorities and two Teaching Agencies. The forms were endless, and it was a case of applying for CRB clearance – again, and again, and again! Still, after half-term she was called out several times, so she was beginning to make some inroads into the Educational Establishment in the area.

In Blackburn I had been invited to join Blackburn West Rotary Club by one of the members at Wilpshire. There were three clubs in Blackburn and Blackburn West got in first! It met on every Tuesday evening in the 'Conservative Club'. The three-course meal was prepared by the Steward and his wife and the cost was a very reasonable £7.00 a head. It was always first rate, the mince and onion pie they occasionally provided was 'to die for'! The after-dinner speakers were always first rate.

My one hesitation about being a member of Rotary was that most members seemed to value their membership more because of the meal than the charitable reasons for which Rotary was founded. Certainly, over the year they spent much more on the meal than they gave to charity.

The original founders of Rotary met in their offices in rotation to share in a simple 'packed' lunch while planning how best to support those in need. One of the members of Blackburn West, who was a member at Revidge Fold URC, resolved, when he was elected as the annual president, to have two or three 'bread and cheese' type meals during his year in office. It didn't happen as the committee vetoed the idea since the members came mainly because of the meals! When I moved to Newcastle-under-Lyme one of the Local Preachers turned out to be a prominent member in Rotary there and when he found out I had been a member in Blackburn I was quickly recruited.

In the run up to Christmas, Christingle, Crib, Toy and Carol Services abounded, but only one Christmas dinner on the horizon – I knew there was another reason I was tempted to stay in Blackburn.

[2006]

In January our first granddaughter arrived. Lois weighed in at 8lb 1oz at 9.37 pm on Sunday 15th January. Liz had a difficult labour that lasted $31^1/_2$ hours. During the year Lois proved to be as bright as a button and quickly developed her own personality. Not content with crawling, by the end of the year she was almost walking on her own. She was a very happy, contented, little girl who has a smile for everyone. It was a privilege to baptise her at St Peter's MC, one of my churches, on 19th March. Despite the fact that we lived so far away Liz and Gareth and Lois visited quite often so we saw more of her than we might have expected.

For the first time for many years, we didn't go abroad for a holiday this year. Possibly having a new granddaughter played a part in that decision. In February we went to York and Lois, only a few weeks old, brought her Mum and Dad to visit and they stayed for a few days. We were in a very modern one-bedroom apartment which meant Liz and Gareth, and Lois, had to sleep on the floor in the lounge. We had some time away after Easter, at a cottage in Anglesey, and Lois and Liz, and Kath's mum, went with us. May half-term break took us to Westbury, in Wiltshire, giving us the opportunity to visit Salisbury and Stonehenge; and Lois and Liz came with us!

We considered going to the States in the summer to visit friends over there, but we hesitated when we saw price of the flights. When we finally decided we would go, we found that the price of flights was even more expensive, so we ditched the idea. Instead, we had three consecutive weeks, first in Ludlow, then Watchet and finally near Tavistock. Kath's Mum came with us for the first week, the last two weeks we had on our own. The cottage we had in Watchet was quaint, being built, in part, over a fairly fast flowing stream.

In the October half-term, we had a week in Chichester, accompanied by (you've guessed it) Lois and Liz, and Kath's Mum. It was Gareth, Lois' Dad, who missed out as he wasn't always able to get time off work at the times we were going away.

We saw quite a bit of Robert in 2006, not least because he came to live with us at the beginning of August for several weeks! He decided he couldn't any longer afford to live in Kendal and the attraction of free board and lodgings with his parents proved irresistible. His intention was to get a job in Newcastle for a few months, until he sorted himself out, then return to the Lake District. However, his stay was shorter than he anticipated. Jobs were not as easy to find as he had hoped and when a friend in the Lakes pointed him in the direction of a job at Brathay Hall near Ambleside, which, although not terribly well paid, included 'board and lodgings', there was no contest. There was also the fact that he missed the boys – and his new girlfriend, Aline!

He met Aline about eighteen months earlier when she was visiting the Youth Worker at St Thomas' Church, in Kendal, where Robert was very involved. She decided to change direction during her first year in University and go for a degree in Youth and Community Work and Applied Theology based at St John's College in Nottingham. This meant her finding a placement. The Youth Worker at St Thomas', who knew her from when he and his wife had lived in Southampton, arranged for a placement at the Church in Kendal. She began there in the September. She made a pre-placement visit in the summer and she and Robert have been 'an item' ever since. Every other weekend, with another student from Preston, she stayed overnight at the manse, on her way to Nottingham for lectures. She was really nice, and she got on really well with both Luke and 'little' Robert. Most months Robert, and more recently Robert and Aline, brought the boys down for a weekend, so, my commitments permitting, we still got to see them quite often.

Kath was still on 'Supply' at a variety of schools up to the February half term. It had certain advantages but some drawbacks in that it tended to be very 'hit and miss', with no sense of continuity. She was then asked to go to Crackley Bank Primary School to cover a fairly lengthy absence caused by a teacher having to go into hospital. It was a difficult school, and she was given a difficult class. She remained there on 'Supply' until the end of the summer term. The head teacher then asked her to return in September, this time on contract. The teacher who had to go into hospital for a hip replacement in the summer term was due to go back in to have his other hip replaced during the next spring term and they had another member of staff ill and unlikely to return soon. Although she found it very hard work, there was a certain satisfaction in dealing with children whose lives outside school were very difficult.

Kath still suffered with a neck problem that the doctor hadn't been able either to identify or help to ease. In the end she went to a sports physiotherapist with very limited success. She wrote to Kath's doctor asking that she have a scan, but with no immediate response.

When I went to the Newcastle (Staffs) Circuit I knew that there were problems, I just didn't know how extensive they were! They had been without a Superintendent Minister for the previous year, so my coming resolved one problem immediately. The 'second' minister, who was due to retire in September 2008, I knew had had health problems. He was soon off work because of ill health and would be for the foreseeable future. That was not anticipated. The Circuit had not been able to attract a 'third' minister in September 2004 and had employed a husband and wife as lay workers. It was a 'job share' but only covered half of the 'third' minister's section, the other half was covered by a Supernumerary minister. This was both expensive and inappropriate.

In September 2005 I persuaded the Circuit to apply for a third minister for September 2006 on the basis that we probably wouldn't get one until September 2007. At the very last minute, in May, to our amazement, we were offered a third minister. This caused all sorts of ripples in some circles, but we invited her, and she began work in the September. She quickly proved to be a tremendous asset. Her coming meant a re-arrangement to my 'pastoral charge'. I gave up responsibility for the Newcastle church so that we could create a town centre section comprising three churches for the new minister. I took on St Luke's church, which was about a mile from St Peter's, which was part of the Local Ecumenical Partnership, in the Westlands. The partnership was a real problem as the Methodist part of the partnership was in decline and there was no account taken of this by the Anglican partner. St Luke's, however, had lots of potential. I seemed to have a baptism almost every time I was there!

During the year that I had pastoral responsibility for Newcastle Methodist Church I had suggested that they consider the possibility of installing a screen and data projector. There was no enthusiasm for the idea, and nothing was done. My successor chose not to pursue the matter. Four years later when I again found myself in pastoral charge of Newcastle MC, I raised the matter again. There were twelve members present at he Church Council. Eleven expressed their reservations. The twelfth said nothing. I promised I could have it installed for under £2,000. When it came to the vote eleven voted in favour and the twelfth abstained. I engaged a company from Keele University who provided the equipment and installed it for £5 under the figure I had said. A month after it came into use several members of the congregation told me they wished they'd had it installed when I first suggested it four years earlier.

Newcastle MC had a Coffee Morning every Saturday and I persuaded them to buy a couple of sets of posters produced by Pauline Books and Media. They made quite an impression since before they were put up the noticeboards around the Schoolroom were either empty or displayed often outdated notices! I also persuaded them to have their notices printed on the blank side of the weekly 'Sunday Link' produced by Redemptorist Publications, and we put one on each table at the Coffee Morning. Low level evangelism!

St Peter's and St Andrew's as 'The Church in the Westlands' was probably the first LEP established just after the failure of the Anglican Methodist Conversations in the 1970s. At the time both churches were of a similar size and St Peter's Methodist

Church, like St Andrew's had a minister in charge who had no other responsibilities.

Both ministers, at the time were of a fairly liberal theological outlook. As successive ministers were appointed to the Circuit responsibilities changed. The minister appointed to St Peter's took on pastoral responsibility for other churches in the Circuit and, in time, the Superintendency. When the Anglican vicar was replaced it was with a vicar, the Rev'd Gerald Gardiner, who was conservative evangelical, a member of 'Reform' and who was also a divorcee! (Reform was started in 1993 to oppose the ordination of women to the priesthood, like Forward in Faith in the Anglo-Catholic tradition, but also focused on advocating a conservative view on homosexuality.) When I was appointed, Gerald had been there for 20 years. He was a really nice guy, but he was not at all committed to ecumenism!

During Holy Week a service was held in St Peter's on the first three evenings with a Communion Service on Maundy Thursday and a service on Good Friday. We invited a guest preacher, one year an Anglican, the next a Methodist. Usually someone prominent, the Bishop or the Chair of District. When it was an Anglican then Gerald prepared the orders of service, when it was a Methodist it was my responsibility. The minister of the other denomination led the service. On one occasion when the guest preacher was the Bishop of Stafford, the Rev'd Gordon Mursell, I was leading the service Gerald had prepared. Gerald had included a Psalm which was set out as in most modern liturgies with alternate verses said by the leader and the congregation. I proposed that we read it as traditionally the

Psalms were intended to be read with each verse split, the first half read by the left side of the congregation and the second half read by the right side of the congregation! Gordon Mursell piped up, "Quite right, it's about time we did it properly"! I got on well with Gordon who would have liked to move Gerald on and see the LEP develop properly but was unable to do so because Gerald's theological position, and the fact that he was a divorcee, made it impossible.

I was approached by that year's president of Rotary to see if I was interested in taking part in arranging a Bible Reading marathon with the proceeds raised to be shared between St Peter's and Newcastle-under-Lyme Rotary Club. It seemed like a good idea. It took some organising. The Bible was to be read from cover to cover by volunteers taking on twenty-minute slots. It would take around seventy hours. All those who volunteered were asked to get sponsors. Members and friends of both the church and the Rotary Club volunteered and we managed to cover all the necessary 'slots' although that meant that I ended up reading my section in the early hours of the morning. We even had the Lord Lieutenant of the County take a turn – unfortunately he drew the short straw and ended up with one of the Old Testament passages that comprised of a very long list of unpronounceable names! Unsurprisingly Gerald declined to be involved. I don't recall now how much we raised but it was several thousand pounds for the two groups involved.

To help preserve my sanity I embarked on an MA in Contextual Theology at Manchester University. I went to a Summer School there on 'Islam in Britain'. This turned out to be one of the modules for the MA and it was suggested that I enrol and produce the necessary assignment. So I did. With one module done, in the first semester I attended the modules on Contextual Theology and Mission History. The next semester I had to tackle the module on World Faiths Encounter. All four assignments would have to be completed by the end of August. That would just leave the Dissertation! The material for that I hoped to gather during my sabbatical, which I was due to take during the next autumn / winter, hopefully visiting India and Malaysia.

[2007]

I was supposed to be starting my sabbatical leave at the beginning of November. The hope was that we would spend Christmas in Singapore, where I had spent the Christmas of 1965 when I was a VSO volunteer in Sarawak. Having taught Hinduism at 'A' level for twenty-seven years without ever visiting India we intended to spend some time in India before Christmas. After Christmas we intended to spend some time in Sarawak, as I'd never been back since I'd left forty years earlier. We were then hoping to go to visit Kath's brother and his family in Australia as we'd never been to see them since they emigrated there a couple of decades ago. November, December, January is the ideal time to visit Asia and Australia because of the climate. That was the plan.

Having begun an MA in Contextual Theology, as a 'part-time' student, in October 2006, and completed the assignments for the four 'taught' units, I was left with a 16,000-word dissertation to write. I decided to look at the 'Growth of the Christian Church in countries where it is a minority faith' so my impending 'sabbatical' seemed an ideal opportunity to gather material. That was the idea.

Then Robert announced that he and Aline were planning to get married on December 15th! So, the 'sabbatical' was moved back by a month to the beginning of December. Then I discovered that the cost of travel and accommodation in India virtually doubles at the beginning of December! Then the head gasket went on the car – nearly £1000 to get it repaired! Suddenly going to Asia and Australia became much less affordable!

So, to Rob and Aline's wedding. They wanted to have the service at St. Thomas's Church in Kendal, which is the Church where they worshipped. However, because the Church would be closed from the beginning of January for six months for a complete refurbishment, and because 'little' Robert would be emigrating to Canada at the beginning of February with Luke and his mum and her new husband, Rob and Aline had opted for a 'short' engagement and a December wedding.

Rob and Aline insisted that I perform the marriage. The vicar was happy to agree, so having officiated at Liz and Gareth's wedding six years previously I would now have the privilege of officiating at Rob and Aline's wedding. Liz and Lois were asked to be 'matron of honour' and 'flower girl' respectively. Having made a sedate entrance Lois spent the rest of the service, and the day, just running around exploring everywhere, everyone thought she was really cute – which, of course, she was! The other two bridesmaids were Aline's sister and her best friend. Gareth and 'little' Robert were ushers along with one of Rob's friends from Church. The service was wonderful – nothing to do with me – Rob and Aline had planned the whole thing; I only did as I was told! The reception was held in the Church Hall, which had been decked out as if we were in a marquee – very atmospheric.

The week before the wedding Rob began a new job as a Mentor at St. Thomas's School in Kendal. On Sunday, after the wedding, Rob and Aline went off to Marrakech 'on honeymoon'. On Saturday, after they returned, they moved into a small house in Kendal to spend their first Christmas together as husband and wife in their own home.

Kath had been having trouble with her neck for the past five years. When we were living in Blackburn, she saw a consultant at Preston who, once he discovered she was a teacher, quickly diagnosed 'stress'! For the past couple of years her head has been pulling more and more to the left, an increasing inconvenience but nothing more. However, it had increasingly become extremely painful as well. Having consulted our GP, she was referred to a consultant neurologist in April. He arranged for her to have an MRI scan in June. She was then booked in for another appointment with another consultant at the end of October, which, when the MRI scan showed up nothing, was moved to the end of November with yet another consultant. This letter mentioned 'dystonia' so Kath immediately made for the laptop and began surfing the net.

When she saw the consultant at the end of November, he confirmed that she was indeed suffering from 'cervical dystonia'. The most effective treatment was a Botox injection every three months. The consultant gave her her first injection there and then explaining that while he could guarantee that it would take away the pain, he could not guarantee that it would take away the 'pull'. However, it was the 'pull' that concerned her most. She hadn't driven since July because she found it so difficult to keep her head straight.

Not long after I changed my car for a Daewoo Tacuma, we changed Kath's car for a Daewoo Nubira. It served her well but not long after we moved to Newcastle-under-Lyme, we found that it needed a lot of work doing on it. The local Kia dealer was a member of one of the churches in the circuit. They offered us a really good deal to trade in the Nubira for a new Kia Picanto so we decided that that was what we would do. At the time the dealer had not realised who Kath was, so the deal was genuine. Unfortunately, because of her dystonia, Kath drove less and less and the Picanto spent more time on the drive than on the raod!

Kath's contract at Crackley Bank Primary School came to an end at the end of August. She was called in once or twice on 'Supply' and managed alright. Then, on the Friday before half-term, the Head asked if she would like a little more supply after half-term – 'Like every day'! The School had taken in so many new children in September that the Year 3/4 and Year 4/5 classes were too big so the Head had decided that there would have to be another class created, so Kath would have a Year 3 class with 20 children in it.

My colleague, who was suffering with health problems, decided to take early retirement on health grounds, and he and his wife moved to Chester. We were able to apply for a replacement, and although we were late in making the application, we were successful, and we welcomed a new minister in September.

Kath and I had a couple of weeks holiday in Spain in the summer. It was an opportunity to simply relax and we thoroughly enjoyed the break. In February we went to Kent, and In May we went to Devon. We took Liz, Gareth and Lois, and Kath's Mum, with us to Devon.

Lois was to be two in January 2008 and, have I already mentioned, she was really cute?! Indulge a doting grandfather! Her first word was 'Gwampa' – much to the annoyance of 'Mummy', 'Daddy' and 'Nanny'! She began walking on her first birthday and hadn't stopped running since. She hated to go to sleep in case she missed anything. It was gone ten o'clock at night on the day of Rob and Aline's wedding before she finally gave up and went to sleep, and she had skipped her afternoon nap – there was just too much going on!

Kath's Mum continued to do well, now aged 82! She baked every week, made Sunday lunch for us each week, went dancing five times a week and ironed all my shirts!

[2008]

On returning from their week's 'honeymoon' in Marrakech Rob began his new job as a 'mentor' at St Thomas' School in Kendal. It was a one-year contract and, with no further funding available, that job had come to an end. So he embarked on a new career. He decided to try his hand at 'Home Improvement, Decoration & Design' – I quote from his business card! Given the state of the economy this might be the worst, or, quite possibly, the best time to be setting up in such a business, only time would tell.

Both Aline and Rob continued to be very much involved in the Youth work at St Thomas' Church in Kendal. Aline was in the final year of her degree course which was linked to her 'part-time' placement as a trainee Youth Worker at the church. Her involvement in the Youth Programme there had increased with the departure of the 'full time' Youth Worker and it was possible that when she graduated, she would be offered the 'full time' post.

February saw 'little' Robert and Luke on their way to Edmonton in Canada with their Mum and her husband Peter who, at one time had been Rob's best friend! We weren't sure how they would cope with the snow – it apparently lasts from around September until May. However, they seemed to be settled, and the boys were both enjoying their new schools – the best thing about them "no uniform and you can chew gum"!

In the summer I was invited to officiate at another wedding in

Kendal, at Stricklandgate Methodist Church, which was the Church we attended when we lived in Kendal. The bride was one of Liz's best friends. Jane had been one of Liz's bridesmaids and was one of Lois's godparents. Needless to say, Lois was invited to be one of Jane's bridesmaids. She, predictably, looked 'cute', thoroughly enjoyed the day, and, again predictably, danced the night away!

Just a few weeks later I was taking part in another wedding, at Keble College in Oxford. This time it was the youngest daughter of our long-time friends, Bill and Jane Phillips from America who was getting married. It had been nearly thirty years since we met Christine's parents on our first Exchange of Pastorates at Gaithersburg in Maryland. Christine was then just a few weeks old. When Christine met Nick in England when she was studying for her degree at Bristol University, she decided to settle here and marry here, and I was invited to take a part of the ceremony.

We combined our trip to Oxford with a couple of weeks holiday, a week near Bath and a week just outside Oxford. Liz, Gareth and Lois came with us as they too were invited to the wedding. The weather was typically British – when the sun shone it was glorious and when it rained it chucked it down! Fortunately, it was beautifully sunny for the wedding day itself – it usually rained when we were indoors, so it didn't matter too much. Bill and Jane had arranged a coach trip to Salisbury and Stonehenge for the many American friends who had come over for the wedding and they invited us to join them. It lashed it down with rain while we were on the coach but when we arrived at

Stonehenge it faired up, so we were able to walk around the site. We each had an audio guide, including Lois and she spent the next hour with it glued to her ear, with the commentary being changed at each stop!

The autumn half term saw us bound for Tantobie in County Durham where, with Kath's mum, Liz, Gareth and Lois we enjoyed a week's break in a beautiful cottage intriguingly named 'John Wesley's Cottage'! It was a very recent conversion of a barn where the first Methodists used to gather over two hundred years previously, hence the name!

Liz was expecting their second child on February 6th. This time they decided they wanted to know the sex of the baby – 'it's a boy!' – although there was always a margin for potential error. They had decided on a name and their choice proved a little controversial with some of the folk who had been told!!!

In May we decided it was time to sell Kath's car as there was no sign of improvement as far as her cervical dystonia was concerned. She hadn't driven for months and it wasn't clear when she might be able to drive again. We decided to trade in both of our cars for a 'nearly new' Kia Carens. It could easily be made into a 'seven-seater', which would prove very useful when we were out and about with Kath's Mum and Liz, Gareth and Lois. I now had to do 'the school run' every day, with the difference being that I was chauffeuring the teacher rather than the children, taking Kath to and from work. She was still having a botox injection every three months and the dosage had been increased each time. It may have helped with the pain, but it hadn't had any effect on the 'pull' to the left which kept her head permanently turned in that direction.

Kath was still teaching at Crackley Bank County Primary School but was now on permanent contract. She was asked to take over the Nursery class in September. It proved to be a real challenge. In the past it had been run by a Nursery nurse, but legislation now required that a qualified teacher be in charge. There was no 'paperwork' in place to meet the requirement of the National Curriculum, so it proved to be a steep 'learning curve', not helped by an Ofsted inspection just a few weeks into term! Her biggest problem was that, because of the new legislation, she had children coming in for the five sessions they were permitted, but that could mean either all mornings or all afternoons or two and a half days but not necessarily the same two and a half days. It made it very difficult to ensure that they all had access to all of the curriculum. Preparing them for the Nativity play proved to be a bit of a nightmare as some of those available for the rehearsals wouldn't be present on the day and some of those who would be present on the day were not there for the rehearsals! Nevertheless, things began to fall into place, and she was beginning to enjoy the challenge.

As for me, my sabbatical came and went, and I didn't! Having completed all four assignments from the 'taught' part of the course I did do some preparatory work for my dissertation without making the proposed visits to Asia. Then, almost before I knew it, it was the end of February and it was 'back to work' and the dissertation was put on one side. Not being able to make the visits I had intended to make I spent some time e-mailing all sorts of people I had come across on various websites, or who had been recommended to me, in order to elicit information that I felt might be helpful with my dissertation – with absolutely no result! It was very frustrating. My hope was that I could really get under way with it in 2009.

The return from my sabbatical saw a change in my pastoral responsibilities in the circuit. Up to that point, as well as being circuit superintendent, I had charge of two churches – St Peter's and St Luke's. My colleague the Rev'd Brian Mifflin, who was 'officially' retired had had charge of Baldwins Gate and Ashley, two of our smaller rural Churches. I now took pastoral charge of these two Churches and Brian became my 'pastoral assistant' across all four of my churches, an arrangement which seemed to be working out well, even though I ended up with more Church Councils and Committees to chair!

[2009]

Most of the highlights of 2009 centred, one way or another, around our holidays, all of which we took in the UK and on all of which we enjoyed good weather, with just the very occasional rainy day.

Since Liz and Gareth were expecting their second baby in early February, we booked a cottage near Clitheroe for the February half-term. It was about 25 miles, about a forty-minute drive, over the moors, from Blackburn. That way, we thought, we could be nearby to help out when the baby arrived. Needless to say, the baby was late, and Liz and Gareth and Lois joined us at the cottage! At least until the Wednesday when we were wandering around Clitheroe and Liz went into labour! We returned to the cottage for tea, Lois stayed with Kath and me, and Gareth took Liz back to Blackburn where after a couple of hours she was admitted to hospital and an hour and a half later gave birth to Cullen. He weighed in at 7lbs 15oz!

I again had the privilege of baptising a grandchild. Liz and Gareth and Lois and Cullen came down to Newcastle-under-Lyme, where family and friends gathered, and Cullen was duly baptised, like his sister before him, at St Peter's Methodist Church.

When it came to the May half-term Kath and I had a holiday on our own in Yorkshire in a cottage in Glaisdale. Talk about isolated. It was a twenty-minute drive into the valley, single track road whichever way you approached it. Our car was an automatic. Quite a number of the roads over the moors were 1 in 3 and I discovered what the 'plus' and 'minus' symbols next to the 'D' on the gear shift lever meant! We did all the touristy things including having fish and chips at Whitby and visiting Goathland, the village of Aidensfield in the TV series 'Heartbeat' We enjoyed the Yorkshire countryside so much that when we were looking for somewhere to go in the summer and spotted an advert in the Methodist Recorder for a holiday apartment in Robin Hood's Bay, we decided to go for it and booked it for two weeks in August.

Liz, Lois and Cullen came with us for both weeks; Gareth

was only able to join us on the Friday for the second week. It turned out that the apartment was one of four in the Methodist Church. We certainly kept fit. Not only was the apartment on the top floor but the Church was at the top of the very steep hill that led down into the village. As we got to the top of the hill after yet another morning on the beach Lois, aged three and a half going on twenty-three and a half, announced, "I'm jiggered!"

Our grandson, Robert, along with his brother Luke and their Mum came over from Canada in August for a visit. Rob and Aline came over to Robin Hood's Bay from Kendal on the 'middle' Friday with young Robert and the caravan in tow! They only stayed for the one night, but it was great to have the whole family together, even if it was only for twenty-four hours! Aline graduated in 2009 and became involved in training Youth Workers across Cumbria and Rob continued in his own business now called 'Changing Spaces'.

Now in my fifth year at Newcastle, with only two years to go until retirement, it was necessary to be 're-invited'. This should never have happened but when I was first appointed the Circuit Stewards failed to produce the necessary documentation to show that my invitation was for seven years. I think 're-invitation' was probably the most stressful process that anyone can be put through! The fact that it was successful, and I was re-invited until August 2012, was little consolation.

My 'retired' colleague, who was looking after two of the Churches which were part of my 'pastoral charge' decided, finally, to retire! This meant some re-organisation, again, since that left me with the largest 'section', with four Churches and the Superintendency. The new arrangements would be fully in place in the New Year. In addition, one of my colleagues was on sabbatical for three months and, for the second time in my ministry I was privileged to be Mayor's chaplain for the current year. Because of what was happening in the Circuit my MA dissertation had to be put on hold – again.

Kath had an incredibly busy year at school. Within a matter of weeks after she took over the Nursery class at the school there was an Ofsted inspection. Despite there being little in place by way of resources and assessment the Early Years Department were judged to be 'Satisfactory'! Because the school overall was judged to be 'Satisfactory' it was clear that Ofsted would be returning within the year. In January Kath and her Reception colleague, Patsy, began planning together and 'team teaching'. An 'Advanced Skills Teacher', Jonathan, started to come in one evening each week to help them resource and re-organise their Department.

The beginning of October was Kath's 60th – so we arranged a 'surprise' party. Kath and I picked up Kath's Mum and went to the Saturday Coffee Morning at the church in Newcastle as usual. Liz and Gareth, Lois and Cullen, and a number of friends, from various parts of the country, arrived clutching balloons and singing 'Happy Birthday' – much to Kath's amazement – it's not often she is lost for words! Everyone brought food and we had a veritable feast back at the manse. Kath's prized present was the purple boa (well lilac boa – we couldn't find a purple one anywhere) and the book of the poem 'When I am old, I will wear Purple'!

Just before the October half-term the school received the dreaded phone call to announce that there would be a full-day inspection sometime during the following twenty working days! That meant that it could be after half-term, a prospect everyone was dreading, as the thoughts of having to worry about an impending inspection over the holiday period was not something any of the staff were relishing. As it transpired the inspector phoned on the eighth day so the whole thing was over and done with by the end of the Tuesday before the beginning of half-term. At the debriefing, the school as a whole was still judged to be 'Satisfactory' because of a number of outstanding issues, but when it came to the Early Years Department the inspector had been very impressed and said that the school should be very proud of its Foundation Unit. The Early Years Staff were over the moon!

So we went off to a cottage near Castle Douglas, in Dumfries and Galloway, in high spirits. Liz, Gareth, Lois and Cullen came with us. The cottage was superb, and huge – even Lois had her own en-suite! The countryside was lovely and, apart from one day, the weather was kind.

It had been a couple of years since Kath had been diagnosed with Cervical Dystonia which caused her head to pull to the left. In November we went to a Dystonia Society day conference in Stafford. One of the speakers had had to withdraw and his place was taken by a Dr Tukmachi who I had heard speak a couple of years previously at a Rotary Meeting. He was an acupuncturist. Kath had tried acupuncture before, at one of those high street shops, but without success. Dr Tukmachi assured us he could help, so Kath went for a consultation. Although at first it seemed to be working the effects were short lived and, in the end, she gave up on the treatment. It had proved expensive! Before abandoning acupuncture altogether Kath had a couple of consultations with a practitioner in Ashley who refused to continue the treatment when it was clearly not effective.

[2010]

Despite the difficulties posed by her condition Kath continued teaching. She made some significant changes to the nursery classroom, not just inside, but also by developing the outside environment. In a recent Local Authority Inspection, the Foundation Unit, of which the Nursery Class was a part, received a 'Very Good'. We had a week's holiday in a cottage near York during the summer half-term. Among the places we visited was Knaresborough where Kath bought some soft toys for her class to take home at weekends and over holidays. We took the rag doll with us when we visited Mother Shipton's cave and recorded the visit.

As for me 2010 proved to be an incredibly busy year. In the spring the Chair of District, asked one of my colleagues to move to fill an appointment elsewhere in the district. This meant her leaving a year earlier than expected and left the circuit without one minister for one year from the September. It was decided to appoint a Circuit Lay Pastoral Worker and that meant a hectic few weeks drawing up a job description, advertising and interviewing to fill the post.

This all came on top of the work already begun to merge our circuit, Newcastle (Staffs), with the neighbouring circuits of Wolstanton & Audley and Kidsgrove. The merger had been agreed the previous year to take place from September 2012, when I was due to retire. However, the need to find a new minister for September 2011 resulted in a major rethink and the decision was taken to bring the merger forward a year. So once again I found myself drawing up another 'profile', this time for a new minister. Bringing forward the merger also meant an increase in the number of meetings necessary to try to ensure a smooth transition to what will become the North Staffordshire Methodist Circuit. Since I was due to retire the year after the new circuit would come into being it was decided that the superintendent minister of one of the neighbouring circuits would take on the role of superintendent minister of the new circuit.

We took our usual quota of holidays again during 2010, and again we did not venture abroad. Unusually, however, we returned to places we had been to before. In February we went back to County Durham and stayed again in John Wesley's Cottage, the barn conversion in Tantobie where the first Methodists used to meet. Although the weather was cold, we thoroughly enjoyed our week. Liz and Gareth and Lois and Cullen came with us and we had fun celebrating Cullen's first birthday.

The week after Easter, again with Liz and Gareth and Lois and Cullen, we went back to stay in two of the studio flats at the Methodist Church at Robin Hood's Bay. This 'return' was prompted by Lois who had frequently asked when we could go back there. Why that holiday had made such an impression on her I had no idea but whenever the topic of holidays came up, she would ask when we were going to go back to Robin Hood's Bay. So, we did, and a good time was had by one and all.

As already mentioned, we spent the summer half-term holiday near York, an opportunity to visit some of the places that were just a little too far away to visit from Robin Hood's Bay. We visited places we have said for years 'we must visit...' Castle Howard, Rievaulx Abbey and one or two properties in York itself.

Cullen wore my favourite tee shirt; it read "Lots of kisses and big hugs for my Grandpa" I know I'm prejudiced but he really looked cute, he must take after his 'big' sister. He was very good natured, and he and his 'big' sister generally got on very well together, though they did have their 'moments'! By and large he gave as good as he got and held his own with Lois. He was getting to the stage of beginning to talk and was constantly learning new words. He loved helping out, taking used mugs away and 'dropping' them in the kitchen sink ready to be washed. He was very much a Daddy's boy, which was not surprising really since Gareth was still working night shifts at Morrisons and then looking after Cullen until Liz came home from school with Lois.

In the autumn Lois started school at Rishton Methodist Primary School, the school where Liz was teaching. In fact, it looked as if she was going to end up in her mum's class, but because of a staff reshuffle Liz was moved from Reception to Year 1. Lois settled in well and loved school. She began learning to sound out words and enjoyed singing. She also enjoyed rehearsing her role as an angel in the school nativity play! She was a bridesmaid – again – during the summer.

In August Kath and I, along with Liz and Gareth and Lois and Cullen, had a week's holiday in a cottage near Aylesbury. This gave us an opportunity to explore 'Midsomer Murders' country and visit the model village at Bekonscot – the oldest model village in the world – which had appeared in an episode earlier in the year. We also had a day visiting Bletchley Park which was really fascinating.

At the end of the week, when the others headed south to London where Lois was to be a bridesmaid at Gareth's sister's wedding, Kath and I headed north for Stratford-on-Avon for a week on our own. We had only visited Stratford on a couple of day visits in the past, so this gave us an opportunity to thoroughly explore the town and neighbouring countryside. The last time I visited the Methodist Church in Stratford was when I was a teenager, the year the church opened! This time they were about to embark on a massive refurbishment scheme.

Kath managed to get an extra week's holiday before we went away in August. She took her mum for a weeks visit to her sister in Northern Ireland. They both had a great time being 'wined and dined' by members of the family over there. Kath's mum was still remarkably fit, as well as knitting and tatting she still went dancing several times a week.

We didn't see much of Rob and Aline during 2010. Kendal was just a bit too far to visit for a day, and weekends weren't really practical given my commitments. Aline continued her training role in the Carlisle Diocese. She reduced her involvement at St Thomas' Church in Kendal; however, she took on additional work running week-long courses in schools in various parts of the country. Rob's business seemed to be doing quite well despite the recession. He had had quite a variety of jobs to tackle, some kitchens to fit, some alterations to do and one or two major decoration jobs, both interior and exterior. Although he had one or two weeks without work, he was generally been kept busy.

[2011]

The anticipated merger of the three circuits happened, but not as expected as the Kidsgrove circuit decided to withdraw so it was just two circuits that came together to form the North Staffordshire Methodist Circuit on 1st September. Not being superintendent of the enlarged circuit meant that my workload should have decreased, however, the retirement in July of my Anglican colleague from the LEP (Local Ecumenical Partnership) of which one of my churches, St Peter's, was a part, meant that, initially at least, I saw no such benefit. To an extent this was resolved with the appointment of his successor who, although of a similar theological persuasion as his predecessor, was much more amenable to doing things together with St Peter's.

The demands of bringing the two circuits together, and a series of quite serious chest infections between December 2010 and April 2011, meant that I ran out of time to complete my MA. I had completed four assignments but failed to complete the final dissertation. However, to my surprise and delight I received notification that I had been awarded a Post Graduate Diploma in Contextual Theology, so all was not wasted.

Kath continued as Nursery teacher at Crackley Bank Primary School. She didn't allow the problem with her dystonia to interfere with her activities with her children. She did, however, acknowledge that now she was 'of a certain age' getting down on the floor with three-year-olds was not quite as easy as it used to be!

On three occasions during the year, we returned for a holiday to places we had already visited. In February we went back to Tantobie in County Durham. Anticipating just the two of us going this time we rented the smaller of the two cottages aptly named 'Methodist Cottage'. In the end we took Liz and Gareth and Lois and Cullen with us and managed quite well. In the past we have usually gone away immediately after Easter weekend for a few days but this year the school holidays were changed so Kath was off school for the two weeks before Easter returning to school on the Tuesday after Easter Monday. This meant we took a few days off before Holy Week and returned to

Stratford-on-Avon to make use of free entry to all the places we had paid to visit the previous August! Despite the fact that I was struggling with the last of my chest infections we still managed to enjoy the break. Kath insisted on having her photograph taken outside the Teddy Bear Shop.

Shortly after Easter we were contacted by the Methodist Ministers Housing Society with a list of properties available for ministers retiring in July 2012. There were very few in the north but there were plenty in the south! The nearest to Liz was the other side of Preston. There was flat in Houghton-le-Spring, a couple of flats in Scarborough and a house in Telford – further south than where we were living in Newcastle! The only other one in the north was a four-bedroom house in Crook in County Durham which sounded very attractive. Kath had always liked the North East, and Crook is only nine miles south west of Durham City, which is where I grew up. We arranged to visit, and we were suitably impressed. It was 'reserved' for us for the next July.

In the light of our decision to retire to the North East we resolved to 'go south' for our remaining holidays. Consequently, in May we rented a cottage near Bury St Edmunds, the town where I was sent as a probationer Methodist Minister in 1971! We had revisited the town only once, briefly, when we were on a holiday in Norfolk about ten years previously. On the Sunday we went into Bury St Edmunds to Trinity Methodist Church and met up with one of my ministerial colleagues from the 1970s who had retired there. We also met Kath's first Head Teacher as well as the minister who followed me at Northumberland

Avenue! I don't know that we would have recognised them if we hadn't been 're-introduced' – mind you, I doubt they would have recognised us either! The rest of the week was spent re-visiting old haunts. In the end we ran out of time so resolved to return to the area again before too long.

We had already booked to go back to Robin Hood's Bay for our summer break and arranged to take Liz and Gareth and Lois and Cullen with us. As before, this was all down to Lois who just loved Robin Hood's Bay! It gave us the chance to take Gareth through to Crook and show him where we hoped to retire. We went on to Durham to have lunch at North Road Methodist Church, the church I attended when I was a teenager. They laid on a lunch every Friday and it was open to anyone who wanted to go. They had an excellent menu, and the prices were reasonable – so that was Fridays sorted for when we retire!

In the autumn half-term Kath and I rented a cottage just outside Barnstaple. The weather was mixed. We drove over to Minehead on one day when the weather was appalling – thick fog and squally rain. By contrast we had a glorious day when we went to Post Isaac, TV 'Doc Martin's' Port Wen! All in all, we really enjoyed the break.

Liz finally decided she'd had enough with teaching and early in the year began attending a course, one evening a week for several weeks, for those wanting to become Registered Child-minders. During the spring and summer Gareth, and Liz, tackled the garden to turn it into a regular adventure playground in anticipation. Once Liz qualified, she handed in her resignation at the end of the academic year and waited...! It was a precarious few months. First one girl every evening after school, then a second for a couple of evenings a week, then a two-year-old boy two mornings a week, and then a twenty-month-old girl for two full days a week starting after Christmas. So, she was getting there, much to her relief. Gareth continued to work the night shift at Morrisons and now that Liz is at home during the day, he was now was getting his regular quota of sleep.

Liz's change of occupation meant that Lois had to change schools since she had been attending the school where Liz was teaching in Rishton. Not surprisingly Lois settled in well at her new school and made really good progress. Cullen continued to grow and, at nearly three, was becoming quite a chatterbox!

The sad news in 2011 was that Rob and Aline had parted company, so Rob was now single again! Thankfully they parted amicably. Aline returned to the south, but Rob remained in Kendal. Earlier in the year he managed to find quite a number of jobs, though most were short term and there were gaps in between. He finally found a long-term job working on a barn conversion which would keep him busy until early the following year.

Kath's mum continued in good health. She still went dancing several times each week, made lunch for Kath and me each Sunday and did the bulk of our ironing! She was planning to go to Australia again in February with Kath's sister to visit Kath's brother and family.

[2012]

The day before Kath's mum was due to leave for Australia, she was clearly unwell. After a great deal of persuasion, we finally managed to get her to go to the out of hours clinic where after due consultation it was decided that she needed to go straight to the Hospital. They insisted she remain there as she was diagnosed with gall stones. She actually felt better and insisted she wanted to be discharged but the doctors insisted she remain. To her chagrin the doctors informed her that there was no way she could continue with her planned trip to Australia. It was too late to stop Pam from coming over from Northern Ireland as she was already on her flight. In the end she stayed with their mum for the five weeks she had planned to be away in Australia. Kath's mum was not pleased to discover that she would not be able to travel by air for at least twelve months after her illness.

For the February half-term week, we booked 'John Wesley' cottage again in Tantobie and took Liz and Gareth and Lois and Cullen with us. On the Sunday we made the half-hour drive over to the Methodist Church at Crook to 'case the joint'. (Actually, it is an LEP – Methodist / URC) We were warmly welcomed and the folk we sat with made themselves known to us and afterwards invited us to stay for coffee in the schoolroom. When we introduced Liz and Gareth as being from Blackburn, we were told that there was one member of the congregation who also came from there and she was promptly introduced. She had been a member at Revidge Fold URC in Blackburn, a partner church in the LEP I was involved with when we lived there, although she had moved to Crook before we went to Blackburn. We had been chatting for quite some time when she stopped, mid-sentence, and asked how come we had driven over from Stanley (Tantobie) to Crook passing several other Methodist Churches on the way. At that point we had to confess that we were anticipating moving to Crook in the August once we retired.

Easter was odd again in 2012 as the school holidays rather than being the week before and the week after Easter were the two weeks before Easter so, again with Liz and Gareth and the grandchildren, we took the first week of the holidays to visit Weston-Super-Mare. It was cold but bright and we had a great time. One of the highlights was visiting to Helicopter Museum just outside Weston-Super-Mare. It was well worth the visit! Kath and Lois especially fancied themselves on the helicopter of the 'Queen's Flight'!

Summer half-term week, which coincided with the Diamond Jubilee celebrations, we decided to re-visit Bury St Edmunds, since, once we moved to the North-East it would be significantly further away as a holiday destination. We watched the celebrations on TV in the cottage we had rented as the weather was so appalling and we didn't fancy standing in the rain to share in some of the open-air events arranged around the area. One thing we did do during the week was to visit the Cathedral. Since we left Bury St Edmunds in 1973 much had changed. A cloister had been added, glazed as any cloister would have been in mediaeval times, though with plain, rather than stained glass. Also, the interior had been completely decorated. The effect was stunning. Although the weather that week was mixed, we had an enjoyable break on our own.

Then it was back to Newcastle-under-Lyme and the countdown to retirement. Just before the half-term break Kath's school had set aside a day to celebrate the Queen's Jubilee in much the same manner as they had celebrated the wedding of Prince William and Kate Middleton the previous year. However, instead of one of the children enacting the main character of the event Kath was chosen to fulfil the role! She was blissfully unaware of this fact until just a few moments before things were due to start when she was whisked aware to be dressed up as 'Queen for the day'! She was also unaware of the fact that I had been invited to play the role of her consort!

There is a 'half' ring-road around the town centre of Newcastle-under-Lyme and there are five roundabouts allowing other roads to join it. In the last few months we were in Newcastle I broke down on each one of the roundabouts! The engine simply cut out and I could not get it restarted. Because the car was an automatic each time it happened, I had to be relayed back to the manse and each time the next day I got into the car it drove perfectly. On most of the roundabouts I was able to coast into a joining road so that I didn't pose a danger, except once and a passing police car pulled up behind me to ensure that traffic moved past smoothly. The garage we baffled. The last time I was relayed the guy said to get the garage to check the exhaust. He was right. The sensor that measured the exhaust fumes was faulty and because it was giving a false reading the engine automatically cut out! Modern technology!

The school staff took Kath out for a farewell meal on the last Thursday evening of term. On the Friday it was the 'Leavers Assembly' and Kath was the 'star turn', the poor Year 6 pupil being somewhat eclipsed by all the fuss that was being made of her. When I collected her from school that evening the car was filled with all sorts of gifts, cards and flowers.

Two days later, on the Sunday it was my last service at Newcastle Methodist Church.

After taking back pastoral charge of Newcastle MC the organist decided it was time to retire. After much debate we bought a Digital Hymnal. Expensive but amazingly versatile. One of our members, who previously had not been actively engaged in doing things for the church volunteered to take responsibility and became very proficient. Not long before my final service an organist from a nearby Methodist Church which had closed, offered to play at an occasional service. He played at my final service. I had chosen 'Born in song' as the first hymn. He mangled the last line of each verse despite the congregation singing it properly. The guy who would have operated the Digital Hymnal later tried to show him where he had gone wrong, but without success.

The service was followed by a lunch which, if anything, exceeded their usual high standard. Afterwards I was presented with an antique bust of John Wesley which I had long admired. It had sat on a windowsill, hidden behind the curtain, in the vestry, and now sits proudly in a display cabinet in our lounge. Apparently, it had been valued in excess of £600! That Sunday evening was the official 'Circuit Farewell' service for one of my colleagues who was moving to a new appointment, and for me. We were both presented with cheques from the Circuit.

The following Sunday was my last Sunday at St Peter's Methodist Church, again followed by an excellent lunch and a presentation, this time of two prints of Newcastle-Under-Lyme which now hang on our lounge wall along with the painting of St Peter's that one of the members of the congregation had done and presented to me during the service. Then we began packing up in earnest, ready to move. Retirement beckoned!

The sixth age...

The sixth age shifts
Into the lean and slipper'd pantaloon,
With spectacles on nose and pouch on side;
His youthful hose, well sav'd, a world too wide
For his shrunk shank; and his big manly voice,
Turning again toward childish treble, pipes
And whistles in his sound.

Crook

[2012-the present]

Liz and Gareth, with the children, and Rob came down for our final weekend in Newcastle-under-Lyme. Although since we had returned from the half-term break, we had been steadily packing, and disposing of various items to the local Oxfam shop, the next couple of days passed in a flurry of last-minute preparations ready for the removers arriving on 31st July. By late afternoon the van was full, and some things had to be left in the garage. We then set off to drive to County Durham. Rob slept on the floor of the house we were moving into so someone would be there when the removers arrived the next day. The rest of us were booked into the Travelodge in Durham City. We got to 6 Peases Way in time to meet the removers. They couldn't believe we were going to fit everything in! Rob and Gareth returned to Newcastle with Rob's van and Gareth's trailer to retrieve the things we had had to leave behind. So, on the 2nd of August we were finally here with all our belongings – boxes everywhere, such that we could barely open the front door when the minister arrived with scones, strawberries and cream to welcome us to Crook.

The weather was good and as a consequence we didn't get too much unpacked as we decided that the grandchildren needed to get out, so had had a trip to South Shields. It wasn't until the family had left that we really got down to it. It would have been easy if we hadn't decided to redecorate the house from top to bottom! We didn't need to do it, but we already had wallpaper sufficient to do two of the bedrooms and, of course, once we had started it seemed sensible to continue.

Liz, Lois and Cullen came to visit again at half-term. Gareth was working so couldn't come with them and he needed the car. So we arranged to collect them from Gareth's parents in Kendal which was about halfway. We awoke on the Saturday morning to about three inches of snow. When we phoned and told them they were really excited. However, only a few miles from Crook and the snow had disappeared and by the time we arrived home later that afternoon the snow here had melted much to the disappointment of the grandchildren!

Nevertheless, we had a good week. Despite the weather being rather cold we took the opportunity again to explore the area. Hamsterley Forest is only a few miles away and the children – big and little thoroughly enjoyed themselves at the play park before we drove through the forest to admire the autumn colours of the trees. Rob came over from Kendal on a couple of occasions. Again, a mixture of work and pleasure as he has the tools and the agility I now lacked to do one or two jobs around the house.

Most Friday's we went into Durham and had lunch at 'North Road Methodist Church, which runs 'Mannas', a café every Friday. Nearly everyone I knew when I attended some 47 years previously had now moved on though it was nice to renew acquaintance with those who remained. When we were there with Rob it was suggested that we visit a new Coffee House, recently opened and run by the son of a URC minister. It turned out that he was the part-time URC minister at Crook.

The church in Crook, St Andrew's Dawson Street, is a Methodist / URC LEP and was very welcoming although it was / is a predominantly elderly congregation. Sadly, the sanctuary is very traditional, and the church has fixed pews. After years of worshipping in churches with the flexibility of having chairs it felt like stepping back in time! The church has a Coffee Morning every Tuesday (Market Day) and they have good uniformed groups for girls, and 'C' club (Messy Church) for children met every first Friday of the month after school. They have a very successful Autumn Fayre and, for the first time held a 'Christmas Tree Festival' on the first weekend of the December of the year we arrived. This latter was already in hand when we arrived, so it wasn't down to us this time! A number of the congregation went out to a local pub for lunch once a month after the Sunday morning service. Sadly this seemed to fizzle out not many months after we arrived.

[2013]

We spent Christmas 2012 with Rob and Liz and Gareth and the grandchildren in Blackburn. Kath and I stayed in the nearby Travelodge, which gave an interesting twist to the Christmas story – there was room in the 'inn' and the prices were very reasonable! We all came back to Crook on Boxing Day for the rest of the 'holidays'.

Some weeks earlier Liz had told us that she had decided that she was going to give up child-minding and, after two years out of the profession, return to teaching, and she was looking for teaching posts in County Durham! An Early Years post came up in Tow Law, just a few miles north of Crook, in a Roman Catholic Primary School. She duly applied and, just before Christmas, the school contacted her to say that they had not appointed as they had had too few applicants. They intended to re-advertise through January and wanted to retain her application for consideration with any others that might be forthcoming.

In January Liz saw another Early Years post advertised at a Primary School in Ferryhill, about a twenty-five-minute drive south of Crook. Again, she sent in an application and, much to her surprise, was called for interview before the end of January. The school was one of three in Ferryhill and had recently had an Ofsted inspection, which rated it as 'outstanding'. There were five candidates interviewed, a half-day for each interview. Liz was last, on the Wednesday morning. She came, with Cullen and Lois, and stayed overnight. After the interview she was told that she would be contacted by five o'clock to be told the outcome. Five o'clock came and went and everyone decided that she hadn't got the job. At twenty past five the phone rang, and Liz retreated with it into the kitchen. When she returned, she couldn't keep her face straight. She had been offered the job, and could she start after half-term, just three and a half weeks away?

Just a few days later she had a letter from Tow Law asking her for interview for that post. We later discovered that there had been forty-five applicants for the post she got at Ferryhill. Needless to say, we were very proud of her.

The next three and a half weeks were hectic to say the least! Liz had to explain to the parents of the children she was 'minding' that she was moving back into teaching – in just three and a half weeks time! In some cases, she had to find alternative Child Minders for them. We were charged with the task of finding a school for Lois and a nursery for Cullen. There was just one place in Year 2 in Crook Primary School, which is just across the road and down a short path from our house. There was just one place in the adjacent, though separate, nursery school. The only drawback was that we could only get Cullen in for 'afternoons only' which was better for him but was a bit limiting for us; we'd have preferred two full days and one-half day, but it couldn't be helped

Liz and the children arrived at the beginning of the February half-term leaving Gareth in Blackburn until he could arrange a transfer from Morrisons there to a Morrisons near Crook.

It was several weeks before a post became vacant at their new store in Consett and then he too moved in. Their house in Blackburn had been on the market since before Christmas, anticipating their eventual move. As it turned out the move came well in advance of the sale, which, given the state of the market, was not completed until almost the end of August.

We took Kath's mum with us for a mid-week break in Lincolnshire during the Easter holidays while Liz was off school and so was able to look after Lois and Cullen. The first chance Kath and I had to get away by ourselves was the last week in August when we used our week of Timeshare in Bowness. In the past we had exchanged our week but now we lived a distance from the Lake District we decided to use it ourselves. We had anticipated that Liz and Gareth and the children would be in their new house by then. However, as it turned out, that proved to be the week they moved into their new house! Fortunately, the previous week, they had moved their furniture out of the Blackburn house into a storage unit just down the road from Crook in Bishop Auckland so, with Rob's help the move went quite smoothly, although they didn't move out of our house until the following week when school began. Rob's business, 'decorating and general handyman', had struggled earlier in the year due to the recession, however, things seemed to have picked up and he suddenly found that he was busy again.

Kath and I had a second, two-week, holiday in September. The first week we were in a cottage just over the Scottish border north of Berwick. This gave us the opportunity to explore north Northumberland, including a day on Lindisfarne. The second week we stayed in a beautiful cottage in Linlithgow, which gave us the chance to visit Sterling and Holyrood Palace and the new Scottish Parliament building in Edinburgh. It also gave us the chance to meet up with David Archer, a colleague from College days who had been my Groomsman when we married.

Cullen had spent all summer eagerly awaiting the start of term. He settled in well and, according to his teacher was making good progress. Lois was also doing well. She was, however, somewhat shy, and reluctant to put up her hand even when she knew the right answer!

Because there was no Sunday School at St Andrew's, most Sundays Liz and the children started to attend St Catherine's Anglican Church where they had a small but lively Sunday School. The children thoroughly enjoyed it and because they started half an hour before St Andrew's they usually had a cup of tea at St Catherine's before crossing the road to St Andrew's to join the folk there for a second drink!

St Andrew's had a very strong Brownie troop that Lois joined in the May. She had the chance to go to Brownie Camp in July but, for weeks, insisted she wouldn't go then changed her mind at the last possible minute. Needless to say, she thoroughly enjoyed herself and declared at the end that she couldn't wait until next year!

Kath and I rediscovered Shakespeare. We went to see a production of 'As You Like It' by the University Drama Group in the Galilee Chapel in Durham Cathedral. It was excellent.

As was the Flower Festival held in the Cathedral at the same time. We also went to see the National Theatre productions of 'Othello' and 'Hamlet' that were live screened to the Gala Theatre in Durham.

Early in the year Kath joined the 'Witness Choir' after seeing their production of 'The Two Sisters' at St Andrew's at Easter. It's a mixed church choir with members from the south of the county and from North Yorkshire. One of our Local Preachers is the conductor. It's actually quite a good choir. I finally capitulated and joined the bass line in the autumn. However, I missed the concert for which we had been rehearsing as I was leading an Advent Study Group for Churches Together in Crook in St Catherine's Anglican Church for five Wednesday evenings through until Christmas.

After a couple of quarters off I started preaching again. I usually gave the West Durham Circuit five or six Sundays each quarter. For the first quarter of 2014 I decided to give some appointments to the neighbouring Durham and Deerness Valley Circuit, which was my 'home' circuit so anticipated that in the New Year I might get the opportunity to preach in my 'home' church for the first time in over forty years!

Liz decided she needed a more reliable car since she was travelling each day to Ferryhill and back. She had spotted a Citroen C1 at a Dealers in Croxdale so we went to have a look. I went along simply to keep the grandchildren occupied. Gareth spotted a Citroen Picasso at a reasonable price and decided that it was perhaps time to change his Tacuma, which to be fair, was getting on a bit. Then I spotted a Citroen Picasso, which was virtually new with only c.500 miles on the clock, and it was automatic, and it was very reasonably priced. So we all came back to Crook having bought 'new' cars. My only hesitation was that I was downsizing from a seven-seater to a five-seater, but my Kia Carens was of an age when the things that were needed renewing were very proving to be very expensive.

The end of 2013 saw Kath planning her visit to Australia with her sister and her mother, to see her brother who lives in Melbourne. They were intending to spend the whole of February there. Although Kath's Mum and sister had been before this would be Kath's first visit so, needless to say, she was very excited about the trip and the prospect of meeting up with her brother, her two nieces, and the three great nieces whom she has never met, except on Facebook!

[2014]

I can't resist retaining the opening paragraph of the Christmas letter for 2014: "Well, that's Christmas Eve, Christmas Day, Boxing Day and New Year's Eve over for another year!!! No, I've not lost the plot. If you haven't guessed, we've just returned from a 'Turkey and Tinsel' week in Perth, in Scotland. The weather was a bit damp and dull, but the company was great, and the food was superb, so much so that we've booked for the 'Turkey and Tinsel' week next year in a village near Aviemore."

Kath, along with her sister and her mum, did indeed jet off to

Australia for the month of February to visit her brother Ray, and nieces Di and Dawn, in Mornington, near Melbourne. She had a wonderful time, visiting many places around the Mornington peninsular and Melbourne itself, plus places further afield such as The Great Ocean Road. One of the delights of the trip was visiting Phillip Island where she watched the Fairy Penguins come out of the sea at night-time and waddle back to their family hutch to feed their young. She was very impressed by the visit to the sand sculptures which were amazing, portraying many stories such as the Mr Men, Postman Pat, Harry Potter, the Flower Fairies plus many more. She was also delighted when she had the opportunity to have her photo taken with a koala bear.

Just before her return home Kath discovered that they were only few minutes away from the set of 'Neighbours'. So she took the opportunity to visit Ramsey Street, and posed for a photo outside the Kennedy's house! However, the biggest delight was visiting the family over there. Kath had only seen Di and Dawn's families through emails and on Facebook, but to be with them for a month was just wonderful. Ray couldn't do enough for them, taking them to different places each day to ensure that nothing was missed. It was with great sadness that the trip came to an end and goodbyes were said.

It seemed that the trip had to be. Just a few months after their return from Australia Kath's sister, Pam, took their mum on a week's holiday in Torquay. The holiday was cut short because her mum wasn't feeling too well. Only a few weeks later she was diagnosed with lung cancer, which was a real shock given that she had lived such a full and active life. The cancer was extensive, and she died just four weeks after diagnosis. She was 89 years old. We were just pleased that she did not have to suffer too long and was looked after extremely well during her last few days by Macmillan nurses. Although a very sad loss we were thankful that she had enjoyed life to the full.

While Kath was at her mum's, along with Pam, looking after her during those last few weeks I was busy re-organising the 'back garden'. When I say, "I was…" I actually had someone in to do it! It wasn't much of a garden to start with – a poor quality lawn that sloped diagonally from one corner to the other and was so small it was hardly worth getting the lawnmower out to cut the grass; a raised area with a shrubbery and a gravelled 'patio' that wasn't big enough to set out our garden furniture on it. One of the guys in the Witness Choir, to which both Kath and I belonged, was a 'general builder' so he came and dug out the lawn and replaced it with a flagged patio with retaining walls made of railway sleepers. We gave the lawnmower to Liz and Gareth and we able to have the garden furniture set out on the patio. It looked great.

Just before the summer half-term we spotted an advert in the Methodist Recorder for a cottage outside Berwick-upon-Tweed. We phoned to see if it was available and when we were told that it was, we duly booked it for the week. Liz and Gareth, and Lois and Cullen came with us and we had a very enjoyable week exploring north Northumberland, including Lindisfarne. We enjoyed the holiday so much that when we arrived home, we checked out dates and phoned to see if the cottage was available at the beginning of August. Much to our surprise it was, so we booked it and spent another enjoyable week in north Northumberland, this time venturing into Scotland as far as Edinburgh.

Kath and I used our 'Timeshare' week in Bowness again at the end of August. We thought we would be on our own but, not entirely unsurprisingly, the family arrived and stayed a couple of days. We managed to visit number of places we hadn't been to for years. When we were at Brockhole the grandchildren had a whale of a time. They were both doing well at school. Cullen, who would be six the next February was tall for his age. Lois, who would be nine next January was small for her age. In other words, they were virtually the same size so look more like twins than older sister and younger brother! Lois was generally quiet and didn't work as hard as she should! Cullen was really boisterous and did work hard – his reading had come on in leaps and bounds.

In September Lois joined 'Natural High', which met in St Andrew's every Friday evening. It was an 'all singing, all dancing' youth club for Years 3–11 and, although it was not a Church group as such, it was run by Maureen Aspey, who also organised 'the Witness Choir', along with a number of other Church folk, including Kath and Liz, as helpers. It was open to any young person with an interest in singing, dance, and drama.

The first three times Lois went she simply sat on the sidelines and watched, then, hesitantly, began to join in and then discovered that she thoroughly enjoyed it. They usually put on a production each year. In 2013, it was the 'Wizard of Oz'. Kath and I went to see their production in Spennymoor Town Hall. It was very good. The next year they were planning to put on a production of "Joseph and his Amazing Technicolour Dreamcoat." They also usually took all the young folk to a show each year. We went with them to see "The Lion King", with the London cast, at the Sunderland Empire. It was a stunning production; the costumes had to be seen to be believed. Cullen couldn't wait to join 'Natural High' however I wasn't sure that the leaders were as enthusiastic about the prospect. Maybe it would calm him down? It had certainly given Lois a confidence she had previously lacked.

In September Kath and I finally got away on our own for a week in Fort William. It was a long drive to get there so we booked a night at a Travelodge on the edge of Glasgow to break the journey. The weather was cool and dull at the start of the week but improved as the week went on. We had intended to take a train trip from Fort William to Mallaig, but it had been fully booked for months, so we drove instead. The road, for the most part, runs alongside the railway so you still get the same views. In the end this turned out to be a better bet as we were able to visit the Glenfinnan monument and see the train on the viaduct – shades of Harry Potter! We wouldn't have had such a view had we been on the train. It was also an interesting time to be in Scotland as it was the week of the referendum on Scottish independence. There were saltires everywhere, along with large placards proclaiming either 'Yes' or 'No'! The result was close but failed to get the necessary majority for independence.

Both Liz and Gareth seemed to be well settled into their now not-so-new jobs. I guess it wasn't so difficult for Gareth since basically he simply moved location, the 'job' was the same. It was more difficult for Liz after two years out of teaching running a child-minding service from home. The income and holidays had helped and we heard nothing of the constant dissatisfaction that marred the last few years she was teaching before resigning to start her child-minding business. The staff seemed to be a really sociable crowd and she didn't seem to have been put off by the increasing administration that seemed to dog the profession!

Robbi, as he now wished to be called, had a better year with his painting and decorating business. Spring and summer kept him busy but with autumn business tailed off. Thankfully he took the initiative and applied for a job as a barista in Caffé Nero in the Market Place in Kendal. Not surprisingly he got the job, after all he had worked for Costa twice in the past, so he had the experience. He seemed to be enjoying it; we only hoped that a regular income would be all the encouragement he needed to stick with it. For the 'Children in Need' appeal he and a colleague cycled from Kendal to Newcastle and back – a round trip of 218 miles! Needless to say, the bikes were stationary, so they never left the coffee shop!

As for me, I enjoyed preaching, on occasion, in the Durham and Deerness Valley Circuit at churches in which I last preached some fifty years ago! As I have always kept a careful record of when, where, and what I preached, on my first occasion re-visiting a church I had previously visited as a young local preacher I usually began by introducing myself concluding with "and the last time I preached here..." To my amazement I kept coming across folk who still remembered me from those days!

[2015]

The New Year saw us deciding to buy a new car – again! Downsizing from a seven-seater to a five-seater had been a mistake with two grandchildren who persist in growing! Also, the 'automatic' on the Citroen left much to be desired. I went online and 'googled' best buy automatic seven-seaters. The first car that came up was a Chevrolet Orlando. There was one on sale in Felling, so we went to have a look. It turned out to be manual, but they assured me that they could source an automatic from their showroom in London. When it arrived a couple of days later it turned out to be 'top of the range' so proved to be a very good buy. So, in January we traded in our Citroen C3 for a Chevrolet Orlando; back to seven seats, and probably the best car we have ever owned!

As already noted, the grandchildren persisted in growing. Lois was nine in the January and Cullen was six in the February! Mind you given that Lois was small for her age and Cullen was tall for his age they were still both the same height so still looked more like twins!

We again enjoyed occasional visits to the Gala Theatre in Durham and during the year particularly enjoyed seeing two Shakespeare productions broadcast live from Stratford-on-

Avon. 'Love's Labour's Lost' and 'Love's Labour's Found' (aka 'Much Ado about Nothing'!) were set before and after World War I using the same cast for both. The productions were outstanding. Some of the comic scenes had the audience in tucks of laughter. We enjoyed them so much that we bought to DVDs so we could watch them again later.

In April we went to the first of two events held in Durham Cathedral. Apparently, it was only the second time that 'Jesus Christ Superstar' had been performed in a cathedral. It was an excellent production but spoiled by the fact that the company, amateur youth and professional adults, chose not to use any staging so, unless you were on the front couple of rows you saw virtually nothing of the performance. Such a pity!

In May we went to see 'Darkness to Light' which was a miscellany of choir, drama, dramatic reading, and much more. It was held to mark the commemoration of the liberation of Belsen concentration camp. Kevin Whately (who played Lewis in the detective series of the same name on TV) and Esther Rantzen were two of the narrators who linked the whole thing together, along with the daughter of one of the Belsen survivors. It was a very moving experience, and we were really glad that we went.

At the last minute we decided to have a week's holiday on our own in early May. We chose to go to Derbyshire and found a quaint two-up two-down cottage in Cromford. We met up with the Revd Keith Bamford, by chance, an ex-colleague from the Chester and Stoke-on-Trent District; a Circuit Steward and

Church Steward, by arrangement (they were on holiday in the area the same week), from Newcastle-under-Lyme; and friends, also by arrangement, from the time we lived in Coalville. We enjoyed some excellent meals out in equally excellent company. It did, however, mean that we would have to return to Derbyshire again as there were a number of places we intended to visit that we just didn't get around to!

At the end of May, with Liz and Gareth and the grandchildren, we went to Lennoxtown, just outside Glasgow, and stayed in what could only be described as a '5 star' bungalow. We visited the Falkirk Wheel, which Kath and I had visited before, several National Trust of Scotland houses – most impressive, as well as the Burrell Collection, which we had long wanted to visit. We also managed a day in Glasgow itself. Again, we decided there would have to be a return visit to the area as there was so much we didn't see.

July 18th was our 45th wedding anniversary. We had booked a nine-day river cruise on the Elbe to celebrate. We were due to fly to Berlin on Thursday 16th then next day transfer to our cruise ship to visit, among other places, Dresden, Wittenberg and Meissen, ending up in Prague. We had extended the trip to spend 4 days in Krakow in order to visit Auschwitz before returning to the UK. On Sunday 12th a message was left on our phone asking us to contact the cruise company which we did on the Monday morning. We were then told that the cruise had had to be cancelled, as the water in the Elbe was too low to allow the cruise to proceed, which was somewhat ironic as the rain was lashing down outside the study window whilst we were on the phone! We were offered a full refund and a significant discount on any future cruise we might book with the company before the end of 2016.

We were at something of a loss to know what to do with ourselves for the next fortnight, however, the Revd Terry Young phoned to say that he and his wife Cathryn were planning to bring their caravan to the area for just over a week. We were kept busy then for the next few days showing them around, including a visit to the Magna Carta exhibition which was on in Durham at the time. Unfortunately, the week ended badly for them as, when we were showing them around North Road Methodist Church Cathryn tripped on the edge of the platform and fell and tore her Achilles tendon and she had to wear the dreaded 'boot' for several weeks.

At the beginning of August, we returned to the holiday cottage near Lindisfarne that we rented on a couple of occasions the previous year. Liz and Gareth and the grandchildren came with us, as before. The weather was a bit mixed, but it didn't stop us getting on to a beach several times, as well as visiting a number of Historic Housing Association properties in the area.

We returned home on the Saturday and the next day Kath and I set off on a four-day coach trip with Weardale Motors, which included a visit to the Royal Edinburgh Military Tattoo on the Monday evening, which was excellent. We also visited Perth and St. Andrews before returning home. When we first retired to Crook, we had booked a coach trip with Weardale Motors on a couple of occasions and both times the trips were cancelled at the last minute due to a lack of numbers. We gave up. Then at a Coffee Morning at St Andrew's a number of folk were talking about Gerald. It turned out that Gerald Bell, who was one of our Local Preachers was a driver for Weardale. Gerald, however, with his partner Vicki, arranged his own coach trips which were always overbooked and never cancelled! Our trip to the Tattoo, was one of Gerald's. He is a fascinating character. He and I got on amazingly well as we discovered that we shared the same theological and liturgical views. Over the next few years, we would go on several of 'Gerald's trips' and we were never disappointed.

On our return from Edinburgh, we had just over a week to get organised before going to Bowness-on-Windermere for our Timeshare week! On the Sunday morning we went to Stricklandgate Methodist Church in Kendal, which gave us an opportunity to renew old acquaintances. We had a sandwich lunch – al fresco – in the Market Place with two friends from Church until Bobbi (another name change – he had now decided that he was a she and was beginning the process of changing gender) had finished her shift at Caffé Nero at two o'clock. She then took us to see her 'new' flat near Oxenholme Station. During the week we spent some time in Bowness, Windermere, the Motor Museum at Newby Bridge and the Priory at Cartmel. The children and grandchildren duly arrived (just to keep us company in case we felt lonely!) and we all went to visit Wray Castle where the children – little and big – had a whale of a time!

The autumn half term saw Lois off to Brownie camp from

the Friday until the Monday. On the Tuesday we all went to Manchester where we had booked into a Travelodge in the city centre for three nights so that on the Wednesday Liz and Lois and Kath and I could visit the Coronation Street set, while Gareth and Cullen went visit Old Trafford on the Thursday. The only Coronation Street tour available was at 8.40 pm! Gareth and Cullen fared better with a 10.30 am tour. On the Friday we stayed over in a Travelodge in Blackburn, an opportunity to visit friends and stock up on curries from the Halal stall in Blackburn Market!

Kath kept busy during the year helping lead Women's Own, and also preparing for, and leading, Messy Church each month at St Andrew's. She still suffered with dystonia and continued with botox injections every three months to try to keep the pain level down. I continued to preach most Sundays, giving several appointments to our two local circuits. On Maundy Thursday I produced a liturgy for a Tenebrae Service and meal for the church in Howden-le-Wear. It went really well and proved to be a memorable beginning to the observance of Good Friday and celebration of Easter Sunday.

At the end of the year Kath and I were in Aviemore in Scotland. No, not on a skiing holiday but on a Turkey and Tinsel week! Christmas Eve, Christmas Day and Hogmanay in as many days! The food and the company were excellent. One of Gerald's trips. The weather was quite good, mostly dry but rather cold. A day in Inverness and visits to Glenfarclas distillery and Speyside Cooperage (where casks are repaired) were the highlights.

[2016]

This was the "Year of the Kidney Stones"! It all began after lunch on Christmas Day 2015 when I started to have severe abdominal pains. By Christmas Day evening I was fine. However, when the pain returned in mid-January, it persisted for a week and was diagnosed as kidney stones. This resulted in my being admitted as an emergency to Sunderland Royal Hospital. The day after admission I had a procedure to insert a stent to bypass the stone. Everything then was fine.

We had a week's holiday at February half-term in a luxury apartment at Budle Bay, just north of Bamburgh on the northeast coast. Again Liz, Lois and Cullen came with us. Although it was cold the weather was fine, so we were able to travel about quite a bit. On the Sunday we visited Seahouses and had fish and chips for lunch! The first time in my life I'd had fish and chips for Sunday lunch. Gareth joined us for a couple of days to celebrate Cullen's seventh birthday.

One of my ex-colleagues from the Lakes School, where I taught for 17 years, arranged a staff reunion at the end of April to mark 50 years since the school's opening. We had a great weekend. It was really good to meet up with old friends, and we enjoyed a fabulous meal on the Saturday evening. It was definitely one of the highlights of the year!

In May Kath and I went on a five-day coach trip, with Gerald, to Dunoon. Among other places we visited Mount Stewart House on the Isle of Bute, one of the finest historic houses we have ever visited. However, we will always remember the trip for the chef's total lack of initiative where Kath was concerned. He had been told well in advance about her dairy allergy, however, while the rest of us were tucking into luxurious profiteroles and cheesecakes with lashings of various sauces Kath was served up a single tinned pear half on the first night, a few tinned peach slices on the second night, and a tablespoonful of tinned fruit salad on the third night! On the last night they excelled themselves, at Kath's instigation, providing fresh fruit and dairy-free sorbet!

Kath and I had always wanted to visit the Isle of Wight so at the beginning of June we headed south. We stayed with Terry and Cathryn in Blackburn overnight then travelled down to stay in a Travelodge in Christchurch before catching the ferry to the Isle of Wight the next morning. We had a wonderful week. The weather was brilliant, and I think we saw everything that was worth seeing on the island. When we returned to the mainland, we visited Beaulieu and, after a night in a Travelodge in High Wycombe, visited Blenheim Palace en route to spend some time with Terry and Cathryn again in Blackburn. We spent three nights there and then set out for home, making a small detour to Kendal to take Bobbi out for her 40th birthday lunch.

On 25th June Liz and Gareth did a sponsored walk for Macmillan cancer support. They walked just short of 26 miles along part of the Roman Wall. It took them 11 hours and 3 minutes (!) and between them they raised just short of £1,000! Needless to say, we were very proud of them.

I was called back to hospital on July 6th (my birthday) to have my kidney stones removed – finally! It was supposed to be half day visit but I was delayed going down to theatre and the procedure took longer than anticipated so I was kept in overnight!

We then had a series of visitors. John and Beryl Challen, who were friends from Kendal days came to visit from Hull. Their daughter, Helen, had been one of Liz's bridesmaids. Then Kath's sister Pam, with husband David, daughter Caroline and granddaughter Holly came to visit from Northern Ireland. So we had some really enjoyable days out showing them the sights around County Durham, including a day in South Shields where they were filming the next series of 'Vera' – so Kath had her photo taken with Brenda Blethyn!

Our August holiday was spent with the family in Hornsea. Apart from a visit to Epworth, the home of John Wesley, which we had visited before, this was an opportunity to visit our friends, Beryl and John Challen, in Hull and a number of places we had not been to before. Hull was well worth visiting, despite the amount of road works going on, by way of preparation to be City of Culture 2017. We spent our last day in Bridlington, on the beach for the sake of the children – young and old! The weather was good all week and on that last day some of us (me) got badly sunburned!

We were home for a week, and then it was off to the Lakes for our annual visit. The idea was for Kath and I to have a week on our own. We went to Stricklandgate Methodist Church on the Sunday morning where we met up again with friends from the time we had lived in Kendal. We took Bobbi out to lunch. Thanks to the 'reunion' earlier in the year, on the Monday we met up with friends from the Lakes School. We had coffee at the Bristly Hog Coffee Shop, where Bobbi was working at the time as a barista. In the evening we were invited to dinner with Ian and Irene Mason. Ian was one of the ministers at Stricklandgate Methodist Church when we had lived in Kendal. They had retired back to Kendal just the previous week. It was really good to catch up. On the Tuesday the family arrived! The rest of the week was spent re-visiting places we had been to a couple of years earlier. On the Friday Liz, Gareth and Cullen left, Lois stayed and came home with us on the Saturday.

Also in August I was called back to hospital to have my stent removed. The procedure took only a few minutes and was fairly painless. That, I thought, was the end of the matter. No more kidney stones! How wrong can you be?

At the beginning of September, I began to have severe abdominal pains – again! After a week I saw the doctor who diagnosed a viral infection! I was no better a week later, and I went to the surgery again, with the same result. Meanwhile Ivor and Judy from Manchester came to visit. Kath was left to entertain them while I sat in my chair, all day and all night, nursing a hot water bottle! A week later I began passing kidney stones – the ones they had supposedly removed some months earlier! Recovery took another three weeks and that meant cancelling our proposed trip to the Republic of Ireland with Great Railway Journeys!

To compensate we booked a holiday for half term in Scotland taking Liz, Lois and Cullen with us. Gareth unfortunately had to work. We stayed in a lodge just outside Dollar. It gave us the opportunity to visit Scone Palace and Perth, also Sterling castle and Sterling. The day we went to Sterling Castle just happened to be the day that Prince William was paying a visit to the museum there, so we hung around outside until he left to make sure that Kath got a photo of him waving to her – well a photo of the car he was in! We also went to the visitor centre at Crieff. Caithness Glass is now situated there, and Lois and Cullen were able to make their own painted glasses.

I was still preaching most Sundays, when we were not away on holiday, and Kath was still organising 'Messy Church'. Both Lois and Cullen were still doing well at school. They would be eleven and eight in January and February 2017 respectively. It was hard to believe that the next September Lois would be starting Secondary School. She was now in Guides, and Cullen would be promoted from Beavers to Cubs in the spring.

At church both Kath and I were involved in 'The Christmas Journey', a dramatic presentation of the nativity for Year 2 children. All five local schools in the area came, around 200 children in all. The schools all declared it a real success. Kath had also been involved in helping to erect the knitted Christmas tree as part of the church's Christmas Tree Festival. To make it, people at church (mainly Kath and our friend Wendy) had been knitting six-inch squares for the previous twelve months. The finished tree looked really good.

Kath and I also went on a weekend coach trip with Gerald to Edinburgh to visit the Christmas Market, apparently on the busiest shopping day of the year! There were times when we simply couldn't move. On the Sunday morning we went to the Methodist Church. The premises had been recently refurbished and they now had a magnificent new organ, and a new cafeteria, where we had Sunday lunch.

[2017]

Spring half-term saw us going south with Liz and Gareth and the grandchildren, to visit the Harry Potter Experience, which really was well worth the visit. We then had a few days in London and then to Leicester to visit friends. We stayed in a Travelodge. There was no cafeteria but on the roadside nearby there was a converted container that produced the most amazing full English breakfasts! At Easter, again with family, we hired a cottage in Tonyrefail, in South Wales. The main reason was to visit the Royal Mint, which was really interesting, sadly there were no freebees, but we did get to 'mint' our own new £1 coin – well, we pressed the button, and the machine did the rest! It also gave us the opportunity to go to St Fagan's National History Museum, and the National Botanic Gardens of Wales.

In April Kath and I went on a Weardale coach trip with Gerald to Nethy Bridge in the Highlands of Scotland. We had been there a couple of years previously and enjoyed it so much we decided it was worth a return visit.

In May Kath's brother Ray, with his new wife Rayma, paid us visit from Australia. They were having an extended honeymoon, visiting Rayma's son in Norfolk, then to visit us in Crook, then to Northern Ireland to stay with Kath's sister, Pam, then holidaying in Wales and Cornwall where we met up with them again, briefly. It was a great week and we all thoroughly enjoyed their visit.

When Ray and Rayma left Kath and I were off on another Weardale coach trip with Gerald, this time to Oban. The tour took in a visit to Iona. Unfortunately, because of mistimings with the ferries, although we got onto the island of Iona, we didn't have sufficient time to visit the Abbey.

We returned from Oban with just a day to spare before setting off for Cornwall. It was the Summer half-term holiday and Liz had signed up for 'Ride the Night', a 64-mile cycle ride around London with 3,000 other women to raise money for three Women's Cancer Charities. Gareth wasn't able to get time off work, so we drove down to London where we dropped off Liz (her bike had gone on ahead with some work colleagues who were also taking part), and we then continued on to Liskeard with the grandchildren. After her cycle ride through the night Liz caught a train from Slough and joined us in Liskeard on the Sunday lunchtime. Among other places we took the opportunity to visit was Port Isaac – Port Wen in the TV series 'Doc Martin.'

To celebrate my 70th birthday in July Kath and I went on a coach trip, organised by Glenton Palmer, to Krakow and Prague, including a visit to Auschwitz. These were places we had anticipated visiting on our ill-fated river cruise two years previously. We really enjoyed Krakow which was a beautiful city. We were there for several nights. The Weiliczka Salt Mine was amazing, and Auschwitz was well worth the visit, even if it was overwhelming, given what had transpired there during World War II. Because of a re-jigging of the itinerary, we didn't have sufficient time in Prague to visit some of the places we would have liked to have visited, but the castle was truly remarkable. The drawback to such a coach trip was that it entailed a long day driving across Europe, there, and back!

In August with Liz, Gareth, Lois and Cullen we stayed in a fabulous barn conversion in Dronfield in Derbyshire. Kath and I had had a holiday in Derbyshire a couple of years previously but despite our best intentions had never got around to visiting Sheffield and Chesterfield, which I last visited in the late 1960s when I spent a year at Cliff College. There were no trams in those days, so it was a new experience to go into the city of Sheffield using their new(ish) means of transport.

In September Kath and I went on another coach trip, again organised by Glenton Palmer, this time to Guernsey and Jersey. Guernsey was amazing. Buses, which were frequent, cost £1.00 a journey, however far you ventured! There was a bus stop just outside our hotel, so we made good use of it. One of the most interesting places we visited was the Occupation Museum. Jersey was quite different – the bus fare was £2.00 a journey to start with, and their routes were not nearly so convenient. Nevertheless, we enjoyed our visit. Among the places we visited on the island were The Jersey War Tunnels, which were really interesting, as was the 'Lalique Church'. On both islands we visited their tapestry exhibitions, very different, but definitely not to be missed.

Later that month Kath and I went on our final trip of 2017 with Weardale Motors, arranged by Gerald. This time to Aberdeen. It was one of the best Weardale tours that we have been on. We visited Haddo House where we had an excellent guided tour of the house, and Fraserburgh where we visited The Museum of Scottish Lighthouses.

Our final holiday, with Liz, Lois and Cullen, was during October half term week. This time we went to north Wales, staying in a delightful cottage in Clynnog-Fawr on the Lleyn Peninsular. Penrhyn Castle filled a whole day, as did our visit to Llanberis and the National Slate Museum. We also visited Caernarvon, Anglesea and Bangor, where Kath did her teacher training back in the late 60s!

When we returned home Kath's sister Pam, along with Caroline and Holly came over from Northern Ireland for a week. Lois and Cullen had great fun with Holly doing Halloween things! We had some very strange food stuffs – mostly coloured green but nevertheless very edible!

Most Sundays – when we are not away on holiday – I was still taking services in various churches in the area; and Kath was still actively involved in Messy Church, both at our church and in a local Primary School. She had also taken up quilting! After making a couple of bags, she made a couple of Christmas table runners, one for Ray and Rayma, and a quilt for Lois for Christmas!

In July we received the news that Heversham Primary School, where Kath had been head teacher, was to close. When Kath was there it was oversubscribed, as it had received an 'Outstanding' Ofsted report, and was rated in the top 100 schools in the country by *The Times*. During her time Kath had had a new hall built on to the school at a cost in excess of £1.5 million. The design was very imaginative as the school was built on a hillside. Sadly, numbers had dropped since she left 16 years earlier to a point where the school was no longer viable, and the decision had been taken to close. The school had arranged an extended weekend of celebrations to mark the 126 years since its founding, and we went over on the Monday. It was an opportunity for Kath to meet up, for one last time, with colleagues from her time there as head.

Bobbi's employment as a barista at The Bristly Hog came to a sudden and unexpected end in the Spring when the couple who owned it split up and put the business on the market. Bobbi decided to try to purchase the business, without success. She tried to rent other premises, again without success. Needless to say, all the premises she tried for remained vacant! In the end she decided to set up a taxi business. She passed 'the knowledge' and purchased a Renault Twingo – yellow of course (with checkerboard pattern on the sides) and got her licence from the Local Authority. She started trading at the beginning of December and already had a regular school run and several Christmas parties booked!

Cullen was now in Year 4 and seemed to be much more settled and was really doing well. He was clearly very bright. His teacher this year seemed to have the measure of him. Meanwhile Lois began Secondary School in the September and she was thoroughly enjoying it. I was a little surprised, however, when her first RE homework was to 'write a letter to a friend explaining the doctrine of the Trinity'! Unfortunately I didn't get the chance to see what she wrote.

[2018]

For a whole variety of reasons, we did not travel about as much 2018. During the spring half-term week in early February, however, we had a week in Dumfries and Galloway with Liz and the grandchildren; a beautiful alpine-style lodge with views over a small loch. The weather was lovely and sunny, but bitterly cold.

The reason we did not travel about as much was because Kath had her left hip replaced on 14th March. She was not allowed to go in a car for six weeks and she was not allowed to go on holiday for three months, which meant we had to cancel the holiday we had booked to visit Peebles in May that included a trip to New Lanark, which we had been particularly looking forward to.

Kath's recovery after her operation was slow but steady. She had a bit of a setback a week after her operation when she had an adverse reaction to the antibiotics she had been prescribed, but that was quickly overcome. Not surprisingly she proved to be an impatient patient! Having heard of people who had been back to normal after just a few weeks she felt that that should have been her!

Our first post-op holiday was at the end of July when we booked a cottage on the outskirts of Bath. We made good use of Park and Ride and had a couple of days in Bath and a couple of days in Bristol. Among the highlights of the week were visits to the Roman Baths, in Bath, and the SS Great Britain in Bristol; the American Museum in Bath and the 'New Room' – Wesley's Chapel – in Bristol. The weather was brilliant – wall to wall sunshine every day!

We were also delighted to have had a number of visitors to stay during the year, some of whom we hadn't seen for years. Jane, from the United States and her daughter, Chrissie from Stornoway; and Lisa, who we knew from our time in Coalville and hadn't seen since Liz and Gareth's wedding, along with Ben, her delightful young son.

Bobbi finally realised her dream when she signed a lease on two small shops in the New Shambles, in Kendal, and spent most of August transforming it into "About Time" – a retro Coffee Bar! This entailed building a bar from old pallets and a trip to London, there and back in a day, to collect a retro Italian coffee machine. The taxi business was consequently abandoned. It hadn't been the success that she hoped for, but with a new business being established, it wasn't practical to continue with 'Bobbi Cabs.'

At the end of August Kath and I had our usual week in Bowness. Liz and Gareth and Lois and Cullen visited as they had in the past. This was the week Bobbi was getting ready to open "About Time", on the Saturday we were coming home. On the Friday Kath ended up on her knees cleaning the furniture and washing the floor ready for the Saturday morning! The shop was finally up and running and seemed to be doing extremely well. Several customers have declared that it's "the best coffee in town." Bobbi also appeared on local BBC TV evening news having signed up to be one of the shops that traded in Lake District Pounds. Her reviews on TripAdvisor were all 5 stars!

Although Kath had her hip operation in the March, she was still struggling a bit and ended up having a cortisone injection, which, it was hoped, would relieve the residual pain in the top of her leg. Sadly, there was no noticeable improvement. Nevertheless, we managed a couple of coach holidays with Weardale Motors. A week in Kent in October, visiting Rochester, Broadstairs and Canterbury. The weather was kind, and the hotel was excellent. Shortly after we were off again, this time to Llandudno. A day in Chester, a trip around Snowdonia and a day in Llandudno itself. Again, the weather was kind, and the hotel was excellent; they were particularly good in catering for Kath's dairy allergy!

October half-term came around and Kath and I had a long weekend in Blackpool, again with Weardale Motors. We travelled there on the Friday and after an early dinner we drove through the illuminations. We were on the front seat of the coach, so we had a splendid view. On the Saturday we spent the day in Liverpool but because Kath's leg was playing up, we didn't get much further than the foyer of the Liverpool Museum. It was Liverpool Irish Week, so we were well entertained by a Ceilidh band and Irish Dancers. We left after breakfast on the Sunday and had a morning at Barton Grange Garden Centre – the Christmas decorations were out of this world! In the afternoon we stopped off for a couple of hours in Bowness before heading home. The weather was amazing, cold, but wall to wall sunshine.

Meanwhile Liz had been learning Spanish in readiness for her trip to Spain during October half-term with a view to teaching the language in school when she returned. She was based at the university in Salamanca. Four hours of intensive language study each morning and guided tours, in Spanish, of the city in the afternoon. She thoroughly enjoyed the experience and gets a certificate to show she's leaned a foreign language in a foreign country!

Kath continued with her quilting classes each Monday and had completed various projects. A couple of table runners, a couple of stoles for me – still unfinished, like the ones she started when she was in college! She then used her time making Christmas decorations. She also joined the WI which meets on the first Monday of each month and she has really enjoyed it. She continued to run 'Messy Church', after school on the first Friday of each month and was again involved in the church's annual 'Christmas Journey' for the six Primary Schools in and around Crook.

We couldn't believe how Lois and Cullen have grown. They were now as tall / taller than Kath. Lois would be thirteen the next January and was now in Year 8 at Secondary School. The highlight of her year was winning an expensive iPad. Having attended every Parents' Curriculum Evening with her mum and dad her name was entered into a draw and she won! Lois continued to enjoy Guides and Natural High. Cullen was in Year 5 and would be ten the next February. Just one more year in Primary School! Time flies! He enjoyed Cubs each week and joined a Computer Club which met each week after school on Tuesdays.

As for me... well most Sundays I was usually preaching in one of the Churches in either the West Durham Circuit or the neighbouring Durham and Deerness Valley Circuit. On alternate Fridays I presided at Table Talk, which included a soup lunch, at St Paul's Centre in Spennymoor. Maureen Aspey who is the Witness Choir's conductor and is in charge of natural High is the Director of St Paul's Centre. The Centre runs all sorts of activities for the local community, especially for those with particular needs. Not long after we retired to Crook Maureen approached me with a view to setting up something that was clearly Christian based, so we came up with Table Talk. Each term we begin with a feature film followed by a discussion. The other sessions we usually follow a Study Series written by Adam Hamilton, a US Methodist Minister who is senior pastor of the Church of Resurrection in Kansas City. He founded the church in 1990. Today it is the largest United Methodist congregation in the world, with a membership of over 25,000 in five campuses and an average weekly attendance for all campuses in 2019 of over 13,000!

[2019]

We usually went away in February half-term but as the grandchildren had grown older it proved more and more difficult to keep them entertained, and there are very few National Trust Properties or Historic Houses open, so this year we stayed at home and had one or two days out instead. It was the first time Cullen had been home for his birthday – ten this year. Lois had become a teenager in the January. Cullen was in his last year in Primary School and Lois began Year 9 in September. She won a Head Teacher's Bronze Award at the end of Year 8, unfortunately she wasn't there when it was presented and when she collected her certificate in the new school year it didn't say why she was awarded it – it was all a bit of a mystery!

'About Time', Bobbi's Espresso Bar was nominated as Best Café in Cumbria for a Cumbria Business Award. She was shortlisted and Liz and Kath and I went over to Carlisle in March for the presentation of the Awards. It was a bit like the Oscars with gold envelopes, drum rolls, and long pauses. There were five establishments named in her category and we were delighted when 'About Time' was named as the winner!

In April we had visitors from Newcastle-under-Lyme. Carol and Marion Reddish had been promising to come and visit since we first retired here but this was the first opportunity that they had had. Carol was one of my Circuit Stewards and Marion was Mayor and I was her chaplain when we were living there. The week was cut short as Kath's sister and her husband had also arranged to visit, so as one lot of visitors went another set of visitors arrived!

Easter Saturday was glorious so Kath and I, with Liz and the grandchildren, drove over to Acorn Bank, a National Trust property near Penrith. I sat outside the house 'people-watching' while the others went off to explore various woodland trails. Well over an hour later I was phoned to say that Kath had fallen over a tuft of grass (!) on their way back to the house! She had hurt her right arm and was in considerable pain. The NT personnel were brilliant – three of them went out, eventually taking a motorized buggy for her to drive herself back to the car. Then it was off to Penrith hospital where they put her arm in a sling and suggested we went to Durham hospital for an x-ray.

It turned out she had broken both bones in her right wrist, so she duly got plastered! Unfortunately, there appeared to have been some nerve damage which, months later, after a series of visits to various consultants, was still causing her considerable pain. After visiting yet another consultant in mid-November it was been decided that she should have a carpal tunnel operation on 17th December – a good excuse to get out of Christmas preparations! Fortunately, the problem resolved itself and the operation was cancelled.

In May Kath and I booked a cottage in Haworth – Bronte country. One reason was to visit the Piece Hall in Halifax, which proved well worth the visit! The other was that the location provided an opportunity to visit friends, Ivor and Judy in Stretford and Terry and Catherine in Darwen, and for friends from Leeds, Shirley and Terry to visit us. Shirley and Terry, we had met on our coach trip to Eastern Europe in 2017.

June was a particularly busy month. First of all, Kath and I went with Gerald again on a Weardale Motors coach holiday to Great Yarmouth. The weather was good, as was the company and it gave us an opportunity to revisit some places in Norfolk and Suffolk that we hadn't been to since we lived in Bury St Edmunds in the 1970s! Next, we took Lois and Cullen to Haggerstone Castle in north Northumberland from Monday to Friday during half-term week, while Gareth was at work and Liz was off to visit a friend in Turkey. We stayed in a very luxurious holiday home – they didn't make caravans like that when we were young! We survived, even though the weather was rather mixed.

Our eldest grandson, Robert, had come over from Canada with his Mum, to stay with his other grandparents in Letchworth. As he usually does, he came to spend a few days with us. It was good to see him, and we were sorry his visit had to be so short, but Bobbi had been given a date by St Pancras Hospital in London for her gender reassignment operation and she was admitted on her birthday, June 12th. Kath went down for a few days, staying with Lisa Davis in London, but had to cut short her time there as our great-niece, from Australia, was coming to spend a week with us after a week in Northern Ireland with Kath's sister's family, and before going to stay with another member of her family who took her off for a few days to visit Disneyland Paris.

That was where Liz and Gareth and Lois and Cullen were going to after the end of the summer term. They extended their visit by a few days in order to have some time in Paris. Their trip, however, was complicated by the fact that Liz had decided to resign from her job after months of what was, in effect, low level bullying, and then their Picasso decided to give up the ghost! So, with just a few days to go they decided that they would have to go in Liz's little Citroen C1! The Picasso was duly revived on their return.

At the beginning of August Kath and I booked an annexe in a house in Fulford, near Newcastle-under-Lyme as Kath had been invited to the wedding of two of her colleagues from the last school she taught in before she retired. It gave us an opportunity to visit St Peter's, one of my churches before I retired, and several friends and relatives of Kath's, including her uncle Arthur who, sadly died in September so we found ourselves making another trip to Staffordshire.

At the end of August, we had our usual week in Windermere. Apart from visiting Stricklandgate Methodist Church on the Sunday, and a day when we drove over to Morecambe, we spent most of the week in and around Kendal. Bobbi's Espresso Bar – About Time – does make the best coffee in Kendal! Before we left, we did spend a day visiting the new Windermere Jetty, the boat Museum, and Blackwell, the Arts and Crafts house.

That week we were chauffeured by Liz in their Citroen Picasso, complete with a reconditioned engine, as my car was in the garage awaiting a new radiator! It remained there for several weeks as there were various problems in getting a radiator and getting it fitted. It wasn't a major problem because at the beginning of September Kath and I were off on another coach holiday with Weardale Motors, this time to Sidmouth in Devon. The Hotel was right on the seafront, the weather was beautiful, and the food was excellent! The only trouble was that it was a long journey, there, and back!

We finally got the car back but then, after just a week, the gearbox packed up, very inconveniently, halfway up Hartside Pass! We were finally relayed back to the Garage we use and didn't see the car again for several more weeks, so it was back to using Liz's little Citroen C1!

At the beginning of October, we went on our penultimate holiday of the year, again with Weardale Motors, this time to the Isle of Man. This was the first coach trip that we'd gone on with Weardale that had not been organised by Gerald. The crossing from Heysham was a little rough and Kath was a little green. However, the hotel in Douglas, and the food, were excellent. We had a trip on the tramway up to the summit of Snaefell, and a tour of the tram depot and workshops – fascinating! The weather was mixed during the week, but the return crossing was smooth, much to Kath's relief, not least because it was her 70th birthday. We went out for a birthday lunch on the Sunday.

Our final holiday of the year was in Douglas – this time in Lanarkshire. We went at the end of October during half-term week, so we hired a cottage and took Liz, Lois and Cullen with us. Since we still were without a car it was Liz who chauffeured us all week in their Citroen Picasso – again! On the Monday we visited New Lanark, which was the reason we chose to go there in the first place. The weather had promised to be poor for the week, but in the end, from Sunday to Thursday, we had glorious sunshine. On the other days we visited most of the Museums in Glasgow all of which were free with free parking!

Kath continued with her quilting, organising Messy Church, and the WI! I was still preaching almost every Sunday and leading 'Table Talk' on alternate Fridays.

[2020]

Since this July we were going to be celebrating our Golden Wedding Anniversary we decided to treat ourselves to a couple of holidays abroad. Our record when it comes to planning such holidays isn't great. The trip we'd planned to mark our 45th Wedding Anniversary was the river trip on the Elbe – cancelled just a couple of days before we were due to go because of a lack of water! When we decided to make up for it a couple of years later with a rail trip round southern Ireland *we* had to cancel because I was ill! Surely this year would be different. So, we planned a rail trip in Switzerland in May and a trip to Spain later in the summer. However, before we paid our deposit the coronavirus hit!

We had also planned a week away in the February half-term with a couple of friends from church, a coach trip Monday to Friday to Bogner Regis. A couple of weeks before we were due to go the coach company cancelled it due to lack of numbers! Was this an omen? Anyway, undeterred we manged to find a cottage near Kendal for the whole week and took Liz and the grandchildren with us. We hoped to help Bobbi out with the refurbishment of her Coffee Shop.

It rained – virtually the whole week. I don't ever recall being on a week's holiday when it rained so heavily and so persistently. We managed a few days out – sort of – because Bobbi was running behind with her refurbishment and so our labour wasn't in the end required. At the same time as she was refurbishing her shop, she was moving from a flat on one side of Kendal to a house on the other side of Kendal. Despite the bad timing it was a good move to a much better property. She finally re-opened her shop, very successfully, and all seemed well set for the future. Then along came 'lockdown', the consequence of the coronavirus pandemic!

Having left teaching last September Liz found a job as a teaching assistant at New College in Durham. It was zero-hours contract, and lousy pay, but she thoroughly enjoyed it. Anyway, just after 'lockdown' began she saw an advert for a Clinical Care Assistant / Ambulance Driver job with the possibility, in time, of becoming a paramedic. It was something she had always wanted to do and, although she had previously applied, unsuccessfully, she decided to try again. This time she succeeded and started her training on 1st June. The next three weeks were spent learning to drive ambulances. There were three in her 'bubble' with their instructor. They drove all over the North East from Edinburgh to York and Sunderland to Kendal. Some of the time on blue lights and often at speed. She passed with flying colours and is now recognised as an 'Advanced Driver' with all the benefits that that could bring! Then she began six weeks of 'Clinical Care Assistant' training.

Meanwhile, in Kendal Bobbi suddenly found that she had to shut up shop! She was not pleased having not long re-opened and was really beginning to see the benefits of her refurbishment. So, it was a case of applying for Government grants and Universal Credit in order to see her through, as rents still had to be paid and she had to live. It was a difficult few weeks, isolated on her own, but it was made easier by the fact that she had moved into a new house with stunning views over Kendal from her balcony, and the weather helped of course. Eventually in June she re-opened for take-aways, having made a number of alterations to the shop to facilitate the 'new normal'.

When the pandemic began, I was one of those who received the dreaded letter to say I was in the 'most vulnerable' category because I have Diabetes and COPD. So, Kath and I were suddenly 'housebound'! I took the car 'off road' and we arranged for Liz to do the shopping and we set about doing all the sorting out we had been putting off for the past eight years. When we first moved in, we decorated, sorted out the furniture and put everything away but we never got around to sorting out the 'everything' as we had intended, before we were caught up in other things. Now was the chance. The garage, which we had never sorted out at all, was left to last since the car was off-road and the tips and charity shops were closed. They reopened, but the garage was still waiting to be cleared! It would have to wait until the next Spring when the weather should be a bit warmer.

Apart from doing the sorting out it was a chance to indulge in some craft activities. Kath knitted several jumpers, including one for Liz's birthday, and a couple of dolls. Meanwhile I finished off a small-ish tapestry wall hanging I hadn't touched for a couple of years, then I did a further four cushions, including one featuring VWs as a Christmas present for Bobbi. She has a thing about VW Campervans. We also began a jigsaw in March – 1000 pieces and no picture. I didn't do much, but Kath refused to let it beat her. It was the end of June before it was finished! Of course, she then got the bug and completed another, then another, then … She also set about learning Spanish. Not sure whether there was an implied hint about possible future holiday venues!

Saturday July 18th was our Golden Wedding Anniversary. With our proposed holidays postponed we decided to take the family to the Fir Tree for a Sunday lunch. We'd gone there for Kath's 70th the previous year. However, 'Shielding' was extended to the end of July so we ended up on our own on the 18th! (Liz dropped the shopping off in the morning and Bobbi arrived in the evening for the weekend.) Sardines on toast for lunch, and cheese and crackers for tea! On the Sunday, however, we did have a family bar-b-q at lunchtime and a buffet tea late afternoon!

In August we tentatively ventured out, though not too far. Lidl and Aldi and Morrisons. I say 'we' by which I mean Kath. The last week in August was our annual visit to the Lake District. We took Lois and Cullen with us. Liz and Gareth joined us on the Thursday. Bowness was busy – social distancing was not much observed. Few places of interest were open, and those that were required one to book. We didn't venture far. Driving from Troutbeck to Ambleside wasn't at much more than walking pace, such was the density of the traffic. Grasmere Methodist Church, where I had often preached in times gone by, closed several years ago. Finally sold it had re-opened as a Bar and Bistro – interesting. We didn't get to go in as, unfortunately, it was closed! We did spend quite a bit of time in Bobbi's coffee shop which she had re-opened for take-aways at the beginning of August and finally, the week we were there, opening up for sit-ins.

September saw Cullen starting Secondary School and Lois returning for the first time since before Easter. September also saw us having a new boiler installed. For several months the hot water had been randomly going cold – not nice when you are in the middle of having a shower. So new boiler – problem solved.

With no sign of Covid 19 disappearing, indeed with its increase and the subsequent re-imposition of 'lockdown', we have become somewhat wary. Liz's job means that, on occasion, she is in contact with people who are likely to have been infected with the virus. In addition, since she is on shift work, and since Gareth is on permanent night shift, Lois and Cullen occasionally have to stay overnight with us, and there have been confirmed cases of Covid 19 at the school they attend!

Liz is thoroughly enjoying her new job and Bobbi keeps adapting to constantly changing circumstances. Church ground to a halt in March. My last service was at the end of March at St Andrew's. Kath and I became used to watching one or other online service on a Sunday morning – it had its attraction – having a cup of coffee while watching, and being able to mute the bits you didn't like!

[2021]

Early in December 2020 I decided to change the car. The Chevrolet was getting to a point where any repairs that needed doing were proving expensive. Covid, plus his wife's illness meant that my regular garage man had decided to retire and that would mean taking the car to the GM dealers in Darlington for servicing and repairs. 20 miles each way and dealership prices! When we were staying in Bowness in the August, I had seen a Kia Niro advertised online at our local Kia dealers at Brandon, just 5 miles away. I was tempted, not least because it was electric, but it was a five-seater. Now that the grandchildren were older perhaps we didn't need a seven-seater any longer? It turned out it was still for sale at the beginning of December, so we decided to have a look.

It looked okay, white, low mileage and in good condition. Standing next to it on the forecourt was a seven-seater Kia Carens, also white, low mileage and in good condition, but diesel like the Chevrolet. After a lengthy discussion with the salesperson, we decided it was no contest and we arranged to buy the Carens. So much for my resolve to 'go electric'! It has proved to be have been a good choice. Mind you, like all new(ish) cars everything is computerised. 'Stop – start' technology has taken a bit of getting used to. Of course, with Covid it meant that we hardly drove anywhere until the spring.

In late January we had a phone call from Kath's brother-in-law to tell us that Kath's sister Pam had died. Tragically she had taken her own life. No one could really work out why. She had a broken arm, but the cast was due to be taken off a few days later, and she'd happily played with her young grandson at his birthday the day before. The family were devastated. To Kath's frustration 'lockdown' meant that she wasn't able to travel to Northern Ireland for the funeral although we were able to be a part of it as it was broadcast online.

Everything at church continued to be closed down so we got used to watching the online service the circuit provided each week courtesy of You Tube. We also 'visited' neighbouring circuits and even ventured as far as Kansas City to share in worship at the United Methodist Church of the Resurrection in Kansas City. The Church has a membership in excess of 25,000 and the senior Pastor, Adam Hamilton, has produced a number of books that I have used in study groups here in Crook and at 'Table Talk' in Spennymoor.

I completed another couple of tapestries which I have subsequently had stretched and framed. Kath meanwhile continued to knit all sorts of things we didn't need! Thankfully she decided to respond to a request for people to contribute to The Methodist Tapestry. The Weardale Museum, which is based in the recently closed High House Chapel, at the head of the dale launched 'The Methodist Tapestry' to be made up of panels telling the story of Methodism in the dales, to be augmented with panels depicting the wider Methodist story. The panels are not strictly tapestry but rather embroidery. Kath suggested that she could do Mow Cop which was closely linked to the beginnings of the Primitive Methodist Connexion and happens to be near to where she was brought up. She was apprehensive at first having rarely done any free embroidery, but in the end she thoroughly enjoyed it.

Although Bobbi was allowed to open 'About Time' for take-aways she was so frustrated by having to constantly remind customers to use the hand sanitizer and wear their masks she decided to close. She then took to wild swimming in Windermere every day. It did wonders for her mental health. She subsequently decided to give the shop an extensive refurbishment, the third in as many years! Still, it kept her going and the results were impressive.

Kath and I had our Covid vaccinations on the 6th February and the 24th April so when restrictions began to ease, we felt a bit more confident about getting back to something approaching normal. The churches began to have some face-to-face services and I found myself with four appointment in July and August.

At the end of August, we went to Bowness for our usual week

in the Timeshare we own there. It coincided with the Bobbi's re-opening and the one glorious week of summer sunshine. It was only marred by the fact that I was waiting for the results of a visit to the Freeman Hospital in Newcastle the week before. In early May Kath had spotted a swelling on my left shoulder blade. I visited the Doctor and he arranged for an ultrasound which proved inconclusive. I was then sent for an MRI scan at Darlington Memorial Hospital and then for an ultrasound guided biopsy at the Freeman Hospital. Once we returned from holiday I was called back to the Freeman and was told that it was a soft tissue sarcoma, and I would need surgery to have it removed.

The operation took around ten and a half hours and took place on October 4th. The cancerous growth was excised. It was around 8 inches by 8 inches. They then took skin and muscle from my left thigh to replace what they had removed from my back, then grafted skin from my right thigh to cover the wound on my left thigh. Three and a half weeks in hospital followed, with strong anti-biotics and daily dressings on both legs. I was finally discharged but with regular returns to the Royal Victoria Infirmary for dressings. It turns out that what I had was one of the rarest and most aggressive of cancers (1%). It doesn't respond well to chemotherapy and does not always respond well to radiotherapy. However, having recovered from surgery I was scheduled to have radiotherapy, Monday to Friday for a period of three weeks beginning in mid-December, initially to ensure nothing of the sarcoma remains around the site where the growth was removed from by back. I wasn't looking forward to traveling an hour each way to the Freeman for a twenty-minute treatment for three weeks, but if that's what it would take…! In the end we discovered a charity 'Daft as a Brush' that provided free transport to and from the Freeman for patients undergoing cancer treatment. They were brilliant. A CT scan has shown that the sarcoma had 'seeded' a few spots on my lungs so, once my three weeks of radiotherapy are completed, then they will then set about treating the spots on my lungs!

I cannot speak too highly of the sarcoma team at the Freeman hospital. The surgical team were fantastic. Everyone who had occasion to examine my back raved over what an amazing job the surgeons had done removing the tumour, replacing it with muscle from my leg, and covering the site with a flap of skin. Every day I was in hospital, and every time I have returned to have the dressing changed on my left thigh, one or other, or both, of the sarcoma nurses, Jo Taylor and Alice Dean, have been there. Their support and encouragement have been appreciated more than they will ever know.

We've had so many cards and e-mails from friends as far apart as Australia and America, as well as from Circuits I have served in, that it is difficult to keep track, but both Kath and I are so grateful for everyone's prayers and good wishes.

Gareth continues to enjoy his work on permanent night shift at Morrisons Supermarket in Consett. Liz also continues to enjoy her work as a Clinical Care Assistant and driver for the North East Ambulance Service although she gets frustrated at times when an ambulance is called by someone who has no intention of going to hospital. Also, some folk seem to think they can only go to A&E by ambulance when there is nothing to stop them getting themselves there. Recently the service has also often been criticised for the length of time some folk have to wait for an ambulance when the problem lies with the hospitals who are so short of beds and staff that often there can be as many as nine ambulances queuing for several hours to transfer their patients. Her shift patterns vary and there are times when her night shifts clash with Gareth's and we end up having the grandchildren staying with us overnight. They are no problem at night since they are glued to their iPads, but when it comes to getting them ready to catch the bus for school in a morning, they drive Kath to distraction!

[2022]

Well, it's now the end of February 2022. Lois celebrated her 16th birthday in January, and Cullen his 13th earlier this month. Both are doing well at school, and their teachers speak highly of them. For Lois it is her GCSE year. Lois was awarded a bronze 'Headteachers Award' several years ago. She gained a silver award a couple of years later and this year gained the gold award! The school they attend has no sixth form provision, so Lois is looking to go on to further education at New College in Durham. At the moment she wants to follow her mum into the ambulance service. Cullen has no idea what he wants to do!

At church Messy Church has not reopened, mainly because the children who did attend are now too old, mind you so too are the staff! Similarly, Women's Own hasn't reopened. Kath is not too disappointed as she feels she is now of an age when she wants to step back from those kinds of responsibilities. However, it doesn't stop her doing her quilting or embroidery! Having finished her embroidery of Mow Cop for the Methodist Tapestry Collection that will go on display at the Weardale Museum she has now undertaken the task of reproducing an embroidery for the bedroom of the Norman Cornish house that has been recreated at Beamish Museum in their 1950s town.

As for me, my operation and the subsequent treatment for my cancer have meant that I've not been able either to preach or preside at the Lord's Supper for several months now. I miss both. I have however continued to prepare and deliver material for Table Talk at St Paul's Centre in Spennymoor; we are currently using Adam Hamilton's course on the Ten Commandments. And all being well, I will be leading the Lent Course for Churches Together in Crook at St Catherine's Parish Church.

I have no idea what the future holds, or how much longer I have before I eventually succumb to my cancer. If this memoir is to be published, then I have to end my reminiscences at some point, and this would seem to be as good a time as any. If you have read this far, thank you, I hope I haven't bored you too much.

The seventh age...

Last scene of all,
That ends this strange eventful history,
Is second childishness and mere oblivion;
Sans teeth, sans eyes, sans taste, sans everything.

I am writing this conclusion in anticipation, since once the "last scene of all" is reached I expect that I will be incapable of recording it! Nevertheless, it is to that part that all the rest leads. Someone once described their retirement home as a 'museum of memories'. I am constantly being encouraged to get rid of those things that my children do not want to inherit. But those things are what give me a sense of identity, a sense of being. To be rid of them before I chose to do so seems to be hastening the inevitable.

It's almost as if they are saying, "When you're gone, I don't want the hassle of getting rid of the things that meant so much to you but mean nothing to me. I'll happily take my share of your estate, but I don't want to have to put myself out in the process." Is the younger generation that much more selfish than our generation or the generations that have gone before us? When I begin to feel that way, I remind myself of a quote I have used more than once in a sermon:

> *The children now love luxury; they have bad manners, contempt for authority; they show disrespect for elders and love chatter in place of exercise. Children are now tyrants, not the servants of their households. They no longer rise when elders enter the room. They contradict their parents, chatter before company, gobble up dainties at the table, cross their legs, and tyrannize their teachers.*
>
> *(Attributed to SOCRATES by Plato, according to William L. Patty and Louise S. Johnson, Personality and Adjustment, p. 277 (1953).)*

I am aware that the bulk of this work at times sounds a bit like a series of holiday journals, for that my apologies. However, certainly when we retired that was inevitable. It does, however, reflect the sense behind Jaques' speech; life is series of encounters, some brief others lifelong. We rarely know the impact such encounters have on others; we can only evaluate their impact on us. Sometimes the people we encounter are well known, at other times they are known only to members of their own community. Whatever, they make a difference to our lives between their "exits and their entrances"!

I guess this final section depends on the eventual outcome of the operation to remove my soft tissue sarcoma which took place on October 4th 2021. When I attended my 'pre-op' where, understandably, the consultant outlined the worst-case scenario, I was advised to make my will, appoint someone with power of attorney, and leave details for my funeral! Thankfully all were already done.

I am now in the position of learning to 'live with cancer'. The wound on my left leg is finally almost healed. Whether the oncologist can slow the spread of the sarcom in my lungs, possibly by chemotherapy, remains to be seen. It is now a case of palliative care. Ah well!

When the time finally comes I want my funeral to be a celebration. To that end I have chosen Karl Jenkins: Palladio and Saint-Saens: Symphony No. 3 "Organ" – Finale to be played before the service and Highland Cathedral and Wesley's Air and Gavotte to be played after the service. I have chosen four hymns, three by Charles Wesley the words from the Methodist Hymn Book to avoid any amendments made in subsequent hymnbooks!

First, 'O for a thousand tongues to sing my great redeemer's praise', to the tune Lyngham. Then, because the words are so appropriate, a hymn we had for our Wedding Service

1   Thou God of truth and love,
     We seek thy perfect way,
     Ready thy choice to approve,
     Thy providence to obey;
     Enter into thy wise design,
     And sweetly lose our will in thine.

2   Why hast thou cast our lot
     In the same age and place,
     And why together brought
     To see each other's face,
     To join with loving sympathy,
     And mix our friendly souls in thee?

3   Didst thou not make us one,
     That we might one remain,
     Together travel on,
     And share our joy and pain,
     Till all thy utmost goodness prove,
     And rise renewed in perfect love?

4   Then let us ever bear

The blesséd end in view,
And join, with mutual care,
To fight our passage through;
And kindly help each other on,
Till all receive the starry crown.

5   O may thy Spirit seal
Our souls unto that day,
With all thy fullness fill,
And then transport away:
Away to our eternal rest,
Away to our Redeemer's breast.

The third hymn, again a hymn we had for our Wedding Service: 'Love divine, all loves excelling' to the tune Blaenwern. The final hymn, one by Stuart Townend and Keith Getty, 'See what a morning, gloriously bright' concludes with the affirmation:

And we are raised with him,
death is dead, love has won, Christ has conquered;
and we shall reign with him,
for he lives; Christ is risen from the dead.

I have chosen three passages of Scripture:

Psalm: Psalm 103:1-4,10-22

Gospel: John 11:17-27

Epistle: *1 Corinthians 15:3-8;12-14;20-22;35-38;42-44;51-57*

It is usual these days to include, usually at the end of the formal order of service, an appropriate poem or prose passage. I have chosen a piece by John Pavlovits, slightly amended, for folk to take away with them and ponder on:

On the day I die a lot will happen.
A lot will change. The world will be busy.
On the day I die, all the important appointments
I made will be left unattended.
The many plans I had yet to complete will remain forever undone.
The calendar that ruled so many of my
days will now be irrelevant to me.
All the material things I so chased and guarded and treasured
will be left in the hands of others to care for or to discard.
The words of my critics which so burdened me will cease
to sting or capture anymore. They will be unable to touch me.
The arguments I believed I'd won here will not serve me
or bring me any satisfaction or solace.
All my noisy incoming notifications and texts and calls
will go unanswered. Their great urgency will be quieted.
My many nagging regrets will all be resigned to the past,
where they should have always been anyway.
Every superficial worry about my body that I ever laboured over,
about my waistline or hairline or frown lines, will fade away.
My carefully crafted image, the one I worked so hard to shape
for others here, will be left to them to complete anyway.
The sterling reputation I once struggled so greatly to maintain
will be of little concern for me anymore.
All the small and large anxieties that stole sleep from me
each night will be rendered powerless.

The deep and towering mysteries about life and death
that so consumed my mind will finally be clarified in a way
that they could never be before while I lived.
These things will certainly all be true on the day that I die.
Yet for as much as will happen on that day,
one *more* thing that will happen.
On the day I die, the few people who really know
and truly love me will grieve deeply.
They will feel a void. They will feel cheated. They will not feel ready.
They will feel as though a part of them has died as well.
And on that day, more than anything in the world
they will want more time with me.
I know this from those I love and grieve over.
I've tried not to squander a priceless moment worrying about
all the other things that will happen on the day I die,
because many of those things are either not my concern
or beyond my control.
Those other things have an insidious way
of keeping you from living even as you live,
vying for your attention, competing for your affections.
They rob you of the joy of this unrepeatable, uncontainable,
ever-evaporating Now with those who love you
and want only to share it with you.
Don't miss the chance to dance with them while you can.
It's easy to waste so much daylight in the days before you die.
Don't let your life be stolen every day, by all that you've been
led to believe matters, because on the day you die –
the fact is that much of it simply won't.
But before that day comes: make sure you live.
John Pavlovitz (2019) – slightly amended

504

When I finally 'shuffle off this mortal coil' will I have any regrets? Well... some I expect. I never did build my model railway. I still have quite a number of books on my shelves I wanted to read, especially on Methodism. Also, CDs of Hancock's Half Hour, The Navy Lark and The Goon Show which I hoped to listen to before my final demise. And then there's a collection of Puzzles I always intended to do!

However, on reflection, I've had a good life. I have a wonderful wife and two wonderful children who seem, finally, to be happy with their lot. A Son-in-law and three grandchildren, one in Canada who we don't see often enough. I hope they will also discover the same delight in living that I have enjoyed. I value all the experiences I have had and hope that my interaction with those whose paths I've crossed has brought as much pleasure to them as it has to me.

How would I like to remembered? I hope, by family and friends, with affection. Essentially, however, I would most like to be remembered as one of Mr Wesley's preachers.

Some Random Thoughts

I wanted to complete my memoir by recording my thoughts on a number of issues, otherwise whoever reads this memoire might well become familiar with what I have done, but never really discover anything about what makes me tick.

If Kath invited you into our home the first thing she would do is apologise for all the 'stuff' that clutters up the house. Given the choice she would probably choose to be a 'minimalist'. Ever since I was around five-year-old and Dad took out a subscription for the Mickey Mouse magazine I have tended to collect things. And ever since Mam finally 'recycled' them just before I discovered their value I have tended to hang on to things! I begin this final section then with references to some of my too many collections. As I have already observed above a retirement home can be a 'museum of memories' and my collections help keep my memories alive and serve to introduce you into what makes me tick.

Collections

I was just a teenager when I first began collecting **stamps**, perhaps because my uncle Jim was the Postmaster at Windy Nook. It made good sense, and it was fun because you collected stamps that were in circulation, even if only for a few weeks, and the number of special issues over a year were limited. I began collecting stamps from all over the world but quickly began to specialise in collecting just British stamps. For a while, when I was teaching 'A' level Judaism I also collected stamps from Israel.

After a while two things happened. Special issues began to appear more often and were in general circulation for a shorter time, if at all, Christmas issues being the exception. This made it much more difficult to collect them oneself. And, in more recent times, e-mail has drastically reduced the number of personal letters being sent. I subsequently took out subscriptions to receive presentation packs of new issues direct from Royal Mail as they appeared. Much later I switched to receive the Annual 'Stamp Book' which made it easier to keep up to date with every commemorative stamp issued. I continued, for a while, to receive presentation packs of definitives, when values or colours where changed. I guess I persisted with my stamp collection because, as someone once commented, 'stamps were masterpieces in miniature', and in many cases they really were.

Initially I only collected **coins** on occasion. It was after we had been burgled when we lived in Kendal, and I made an attempt to replace some of the sets that had been stolen that I began to collect coins seriously. The same with coins as with stamps. Once the only way to collect them is by purchasing them direct from the Royal Mint the fun goes out of collecting. It is no way to encourage children and young people to get into collecting. The Royal Mint recently produced a series of 10p coins, each bearing a letter of the alphabet. They don't appear to have ever been in circulation. What an opportunity missed. The US Mint did something similar with State quarters. However, they were in general circulation for quite some time, and it did encourage folk to collect them by regularly checking their change. Also, by way of collecting souvenirs I have kept a set of notes and coins from the various countries we have visited on holiday.

I began collecting **Methodist Memorabilia** when I was in theological college. One of our students, who came from, and had worked in, the Potteries, commissioned a Hartley Victoria College commemorative plate showing a picture of John Wesley. Nearly everyone ordered at least one plate. I ordered three! Not long after he had two plaques made of black Wedgwood, relief portraits of John Wesley and Hugh Bourne. Methodist Central Hall Westminster produced a china beaker. I bought two so I could display both sides. So my collection began. It continued, in somewhat random fashion over the years.

Our visit to the USA on our first Exchange of Pastorates coincided with the Bicentenary of American Methodism and the opportunity to add to my collection of memorabilia. Then, and on later visits, churches sold 'cut-outs' of their church buildings. The first Methodist plate I added was a Primitive Methodist centenary plate given to me by one of Kath's aunts. When I returned to circuit ministry, until I retired, I added plates, and mugs, issued by each successive annual Conference. Along the way a number of other items were added – replicas of John Wesley's crockery reissued by Wedgwood for the US market and a number of 'statues' and busts of John Wesley. The last addition was the antique bust of John Wesley, valued at c.£650, which was given to me on my retirement by Newcastle-under-Lyme Methodist Church.

Shortly after we were married, we decided to embark on a collection of annual **Wedgwood Calendar Plates** and Dartington Glass Tankards. With the advent of a family, we abandoned both collections after only around a half dozen of each. When I went back into circuit ministry, we moved into a manse in Lammack that had a delft rail around the hall. It appeared somewhat bare after we had put onto it the few plates that we had. Shortly after we moved in we were on holiday in Cornwall and on a rainy day found ourselves in a covered market hall where there was a stall selling Wedgewood calendar plates. It gave me the opportunity to fill in a couple of gaps and the stall holder took my details and from time to time contacted me with details of other plates he had come across. Between that contact and the internet, I was able to bring the collection up to date and began collecting them again each year until production stopped. Dartington stopped production of their tankards shortly after we stopped collecting them.

Teaching Judaism at 'A' level GCE led me to arrange a series of visits to Israel and that inevitably led me to start collecting **Jewish memorabilia,** in the main as teaching aids to use in the classroom when we introduced Judaism in the lower school. In the souks in Jerusalem, it was usual to haggle over the price of anything one purchased. On the day we were leaving after our first visit we wandered through the souks and I spotted a brass chanukiah menorah which I rather fancied. The stallholder wanted far more than I had left in Israeli shekels. I wouldn't budge despite his insistence that I pay more than I actually had. A crowd gathered. In the end I walked away. The stallholder called me back and accepted the price I had offered. Several people in the crowd muttered that I had managed to get the menorah at an amazingly low price!

Some of the pictures that have ended up on our staircase walls were gifts from various parties we have taken to Israel, as well as items we have bought ourselves. One small low relief sculpture of a Jewish wedding was by Ruth, an up-and-coming Israeli artist. We were assured that one day it might even be valuable!

When I was teaching at the Lakes School, I came across a toyshop in Windermere that sold **Models of Yesteryear**. Only a few were produced each year and collecting them seemed like a good idea at the time. Then suddenly, like commemorative stamps and coins, they started to appear almost every other week. Never mind having to find the display space I couldn't afford such an outlay, so I gave up what was otherwise an interesting collection.

When I was teaching at King Edward VII College in Coalville David Fisher, the Head of Music, told me he collected anything associated with Kingfishers. At about the same time in one of the Sunday papers there was an advert for a Kingfisher plate. I couldn't resist, so I ordered it. Three more plates followed and one or two other items featuring Kingfishers. Fortunately, I didn't pursue this interest!

Over the years Kath has collected **thimbles** and **fridge magnets** as souvenirs of places we have visited, or for special occasions. The idea was that because they were small, they wouldn't take up too much space. That is true, but, nevertheless, over time they have turned into substantial collections.

Politics

I was brought up to believe in democracy. I keep hearing it said that we live in the oldest democracy in the world. I am, however, far from convinced that the United Kingdom is a democratic society. It can hardly be called democratic when, more often than not, we have a Government in power elected by a minority of voters! Unless you happen to have voted for the party in power your vote counts for nothing and is in effect a wasted vote!

I recall in my teens in Durham watching the results of a General Election coming in on TV. What became apparent quite quickly was that whilst the majority of MPs elected were either Labour or Conservation a significant proportion of the votes cast were for Liberal Party candidates. On the basis of the number of votes cast there should have been Liberal MPs in three figures rather than the single figures they ended up with. The result was clearly unfair. The 'first-past-the post' voting system undoubtedly favours the bigger parties. Today the only European nation to retain a 'first-past-the-post' voting system for national elections is Belarus! As the Liberal Party campaigned for proportional representation it, not unsurprisingly, became the party I chose to support through most of my life. When we were living in Kendal I became a member of the Liberal Democrats for a number of years and was invited to stand for election for the County Council on their behalf. However, because of my church and school commitments I felt unable to accept.

So often major changes brought in by successive Governments are merely ways of extending and underpinning their own position. Whatever might be said by the government of the day, the redrawing of constituency boundaries always seems to favour the party in power. How can that be said to be democracy? We see that the same thing pertains in the House of Lords. Successive Governments have promised to reform the House of Lords. It has never happened. Instead, the number of unelected members in the Lords is increased as the incumbent government seeks to shift the balance of power in the Lords in their favour.

Perhaps with 'devolution' and the creation of national Parliaments it would make more sense for the House of Commons to become the English Parliament and the House of Lord's to become an elected body representing the four nations that make up the UK?

It is hardly surprising that many people either vote 'tactically' in a, usually, vain effort to shift the balance of parties in Parliament or choose not to vote at all. Is it perhaps also time to introduce mandatory voting, in much the same way as they have in Australia, along with proportional representation, making sure that that way every vote really does count! I recognise, of course, that there a several possible types of proportional representations but it should not be beyond the grasp of any government to choose one that gives real choice and power to the voting public.

All that, of course, presumes a government that is free of the kind of corruption that bedevils so many governments across the world. There's the rub. What we see increasingly are governments in general, and individual ministers in particular, concerned only with satisfying their own particular greed. No one party is exempt. Labour lost he last elections because they put their own particular ambitions before the socialist principle on which the party was founded. How someone like Tony Blair can claim to be a socialist when he has amassed such a personal fortune as a result of his premiership beggars belief.

I suspect we also need to (re)introduce 'politics' and 'logic' into the school curriculum. After the result of the Hartlepool by-election saw the seat pass from Labour to Conservative one man who was interviewed about his change from being a life-long Labour voter to a first-time Conservative voter maintained that this was because Labour had failed, over the past decade, to combat the consequences of austerity. He clearly had no recognition of the fact that the decade of austerity was the consequence of Conservative Government policy about which Labour, nationally and locally, was powerless to contest!

The Internet has become effective in bringing to a broader public political issue that might otherwise not gain a hearing except in the hallowed halls of Westminster. A number of groups have recently emerged that encourage readers to sign **petitions** that will eventually reach the House of Commons, or some instances the CEOs of various multi-nationals. What is worrying is that more often than not, despite large numbers signing such petitions, nothing is done. The unwillingness of those in power to behave in a moral manner is of considerable concern.

Brexit

I still cannot get my mind around what a disastrous decision this was, and how no-one seems capable of challenging it even in the light of all that is known about the initial campaign and the likely consequences for generations to come. To have a referendum at all was simply a means to quell rebellion in the Conservative Government's ranks. It was ill conceived and led to a campaign that by anyone's reckoning was based on lies designed to curry support among the masses. It was never clear whether the referendum was either advisory or legally binding. And, in a democracy, surely a two-thirds majority should have been required, not simply 51% of the vote needed for success.

I suspect many voted on the basis of their mistaken perception that independence from Europe would somehow restore the 'Golden Days of Empire'. What they failed to recognise was that since those 'glory days' British society has changed out of all recognition. The days of being a manufacturing society are long gone. From cars to TVs most companies had been bought out by German or Japanese companies. They might still display a British marque but the profits from those companies go abroad. All the result of Tory Government policies. The same is true where utilities are concerned; privatisation, again a Tory government policy, has meant that European companies, and governments, were able to buy them up so that any profits go outside our borders. Such industry that remains, farming and hospitality, prospered only because of seasonal workers from Europe, who, for the most part, are now excluded from our shores because of Brexit!

I include here a piece that I came across on Facebook. It had no attribution, so I assume it is OK to reproduce it. It's a pity it wasn't circulated more widely before the Brexit referendum. Don't worry if you don't read all 98 reasons, after just a few you'll get the drift

98 Reasons to Stay in the EU: Benefits of Membership for the UK

With the Brexit deadline fast approaching and no deal in sight, we thought now might be a good time to take a look at 98 benefits of EU membership for the UK.

The Bank of England estimates that the fallout of a No Deal Brexit will be worse than the 2008 financial crisis. Needless to say this will likely be very bad for UK small businesses.

However, the UK can unilaterally revoke article 50 at any time to stop this madness.

Here are 98 reasons why we should:

1. Membership of the world's largest trading bloc with over **500 million** consumers, representing **23%** of global GDP
2. The UK has greater global influence as a member of the EU
3. The EU provides a counterweight to the global power of the US, Russia and China
4. With Trump in the White House the UK's strongest natural allies are France, Germany and our other West European neighbours
5. Tariff-free trade within the EU
6. The abolition of non-tariff barriers (quotas, subsidies, administrative rules etc.) among members
7. Participation in free trade agreements with Japan and Canada as an EU member
8. The EU accounts for **44% of all UK exports** of goods and services
9. The EU accounts for **53% of all UK imports** of goods and services
10. Cheaper **food and alcohol** imports from continental Europe
11. As a member of the EU the UK maintains a say in the

shaping of the rules governing its trade with its European partners

12. **3.1 million jobs** in the UK are directly linked to exports to the EU

13. Free movement of labour has helped UK firms plug skills gaps (translators, doctors, plumbers)

14. Free movement of labour has helped address shortages of unskilled workers (fruit picking, catering)

15. The Single Market has brought the best continental footballers to the Premier League

16. The EU accounts for **47% of the UK's stock** of inward Foreign Direct Investment (FDI), worth over **$1.2 trillion**

17. Access to the EU Single Market has helped attract investment into the UK from outside the EU

18. No paperwork or customs for UK exports throughout the single market

19. Price transparency and removal of commissions on currency transactions across the Eurozone

20. FDI into the UK has effectively doubled since the creation of the EU Single Market

21. The UK's net contribution to the EU budget is around **€7.3bn, or 0.4% of GDP** (less than an eighth of the UK's defence spending)

22. No time-consuming border checks for travellers (apart from in the UK)

23. The City of London, as a global financial hub, has acted as a bridge between foreign business and the EU

24. British banks and insurance companies have been able to operate freely across the EU

25. Cornwall receives up to £750 **million per year** from the

EU Social Fund (ESF)

26. Structural funding for areas of the UK hit by industrial decline (South Wales, Yorkshire)

27. Support for rural areas under the European Agricultural Fund for Regional Development (EAFRD)

28. EU funding for infrastructure projects in the UK including **£122 million** for the "Midlands engine" project

29. Financial support from the EU for **over 3,000** small and medium enterprises (SMEs) in the UK

30. EU funding for the British film industry

31. EU funding for British theatre, music and dance

32. EU funding for British sport, including football apprenticeships, tennis and rugby league

33. Glasgow (1990) and Liverpool (2008) benefitted from being European capitals of culture, stimulating their local economies

34. EU competition laws protect consumers by combatting monopolistic business practices

35. Strict controls on the operations of Multinational Corporations (MNCs) in the EU

36. Human Rights protected under the EU Charter of Fundamental Rights

37. The death penalty can never be reintroduced as it is incompatible with EU membership

38. Minority languages such as Welsh and Irish are recognized and protected under EU law

39. The **right to reside** in any EU member state

40. The **freedom to work in 28 countries** without visa and immigration restrictions

41. The mutual recognition of professional qualifications has

facilitated the free movement of engineers, teachers and doctors across the EU

42. The mutual recognition of educational diplomas

43. The Common European Framework of Reference for Languages (CEFR) has standardized assessment of language proficiency across the EU

44. The freedom to study in 28 countries (many EU universities teach courses in English and charge lower fees than in the UK)

45. The Erasmus programme of university exchanges (benefitting 16000 UK students a year)

46. **The freedom to set up a business in 28 countries**

47. The ability to retire in any member state

48. Pension transferability

49. The right to vote in local and European Parliamentary elections if resident in any member state

50. EU laws making it easier for British people to buy property on the continent

51. The right to receive emergency healthcare in any member state (EHIC card)

52. Consular protection from any EU embassy outside the EU

53. The EU has played a leading role in combatting global warming (Paris 2015 climate change conference)

54. Common EU greenhouse gas emissions targets (19% reduction from 1990 to 2015)

55. Improvements in air quality (significant reductions in sulphur dioxide and nitrogen oxides) as a result of EU legislation

56. Reductions in sewage emissions

57. Improvements in the quality of beaches and bathing water

58. EU standards on the quality of drinking water
59. Restrictions on landfill dumping
60. EU targets for recycling
61. Common EU regulations on the transportation and disposal of toxic waste
62. The implementation of EU policies to reduce noise pollution in urban areas
63. EU policies have stimulated offshore wind farms
64. Strict safety standards for cars, buses and trucks
65. Protection of endangered species and habitats (EU Natura 2000 network)
66. Strict ban on animal testing in the cosmetics industry
67. Membership of the European Medicines Agency (EMA) which monitors the quality and safety of medicines (until recently located in London)
68. **13% of EU budget** earmarked for scientific research and innovation
69. The UK receives **£730 million a year** in EU funding for research
70. EU funding for UK universities
71. Cooperation in the peaceful use of nuclear energy as a member of Euratom
72. Minimum paid annual leave and time off work (Working Time Directive)
73. Equal pay between men and women enshrined in European law since 1957
74. The right to work no more than 48 hours a week without paid overtime
75. Minimum guaranteed maternity leave of 14 weeks for pregnant women

76. Rights to a minimum 18 weeks of parental leave after child birth
77. EU anti-discrimination laws governing age, religion and sexual orientation
78. EU rules governing health and safety at work
79. The rights to collective bargaining and trade union membership are enshrined in EU employment law
80. The UK enjoys an opt out from the single currency and maintains full control of its borders as a non-member of the Schengen area
81. Since 1985 the UK has received a **budget rebate equivalent to 66%** of its net contribution to the EU budget
82. EU cross-country coordination offers greater protection from terrorists, paedophiles, people traffickers and cyber-crime
83. The European common arrest warrant
84. Europe-wide patent and copyright protection
85. EU consumer protection laws concerning transparency and product guarantees of quality and safety
86. Improved food labelling
87. A ban on growth hormones and other harmful food additives
88. Cheaper air travel due to EU competition laws
89. Common EU air passenger rights
90. Deregulation of the European energy market has increased consumer choice and lowered prices
91. Mutual recognition of the common European driving license
92. The introduction of the European pet passport

93. The abolition of mobile telephone roaming charges
94. The EU acts as a guarantor of the Irish Good Friday Agreement
95. A frictionless Irish border
96. The EU acts as a guarantor of the special status of Gibraltar
97. The EU helped support and maintain democracy in Spain, Portugal and Greece from the 1970s and these countries have become major destinations for British tourists
98. EU membership has helped facilitate intercultural dialogue

Modern Life

Let's start with a niggle! I cannot get used to, or condone, the increasingly popular practice of **applauding oneself**. It can be seen in most TV shows, especially Quiz shows. I was always of the view that to applaud was a way of recognising something someone else had achieved!

I think, if I had not taken the path in my life that I did, I would have been tempted into something to do with English **language**. I know I constantly irritate my family when watching TV by 'correcting' the English grammar of the presenter. I reckon I could have made a fortune correcting the mistakes contained in many translations on menus posted outside restaurants in countries abroad, and occasionally in the UK! I know English is a difficult language, but still . . . . There is a poem I first came across when I was in Primary School, and I thought it was worth sharing so I've included it here:

TOMMY GOUGH IN ENGLISH

When first the new boy came to school,
His name was not announced,
The children knew how it was spelled,
But not how 'twas pronounce.
"'Tis easy to decide," quoth one,
"Of course, it rhymes with rough,
I'm positive in my own mind,
That that boy's name is Gough!"
"You may be right," a second said.
"'Tis possible, although
I rather think, if he was asked,
He'd say his name was Gough!"
"Pooh, pooh!" a loud voice called in scorn,
"With nonsense let's be through,
That I am right you must allow –
We'll call the new boy Gough."
"That's as you please," replied a fourth,
While swinging on a bough,
"And yet I see no reason why
His name should not be Gough."
But here the boy himself appeared,
And said with bashful cough,
"Say, fellows, can I play with you?
My name is Tommy Gough!"

Pauline Frances Camp.

523

Staying with matters of language for a moment. Why is it that novelists have, over my lifetime at least, more than doubled the length of the average novel? Two hundred pages was usual, now most novels range between five and six hundred pages long!

And then there is the 'f' word. Now I am neither a snob nor a prude, but I can't say I am happy about how often the 'f' word is being used in TV dramas these days. It just seems so unnecessary. I've even taken to giving up on some, otherwise, excellent TV series because the 'f' word is used in almost every conversation. Still I have a large collection of DVDs to fall back on.

And then there is **metrication!** I was never convinced of the need for it. But, again, it was a Tory Government's policy. In the early days it led to a number of ludicrous anomalies. You bought petrol by the gallon, but oil by the litre. You bought paint by the litre, but wallpaper by the yard! All was going well until the then PM, Margaret Thatcher, announced that we didn't need to go metric in everything after all. The school I was teaching in at the time had just got rid of all its Maths books that were in imperial and replaced them with textbooks that were exclusively metric. Being told that exams in future would be in both measurements necessitated the massive expense of purchasing another set of new textbooks that also included imperial measurements! I still find it irritating that often on TV news reports the two are used interchangeably, often, confusingly, in the same report. Odometers still measure speed in miles per hour and signposts tell you how many miles it is to your destination, but you now buy petrol in litres (although beer is still sold in pints!). To underline the point, I've just been looking at fence panels with a view to adding two to the side fence. Several firms advertise panels as e.g. 6ft x 1500mm. You couldn't make it up!

I can't get my head around the **increasing gap between rich and poor**. Surely in the twenty-first century the gap should have narrowed, not widened. When I was growing up food banks were unknown. They simply didn't exist. What went wrong? The answer, it seems to me, is simple – greed! Many youngsters today if asked what they want from life seem to sum it up in two words, 'fame' and 'fortune'. Footballers and TV celebrities alike make unbelievably, often obscene, salaries. It seems to be true that the rich do get richer and the poor do get poorer. The Revd Brian Mifflin, a colleague when I was Superintendent minister in Newcastle-under-Lyme, recalled a conversation, some years earlier when he was attending a connexional committee in London. They were discussing 'the minimum wage' which at that time did not exist. A colleague remarked to Brian that "to resolve the problem of poverty what is needed is a 'maximum wage'"! I think he was right. Whilst I am aware that they are facing some problems currently, I do admire the John Lewis Partnership which seems to be remarkably democratic in its structure and has both a minimum and a maximum wage so that the CEO receives an annual salary at most 75 times that of the average pay of workers. So, it can be done.

The NHS was born out of a long-held ideal that good healthcare should be available to all, regardless of wealth. At its launch by the then minister of health, Aneurin Bevan, on 5 July 1948, it had at its heart three core principles: a) that it meets the needs of everyone; b) that it be free at the point of delivery; c) that it be based on clinical need, not ability to pay. It's that second principle that bothers me most. In recent years hospitals have started to charge for parking. The charges apply not only to visitors but also to staff. Recently they have also been applied to 'Blue Badge' holders even though it has already cost to have a Blue Badge. And it's not as if the payments go to the hospitals, often it is a case that private companies run the car parks and pocket the fees! If people boycotted the car parks, thus forcing the hospitals to provide transport how quickly might such parking charges be abolished?

Of course, the above assumes that you can even find a parking space in the first place. Why are new hospitals built several stories high with limited surface parking for staff and visitors alike? Some hospitals now no longer allow a minister to visit outside visiting hours which means making pastoral visits when car parks are most likely to be full and the full allocation of permitted visitors per bed is taken up by relatives. On more than one occasion I have had to abandon a visit to a church member in hospital having been unable to find somewhere to park!

The problem is exacerbated by the fact that more often than not the patient is having to travel some distance for treatment. Since living in Crook I have to take Kath to Walkergate Hospital in Newcastle-upon Tyne (via the Tyne Tunnel which requires the payment of a toll). She had her hip replacement done in Darlington Memorial Hospital. She also on one occasion had to go to Shotley Bridge Hospital. For my kidney stones I had to attend Sunderland Royal. I have also, on occasion, been referred to Durham University Hospital and Bishop Auckland General Hospital. I have also had to attend Peterlee Community Hospital and the University Hospital of North Tees. To have very minor surgery, in the past done at my local surgery, I have to attend Sedgefield Community Hospital. And now I find myself having to attend the Freeman Hospital and the Royal Victoria Infirmary in Newcastle. All of these visits not only involve parking charges but also considerable expense in both fuel costs and time commitments. The NHS, it seems to me, falls very far short of its core principle – 'free at the point of delivery'. Bear in mind also that it is the elderly, many of whom are less well off and have perhaps given up driving because of their age, who make a disproportionate use of hospital facilities.

In my last appointment, on one occasion, I wasted a whole day trying to track down a patient I planned to visit. I spent ages tracking her from ward to ward only to discover in the end that she had been moved to a hospital fifteen miles away! I adopted the UMC pattern of having a 'pastoral assistant' who was responsible for arranging all my pastoral visits and keeping a record of them, and accompanying me on my visits. It was time consuming for the person appointed but freed me up to use my time more effectively.

I am also appalled at the amount of waste in the NHS. Letters sent out by post when a text message would suffice. I have just received two notifications of the same appointment, by post, one printed single-sided on best quality paper. I now receive a full copy of all my repeat prescriptions enclosed with every lot of medicines dispensed, even if it is a one-off prescription and usually the final page is blank! Medications incorrectly dispensed cannot be returned to the pharmacy, or if they are, they are destroyed, even if they have not been opened. Add all that to the cost of transporting patients to hospitals because medical care is being centralised rather than consultants moving between hospitals. And yes I know there are very good reasons for creating centres of excellence but I'm not sure that the consequences are always thought through.

For years I used an Accu-Chek blood glucose meter. It was decided that they would no longer dispense the test strips, instead dispensing test strips for Gluco RX. A new meter was supplied, admittedly free of charge. It was twice the size of the one I had been using. Two years later I was informed that different test strips would now be dispensed, also Gluco RX but it entailed a new meter, smaller but not as easy to use as the old one. So, for the sake of saving a few pence on the test strips, perfectly good meters, which must cost to produce and supply, end up in landfill. Shouldn't the NHS be more sensitive to longer term savings and the impact of their decisions on the environment? Like so much that happens in today's society there seems to be little thought given to long term consequences.

Political Correctness seems to have gone mad in recent years. At first it was humorous. I remember when Robert came home from school one day to tell us that his English teacher, who was a rabid feminist, had declared that 'manhole cover' had to be replaced with 'personhole cover'! Once in Newcastle-under-

Lyme, when attending a local health centre for a blood test I discovered that I would not feel a 'p***k' but rather a 'scratch', which didn't describe at all what I might expect. One nurse however, refused to use the word 'scratch' instead using the, much more appropriate, word 'sting'! Is there a person in some obscure government office being employed to find politically incorrect words and come up with inappropriate substitutes?

It does have more serious implications. In the New Testament Jesus' feeding of the five thousand refers to 'men' – a literal translation from the Greek. In modern translations this is often rendered as 'men and women' which is misleading. Women and children were not counted in Jesus' day so the likely number present would have been in excess of fifteen thousand!

And where do you draw the line? A couple of years ago Kath and I attended a live streaming of a Shakespeare play the Gala Theatre in Durham. A 'white' actor, a 'black' actor and an 'Asian' actor made up one family – it was rather confusing. In some instances, of course, it doesn't make a great deal of difference, but there are limits. Whilst in no way denying the undeniable ability of the 'black' actress (or should that be actor to be politically correct), casting her in the role of Ann Boleyn in a recent TV series, seemed to me to be totally inappropriate.

And, before moving on, there's the whole matter of **computers** and modern **digital technology**. When computers first made their way into schools a number of colleagues expressed delight. I confess I did not share their enthusiasm. They felt that it would result in less paperwork. I suspected it would result in more. I was proved right. Because computer programmes were able to make calculations previously unthought of we were suddenly expected, for example, to produce evidence of 'value added' – I didn't understand it then and I don't' understand it now! All I know is that it meant more work! Reports, which for generations consisted of a line or two for each subject were now to be substantial booklets – and teachers were forbidden to record anything negative about a pupil! And how often do computers refuse to do what you want them to do? And that's without getting into the whole issue of scams and the like.

And now we have smart TVs with things like BBC iPlayer or My5 so you can catch up on programmes you might have missed. The number of times you try to access a programme and find that it's 'buffering' and you have to give up! Of course there's always Netflix and the like – at a cost, of course.

The Environment

The planet seem intent on self-destruction. As usual the politicians are concerned primarily with their own agenda and that seems to be true whether we are talking about the US, or Europe, or Russia, or China! I am impressed with the efforts of Greta Thunberg, the young Swedish environmental activist who now is internationally known for challenging world leaders to take immediate action for climate change. She initially gained public attention because of her youth and her straightforward speaking manner, both in public and to political leaders and assemblies, in which she criticised world leaders for their failure to take sufficient action to address the climate crisis. Her activism began by persuading her parents to adopt lifestyle choices that reduced their own carbon footprint.

In August 2018, at age 15, she started spending her school days outside the Swedish Parliament to call for stronger action on climate change by holding up a sign reading *Skolstrejk för klimatet* (School strike for climate). Soon other students engaged in similar protests in their own communities. Together they organised a school climate strike movement under the name *Fridays for Future*. After Thunberg addressed the 2018 United Nations Climate Change Conference, student strikes took place every week somewhere in the world. In 2019, there were multiple coordinated multi-city protests involving over a million students each. To avoid energy intensive flying, Thunberg sailed to North America where she attended the 2019 UN Climate Action Summit. In the past couple of years little has been heard from her and the world still turns!

It is clearly essential that we reduce our carbon footprint. That means a move away from gas and towards electric power generated by renewal means. Sounds good in theory but... Recent storms resulted in many homes being without power for several days. In some instances they were the homes of the elderly and the vulnerable. Clearly power lines need to be buried. That will prove to be costly and time consuming.

A separate, though linked, issue is the internet. Without electricity there is no internet, so communication becomes impossible. Of course, there are still far too many places, particularly in rural areas where there simply is no internet.

Within the next few years all new cars sold in the UK have to be powered by electricity. So now there is a scramble to provide sufficient charging points and manufacture batteries that will provide extended mileage. Has anyone worked out how to provide charging points for folk who live in terraced houses with front door that open straight onto the street?

What of **recycling**? Clearly part of addressing the issue of climate change is the fact that we cannot afford to continue producing waste in the quantities that we do. We are rapidly running out of possible sites for landfill and burning waste impacts on climate change. In Crook recently 'The Bread and Butter Thing' has started up offering food destined for landfill. For £7.50 you receive c. £30.00 + worth of food. The only drawback is that you take what you are given, there is no choice. Usually it's OK, occasionally you end up with a surfeit of one particular product that should be used within a day or two! No matter how good they are a couple of boxes of Pukka Pies, each containing a dozen pies can be a bit much! Nevertheless, it's better than seeing so much perfectly good food being consigned to landfill.

One thing we noticed when we first visited the US, and subsequently, was that supermarkets packed the goods you purchased in free paper bags that were then used to line rubbish bins at home. In the UK we chose instead to use plastic!

When we were living in Newcastle-under-Lyme the Borough received a national award for recycling. Mind you it demanded that householders sort out their recyclable rubbish. A bin for garden waste; a box for cardboard waste; a box for glass; a bag for paper; a bag for cardboard; a sack for plastics; a small sack for food waste; and of course, a bin for non-recyclables! It was a bit of a hassle but we quickly became used to it.

On a couple of occasions recently 'The Green Thing' has appeared on Facebook, with no attribution, so I thought it was worth including. It is a salutary reminder that we need perhaps to reassess what we have called 'progress' over my lifetime

THE GREEN THING

In the line at the checkout, the cashier told an older woman that she should bring her own grocery bags because plastic bags weren't good for the environment.

The woman apologized to him and explained, "We didn't have 'the green thing' back in my day."

The clerk responded, "That's the problem today. Your generation did not care enough to save the environment."

He was right – our generation didn't have 'the green thing' in its day.

Back then, we returned milk bottles, pop bottles and beer bottles to the shop. The shop sent them back to the plant to be washed and sterilized and refilled, so it could use the same bottles over and over. So they really were recycled.

But we didn't have 'the green thing' back in our day.

We walked up stairs, because we didn't have an escalator or lift in every shop and office building. We walked to the grocery shop and didn't climb into a 300-horsepower machine every time we had to go two streets down the road.

But she was right. We didn't have 'the green thing' in our day.

Back then, we washed the baby's nappies because we didn't have the throw-away kind. We dried clothes on a line, not in an energy gobbling machine burning up 220 volts – wind and solar power really did dry the clothes. Kids got hand-me-down clothes from their brothers or sisters, not always brand-new clothing. But that old lady is right; we didn't have 'the green thing' back in our day.

Back then, we had one TV, or radio, in the house – not a TV in every room. And the TV had a small screen the size of a handkerchief (remember them?), not a screen the size of a US State. In the kitchen, we blended and stirred by hand because we didn't have electric machines to do everything for us.

When we packaged a fragile item to send in the post, we used scrunched up old newspaper to cushion it, not Styrofoam or plastic bubble wrap.

Back then, we didn't fire up an engine and burn petrol just to cut the lawn. We used a push mower that ran on human power. We exercised by working so we didn't need to go to a health club to run on treadmills that operate on electricity.

But she's right; we didn't have 'the green thing' back then.

We drank from a tap or a water fountain when we were thirsty instead of using a cup or a plastic bottle everytime we had a drink of water.

We refilled pens with ink instead of buying a new pen, and we replaced the razor blades in a razor instead of throwing away the whole razor just because the blade got dull.

But we didn't have 'the green thing' back then.

Back then, people took a bus and kids rode their bikes to school or walked instead of turning their parents into a 24-hour taxi service.

We had one electrical outlet in a room, not an entire bank of sockets to power a dozen appliances. And we didn't need a computerized gadget to receive a signal beamed from satellites 2,000 miles out in space in order to find the nearest MacDonald's.

But isn't it sad the current generation laments how wasteful we old folks were just because we didn't have 'the green thing' back then?

War and Peace

Do we really need to spend the monies we do on the **Armed Forces**? When we had a significant role on the world's stage, perhaps – but today? … I can't help but feel that such money could be much better spent. According to the CIA Handbook there are 36 countries that do not have a standing army. Some rely on the protection of neighbours others on their own Police Force.

Costa Rica has had no standing army since 1949. The country, which is often referred to as "Switzerland of Central America", proclaimed its permanent and unarmed neutrality in 1983. In fact, Costa Rica is protected by the US. It has used the savings from defence spending to improve education, health care and a durable social safety net. This Central American country is home to the greatest density of species in the world. It takes pride in its ecologically friendly policies that attract tourists to its lush jungles. It also enjoys a standard of living that is about double that of other Central American nations with the exception of Panama, which profits from the Panama Canal. Maybe we could learn from them?

It puzzles me that the UK seems determined to engage in conflict somewhere in world as if it mattered. Surely conflicts are better resolved by diplomacy. Why do some countries manage to maintain their status as neutral in any conflict whereas we are determined to engage? Was the Falklands War really necessary or was it simply a convenient distraction from what was happening in our own country? What about the conflicts in Iraq and Afghanistan? Was Putin right when he said he has no intention of invading Ukraine and that it was 'the West' that was fuelling the possibility of conflict by its insistence that there was likely to be a war. Since the conflict has now begun, we may never know. And like previous areas of conflict what has it got to do with us, or again is it simply a way of distracting our population from what is happening in our own country?

In the present conflict in Eastern Europe NATO persists in refusing to establish a no-fly zone over Ukraine on the grounds that they are not a member of NATO. We seem to have (conveniently?) forgotten about the Budapest Memorandum on Security Assurances. It comprised three identical political agreements signed at the OSCE (Organisation for Security and Co-operation in Europe) conference in Budapest on 5th December 1994 and included security assurances against threats, or the use of force against the territorial integrity or political independence of Ukraine, Belarus, and Kazakhstan on condition that they relinquished their nuclear weapons and acceded to the Treaty on the Non-Proliferation of Nuclear Weapons (NPT). This they agreed to do. The Memorandum was originally signed by three nuclear powers: the Russian Federation, the United Kingdom and the United States. China and France later gave similar assurances in separate documents.

All of the above, however, begs the question: when have we ever left a country, where we have actually engaged in conflict, in a better state than before we became involved? Afghanistan is only the latest example.

Consider **Israel / Palestine.** Over several years I took six trips to Israel while I was teaching at the Lakes School. Every trip was different, and every trip was worthwhile. I decided to stop, however, when Israel persisted in speeding up the development of settlements in the occupied territories even though this was in direct contravention of International Law. As of 30th January 2020, there were about 130 government-approved settlements, and 100 unofficial ones, which are home to around 400,000 Israelis in the West Bank, with an additional 200,000 Israelis residing in 12 neighbourhoods in East Jerusalem.

The origins of the problem can be laid firmly at the door of the UK. The Balfour Declaration established the possibility of a homeland for the Jews in Palestine but made no attempt to say how that homeland might be achieved. The events of the Holocaust gave impetus to the Zionists' demand for a Jewish homeland.

Criticism of Israel is often seen as 'anti-Semitism'. I do not agree. I cannot see how supporting the Jews means supporting the government of Israel in its determination to effectively deny the Palestinians their homeland. This was one of the issues that sadly brought about the downfall of Jeremy Corbyn as Labour Party leader in 2019! The situation is complicated by the fact that the media so often fail to distinguish between 'Jews' and 'Israelis' (many of whom have no faith, and some of whom are Christian or Muslim) and 'Muslims' and 'Palestinians' (some of whom have no faith or are Christian). If Israel is to be a 'Jewish' State it has a fundamental problem. For the most part Israeli families comprise 2 adults and 2 children. Palestinian families comprise 2 adults and up to 7 children. Absorbing 'Palestine' into Israel therefore cannot be countenanced – you do the maths! Israel, it appears, cannot tolerate a two-state solution, even though that is an obvious way forward.

And that brings us neatly to:

Religion

I think when I left school in 1965 and set out for my year on VSO in Sarawak that I was unaware of any 'World Faiths' other than Christianity. I think I believed that Judaism had disappeared after the events recorded in the pages of the New Testament. It came as something of a shock to the system when, stranded for four days in Singapore, I found myself visiting Hindu and Buddhist Temples and Shinto shrines. When I finally arrived in Sibu I was wakened each morning by the Imam's first 'call to prayer' broadcast from the minaret of the mosque just down the road from the school. And what to make of the fact that in the Methodist School where I was teaching there were a significant number of Muslim students who regularly won the annual Qur'an Reading Competition? I have a photograph of the students who took part that year under a banner that oldy proclaims 'Methodist Secondary School: Qur'an Reading Competition Winners'

Teaching in Coalville gave me the opportunity to visit various faith communities in Leicester which was, and as far as I know still is, the most multi-faith community in the UK. When the

Sikh Gurdwara opened their Langar, their kitchen from which they serve free meals to anyone who chooses to turn up, the Christian clergy suddenly found that the number of folk who turned up on their doorsteps begging for money for a meal, dropped to zero! There was also a certain irony in the fact that the first Hindu Temple established in Leicester was previously Carey Baptist Church, named after the Baptist missionary who had been a member there before setting out for India to evangelise among Hindus. The Hindu community had cleared the ground floor of the church to accommodate the images of their gods. The gallery was, initially, left untouched but round the front of the gallery were hung pictures of various influential religious figures, including a portrait of Jesus!

When I was doing my MA in Contextual Theology (which, sadly, I did not complete) our principal lecturer was the Rev'd Dr John Parry, a URC minister. His particular interest was Sikhism. He told us how, in his researches for his PhD, he had cause to examine archives of the Missionary Societies associated with the Congregational Church. What he found was enlightening. The missionaries found, when they arrived in the Punjab, a religious society in which there was much that resonated with the Christian Faith, especially the idea of 'grace'. Consequently, whilst the missionaries established schools and hospitals and were welcomed into the community, there were very few who actually converted to Christianity. The home churches, who were funding their missionary activity, were primarily concerned with the very few numbers of converts. It made requests for funding difficult, to say the least!

Studying John Robinson's 'Honest to God' in our Fellowship group the year I spent in Sarawak, along with my experience of meeting people of other faiths meant that I began a lifelong exploration of how my Christian faith fitted into the world of Faiths. I discovered, over the years, that most Faiths shared certain fundamental beliefs about God and daily living. I recall a series of posters advertised for use in schools which set out 'the Golden Rule' as it appears in each major World Faith. Also, each Faith has always struggled to 'explain' God. In Judaism this is expressed in the Shema "Hear, O Israel: The Lord is our God, the Lord alone. You shall love the Lord your God with all your heart, and with all your soul, and with all your might."

(Deuteronomy 6:4-5 NRSV). For Christians it finds expression in the doctrine of the Trinity, which it has to be said, is not Biblical. Islam has 99 names for God (the 100th is known only to the camel!) since we can never know God in all his fullness. For Hindus their 330 million gods are all expressions of the one God. Buddhists, for the most part avoid the problem altogether, concentrating instead on how to lead a fulfilled life in the present – they have a point!

Sadly, in all Faiths there is an element that persists in an adherence to fundamentalism. This has had a negative impact, often bringing about division within a faith and antagonism between faiths; all too often finding expression in violence and killing. It could well result in the demise of those faiths in which it is most prevalent. We have seen this in Christianity with the Crusades and the Reformation. In Judaism with the growth of ultra-orthodox communities and secular Zionism. In Islam between Sunni and Shia. Most modern-day conflicts have their roots in the fundamentalist traditions of the predominant faith in their communities.

God

It seems to me that the biggest problem facing all religions today is how to understand and communicate the idea of God in a post-modern world. In a way it has always been a problem and religions have struggled to make sense of the idea of God. In the past, however, the prevalent world view has permitted acceptable answers. With the earth unique and at the centre of a very limited universe it was not difficult to envisage a 'god', usually in anthropomorphic terms, and identify the place of 'his' dwelling as just out of reach above the sky. Many Christians and many who live in the developed world with a Christian heritage still see God as a grey-haired old man sitting on a throne in heaven above us.

Today, however, we know that we live on a planet which is part of a solar system, which is part of a galaxy known as the Milky Way. Scientists have identified 2,500 stars in our galaxy with planets orbiting them – so far! The Milky Way is 100,000 light years across. A light year is the distance that light travels in empty space in one year. Since the speed of light is about 186,000 miles per second, then a light year is about 6 trillion miles – 6 million million miles. The Milky Way is an average sized galaxy with around 100 – 400 billion stars. The universe is made up of around 100 – 1000 billion galaxies – a billion is one thousand million

If it helps . . . 1,000 seconds is equal to almost 17 minutes. It would take almost 12 days for a million seconds to elapse and 31.7 years for a billion seconds. Therefore, a trillion seconds would amount to no less than 31,709.8 years.

So where do we place 'God' in the vastness of the universe and what do we mean by 'God' and how do we describe 'him'? (When I was teaching, I was often asked, "Sir, do you believe in God?" My standard response was "You tell me what kind of God you are talking about and I will tell you whether or not I believe in her.")

Islam is one of the three Abrahamic religions which share a common ancestry and a common belief in monotheism. Muslims refer to God as 'Allah' which is simply the Arabic word for God, and not, as some Christians believe a name for God. In Malaysia all faiths, including Christianity, are required to use the word Allah when referring to God. As we have already noted Islam lists 99 names for God in a valiant attempt to recognise that if God is God he defies definition since we can never know God in all his fullness!

By contrast Hinduism is seen as a polytheistic religion with its 330,000,000 'gods' each one an aspect of what we might attribute to a single being beyond our understanding. Sikhism, no doubt in part a consequence of an encounter with Islam, is monotheistic.

In the Christian west during the twentieth century the issue of 'God' has been addressed by a number of prominent theologians. When I was training for the ministry Karl Barth was the theologian of choice by the Rev'd Dr Percy Scott who was College Principal and our theology lecturer. The focus of Barth's teaching was the Sovereignty of God. We were also referred to Rudolf Bultmann whose principal concern was demythologization. We were also encouraged to read Dietrich Bonhoeffer, a Lutheran Pastor who was martyred in Germany just weeks before World War II ended. His writings explored radical discipleship and religionless Christianity.

Among other theologians of note are Paul Tillich who, in his famous phrase taught that God is "the ground of being". Hans Kung, a prominent Roman Catholic theologian. Gustavo Gutierrez whose principal concern was the plight of the poor, and John Hick who addressed traditional theological issues and also the relationship between Christianity and other World Faiths.

At a popular level J B Phillips published his very readable book appropriately entitled "Your God is Too Small". And of course, Bishop John Robinson attempted to provoke Christians to think about the problem with his book "Honest to God". Don Cupitt, who was instrumental in establishing the 'Sea of Faith' movement, tackled the issue of Christianity in a postmodern world. (I met him once when he was guest lecturer at Lincoln Theological College. Peter Robinson and I were there from Hartley for Holy Week. I had an interesting debate with Don Cupitt about John Wesley's Aldersgate experience!)

Most recently I have been reading 'Keeping Alive the Rumor of God: When Most People Are Looking the Other Way' by Martin Camroux which again addresses the issue of our understanding of God in the twenty-first century. I cannot commend it too highly.

As a beginning perhaps we need to revisit the traditional arguments for the existence of God. When I was teaching, I produced 'Handbooks' for my GCSE students. Reproduced below is the section I included on:

Proving God's Existence

Proof can take two forms:

1. Deductive – this assumes something as a premise and works out the implications of the premise, Thus in mathematics one can assume certain things about numbers or angles and draw conclusions from them that are certain. For instance, from the premise that there are 360o in a circle we can discover truths about triangles. Or, to take another example, from the premises that 'the Eiffel Tower is in Paris', and 'Paris is in France', we can conclude that therefore 'the Eiffel Tower is in France'. This sort of proof only works with logical or mathematical statements. If God is seen as an impersonal force or like an absolute number, then it could possibly have an application therefore into proving God's existence.

2. Inductive – this is a form of proof that reaches general conclusions on the basis of individual examples and is the sort of proof used in science. It is based on observation, from which a theory is formed and then tested and on which predictions can be made. For example, from the premises that 'if it rains, I shall get wet', and I get wet, we might conclude that 'therefore it rained'! However, that conclusion doesn't necessarily follow – I might get wet because someone threw a bucket of water over me! It can never give an absolute assurance, but only highly probable conclusions. If God is regarded as personal, then this is the only sort of proof that is relevant.

The Ontological Argument

The word 'ontological' means 'concerned with being' and is an argument based on what the word God means. It is associated with Anselm, the eleventh century Archbishop of Canterbury. He maintained that if God is the object of supreme devotion, then God must be regarded as the Supreme Being, (the greatest imaginable being). Anyone who talks about the concept of God must know what they mean by it and therefore everybody must have the concept. From this he worked out a logical argument:

a. God is defined as the greatest possible being.
b. Everybody can, at least, understand what (a) means and therefore we can have an idea in our minds of what God is like.
c. Something that exists in the mind, or imagination, is

not as great (real) as something that exists in the world (reality)

d. Therefore, if God only existed in the mind, he would not be the greatest possible being.

e. Therefore, God must also exist in the real world.

One of the original objections to this argument was that you can imagine the 'greatest possible' of anything, but this does not prove that that thing exists. For instance, you could imagine the greatest possible island, but that would not make it a real island. Anselm replied by saying that this is a misunderstanding of what he is saying. You cannot have the greatest possible island because it is always possible to think of things that could make it better, like a better climate or more palm trees. It is different with God because God is a unique being whose powers cannot be bettered. For instance, God is all-powerful and all-knowing, and one cannot improve on omnipotence and omniscience.

The real objection to the argument was put forward by a later philosopher, Immanuel Kant, who pointed out that existence is not a predicate describing something but merely asserts that what we have been describing really does exist. For example, if we are describing a tiger, we can say things about it like it is a big cat, has stripes and lives in India, but when we say that a tiger exists, we do not add to our description of a tiger but merely point out that there is something that answers to the description. If we say that a being called God actually exists, we are saying that such a being must have all the superlative qualities, but not that the existence of the superlative qualities in themselves proves that God exists.

This argument is the only one that is a deductive proof and would therefore be more appropriate as an argument for an impersonal God rather than a personal one.

The Cosmological Arguments

These start from the acceptance that the universe (cosmos) exists and needs explaining. The argument is usually associated with St. Thomas Aquinas who said that *something* could not come from *nothing* and therefore everything has a cause and the universe itself must have a cause. If we are to avoid an unending series of causes and effects there must be an original uncaused cause, which / who is outside of the process, namely God. Aquinas put forward five different arguments or ways to prove this. One of them, the third way, can be written like this:

a. In nature things have the possibility of not existing. For instance, animals are born and die, just as buildings are erected and ultimately disintegrate.
b. If everything has the possibility of not existing then at some time it did not exist.
c. If (b) is true then there was a time when nothing existed.
d. But if there was a time when nothing existed and everything depends for its existence on something else, then nothing could possibly exist for there would have been nothing to have caused it to exist.
e. Therefore, there must be an eternal being (God) to whom ultimately everything owes its existence.

If this argument is concerned with time, then it can be defeated. Everything had the possibility of not existing and we could say that *at any one time* each thing did not exist. What we cannot say is that there was never a *particular time* when nothing existed because each thing could exist at *different times* and no two things need exist at the *same time*. Besides, the universe itself could be eternal.

The Teleological Argument (argument from design)

This is a development of the cosmological argument. The word 'teleological' comes from the Greek word telos, which means 'end', and refers to the belief that if it can be shown that the universe is working towards a predetermined end then it must have been designed by a designer.

It has always concerned me that so many of the folk in our churches, ordained and laity alike are unfamiliar with such arguments for the existence of God while for my year 10 and 11 students such arguments were fundamental to their understanding of Christianity. Such arguments are only one way of seriously tackling the issue of what we mean by the word 'God'. The real issue is the need to recognise that for many in our so-called postmodern society God is imply dismissed as of no relevance!

It must also be said that the arguments outlined above are not exhaustive. Try 'googling' 'Arguments for the existence of God' and, as well as the 'Logical Arguments' outlined above there are also 'Empirical Arguments' – from beauty / from consciousness / from design, and 'Arguments from Historical events and Personages / from testimony' and 'Arguments grounded in personal experiences.'

It is clear that despite the vast amount of material that relates to this issue, in a world that for the most part no longer recognises a need for God, Christians are ill equipped to commend a belief in God in a way that makes sense in postmodern society.

For me, I find both Shakespeare and the Psalmist to be a helpful starting point when trying to make sense of God:

"What a piece of work is a man! How noble in reason, how infinite in faculty! In form and moving how express and admirable! In action how like an angel, in apprehension how like a god! The beauty of the world. The paragon of animals."
(**Hamlet** Act 2 Scene 2)

Psalm 8

1 O Lord, our Sovereign,
how majestic is your name in all the earth!
You have set your glory above the heavens.
2 Out of the mouths of babes and infants
you have founded a bulwark because of your foes,
to silence the enemy and the avenger.
3 When I look at your heavens, the work of your fingers,
the moon and the stars that you have established;

4 what are human beings that you are mindful of them,
mortals[a] that you care for them?
5 Yet you have made them a little lower than God,[b]
and crowned them with glory and honour.
6 You have given them dominion over the works of your hands;
you have put all things under their feet,
7 all sheep and oxen,
and also the beasts of the field,
8 the birds of the air, and the fish of the sea,
whatever passes along the paths of the seas.
9 O Lord, our Sovereign,
how majestic is your name in all the earth!

Footnotes

a. Psalm 8:4 Heb *ben adam*, lit. *son of man*
b. Psalm 8:5 Or *than the divine beings* or *angels*: Heb *elohim*

Jesus

We are probably on safer ground when it comes to Jesus. The 18th century saw the beginnings of 'The Search for the Historical Jesus'. The results are significant. Not only were the Gospels subject to significant scrutiny so too was Paul who made no claim to have encountered Jesus in the flesh. Sources outside the Biblical record have also been scrutinised and their contribution to the debate is important. first century Josephus and Roman historian Tacitus.

In Books 18 and 20 *of Antiquities of the Jews*, written around AD 93 to 94, the Jewish historian Josephus twice refers to the biblical

Jesus. The general scholarly view holds that the longer passage, known as the Testimonium Flavianum, most likely consists of an authentic nucleus that was subjected to later Christian interpolation or forgery. On the other hand, Josephus scholar Louis H Feldman states that "few have doubted the genuineness" of the reference found in Antiquities 20, 9, 1 to "the brother of Jesus, who was called Christ, whose name was James".

Tacitus, in his *Annals* (written c.115 CE), book 15, chapter 44, describes Nero's scapegoating of the Christians following the Fire of Rome. He writes that the founder of the sect was named Christus (the Christian title for Jesus); that he was executed under Pontius Pilate; and that the movement, initially checked, broke out again in Judea and even in Rome itself.

The Mishnah (c. 200 CE) may refer to Jesus as it reflects the early Jewish traditions of portraying Jesus as a sorcerer or magician. Other references to Jesus and his execution exist in the Talmud, but they aim to discredit his actions, not deny his existence.

Taken with the Gospels and Paul such testimony only serves to affirm the existence of Jesus as an historical figure. Someone once commented, with perhaps a degree of truth, that there is more evidence for the existence of Jesus than for the existence of Julius Caesar!

The problem is not whether Jesus existed, that he did is largely beyond doubt, but rather the problem is what are we to make of Jesus in his context and how relevant is he for the world of the 21st century?

During my lifetime our understanding of Jesus has expanded considerably. In Sunday School I was surrounded by pictures of Jesus as a white European. It was a bit of a shock when, as an eighteen-year-old, in Sarawak, I received Christmas cards that showed the Holy Family as Chinese rather than European. Today most Christians recognise that Jesus was likely to have been middle eastern and therefore brown, rather than, white skinned. Similarly, we have, finally moved away from the 'Gentle Jesus, meek and mild' of earlier times to recognise Jesus as a man with very human emotions, not least anger, as evidenced in his 'cleansing of the Temple'.

What is not resolved, however, is how we understand Jesus in terms of his role in God's plan. I spent the final year on my degree course studying just two units. One was on Hinduism; the other was on the Christian Doctrine of the Atonement. In reality there are several theories relating to the Christian understanding of the Atonement. I've outlined them, briefly, below:

1 The Moral Influence Theory

One of the earliest theories for the atonement is the Moral Influence theory, which simply taught that Jesus Christ came and died in order to bring about a positive change to humanity. This moral change comes through the teachings of Jesus alongside his example and actions. The most notable name linked to this theory is that of Augustine from the 4th century. His influence has almost single-handedly had the greatest impact upon Western Christianity. He affirmed the

Moral Influence theory as the main theory of the Atonement (alongside the Ransom theory as well).

According to this theory the death of Christ is understood as a catalyst to reform society, inspiring men and women to follow his example and live good moral lives of love. The Holy Spirit comes to help Christians produce this moral change. After death the human race will be judged by their conduct in life.

This theory focuses on not just the death of Jesus Christ, but on his entire life. This sees the saving work of Jesus not only in the event of the crucifixion, but also in all the words he has spoken, and the example he has set. The cross is merely the consequence of the moral life of Jesus. He is crucified as a martyr due to the radical nature of his moral example.

2 The Ransom Theory

This is one of the first major theories of the Atonement. It is often held alongside the Moral Influence Theory, and usually deals more with the actual death of Jesus Christ, what it actually means and the effect it has upon humanity. This theory finds its roots in the Early Church, particularly in Origen from the 3rd century. Essentially it teaches that Jesus Christ died as a ransom sacrifice, paid either to Satan (the most dominant view) or to God the Father. Jesus' death is seen as a payment to satisfy the debt we inherited from Adam's original sin.

Redemption in this theory means to buy back the human race from the clutches of the Devil. The main problem with this theory lies with the idea that the crucifixion is about paying off the Devil. Some advocates of this theory prefer to understand that in this act of Ransom Christ frees humanity from the bondage of sin and death. In this way, Ransom relates to the Christus Victor theory.

3 Christus Victor

The Christus Victor theory of Atonement is widely considered to be the dominant theory for most of the historical Christian Church. In this theory, Jesus Christ dies in order to defeat the powers of evil (such as sin, death, and the devil) in order to free mankind from their bondage. This is related to the Ransom view with the difference being that there is no payment to the devil or to God. Within the Christus Victor framework, the cross did not pay off anyone but defeated evil thereby setting the human race free.

Gustaf Aulen argued that this theory of the Atonement is the most consistently held theory in church history, especially in the early church up until the 12th century when Anslem's satisfaction theory came along. He writes that "the work of Christ is first and foremost a victory over the powers which hold mankind in bondage: sin, death, and the devil."

4 The Satisfaction Theory (Anselm)

In the 12th century, Anselm of Canterbury proposed a satisfaction theory for the Atonement. In this theory, Jesus Christ's death is understood as a death to satisfy the justice of

God. Satisfaction here means restitution, the mending of what was broken, and the paying back of a debt. In this theory, Anselm emphasizes the justice of God and claims that sin is an injustice that must be balanced. Anselm's satisfaction theory says essentially that Jesus Christ died in order to pay back the injustice of human sin and to satisfy the justice of God.

This theory was developed in reaction to the historical dominance of the Ransom theory, that God paid the devil with Christ's death. Anselm saw that this theory was logically flawed, because what does God owe Satan? In contrast with the Ransom theory, Anselm taught that it is humanity who owes a debt to God, not God to Satan. This theory suggests that Jesus Christ pays God back by his death on the cross. This is the first Atonement theory to bring up the notion that God is acted upon by the Atonement (i.e. that Jesus satisfies God).

5 The Penal Substitutionary Theory

Penal Substitutionary Atonement is a development of the Reformation. The Reformers, specifically Calvin and Luther, took Anselm's Satisfaction theory and modified it slightly. The result is that within Penal Substitution, Jesus Christ dies to satisfy God's wrath against human sin. Jesus is punished (penal) in the place of sinners (substitution) in order to satisfy the justice of God and the legal demand of God to punish sin. In the light of Jesus' death, God can now forgive the sinner because Jesus Christ has been punished in the place of the sinner, in this way meeting the retributive requirements of God's justice.

This theory of the Atonement contrasts with Anselm's Satisfaction Theory in that God is not satisfied with a debt of justice being paid by Jesus, but that God is satisfied with punishing Jesus in the place of mankind. The notion that the cross acts upon God, conditioning him to forgiveness, originates from Anslem's theory, but here in Penal Substitution the means are different. This theory of the Atonement is perhaps the most dominant today, especially among the Reformed, and the Evangelicals.

6 The Governmental Theory

The Governmental Theory of the Atonement is a slight variation upon the Penal Substitutionary theory, which is notably held in Methodism. The main difference here is the extent to which Christ suffered. In the Governmental Theory, Jesus Christ suffers the punishment of our sin and propitiates God's wrath. In this way, it is similar to Penal Substitution. However, in the Governmental Theory, Jesus Christ does not take the exact punishment we deserve, he takes a punishment. Jesus dies on the cross therefore to demonstrate the displeasure of God towards sin. He died to display God's wrath against sin and the high price which must be paid, but not to specifically satisfy that particular wrath. The Governmental Theory also teaches that Jesus died only for the church, and if you by faith are part of the church, you can take part in God's salvation. This view contrasts with both the Penal and Satisfaction models but retains the fundamental belief that God cannot forgive if Jesus does not die a propitiating death.

7 The Scapegoat Theory

The Scapegoat Theory is a modern Atonement theory rooted in the philosophical concept of the Scapegoat. The key figures are Rene Girard and James Allison. Within this theory of the Atonement Jesus Christ dies as the Scapegoat of humanity. This theory moves away from the idea that Jesus died in order to act upon God (as in Penal Substitution, Satisfaction, or Governmental theories), or as payment to the devil (as in Ransom). Scapegoating therefore is considered to be a form of non-violent atonement, in that Jesus is not a sacrifice but a <u>victim</u>.

There are many Philosophical concepts that come up within this model, but in a general sense, we can say that Jesus Christ as the Scapegoat means the following. 1) Jesus is killed by a violent crowd. 2) The violent crowd kills him believing that he is guilty. 3) Jesus is proven innocent, as the true Son of God. 4) The crowd is therefore deemed guilty.

At the end of a year studying 'The Doctrine of the Atonement' the only conclusion we arrived at was that there wasn't one! There were several – 'you pays your money and you makes your choice!' I did consider copying from my GCSE handbook the section I prepared on the Doctrine of the Atonement but realised that it would have taken up far more space than I would have liked so I offer the above, brief, summary. Why bother? Well, if we are to be true to our calling to proclaim the gospel, we have to attempt to make sense of Jesus' death as relevant to the world we now live in. I suspect the development of this doctrine in incomplete. The danger is that this doctrine can become a distraction from holding Jesus before our contemporaries as someone worth following because of his burning desire for justice for all.

Methodism
Meetings and Minutes

Let me begin with a couple of relatively trivial things. Why ever did Methodism merge the Trustees Meeting and the Society Meeting? I know the arguments but, on reflection, I am not convinced that it was a wise move. It may make us look like other churches to have a Church Council, but the move has, I believe, been detrimental both to the maintenance of our buildings and the furtherance of our mission.

With the meetings combined it is too easy for property matters to be neglected, especially when finances as stretched. I am also not at all sure that members of the Church Council are aware of the legal obligations imposed on them as trustees of the property. When I pointed this out at one of my churches several members resigned from their posts and consequently from the Church Council!

And when did we get into the bad habit of producing the Minutes of Meetings on the eve of the next meeting? Surely the idea is for minutes to be available as soon as possible after the meeting so that members can have a written record of their decisions and set about fulfilling the tasks they have committed themselves to at the meeting?

Resources

Since my late teens I have been aware of the way in which the United Methodist Church resources its members and ministers. In the UK not only has the Epworth Press disappeared but publications from The Methodist Publishing House are now only available from Hymns Ancient and Modern! Cokesbury is the main distributor for The United Methodist Publishing House and serves United Methodists in the United States and overseas as well as other denominations and independent churches. They distribute material produced by Abingdon Press (the US Methodist Publishing House).

Each year they produce a 'Preaching Annual' and a 'Worship Annual' containing material for every Sunday of the year. Among recent Methodist material they have produced is a Comic Book entitled 'Submitting to be More Vile' – The Illustrated Adventures of John and Charles Wesley, and a download package entitled 'The Wesley Challenge Campaign'. They also produce study material for use in local churches covering seasons such as Advent and Lent along with other topical material. Importantly the material produced reflects its Methodist origins. Most weeks I get one or more e-mails from Cokesbury in the US advertising new material. What's more such material it appears, more often than not, is actually used in the churches! Cokesbury also makes available first-rate material for Sunday School work.

I have used number of study series produced by the Rev'd Adam Hamilton who is senior pastor of the UM Church of the Resurrection in Kansas City. A church with a membership today of c. 20,000 spread over 5 campuses. He founded the church as a 'church plant' with 10 people in 1990 with the goal of welcoming thinking people not actively involved in a church and is committed to the renewal of mainstream church, in particular Methodism. Given the church's phenomenal growth he is clearly doing something right.

For years, each week I have received an e-mail from Discipleship Ministries for the United Methodist Church with suggestions for worship and preaching in the coming weeks. It is only recently that with the advent of Singing the Faith Plus that we are beginning to see similar resources becoming available in British Methodism. But we are still a long way from producing books like those in the Preachers Library which were so useful in the 1960s before they were discontinued.

Ecumenism

On the basis of a suggestion by Archbishop Geoffrey Fisher in 1946 that unity between the C of E and the Free Churches might be achieved if the latter would accept episcopacy, the Methodist Conference and the Convocations of Canterbury and York in 1955 agreed to enter conversations. The final report was published in 1968, in two parts: The Ordinal and The Scheme. It was accepted by the Methodist Conference but failed to gain the necessary majority in the Convocations in 1969 and in the General Synod in 1972. The House of Bishops and the House of Laity accepted to the report, but the House of Clergy declined it. New talks were initiated in 1995, and a 'covenant' was signed in 2003. There was a time, then, when I hoped to cease being a Methodist in favour of being in a United Church. That time has passed. The 2003 Covenant proved to be a damp squib. The heady days of ecumenism have been replaced with a desperate scabble for simple survival.

In the developed world Christianity is in decline. It doesn't surprise me. Despite the warnings of scholars like Bishop John Robinson and Bishop David Jenkins we have failed to find a way of talking about God in a way that makes sense in the modern world. We seem to be trapped in a medieval world view that science and society have long since abandoned. Similarly, we seem to have been unable to abandon the conservative evangelical view of Jesus as a personal saviour and reconnect with the gospel image of a Jesus whose overriding concern, in keeping with the Old Testament prophets, was social justice – something the world is crying out for.

Methodist Conference

"In June 1744, I desired my brother and a few other clergymen to meet me in London, to consider how we should proceed to save our own souls and those who heard us. After some time, I invited the lay preachers that were in the house to meet with us. We conferred together for several days and were much comforted and strengthened thereby." (John Wesley)

The conference got underway at the Old King's Foundry, which the Methodists had converted into a chapel. When the meeting opened on June 25, 1744, in attendance were John and Charles Wesley and four other clergymen. However, these six leaders quickly agreed to bring in four traveling preachers, "lay brothers."

"The first preliminary question was then proposed; namely, how far does each of us agree to submit to the unanimous judgment of the rest in every practical point, so far as we can without wounding our consciences."

They then took up their three main agenda items: 1. What to teach. 2. How to teach. 3. How to regulate doctrine, discipline, and practice. Under doctrine, they took up such issues as faith, justification, assurance of salvation, and sanctification. Afterwards they discussed discipline and organization for their growing following.

Over the years the structure of Conference has changed significantly. With the ordination of his 'travelling preachers' the early conferences were exclusively clerical. Later a lay 'representative' body was added, and that body today is given the most time when conferring!

In 2000 the Conference approved the report that resulted in "Our Calling" summarised below:

The calling of the Methodist Church is to respond to the gospel of God's love in Christ and to live out its discipleship in worship and mission.

It does this through:

Worship: The Church exists to increase awareness of God's presence and to celebrate God's love

Learning and Caring: The Church exists to help people to grow and learn as Christians, through mutual support and care

Service: The Church exists to be a good neighbour to people in need and to challenge injustice

Evangelism: The Church exists to make more followers of Jesus Christ

'Our Calling' prompted a series of Circuit and Church Reviews that rarely resulted in any action being taken.

Conference 2004 extended 'Our Calling' by identifying the 'Priorities of the Methodist Church':

Priorities for the Methodist Church:

- In partnership with others wherever possible, the Methodist Church will concentrate its prayers, resources, imagination and commitments on this priority:
- To proclaim and affirm its conviction of God's love in Christ, for us and for all the world; and renew confidence in God's presence and action in the world and in the Church
- As ways towards realising this priority, the Methodist Church will give particular attention to the following:

- Underpinning everything we do with God-centred worship and prayer
- Supporting community development and action for justice, especially among the most deprived and poor - in Britain and worldwide
- Developing confidence in evangelism and in the capacity to speak of God and faith in ways that make sense to all involved
- Encouraging fresh ways of being Church
- Nurturing a culture in the Church which is people-centred and flexible

Again, there was a flurry of Circuit and Church Reviews. Again, nothing much changed.

Conference in 2018 re-affirmed 'Our Calling'. To what end? It also proposed to produce 'A Methodist Way of Life'. I cannot commend it too highly even if the recognition that there is such a thing is, arguably, several decades too late!

The Conference Handbook for 2021 comprised four volumes, three of which are 'The Agenda'. In total it ran to almost 1,000 pages! In the eight days of Conference, it was expected that no less than 62 reports would be dealt with. The reports coming to the Conference included *God in Love Unites Us*, *Changing Patterns of Ministry*, *Holy Communion and Online Worship*, *The Theology of Safeguarding* and *Oversight and Trusteeship*. Conversations would also include the response of the Methodist Church to climate change and becoming a church focused on Justice, Dignity and Solidarity.

One of the reports that came to the 2021 Conference dealt with the proposal to establish 'Lay Pastors'. As a teenager I recall Methodism abolishing Lay Pastors, inviting them to become ordained! Joe Kidd's brother, Caleb, was a Lay Pastor in Danby and I recall him opting to train and be ordained, so he became the Rev'd Caleb Kidd. Another example perhaps of Methodism ignoring the lessons to be learned from its past?

I cannot help but wonder what our founding fathers (is that politically correct?) would make of it all! Conference Agendas of c.1,000 pages in three volumes, and CPD (Constitutional Practice and Discipline of the Methodist Church) of c.1,000 pages in two volumes! We seem to be a long way removed from:

John Wesley's "Twelve Rules for Helpers"

(As Wesley began to train and equip lay men for the task of preaching, he outlined for them "12 Rules for Helpers".)

1. Be diligent. Never be unemployed a moment. Never be triflingly employed. Never while away time; neither spend any more time at any place than is strictly necessary.
2. Be serious. Let your motto be, "Holiness to the Lord." Avoid all lightness, jesting, and foolish talking.
3. Converse sparingly and cautiously with women; particularly, with young women. 4. Take no step toward marriage, without first consulting with your brethren.
4. Believe evil of no one; unless you see it done, take heed how you credit it. Put the best construction on

everything. You know the Judge is always supposed to be on the prisoner's side.

5. Speak evil of no one; else your word especially would eat as doth a canker. Keep your thoughts within your own breast, till you come to the person concerned.

6. Tell every one what you think wrong in him, and that plainly, as soon as may be; else it will fester in your heart. Make all haste to cast the fire out of your bosom.

7. Do not affect the gentleman. You have no more to do with this character than with that of a dancing-master. A Preacher of the gospel is the servant of all.

8. Be ashamed of nothing but sin: Not of fetching wood (if time permit) or drawing water; not of cleaning your own shoes, or your neighbour's.

9. Be punctual. Do everything exactly at the time. And in general, do not mend our Rules, but keep them; not for wrath, but for conscience' sake.

10. You have nothing to do but to save souls. Therefore, spend and be spent in this work. And go always, not only to those that want you, but to those that want you most.

11. Act in all things, not according to your own will, but as a son in the Gospel. As such, it is your part to employ your time in the manner which we direct; partly, in preaching and visiting from house to house; partly, in reading, meditation, and prayer. Above all, if you labour with us in our Lord's vineyard, it is needful that you should do that part of the work which we advise, at those times and places which we judge most for his glory.

When Conference is over the decisions made are incorporated into the latest version of **CPD** (Constitution, Practice and Discipline). This is a volume larger than the Bible! It contains all the rules and regulations relating to Methodism today. Yes, I know it has to cover all sorts of legal questions that are the result of becoming a church with considerable assets invested in property. And, issues relating to Safeguarding, Data Protection, Diversity and Charity Law, were unknown in Wesley's day, but are part and parcel of the society in which our Church operates today.

Nevertheless . . . We seem to have fallen foul of what is happening in much of the world at large. We produce endless reports stating the problem but rarely get around to actually doing anything about them. There seems to be a serious disconnect between the 'Westminster Bubble' and the rest of Methodism. It was not always so. Until relatively recently Conference moved around the Connexion and ministers and representatives stayed in the homes of Methodist members. Preachers, ordained and lay, took services in churches in the vicinity. I can remember my parents hosting the Rev'd J Neville Ward, when Conference was near Durham and Kath's parents hosted the Rev'd Kathleen Richardson when Conference was in the Potteries. It all helped 'ordinary' Methodists to feel part of something bigger. Today those attending Conference are usually put up in an hotel and Conference is increasingly being held in the Midlands each year with the possibility of finding a permanent location!

Membership of the Methodist Church

I remember hearing an Anglican Bishop when he addressed a District Synod refer to his elderly father, who was a Methodist. He was proud to be a Methodist as he considered himself, even, in old age, to still be seeking the truth. That idea was explicit in Wesley's statement of 1743, and was still the basis of membership when I became a member of the Methodist Church in the early 1960s, encapsulated in the phrase those "who sincerely desire…" (See below) The change in the 1980s may have been intended to consolidate our claim to be a Church in the accepted definition of the word, but, I would maintain, it leaves us open to the claims of the modern conservative evangelical which are, I believe far removed from the origins of the Methodist movement.

Below are four extracts from Methodist publications which demonstrate a move from welcoming those who are 'seeking' to those who have 'arrived'!

"4 There is only one condition required in those who desire admission into these societies; viz *'a desire to flee from the wrath to come, to be saved from their sins.'* But wherever this is really fixed in the soil it will be shown by its fruits." ('Rules of the Society' – John & Charles Wesley May 1st, 1743)

"1. All persons are welcomed into membership of the Methodist Church who sincerely desire to be saved from their sins through faith in the Lord Jesus Christ and evidence the same in life and conduct and who seek to have fellowship with Christ himself and his people by taking up the duties and privileges of the Methodist Church." (p.42 – Joining the Church – A Manual of Membership for Methodists – Epworth Press 1968)

"69. Who are received as full members of the Methodist Church? – All those who confess Christ as Lord and Saviour and accept the obligation to serve him in the life of the Church and the world are welcome as full members of the Methodist Church." (A Catechism for the use of the people called Methodists – Methodist Publishing House – undated but possibly 1986)

"69. Who are received as members of the Methodist Church? – All those who confess Jesus as Lord and Saviour and accept the obligation to serve him in the life of the Church and the world are welcome as members of the Methodist Church." (A Catechism for the use of the people called Methodists – Methodist Publishing – 2018)

It is also worth noting that nowhere does the Methodist Church suggest that the Bible *is* the Word of God. Clause 4 in the Deed of Union is clear: "The doctrines of the evangelical faith which Methodism has held from the beginning and still holds are *based upon* the divine revelation *recorded in* the Holy Scriptures." (my italics)

We seem to have forgotten our heritage and espoused a version of the Christian Faith that would not be recognised by our founding fathers.

Members of John Wesley's Holy Club, over 200 years ago, asked themselves 22 questions each day in their private devotions. I wonder, today, how many of our members make daily devotions and whether they are even aware of Wesley's questions? Might they make their way, in some form or another into 'A Methodist Way of Life' I wonder.

Wesley's Questions

1. Am I consciously or unconsciously creating the impression that I am a better person than I really am? In other words, am I a hypocrite?
2. Am I honest in all my acts and words, or do I exaggerate?
3. Do I confidentially pass on what I was told in confidence?
4. Can I be trusted?
5. Am I a slave to dress, friends, work or habit?
6. Am I self-conscious, self-pitying, or self-justifying?
7. Did the Bible live to me today?
8. Do I give time to speak to me every day?
9. Am I enjoying prayer?
10. When did I last speak to someone else of my faith?
11. Do I pray about the money I spend?
12. Do I go to bed on time and get up on time?
13. Do I disobey God in anything?
14. Do I insist on doing something about which my conscience is uneasy?
15. Am I defeated in any part of my life?
16. Am I jealous, impure, irritable, touchy or distrustful?
17. How do I spend my spare time?
18. Am I proud?

19. Do I thank God that I am not as other people, especially as the Pharisee who despised the publican?
20. Do I grumble and complain constantly?
21. Is Christ real to me?

Despite everything that has been said and written over the years about what it means to be a member of the Methodist Church churches rarely remove anyone from the membership lists. Of course, there are those who because of age or infirmity can no longer fulfil the duties of membership. However, there are many whose names are retained on the flimsiest of excuses. "They always support the Christmas Fayre." "Although they never come to church, they do send a donation occasionally." "We can't remove their name, their parents would be upset."!

Pastoral Visitors

Wesley organised his societies into Bands and Classes. Class Leaders would have a class of no more than a dozen folk with whom they would meet regularly, usually weekly. They would meet to confess their failings, to share in prayer and Bible Study and make their weekly monetary contribution to the upkeep of the Society. The Class Leaders would also issue to each of their members a quarterly Class ticket, usually bearing a verse of Scripture. By the time I became a member few Methodists met in Classes though most were members of a regular weekly meeting for fellowship. The 'Women's Own' or something similar, perhaps with a different name usually met weekly. Men's meetings were more often than not monthly.

Mixed groups, like The Wesley Guild or Christian Endeavour or Youth Fellowship met weekly. Class Leaders still delivered the quarterly Class Ticket, a convenient excuse for making a regular pastoral visit.

Before the end of the century Class Leaders were renamed Pastoral Visitors and, while some still take their role seriously, for the most part many Pastoral Visitors today do little more than distribute the annual Membership Ticket, often just pushing it through the letterbox!

Local Preachers and Worship Leaders

As a 16-year-old Local Preacher on Trial my Superintendent gently but firmly pointed out that unless I had a prior, unavoidable, commitment he expected me to offer every Sunday each Quarter – not that he intended to plan me every Sunday but so that he had the flexibility to make the Preaching Plan. In practice we have made the requirements for preaching much less onerous. Such that when I was a Superintendent with responsibility for making the Plan, I had preachers who told me they would give no more than one or two appointments and / or they would stipulate which churches they were prepared to preach in! Again, their training has been made easier, two schemes ago a required study of a World Faith was abandoned just when we were becoming an increasingly multi-faith nation! The latest scheme has moved online thereby excluding those who either have no computer or whose access to the internet is very limited, possibly by virtue of where they live.

From CPD: **563 Duties and Rights of Local Preachers.**

(1) Preachers are called of God, to be worthy in character, to lead God's people in worship and to preach the gospel. This places duties on, and gives rights to, local preachers.

(2) As to worship, it is the duty of local preachers:

i.   to lead worship and preach with knowledge, conviction and competence;

ii.   to preach nothing at variance with our doctrines (the term 'our doctrines' refers to those truths of salvation which are set forth in the Methodist doctrinal standards);

iii.   to be available for an appropriate number of appointments each quarter, having regard to the situation of the local preacher and of the Circuit;

iv.   to inform the Superintendent of any occasions on which they cannot be available for appointments on the forthcoming circuit plan;

v.   to fulfill all appointments given on the circuit plan;

vi.   if unable to fulfill an appointment, to arrange for a suitable substitute, informing the Superintendent and a church steward of the Local Church concerned;

vii.   to take overall responsibility for an act of worship when appointed on the circuit plan;

viii.   to seek to work collaboratively with others in leading worship.

For the doctrinal standards see cl. 4 of the Deed of Union (Book

II, Part 1). For the circuit plan see S.O. 521.

(3) As to fellowship and training, it is the duty of local preachers:

i.   to attend the Local Preachers' Meeting on each occasion (or to tender an apology for absence to the secretary if unable to attend for good reason);

ii.   to continue to develop in their personal spiritual life, in knowledge and understanding, and in preaching and leading worship;

iii. if admitted as such after the year beginning 1st September 1995, to participate in a programme of continuing local preacher development;

iv.   to attend a class, housegroup, or similar fellowship group if possible.

(4) As to membership of the Local Church, it is the duty of local preachers regularly to attend public worship (as appointments permit) and receive the Sacrament of the Lord's Supper (normally in a Methodist church or an approved local ecumenical partnership).

(5) It is the right of local preachers:

i.   to retain local preacher status while they remain members of the Methodist Church (this right continues if they are no longer able to lead worship and preach by reason of age or infirmity, but is subject to Sections 113 to 115);

ii.   upon removal from one Circuit to another, upon

production of a copy of the current circuit plan from their former Circuit, to be received in the new Circuit as local preachers;

iii.   to have the year of their admission as a local preacher recorded by the Circuit.

Below I have reproduced another excerpt from "College, Chapel and Culture in Edwardian Manchester" by Rachel Larkinson. I have no doubt that my father would recognise what was demanded of a Local Preacher in training. What a Local Preacher in training would make of it today I cannot imagine.

Primitive Methodist Church:
Darlington & Stockton District Local Preachers' Training Committee Correspondence Classes, 1909-10

The arrangements for the coming Sessions are now complete.

You are asked to select one, two, or three of the following Text Books, and order them as early as possible. Your minister can supply them.

Questions on each book will appear in the "Teacher and Preacher" each month, September to march. Send you answers *to me* during the last week of the month if possible.

Your answers will be corrected by one of the sub-tutors, and returned to you.

Let me know which books you will study, and I will send you

full rules and suggestions. Reply early.

Please make Classes known as much as you can. Send me the names and addresses of any likely Students.

TEXT BOOKS

1. *Primitive Methodist History and Polity,* by Kendall $4^1/_2$d
2. *Preaching (Homiletics),* by Fletcher 1s $1^1/_2$d
3. Gill's *English Grammar* 1s
4. *Our Lord's Teaching* Guild Series 6d
5. *New Testament and its Writers* 6d
6. *Manners and Customs of the Bible* 6d
7. *Christian Character* 6d
8. *Christian Doctrine* 6d

Advanced Section

- 10. *Unto This Last,* by Ruskin
- 11. *Romans,* hy Garvie 2s 6d
- 12. *Outlines of Theology,* by Clarke 5s 8d

1/- (1909) = £5.60 (2017) 6d (1909) = £2.80 (2017) 1d (1909) = 46p (2017)

Extracts from Appendices of "College, Chapel and Culture in Edwardian Manchester." Edited by Rachel Larkinson.

When I was training as a Local Preacher the Methodist Church published and annual series of books in the 'Local Preacher's

Library'. They were first rate and, without doubt, were valued. Sadly, they simply ceased to be produced, for no good reason that I can recall. It left the way open for preachers, if they read anything at all, to choose books that re-enforced their particular theological perspective rather than being challenged to understand Methodism's position.

The introduction of Worship Leaders, like the Diaconal Order was, I believe, ill-conceived. The expectation now is that Ministers and Local Preachers will make use of Worship Leaders when they are planned to conduct worship. However, being a Worship Leader is surely part of what it means to be a Minister or Local Preacher. (See **563 Duties and Rights of Local Preachers** (2) (i) above). No one would offer for either Office on the basis that they did not want to be a leader of worship! With the increasing problem of filling pulpits, it would make more sense for Worship Leaders to take on the role traditionally given to Readers. Leading worship and reading an approved, prepared sermon available either from the Connexion or from the Circuit. To my mind this is yet another example of Methodism being re-active rather than pro-active, and in the process dumbing down yet further!

Today it almost as if preachers and leaders of worship are doing the church a favour by offering to fill the pulpit on occasion rather than being a response to a calling which imposes a certain discipline.

It still baffles me why we persist in setting out the **Duties and Rights of Local Preachers** yet ignore the fact that there are many on a Circuit Plan who make no effort to accept the discipline of the office. In one circuit where I was superintendent, I removed three preachers who had never attended worship or lead worship for years. One simply accepted it. One kicked up a fuss and couldn't understand why he was being removed from the list despite the fact that by his own admission he had no intention of attending worship again! Interestingly the third began to re-evaluate his faith and in time requested to be re-instated. Which we were happy to accept.

I remember when I was training as a preacher, we were advised to dress formally to conduct worship. All that seems to have gone by the board and our younger preachers now dress casually! Strangely at baptisms, weddings and funerals, the last thing the guests do when they come to church is to dress casually. They see such events in church as special, and dress accordingly. Perhaps that is something our younger preachers might care to consider!

Worship

When I was training for the ministry, I spent my first year in Theological College on the College course, part of which led to a Certificate of Biblical Knowledge, awarded by the University of Manchester. Having, finally meet the requirements, I embarked on a degree course, leading to a BA (Theol), at Manchester for my remaining three years of training for the ministry. The only thing I was then required to do in College was attend evening sessions on 'Worship and Preaching' led by the Rev'd

Dick Jones. I confess, I was rebellious, and after a couple of sessions I refused to continue attending as I could see no value in simply 'fiddling about' with the order of what happened in worship. Nothing much has changed.

The pandemic has led to a demand from some folk to look again at how worship must now change as churches begin to return to 'in church' rather than 'online' services. This seems to me to be a thinly veiled attempt by modern conservative evangelicals to demand that worship should be in a form that suits them better, primarily more 'modern' hymns.

Over my lifetime worship has been constantly changing. 'Thees' and 'Thous' have been replaced in prayers (although there has been a marked reluctance to adopt the modern form of the Lord's Prayer). The AV has fallen out of fashion in favour of more modern translations of the Bible. Drama has often been utilised as a means of communicating either the Scripture or the message. A variety of instruments have replaced the organ in accompanying hymns. Modern technology has allowed leaders of worship and preachers to use pictures and videos to enhance worship. What more is there to say? That only leaves 'the sermon'. That has often become shorter and often is not well used as a means of both teaching and challenging the hearers. And I deplore the fact that the pulpit has often been removed or is ignored in favour of using a lectern, and sermons are replaced with reflections; they are not the same thing! Jesus preached sermons; he didn't offer reflections!

The Sermon

'Of all preaching, what is called gospel preaching is the most useless ... A harangue on the sufferings of Christ or salvation by faith speaks little of the commands of Christ ... It is an unconnected rhapsody of unmeaning words containing neither sense nor grace ... The essence of a Methodist sermon is holiness of heart and life.'

John Wesley (in a letter to his brother, Charles, 4th November 1772)

If we have failed anywhere, I believe it is here. Sermons have all too often become little more than a rehearsal of anecdotes. Preachers, lay and ordained, have consistently failed to communicate the challenge of the gospel to their hearers. The difficulties of understanding the person and nature God in the changed world view of the past century is not something we chose to grapple with. Nor are the implications of Jesus' teaching and ministry in a world where poverty and injustice abound. We are often told that preachers shouldn't get involved in the world of politics – try telling that to Lord Soper! Indeed try telling that to Jesus!

Hymns

In my last appointment several of the churches in the circuit were keen to buy the latest edition of Songs of Fellowship as a supplement to Hymns and Psalms. I did my utmost to dissuade them on the basis that the Methodist Church was about to publish a new Hymn Book, 'Singing the Faith'. I consider it to have been a big mistake.

I know that complaining about hymns that are omitted is not unusual, but I do feel that a lot of excellent hymns have been left out, more so than in previous 'new' hymn books. Whilst I am the first to commend the editors for their inclusion of some excellent new hymns, in particular in relation to areas that were missing from previous hymn books, I am not convinced that the inclusion of popular, brief, repetitive songs, does much to enhance worship.

But my main complaint is the 'modernisation' of some well-known traditional hymns. In the first place it is, I think, disingenuous to presume to alter the wording of traditional hymns. We wouldn't dream of changing the words of well-known poems to 'make them more up-to-date'. Simply changing 'thees' to 'yous' doesn't cut it! And more extensive revision can, and often does, alter the theological meaning. The classic example is the revision of the so-called 'Wesley's conversion hymn. The whole argument for 'modernisation', however, falls flat because the whole thing is random. Some of Wesley's hymns are modernised, others are not, the whole thing appears to be purely arbitrary. There is also, I think, an argument, on ecumenical grounds. Why make it more difficult to choose hymns on ecumenical occasions? It was irritating enough in the past when hymns like 'Guide me O thou great Jehovah', or should that be 'Redeemer' were chosen on such occasions. It was a distraction, however you looked at it.

Do we even need hymnbooks when an increasing number of churches have the means to project their services either on screens or via TV monitors? When the Methodist Church was producing Hymns and Psalms, I remember receiving a flyer from and independent publishing house – Mayhew McCrimmon (?) advertising a loose-leaf hymn book. The idea was that a church could add to a basic collection of hymns both traditional hymns and new hymns as they became available. The project came to nothing as most churches were committed to produce 'new' hymn books around the same time. The same principal could be applied using modern technology.

Services Peculiar to Methodism

Interestingly neither of the two services most often associated with Methodism have their origins in the Methodist movement.

The origins of **the Love Feast** in the early church are closely interconnected with the origins of the Lord's Supper, the two services became quite distinct and should not be confused with each other. While the Lord's Supper has been practically universally adopted among Christians throughout church history, the Love Feast has appeared only at certain times and among certain denominations.

The modern history of the Love Feast began when Count Zinzendorf and the Moravians in Germany introduced a service of sharing food, prayer, religious conversation, and hymns in 1727. John Wesley first experienced it among the Moravians in Savannah, Georgia, ten years later. His diary notes: "After evening prayers, we joined with the Germans in one of their love–feasts. It was begun and ended with thanksgiving and prayer and celebrated in so decent and solemn a manner as a Christian of the apostolic age would have allowed to be worthy of Christ."

It quickly became a feature of the Evangelical Revival and a regular part of Methodist society meetings in Great Britain and throughout the English–speaking world. As Methodists immigrated to North America, they made Love Feasts an important part of early American Methodism. The UMC still have an Order of Service for a Love Feast in their 'Book of Worship'.

In 1663 Puritan Pastor Richard Alleine published *Vindiciae Pietatis:* or, A Vindication of Godliness in the Greater Strictness and Spirituality of It. On many occasions John Wesley republished Alleine's work in his A Christian Library in 1753, and on August 11, 1755, used a chapter from the book, "Application of the Whole", in what was probably the first celebration of **the Covenant Service** in the Methodist movement.

We say the Covenant Prayer each year, but I wonder whether we really mean it!

'I am no longer my own but yours.
Put me to what you will, rank me with whom you will;
put me to doing, put me to suffering;
let me be employed for you, or laid aside for you,
exalted for you, or brought low for you;

let me be full, let me be empty,
let me have all things, let me have nothing:
I freely and wholeheartedly yield all things to your pleasure and
disposal.
And now, glorious and blessed God, Father, Son and Holy Spirit,
you are mine and I am yours' So be it
And the Covenant now made on earth, let it be ratified in heaven
Amen'.

Children in Worship

In the 1960s I went with my parents to the Sunday morning service. I crawled around on the floor under the pews and did lots of drawings on scrap paper! Eventually I took an interest in the 'Children's Address' and by the time I was in my teens I also began to relate to the sermon. Sunday School was at 2.00 pm and we used the Sunday School Hymnbook.

In the 1970s Sunday School was moved to the Sunday morning with children in worship for the first 10 minutes or so with "appropriate" hymns. The Sunday School Hymnbook was abandoned by Methodism. In my first appointment, at Northumberland Avenue in Bury St Edmunds, the Sunday School was so large that we had to 'cream off' the top class and we made them a 'Junior Fellowship', meeting after the Sunday morning service in the same way the 'Youth Fellowship' met after the evening service. In both cases attendance at the service preceding the Fellowship was expected! After a year when we reviewed the situation the children were very happy with the arrangement – the only negative comment was that they 'didn't know the hymns' used in the morning service having been used to more child appropriate hymns when they were only in for the first 10 minutes or so. I believe that did our young folk a great disservice, in effect discouraging them from graduating into so-called 'adult' worship.

I am mindful of the story recorded in Acts:

A young man named Eutychus was sitting in the window. He was sinking into a deep sleep as Paul talked on and on. When he was sound asleep, he fell from the third floor and died. Paul went down, fell on him and embraced him, then said, "Don't be alarmed. He's alive!" (Acts 20:9-10 CEB)

Perhaps someone should have talked to Paul about 'All age worship' or as it now known as 'Inter-generational worship'. (Does changing the name actually make any real difference?) I know, those were different times, but . . .

Ten years ago when I retired to Crook I divided my preaching appointments between the West Durham Circuit, where I live, and the Durham and Deerness Valley Circuit which was circuit where I grew up and from which I candidated for the ministry. As I have preached in the various churches in the Durham and Deerness Valley Circuit I have come across folk who remember me, and who I remember, from 50 years ago. Without exception the are folk, who, like me first attended Sunday morning worship with their parents and went to an afternoon Sunday School!

Ordained Ministry

For most of my life what I have witnessed what I believe to be a dumbing down of Methodism. It began with our Colleges. When I was accepted for ministerial training, we had several Methodist Colleges. Cliff College was a lay training College, offering a one-year course. Ministerial training was offered in five Colleges and was usually a four-year course, and involved Biblical and Theological studies, in depth! We also had a deaconess training College in Ilkley. We now have only two Colleges, one of which is Cliff, the other, an ecumenical institution, Queens, is in Birmingham. The training is usually completed in months rather than years, often by 'distance learning'. In the 1960s the tutors were often scholars of some repute, academics recognised and employed by the University with which the College was linked. We now have few Methodist scholars of international repute in British Methodism. Of course the Church must change with the times, but too often I believe we have embraced change without considering the implications, sometimes with detrimental consequences.

A couple of years ago I came across "College, Chapel and Culture in Edwardian Manchester" by Rachel Larkinson. The couple of extracts below are reproduced from Larkinson's book which is primarily a record of, and commentary on a surviving portion of her grandfather's diary which he kept whilst training for the ministry at the Primitive Methodist Theological Institute in Manchester.

The first extract sets out details of the curriculum for students along with what is expected of them. I wonder how thorough today's curriculum is and what we expect of candidates today?

THE CONSOLIDATED RULES
of the PRIMITIVE METHODIST CONNEXION
REVISED BY ORDER of the EIGHTY-THIRD ANNUAL
CONFERENCE held at HULL, JUNE 11-20, 1902
Ministerial Education

THEOLOGICAL INSTITUE AT MANCHESTER

Curriculum for Students

562.   The curriculum shall include the following subjects:-

a. First year's Students: Systematic Theology, Pastoral Theology, including Homiletics, Logic, Church Government, Greek (New Testament), Old Testament Introduction, Old Testament Exegesis, Old Testament Theology, New Testament Introduction, New Testament Exegesis, New Testament Theology, History of Doctrine, Hebrew, and Classical Greek (optional).

b. Second year's Students: Systematic Theology, Pastoral Theology, including Homiletics, Psychology, Church Government, Greek, Old Testament Introduction, Old Testament Exegesis, Old Testament Theology, New Testament Introduction, New Testament Exegesis, New Testament Theology, History of Doctrine, Hebrew,

c. Third year's Students: Hebrew, Classical Greek, Systematic Theology, Philosophy, Comparative Religion, Church

History, Apologetics, Biblical Work.

d. German may be taken each year, but shall not be compulsory.

e. English language and English Literature shall be taught should the Principal and Tutors so decide.

Students

565. No person shall be, admitted as a student unless he is a Local Preacher, and has been recommended by the Quarterly Meeting of the station to which he belongs, by the Candidates Examining Committee and the Conference.

566. On entering the Institute each student shall be required to sign a document stating (1) Whether he offers himself for Home, Colonial, or foreign work. (2) That should he leave our ministry within six years of his entrance on probation he will pay the Committee the sum of £30 (£11,600 in 2017).

567. Students must remain in the Institute two years at least. The fees for each student shall be £15 per annum (£5,800 in 2017), which shall be paid half-yearly in advance.

568. Half-yearly examinations of the students shall be conducted in December and May by Examiners appointed by the Conference. Arrangements as to the method of conducting the examinations shall be made by the Tutors, Examiners, and Committee of Management.

The second extract is a brief summary of the life of A S Peake who was highly thought of in both church and academia. His position in no way undermined the Primitive Methodist Church's commitment to evangelism but he did prevent it going down the road of what today we would recognise as 'conservative evangelicalism'.

"Arthur Samuel Peake MA (1865-1929)

Arthur Samuel Peaks was said to be the greatest biblical scholar of his generation. His presence at Hartley College from 1892 for over thirty years had a profound effect on the quality of academic training given at the College and the biblical understanding with which students were equipped to go out to serve their circuits.

Arthur had been brought up in the evangelical Primitive Methodist religious environment, but during his years at Oxford he had been much influenced by those who taught him and from whom he learnt the value of an historical-critical approach to Biblical Studies.

In May 1891 he was approached by William Hartley to consider moving to Manchester to take up a position as a tutor at the Manchester Primitive Methodist Theological College. Hartley was offering to fund the appointment for five years.

In addition to lecturing, he was the author of many publications; beginning in 1902 with is commentary on *Hebrews*. However, he is best remembered for *Peake's Commentary*, which was published in 1919, in which he sought to 'put before the reader in a simple form … the generally accepted results of Biblical Criticism, Interpretation, History and Theology'.

His personal piety, his scholarship and honesty in seeking the truth, along with his gracious nature, meant that he held the confidence of his denomination, enabling PM ministers to accept critical biblical scholarship without losing their faith, and the same was true of many other church leaders. In the words of the Wesleyan, George Jackson, echoed by the New Testament scholar, C. H. Dodd, he 'saved the English Church from a fundamentalist controversy'."

"College, Chapel and Culture in Edwardian Manchester" by Rachel Larkinson

I digress, briefly, to include a Facebook post from my childhood friend. We played together in the manse garden in Prudhoe until I moved to Durham when I was six. Our paths have never crossed again until very recently when we 'met' again on Facebook. Our positions on politics and faith are remarkably similar!

The term evangelical is much tossed about. Often with the assumption that the preceding word is "conservative" though left silent! My understanding is that to be evangelical is to be

someone with a passion to share the "Gospel", the good news, revealed in the stories told by and about Jesus in scripture. That passion leading to a commitment to ministry and mission. What it does not require is one way of understanding and studying scripture. Methodism is evangelical despite including those with varied approaches to the scripture that they have that passion to share. So, you can have "radical" and "liberal" and "traditional" and "mainstream" and "conservative" evangelicals. All with the same passion based on reading and studying the same scriptures. Personally, my whole life outside of my school career has been as an evangelical, preaching, teaching, and tutoring, and so encouraging, affirming, and challenging congregations with sermons rooted in scripture, enhanced by the quadrilateral dance with tradition, reason and experience joining in the dance of faith. Perhaps less time claiming that any one group are the "real" evangelicals, and more time listening to others, might help.

Geoffrey Best

15 June 2021

The Wesleyan Quadrilateral

Wesley and his spiritual successors stand firmly within the Evangelical tradition of the Christian Church. However, that term needs careful definition as it has been hijacked and reinterpreted in recent times and I am not sure Wesley would want to own it in the 21st century.

Wesley considered the Bible to be the primary source for Christian belief and life. He wrote, *"I will not, I dare not vary from this book, either in great things or small. I have no power to dispense with one jot or tittle of what is contained therein. I am determined to be a Bible Christian, not almost but altogether"* *(Sermon, "Causes of the Inefficacy of Christianity," 1787).*

However, on an examination of Wesley's work, 20th century American Methodist Albert C Outler identified four different sources that Wesley used in coming to theological conclusions:

- Scripture - the Holy Bible (Old and New Testaments)
- Tradition - the two millennia history of the Christian Church
- Reason - rational thinking and sensible interpretation
- Experience - a Christian's personal and communal journey in Christ

In his introduction to his 1964 collection 'John Wesley', Outler coined the term 'the Wesleyan Quadrilateral' to describe these sources.

The United Methodist Church, asserts that "Wesley believed that the living core of the Christian faith was revealed in Scripture, illumined by tradition, vivified in personal experience, and confirmed by reason. Scripture [however] is primary, revealing the Word of God 'so far as it is necessary for our salvation.'" (The Book of Discipline of the United Methodist Church-2004, p. 77).

It must be understood, then, that for Wesley, Tradition, Reason, and Experience do not form additional "sources" for theological truth, for he believed that the Bible was the sole source of truth about God, but rather these form a matrix for interpreting the Bible.

Ministers

Once the Methodist Diaconal Order was established, I suppose it was inevitable that ministers would be rebranded 'Presbyters'! A term that conveyed little or nothing to Methodists, or indeed to members of other denominations. And, a passing thought, why does British Methodism not produce a 'certificate' for those ordained like the United Methodist Church does in the US? I know we are given a Bible, but I have been impressed, when on an Exchange of Pastorates, to see such a certificate of ordination prominently displayed in the Pastor's Office in churches where I have been the visiting pastor.

The Methodist Diaconal Order

I am indebted to the Methodist Church website for some of this material. This section is perhaps longer than the others because I wanted to show how, what I consider to be 'dumbing down', is illustrated by reference to one area of Methodism in some detail.

In the 1870s and 1880s the Rev Thomas Bowman Stephenson

developed what was to become the National Children's Home (NCH), today rebranded as 'Action for Children'. Alongside this he founded the Sisters of the Children who worked in the homes and in some way fulfilled his vision of an order of women used by the Church.

In 1890 Stephenson outlined his vision for a deaconess order within the Wesleyan Church. The Sisters of the Children would become the core of the new Order committed to any Christian work, except that of the pulpit.

Stephenson proposed three essential principles:

- There should be vocation but no vow; but he insisted that the sisters should be paid.
- There should be discipline but not servility
- There should be association, but it should not exclude freedom.

He described three fields of usefulness:

- moral and spiritual education (in connection with orphanages and industrial schools)
- ministry to the sick, especially the sick poor
- evangelistic visitation in connection with circuits, congregations and missions.

The United Methodist Church had an order based on similar lines, founded in 1891 by the Rev T. J. Cope, with its headquarters in Wandsworth, London. In the Primitive

Methodist Church, the Rev J. Flannigan, founder of St. Georges Hall in the Old Kent Road, began to train Sisters, and later the appointments came under the general care of Home Missions.

The work of Wesleyan Deaconesses developed quickly and in 1894 the first sister was sent to work in South Africa. This began a long tradition of overseas service and the founding of deaconess orders in other countries.

In 1900 Stephenson became Superintendent of the Ilkley Circuit. Whilst there, Conference agreed that what had become the Wesley Deaconess Order be fully acknowledged, and Stephenson appointed its Warden. In 1902 he purchased a house that was to become the Deaconess Institute College, and it opened that September with 17 students.

At Methodist union in 1932 the Wesleyan Deaconess Order (304 deaconesses) was joined by the United Methodist Order (45 deaconesses), and a year later by 24 Primitive Methodist Sisters to become the Wesley Deaconess Order of the Methodist Church. Four years later the new Methodist Book of Offices included a service of ordination for deaconesses until then they had been consecrated.

The 1950s saw new challenges with society offering new avenues of work for women, and it was felt that the Order was not offering deaconesses the scope and responsibility enjoyed in other professions. In the 1960s it was agreed that ordination into the Deaconess Order is for life, so ordination can be terminated only by resignation. (Up to that point, women had been obliged to leave the Order upon marriage.)

In 1968 the house in Ilkley closed and the training of deaconesses moved to Handsworth College in Birmingham, where it was united with the training of presbyters. Two years later Handsworth itself closed and the deaconesses transferred their training to the ecumenical Queens College, also in Birmingham.

The event that probably had the most profound effect on the Order was Conferences decision in 1973 to open presbyteral ministry to women. The Church ceased recruitment for the WDO from 1978. The work of the deaconess was becoming increasingly church-based, they were increasingly being used to fill the gap left by the reduction in ministerial posts.

In 1986 the Methodist Church agreed to re-open the Wesley Deaconess Order to men and women. In 1989 the Wesley Deaconess Order became the Methodist Diaconal Order and admission into full membership of the Order was by ordination. Subsequently the title deacon was agreed for all members.

Deacons today are trained alongside presbyters, paid the same as presbyters and like presbyters are entitled to a manse. They are largely used to fill presbyteral posts and are now expected to be preachers. The only thing, in practice, that marks a deacon out as different to a presbyter is that they are not able to preside at the Lord's Supper, though of course they are able to take 'extended' communion to churches and members as appropriate. All this, to my mind, raises questions about the validity of the MDO. It is far removed from the intentions of the founders of the Wesleyan Deaconess Order and, as such, means that the church is missing out on an invaluable opportunity for taking mission into society.

Supernumeraries

I'm not sure that Methodism knows what to do with its Supernumeraries. When I retired to Crook ten years ago there was a constant complaint that there were too many funerals for the Circuit staff to deal with. I volunteered my services and have been approached just three times. Twice I couldn't help as we were on holiday, so I have actually taken only one funeral! I did, however, after two quarters 'off' split my Sundays between this circuit, West Durham, and my 'home' circuit, Durham and Deerness Valley, so most Sundays, before the advent of Covid and the discovery of my cancer, I was preaching, often presiding at Holy Communion. I have also, over the years led a number of study groups, Advent and Lent for Churches Together in Crook, and throughout the year for Table Talk at St Paul's Centre in Spennymoor. I know of other Circuits who have used their supernumeraries far more constructively

The genius of the Wesleys

What Wesley recognised at his Aldersgate Street experience was that the consequence of accepting God's grace inevitably leads to a change of lifestyle and this led him to affirm that Methodism was raised up to "spread Scriptural holiness" throughout the land! Being a Christian is about being changed and in turn bringing about change in society! It's about "works of piety" and "works of mercy" – for Wesley it was always about 'both' / 'and' and not 'either / 'or'!

"Works of piety" – 'the means of grace' – include searching the scriptures; prayer; fasting; the Lord's Supper; fellowship; public worship; avoiding evil – all these are about 'inward holiness'!

However, genuine inward holiness must show itself in outward holiness.

"Works of piety" were worthless without "works of mercy." Faith without works of love, Wesley stated, is the "grand pest of Christianity" (see *James 2:14-26)*. Talking about our faith isn't enough. It must manifest itself in our dealings with others. It must be a faith filled with the energy of love *(Galatians 5:6)*. It is our duty and our privilege to "do good" to others, to engage in "works of mercy." The works are:

> feeding the hungry,... clothing the naked,... entertaining or assisting the stranger,... visiting those that are sick or in prison,... comforting the afflicted,... instructing the ignorant,... reproving the wicked exhorting and encouraging the well-doer; and if there be any other work of mercy, it is equally included in this direction.

> (Sermon, "Upon Our Lord's Sermon on the Mount, VI," 1748)

If all we are offering is a variation on the same theme that every other Church in the land is offering, then how do we justify our existence? Shouldn't we then be working together with our Christian neighbours to be an effective witness in our Community? Or are we simply trying to find ways to keep our buildings in existence to satisfy our own sense of power? Didn't Jesus say "All who want to save their lives will lose them. But all who lose their lives because of me and because of the good news will save them." (Mark 8:35 CEB)

Looking to the Future

In the current round of church and circuit reviews there seems to be not only an understandable emphasis on looking to the future but a steadfast refusal to consider what has gone before.

Spanish philosopher George Santayana is credited with the aphorism, "Those who cannot remember the past are condemned to repeat it." This often quoted in relation to occasions where conflict occurs. If we ignore the Holocaust, then new examples of genocide often emerge. That may well be true, but there is more to remembering the past that simply avoiding 'repeating the mistakes' that were made previously. There are things in the past that were positive and clearly worth recalling and, indeed, repeating!

If we choose to ignore the past and look only to the future, it leads to the kind of letter that recently appeared in an edition of the Methodist Recorder suggesting that the time had come for the Christianity to abandon the Old Testament since as it is of the past it is therefore no longer relevant! It could also be argued that the same is also true of the New Testament!

The mid-twentieth century saw the emergence of mass evangelism with several visits to the UK by Dr Billy Graham. Whilst I would be the first to acknowledge that his rallies had a very positive impact on both church and society, I would also suggest that, in retrospect, they marked the beginning of the rapid decline of the Christian faith in our country. Their emphasis on 'personal salvation', based on a conservative evangelical view of Scripture, led to a neglect of other aspects of the Christian faith. In Methodism this resulted in an inevitable abandoning of a traditional understanding of Wesleyan Evangelicalism.

The demand that Jesus be accepted as a personal saviour is to be found nowhere in the Gospels. All Jesus ever asked of those with whom he came into contact was, "How can I help?" Nowhere, when he is asked for help or healing, does Jesus demand a profession of personal faith. The only demand he ever made was, "Follow me".

The problem with 'personal salvation' is that there is little reference to it in Scripture. Verses quoted in support are few and far between, and even fewer can be attributed to Jesus. Often they are quoted with no reference to their context. John Wesley was well aware of the problem:

> "And first let us inquire, 'What is salvation?' The salvation which is here spoken of is not what is frequently understood

by that word, the going to heaven, eternal happiness. It is not the soul's going to paradise, termed by our Lord, 'Abraham's bosom'. It is not a blessing which lies on the other side death, or (as we usually speak) in the other world. The very words of the text itself put this beyond all question. 'Ye are saved.' It is not something at a distance: it is a present thing, a blessing which, through the free mercy of God, ye are now in possession of. Nay, the words may be rendered, and that with equal propriety, 'Ye have been saved.' So that the salvation which is here spoken of might be extended to the entire work of God, from the first dawning of grace in the soul till it is consummated in glory."
– John Wesley (Sermon 43: "The Scripture Way of Salvation")

Two modern quotes are worthy of note:

"I accept Jesus Christ as my Saviour" diminishes the Gospel into an introverted and self-centred individualism. (Jurgen Moltmann)

"Jesus didn't ask to be let into people's hearts; he told them to follow him – dedicating his life to the most vulnerable in society. Following Jesus wasn't a call to private piety disconnected from society. Following Jesus was relational, social, and it involved justice." (Kat Armas)

In a recent article in the Methodist Recorder the Rev'd Brian Beck made the following observation:

"Part of our problem in British Methodism is that generally

we know too little about him (John Wesley). For most, I guess, he is the one who started it all. He may be referred to on Aldersgate Sunday, recalling his experience on May 24, 1738. Local preachers and ministers in training have to read some of his sermons (far fewer than was once the case), but how often do most preachers (myself included) refer to him in preaching? But there is more to Wesley than his 44 sermons and Notes on the New Testament."

Although I have never been a great fan of Paul, I cannot help but applaud his defence before King Agrippa when he succinctly states his perception of the Gospel in words I suspect would resonate with John Wesley:

"So, King Agrippa, I wasn't disobedient to that heavenly vision. Instead, I proclaimed first to those in Damascus and Jerusalem, then to the whole region of Judea and to the Gentiles. My message was that they should change their hearts and lives and turn to God, and that they should demonstrate this change in their behaviour. (Acts 26:19-20 CEB)

So how should we understand the Gospel today? At the risk of being accused of looking to the past I am constantly drawn to what has sometimes been referred to as 'Jesus' Manifesto:

16 Jesus went to Nazareth, where he had been raised. On the Sabbath he went to the synagogue as he normally did and stood up to read. **17** The synagogue assistant gave him the scroll from the prophet Isaiah. He unrolled the scroll and found the place where it was written:

> **18** *The Spirit of the Lord is upon me,*
> *because the Lord has anointed me.*
> *He has sent me to preach good news to the poor,*
> *to proclaim release to the prisoners*
> *and recovery of sight to the blind,*
> *to liberate the oppressed,*
> **19** *and to proclaim the year of the Lord's favour.*

20 He rolled up the scroll, gave it back to the synagogue assistant, and sat down. Every eye in the synagogue was fixed on him. **21** He began to explain to them, "Today, this scripture has been fulfilled just as you heard it." (Luke 4:16-21 CEB)

Following Jesus is about a life of faith worked out in establishing social justice in the society in which we live. This was what God demanded of his chosen people Israel. Perhaps most clearly expressed by the prophet Micah:

> What does the Lord require of you
> but to do justice, and to love kindness,
> and to walk humbly with your God? (Micah 6:8 NRSV)

Other prophets proclaimed a similar message (Isaiah 1:14; Hosea 6:6; Amos 5:21). It was always the case that God intended his message for the whole world, with Israel charged with communicating it. That had never happened. Jesus laid claim to the same message but in his ministry did what God had always wanted by taking it outside Israel, both in word and deed. Much of his ministry was in the Galilee of the Gentiles, the clue is in the name. He also ventured north into what is modern-day Lebanon and east in what is modern-day Jordan, neither territory was Jewish. He accepted Romans, women and those who were ill, mentally or physically, without any precondition, and treated them with respect as equals.

Has the church failed / is the church failing, when it comes to establishing the Kingdom / proclaiming the Gospel? I think not. I never cease to be amazed by the generosity of people, whether they be people of faith or not. There are around 166,000 registered charities in the UK offering help to people in need. That aside, you only have to consider the response to the current conflict in Ukraine. Apart from in excess of £100 million pounds raised in just a few days, countless individuals have driven the 1,500 miles to Ukraine in vans laden with essential goods destined for refugees forced out of their homes by the conflict. One TV commentator observed that, unlike any other war zone from which they had reported in the past, there was a notable absence of refugee camps despite the fact that there were, to date c. 2 million people forced from their homes. The reason – people from neighbouring states were opening their homes to receive refugees, often whole families, fully accepting that they may be with them for the foreseeable future.

Of course, evil has not been eradicated, otherwise the Ukraine conflict would never have occurred, but it has only served to further emphasise the fact that many people are increasingly moved to 'love one another' even if they have no idea who first made that demand. And clearly there is still the task of calling people to "change their hearts and lives and turn to God" that remains to be fulfilled, but I've already made reference to that above.

As one of Mr Wesley's preachers it would seem appropriate to let John Wesley have the last word. The significance of the quote lies in the last sentence. We may hold fast to the doctrine and spirit, but where we have failed, I believe, is in our abandoning the disciple that was so much a feature of early Methodism. Therein, I contend, lies the root of our demise.

A Last Word – from John Wesley

I am not afraid that the people called Methodist should ever cease to exist either in Europe or America. But I am afraid, lest they should only exist as a dead sect, having the form of religion without the power. And this will undoubtedly be the case, unless they hold fast both the doctrine, spirit, and discipline with which they first set out.

John Wesley 1786